LIVES IN TRANSITION

CARLETON LIBRARY SERIES

The Carleton Library Series publishes books about Canadian economics, geography, history, politics, public policy, society and culture, and related topics, in the form of leading new scholarship and reprints of classics in these fields. The series is funded by Carleton University, published by McGill-Queen's University Press, and is under the guidance of the Carleton Library Series Editorial Board, which consists of faculty members of Carleton University. Suggestions and proposals for manuscripts and new editions of classic works are welcome and may be directed to the Carleton Library Series Editorial Board c/o the Library, Carleton University, Ottawa K1S 5B6, at cls@carleton.ca, or on the web at www.carleton.ca/cls.

214 *Inventing Canada*
Early Victorian Science and the Idea of a Transcontinental Nation
Suzanne Zeller

215 *Documents on the Confederation of British North America*
G.P. Browne

216 *The Irish in Ontario*
A Study in Rural History
Donald Harman Akenson

217 *The Canadian Economy in the Great Depression* (Third edition)
A.E. Safarian

218 *The Ordinary People of Essex*
Environment, Culture, and Economy on the Frontier of Upper Canada
John Clarke

219 *So Vast and Various*
Interpreting Canada's Regions in the Nineteenth and Twentieth Centuries
Edited by John Warkentin

220 *Industrial Organization in Canada*
Empirical Evidence and Policy Challenges
Edited by Zhiqi Chen and Marc Duhamel

221 *Surveyors of Empire*
Samuel Holland, J.F.W. Des Barres, and the Making of The Atlantic Neptune
Stephen J. Hornsby

222 *Peopling the North American City*
Montreal, 1840–1900
Sherry Olson and Patricia Thornton

223 *Interregional Migration and Public Policy in Canada*
An Empirical Study
Kathleen M. Day and Stanley L. Winer

224 *How Schools Worked*
Public Education in English Canada, 1900–1940
R.D. Gidney and W.P.J. Millar

225 A Two-Edged Sword
The Navy as an Instrument of Canadian Foreign Policy
Nicholas Tracy

226 *The Illustrated History of Canada*
25th Anniversary Edition
Edited by Craig Brown

227 *In Duty Bound*
Men, Women, and the State in Upper Canada, 1783–1841
J.K. Johnson

228 *Asleep at the Switch*
The Political Economy of Federal Research and Development Policy since 1960
Bruce Smardon

229 *And We Go On*
Will R. Bird
Introduction and Afterword by David Williams

230 *The Great War as I Saw It*
Frederick George Scott
Introduction by Mark G. McGowan

231 *The Canadian Oral History Reader*
Edited by Kristina R. Llewellyn, Alexander Freund, and Nolan Reilly

232 *Lives in Transition*
Longitudinal Analysis from Historical Sources
Edited by Peter Baskerville and Kris Inwood

Lives in Transition

Longitudinal Analysis from Historical Sources

EDITED BY
Peter Baskerville and Kris Inwood

Carleton Library Series 232

McGill-Queen's University Press
Montreal & Kingston • London • Ithaca

ISBN 978-0-7735-4466-6 (cloth)
ISBN 978-0-7735-4467-3 (paper)
ISBN 978-0-7735-9668-9 (EPDF)
ISBN 978-0-7735-9669-6 (EPUB)

Legal deposit first quarter 2015
Bibliothèque nationale du Québec

Printed in Canada on acid-free paper that is 100% ancient forest free (100% post-consumer recycled), processed chlorine free

This book has been published with the help of a grant from the Canadian Federation for the Humanities and Social Sciences, through the Awards to Scholarly Publications Program, using funds provided by the Social Sciences and Humanities Research Council of Canada.

McGill-Queen's University Press acknowledges the support of the Canada Council for the Arts for our publishing program. We also acknowledge the financial support of the Government of Canada through the Canada Book Fund for our publishing activities.

Library and Archives Canada Cataloguing in Publication

Lives in transition : longitudinal analysis from historical sources / edited by Peter Baskerville and Kris Inwood.

(Carleton library series; 232)
Includes bibliographical references and index.
Issued in print and electronic formats.
ISBN 978-0-7735-4466-6 (bound). – ISBN 978-0-7735-4467-3 (pbk.)
ISBN 978-0-7735-9668-9 (EPDF). – ISBN 978-0-7735-9669-6 (EPUB)

1. Emigration and immigration – History – 19th century. 2. Emigration and immigration – History – 20th century. 3. Migration, Internal – History – 19th century. 4. Migration, Internal – History – 20th century. 5. Immigrants – Social conditions – 19th century. 6. Immigrants – Social conditions – 20th century. I. Baskerville, Peter A. (Peter Allan), 1943–, author, editor II. Inwood, Kris E., 1951–, author, editor III. Series: Carleton library series; 232

JV6029.L59 2015 304.809'034 C2014-906563-9
C2014-906564-7

This book was typeset by True to Type in 10.5/13 Baskerville

Contents

Tables and Figures vii

Acknowledgments xiii

1 Introduction 3
Peter Baskerville and Kris Inwood

PART ONE TRANSNATIONAL MIGRATIONS

2 A Test of Character: A Case Study of Male Convicts Transported to Van Diemen's Land, 1826–38 19
Rebecca Kippen and Janet McCalman

3 Sickness and Death on Convict Voyages to Australia 43
Hamish Maxwell-Stewart and Rebecca Kippen

4 Wanderlust: The Multiple Migrations of New Zealand's Scots, 1840–1920 71
Rebecca Lenihan

PART TWO MOBILITY IN THE RURAL WORLD

5 Lives in Motion: Revisiting the "Agricultural Ladder" in 1860s Ontario, A Study of Linked Microdata 93
Gordon Darroch

6 Change amid Continuity in Canadian Work Patterns during the 1870s 120
Luiza Antonie, Peter Baskerville, Kris Inwood, and J. Andrew Ross

7 Wilson Benson Revisited: Movement and Persistence in Rural Perth County, Ontario, 1871–81 141
Peter Baskerville

8 Revisiting Wealth on the American Frontier: Farm Growth, Inequality, and Social Persistence in Kansas, 1875–1940 165
Kenneth M. Sylvester and Susan Hautaniemi Leonard

PART THREE MOBILITY IN THE URBAN WORLD

9 Ladders of Mobility in a Fast-Growing Industrial City: Two by Two and Twenty Years Later 189
Sherry Olson

10 Moving around the City: Residential and Economic Mobility in Chicago, 1925–30 211
Evan Roberts

PART FOUR ETHNICITY AND WAR

11 Genes, Class, or Culture? French-English Height Differences in Canada 233
John Cranfield and Kris Inwood

12 Aboriginal and Mixed-Race Men in the Canadian Expeditionary Force, 1914–18 254
Allegra Fryxell, Kris Inwood, and Aaron van Tassel

13 Tracing "The Trail of Infected Armies": Mobilizing for War, the Spread of the 1918 Influenza Pandemic, and the Case of the Polish Army Camp at Niagara-on-the-Lake, 1917–19 274
Kandace Bogaert, Jane van Koeverden, and D. Ann Herring

Notes 293

Bibliography 333

Contributors 371

Index 377

Tables and Figures

TABLES

2.1 Ship and year of arrival 25
2.2 Sentence, crime, and background characteristics 26
2.3 Behaviour and punishment under sentence 30
2.4 Life after sentence 34
2.5 Logistic regression: variables associated with behaviour and punishment under sentence 36
2.6 Logistic regression: variables associated with outcomes after sentence 39
3.1 Loading and mortality 53
3.2 Mortality and morbidity classified according to cause or symptom 56
3.3 Morbidity rate and risk 58
3.4 Statistical analyses of the relationship between convict voyage characteristics and days in voyage sickbay, voyage deaths, and deaths in arrival year 67
3.5 Statistical analyses of the relationship between convict voyage characteristics and days in voyage 69
4.1 Proportion of New Zealand immigrants from each region of Scotland, with indices of representation based on the Scottish population distribution in 1871 75
4.2 Proportion of migrants from each region of Scotland who died outside of the New Zealand province in which they first arrived 83
5.1 Linkage, population turnover, and adjusted outmigration estimates, south-central Ontario, 1861–71 96

5.2 Occupational distributions for men aged fifteen and up in 1861, linked in central Ontario, 1861 and 1871 98
5.3 Decadal occupational mobility of men aged fifteen and up, 1861–71, central Ontario 100
5.4 Household status transitions of new farmers (men aged fifteen and up) in 1871, by 1861 occupational origins 104
5.5 Intertownship (town) migration, men aged fifteen and up in 1861, by occupational mobility, 1861–71, central Ontario 106
5.6 Farm acreage, improvement, and tenure among farmers (men aged fifteen and up) in 1871, by 1861 occupational origins, central Ontario 110
5.7 Logistic regressions for the odds of entering farming or nonfarming among all 1861 nonfarmers, among all mobile 1861 nonfarmers, and of tenure among 1871 farmers, men aged fifteen and up, central Ontario, 1861–71 113
5.8 Occupational distributions for men aged fifteen and up, central Ontario in 1861 and 1871, full samples for each year and linked sample across the decade 119
6.1 Distribution of occupations from published tabulations, Canada, 1871 and 1881 122
6.2 Distribution of occupations from published tabulations and from linked microdata, old Canada, 1871 and 1881 126
6.3 Age distribution of 1871 population and linked women and men 127
6.4 Distribution by nativity and ethnicity in the 1871 population and in linked records 128
6.5 Share of linked records with occupation, by age and sex 130
6.6 Occupational transitions 1871–81 of linked women with occupations, by age 131
6.7 Occupational sectors of linked men in 1881 by province of residence in 1871, with change from 1871 132
6.8 Occupational transitions 1871–81 of linked men with occupations, by age, Canada 133
6.9 Occupations of linked men in 1881 by birthplace and age, with change from 1871 to 1881 135
6.10 Occupational sectors of linked men in 1881 by ethnic origin and age cohort, with change from 1871 to 1881 136
6.11 Occupational sectors of linked Irish-origin men in 1881 by birthplace and age cohort, with change from 1871 137

7.1 Birthplace and origin: household heads, Logan Township, 1871 143
7.2 Some community studies of mobility: Canada and the United States, 1850–80 146
7.3 Logistic regression with linked/not linked as the dependent variable: all household heads, Logan Township, 1871 147
7.4 Logistic regression with move/stay as the dependent variable 149
7.5 Variables compared between logistic regressions on odds of being linked and odds of moving: Logan household heads, 1871 150
7.6 Stockholding: German Lutheran farms compared to all other farms, Logan Township, 1871 155
7.7 Crop cultivation: German Lutheran farms compared to all other farms, Logan Township, 1871 156
7.8 Ethno/religion by tenant/owner: household heads, Logan Township, 1871, nominal level census 157
7.9 Tenants and landlords: Logan Township, Perth County, 1871 160
7.10 Landholding patterns by ethnicity: Logan Township, 1840–1911, (household heads, 1871 census cohort) 161
8.1 Number and per cent of occupations reported by persons aged twenty and older, 1860 to 1930, Kansas townships 172
8.2 Proportion of farmers who were tenants by age group, 1850–1930, expressed in rates per thousand, contiguous United States 174
8.3 Proportion of farmers who were owners and renters, rates per thousand, by age group, Kansas, 1885 and 1920 175
8.4 Social persistence, measured as the proportion of household heads in the population censuses linking forward over time, 1860–1930 178
8.5 Multilevel panel estimates of farm size growth, segmented by period, 1875–1940 183
9.1 Retrieval of persons fifteen to twenty-four versus all other ages, by gender and cultural community 190
9.2 Retrieval rates by characteristics of the individual and household in 1881: ethnicity, sex, age, relatedness, marital status, residential, and occupational status 192

9.3 Street segments rated and standardized by median rent level, 1881 and 1901 194
9.4 Rent level indicators of social status for household heads of selected occupations 194
9.5 Rent level indicators of social status by cultural community 195
9.6 Characteristics of populations sought and recovered, split by ages 198
9.7 Rates of retrieval in 1901 of census populations of 1881 by age and ethnicity, surname samples compared with entire population of Montreal, both sexes combined 200
9.8 Distance from nearest related household 1901, by cultural community and rent level 204
9.9 Living arrangements of persons fifteen to twenty-four in 1881 versus other age groups 207
10.1 Comparison of Houghteling families with 1920 census and 1925 Department of Public Welfare survey 220
10.2 Home ownership in 1925 and 1930 222
10.3 Changes in exact occupation and industry 226
10.4 Changes in major group occupation and industry 226
10.5 Occupational transitions of head of household 227
10.6 Industrial transitions of heads of household, 1925–30, industry in 1930 228
11.1 Percentage distribution of characteristics of the linked sample, all soldiers, and all Canadian men in the 1901 census 239
11.2 Comparison of CEF soldier's occupation to head's occupation in 1901 241
11.3 Truncated regression results for linked records with all census variables 244
11.4 Oaxaca decomposition of mother tongue height differential 248
11.5 Estimated stature differentials, Quebec born and Quebec resident, various surveys, 1985–2005, by age and sex 250
11.6 Estimated stature differentials, French origin and French language, various surveys, 1985–2005, by age and sex 251
11.7 Truncated regression results for linked soldiers with alternate sources for occupation 252
11.8 Truncated regression results with urban/rural split 253
12.1 Distribution of ages at enlistment 260
12.2 Occupations of the heads of soldiers' households in 1901 260
12.3 Links and "enlistment rates" by Aboriginal groups 263

12.4 Mother tongue and mixed race versus pure blood, by region and all Canada 266
12.5 Characteristics indicating the extent of social integration, by region 268
12.6 Quality codes for positive links from census to CEF 272
12.7 Average length of service for those who died 273

FIGURES

3.1 Death rates at sea and during the first year in the colony for male and female convicts arriving on voyages to VDL, 1830–53 50
4.1 Proportions of Scots residing in only one country other than Scotland prior to migration to NZ 81
4.2 Last country of residence for Scots with more than one country of residence prior to emigration to New Zealand 82
5.1 Central Ontario main study region, 1861–71 linked data 95
5.2 Distribution of new farmers by age in 1871, by 1861 occupational origins, for males aged fifteen and up 101
5.3 Age of new farmers, 1871, by occupational origins, for Canadian-born and foreign-born males aged fifteen and over, 1861 103
5.4 Intertownship (town) migration, men aged fifteen and up, by occupational mobility, 1861–71, central Ontario 107
6.1 Occupational transitions of linked men (aged fifteen to fifty-five) from 1871 to 1881 134
7.1 Tenancy rates: Logan Township, Perth County, 1840–1911 142
7.2 Number of chattel mortgages, Perth County, 1871–80 144
7.3 Number of mortgages, Logan Township, 1870–79 145
7.4 Ethnic Concentration, Logan Township, 1879 154
7.5 Leasing Logan, the Canada Company as land owner/lessor, Logan Township 1849 158
7.6 Leasing Logan, the Canada Company as land owner/lessor, Logan Township 1869 159
8.1 Sample townships by county and land-use region 168
8.2 Township Gini coefficients, by region and year 179
8.3 Two-way scatter of farm sizes by age, segmented by region and time period, fitted with quadratic curves: Kansas sample township farms 1,500 acres or smaller 180
10.1 Cost of houses in 1925 versus value of house in 1930 (all families) 222
10.2 Cost of houses in 1925 and 1930 for families in the same house 223

10.3 Monthly rents in 1925 and 1930 224
10.4 Distribution of rents in 1925 and 1930 224
11.1 Mean stature (inches) of Canadian-born WWI and WWII soldiers, by region of birth 234
11.2 Mean height (inches) of men aged five to sixty-seven years, resident Quebec and in the rest of Canada, 1953 Survey 235
12.1 Rate of enlistment by attestation year 259
12.2 Province of birth for Aboriginal-born CEF 261
12.3 Province of birth for all Canadian-born CEF 262
12.4 Aboriginal "enlistment rates" 264
13.1 Recruiting poster, "Armia Polska we Francyi/Polish Army in France." Library and Archives Canada, Acc No 1983-28-3798 277
13.2 Emergence of the Polish Army in France 278
13.3 Niagara-on-the-Lake, Ontario, Camp Niagara and Polish soldiers cemetery 280
13.4 Polish soldier mortality and camp strength, September to December, 1918 288
13.5 Polish soldiers memorial. Photo by K. Bogart 289

Acknowledgments

The research reported in this volume has been enriched by collaboration with family history and genealogical groups including the Hobart Female Convict Research Centre, New Zealand Society of Genealogists, the Quebec Family History Society, Ontario GenWeb, Ontario Genealogical Society, Timmins Martelle Heritage Consultants, and Family Search (Church of Jesus Christ of Latter-day Saints). We have relied critically on the expertise of librarians and archivists on three continents and on financial support from the Australian Research Council, Tasmanian Archive and Heritage Office, US National Institutes of Health, Canadian Foundation for Innovation, Canadian Institute for Health Research, Social Sciences and Humanities Research Council of Canada, Sharcnet, Google, and the universities to which the authors are affiliated. Finally, we wish to acknowledge the superb editorial assistance of Sierra Dye and much appreciated encouragement and support from the College of Arts and College of Business and Economics at the University of Guelph.

LIVES IN TRANSITION

1

Introduction

PETER BASKERVILLE AND KRIS INWOOD

The child is father of the man: Woodsworth's truism has many echoes in scholarly discourse and popular common sense. The social class, ethnicity, or culture of the child may limit, or even predetermine, the fate of the adult – and that of subsequent generations. One of the great challenges of research today is to understand change over the life course and across generations. The challenge has wide cultural and scholarly resonance: it is encapsulated in the great British television series known as *Up*, which tracks the lives of fourteen British children, selected from a range of socio-economic backgrounds. The documentary is a simple example of longitudinal cohort analysis, in which a population sample is tracked over time (since 1964 for the fourteen children) to measure the relative weight of starting conditions and of subsequent events upon the entire life course. But what if we could perform an analogous longitudinal analysis for large numbers of people, for entire populations at a local, national, or even transnational level? Success at meeting this challenge would transform research into the human condition. The chapters in this book respond to that challenge.

The evidence needed to support this kind of research is elusive. Because no single source is available to describe people at multiple points in their lives, typically we have to link together different sources in order to develop the longitudinal profiles. This is why linked microdata have become an essential tool for research focusing on the post-1950s universe. Social scientists, medical investigators, and public policy practitioners commonly employ longitudinally linked data in pursuit of answers to a myriad of questions. Such resources, however, are limited in terms of chronology and restricted by regulations governing privacy. Linked historical microdata files are not subject to the same limitations. Social scientists interested in questions the answers to which benefit from a deeper time perspective are beginning to construct longitudinally linked historical microdata files. These files enable innovative research on any social, economic, or health outcome that must assess the importance of family and ancestral inheritance, early life conditions, migratory movements, and subsequent events upon the life course.

The chapters in this book point to the broad range of interesting and exciting research questions that can be answered by employing longitudinal data. While censuses are the central sources for the linkage of individual-level data, the papers gain a great deal of their strength through linking to a complementary source: enlistment records, convict records, welfare surveys, crop surveys, land records, and sundry qualitative sources. These multiple links deepen one's understanding of context and human behaviour. The authors focus on the dynamics of movement: initial decisions, where movers came from, the routes they took, where they stopped, and where they went next. The moves were multiple: in and out of work, in and out of farming, in and out of marriage, in and out of ownership, and out and back to one's home country. Each paper offers substantive interpretations that sometimes corroborate but most often go beyond current understandings and open up new avenues for exploration. Indeed, taken as a whole, the book can be seen as a primer for the "doing" of longitudinal historical research. As far as the editors are aware, this is the first book that provides a *discussion* of the possibilities for new knowledge that can be realized through linking individual-level data for large numbers of people between two or more points in time and also *demonstrates* through actual research how such a procedure can lead to new and enhanced understandings of important aspects of our collective past.

INTELLECTUAL CONTEXT

The construction and use of longitudinal data for historical populations draws from several distinct methodological traditions. Before introducing each paper, it is useful to situate our vision of the field more clearly within a broad intellectual context.

For many people the most familiar historical genre is biography, through which a narrative of someone's life is fashioned. Most biographers draw from a wide variety of sources some of which are rich in detail and context. We can extend the idea of following one person through her or his life to a group of individuals, or collective biography. Looking at a large group of people, however, makes it difficult to use the same number and diversity of sources for each individual. *Collective* biography, therefore, tends to focus on particular dimensions of life and to rely on sources that are less rich individually. The advantage, of course, is being able to compare different kinds of people and to generalize across the experience of many people rather than being restricted to the one person who happened to leave behind the sources needed for a biography.

An important step in the development of collective biography was the emergence during the early twentieth century of *cohort* data. A typical study in this genre collected information from a selected group of people at multiple points through their lives in order to develop generalizations on topics of interest to social and medical science. There was some reliance on retrospective data collection, but since everyone being studied was still alive, the most useful information was that emerging from the process of monitoring the cohort of individuals as their lives unfolded. The genre continues and indeed has had a renaissance of sorts in recent decades as interest has grown in research about childhood, old age, labour market transitions, and the early life origins of adult health. Most important national statistical agencies now maintain a longitudinal survey, which is updated on a continuous basis.

Separately, researchers in historical demography have engaged in *family reconstruction*, often within a local community or parish, in order to follow a set of individuals in the past from cradle to grave. Very often the analytical purpose of this research was to compare the experience of the entire life course in one generation to that of the next and to assess the socioeconomic circumstances in which one generation married early or later, had fewer or more children, etc.

Another conceptually distinct genre of research examines a large number of people at a single point in time or in a single source. Here the cross-sectional variety of personal characteristics and circumstance allows rich analysis of individual-level experience that contributes to and is influenced by a group process. If we assemble cross-sectional snapshots at different points in time we can study *synthetic cohorts* in which the lifetime experience of a group of people is understood by extracting information from multiple snapshots in a way that ensures maximum comparability. A synthetic cohort analysis might compare at different points in time people with the same birthdate; for example, fifteen-year-olds in 1985 are compared with thirty-five-year-olds in 2005. Here we are comparing the same kinds of people at different dates rather than following exactly the same people through their lives. The latter, a true cohort analysis, is more precise insofar as entrance into the group (immigration) or exit (death, emigration) does not influence outcomes.

In recent years all genres of research have acquired the power to address larger and larger databases, as the cost of data acquisition has diminished and the power of hardware and software to store and analyze the data has increased. The number and size of cross-sectional databases have increased to the point that it is now possible to employ computer science-based techniques of data mining or machine learning that will identify exactly the same people in two large bodies of data. Observing someone in two databases, at different times, effectively creates longitudinal data for that individual. And because we can do this for thousands and millions of people, we are able to generate longitudinal or cohort data on a large scale. The process relies critically on advanced computing capacity and techniques. It would not be possible for an individual, even someone very hard-working, to review and identify matches (that is, find the same people in two sources) if the relevant sources are 100 million records of the 1900 United States census and 120 million records from 1910. The right computer software, however, can do it. Many of the papers in this volume draw from this kind of methodology to generate large samples of cohort or longitudinal data for past populations.

THE PAPERS IN THIS VOLUME

Nearly all the papers deal with "settler societies" in an era of quickening and cheapening ocean transport and increasing continental expansion made possible by railways. Accordingly, the book begins in Part One, "Transnational Migrations," with an examination of the lives of women and men who travelled from Britain to the south Pacific during the nineteenth century. The movement of British people to Australia and New Zealand was the longest and most arduous of all the nineteenth-century migrations. The voyage was challenging in different ways for those who were transported as convicts, the subject of the first two papers, and those who decided freely to migrate, considered in the third paper. The chapters underline that migration was a risky process: whether risks were enforced (as with convicts) or accepted (as with the travellers to New Zealand), migrants were risk takers.

The first paper, by Kippen and McCalman, reconstructs the lives of men transported to Van Dieman's Land during the late 1820s and 1830s. The authors draw upon a collaboration with genealogists and other volunteers that has digitized and linked together extensive British government information about each of the convicts. In this paper Kippen and McCalman overturn a widely held belief of Australians about their past. The authors argue that the transported convicts were *not* typical English, Scots, Welsh, and Irish of the sort beginning to migrate freely to the Australian colonies at this time. Rather, the temperament, behaviour, and moral quality of convicts were conspicuously problematic following impoverished early lives and the compounding effects of subsequent experience.

Kippen and McCalman develop a window into the character of transported convicts through a structured comparison of 330 rural workers imprisoned for protesting a loss of land with more typical convicts whose offences were theft and related crimes. The lives of both groups are reconstructed in remarkable detail. The men imprisoned for political protest escaped the worst excesses of physical and psychological punishment and won their freedom more quickly. The transgressions of the more typical prisoner prior to and within the convict system exposed him to severe physical and psychological punishments and longer sentences that, cumulatively, created considerable stress. Both character and experience contributed to a reduction in the prospects for marriage and an increased risk of early death for the convicts. This persuasive challenge to one of the foundational myths of Australian history would not be possible without the information resources of the larger project, a sophisticated combination of qualitative and quantitative analysis and the conceptual framework of life course analysis.

Maxwell-Stewart joins Kippen to examine sickness and death on the voyage to Australia and after arrival. They show that while early nineteenth-century ship travel was hazardous to health, especially on long voyages, medical regulation and support made convict voyages *safer* than the maritime experience of free or voluntary migrants. This is unexpected because it is generally believed that doctors and medical knowledge at the time had little to offer. Travel in winter months was less healthy but, another surprise, crowding aboard ship did not seem to affect the risk of sickness and/or death.

The authors observe a remarkable pattern of gender differences. The ships carrying female convicts had a higher mortality rate, but the risk of death in the months after arrival in Australia was greater for men. The presence of children and accompanying diarrheal disease on the female convict voyages provides part of the explanation. Equally interesting, though, is the insight afforded by a longitudinal perspective. By following large numbers of individual convicts over time Kippen and Maxwell-Stewart show that women were typically in poor health before boarding the ships – because of their social class, living conditions, and gender discrimination in their home lives and because many travelled longer and farther than men in order to reach the port. Male convicts may have been healthier than women before boarding and on the voyage, but the severe punishment regime for men after arrival damaged their life prospects disproportionately.

The third article in this part, by Rebecca Lenihan, again builds on collaboration with genealogists, in this case following the lives of many thousands of Scots who moved to New Zealand. This migrant flow was especially important for both countries, as European settlers in New Zealand were disproportionately Scottish. Lenihan argues that while the sheer length of the voyage understandably focuses attention on the oceanic passage, a careful examination of migrant lives reveals a complex and more varied pattern. A large number of migrants moved within Scotland at least once before departure or travelled elsewhere in the British Empire before settling in New Zealand. Many families relocated one or more times after arrival in New Zealand, and some returned to Scotland. Lenihan's life course perspective allows her to argue that, for many, migration was more than a long and hazardous voyage. Rather, migration was a multistep experience encountering obstacles and complications that stretched over several years and often involved interim settlement in other countries and family relocations at home and in the country of eventual settlement.

In Australia and New Zealand, as elsewhere in the overseas British Empire, more people lived in rural areas than in towns and cities. It is therefore particularly appropriate to focus on rural society and the experience of agricultural change. Papers in the next part of the book, "Mobility in the Rural World," examine people living in the North American countryside. Three papers examine spatial and social mobility in Ontario and Canada between 1860 and 1880, and the final paper, by Sylvester and Leonard, focuses on land tenure changes in Kansas 1874–1941.

Gordon Darroch, author of the first paper in this part, was in the forefront of those who questioned an older literature which had argued that as early as the 1860s large numbers of people moved out of agriculture and into more "modern" manufacturing jobs. In this paper, Darroch revisits the flow of people into and out of occupations in the 1860s and looks as well at the degree to which this social mobility was accompanied by movement across space. Darroch suggests that the traditional – "long in the tooth" – argument that movement into farm ownership was akin to climbing the rungs of a single ladder one step at a time is both overly simple and somewhat whiggish or, in Darroch's words, "a rather unadorned upward mobility thesis." Using one of the first large longitudinal databases ever constructed – some 14,000 people who lived in central Ontario in 1861 who were found on the census living in central Ontario in 1871 – Darroch uncovers a "culture of mobility" both spatial and social. Not only did men from all walks of life change their jobs over the decade but they also changed their residences. New jobs went hand in hand with new living quarters. A large number moved into farming but, as Darroch notes, 20 per cent of farmers became nonfarmers over the decade. By linking a large number of individuals across time, Darroch demonstrates that movement into farming occurred from many quarters – the labouring segment, native born, immigrants, tenants, farmer's sons, and even merchants. Thus he suggests that the dominant metaphor of a single ladder needs to be modified, if not discarded. There were many possible ladders to scale or paths to traverse as individuals sought out new employment opportunities and new places to set up a home.

Antonie et al. pursue similar questions for the decade of the 1870s with a sample of 32,699 people found on the 1871 national census who were linked to the 1881 national census. They outline the construction of this first Canadian national database of linked individuals and employ the data to examine change versus continuity in work patterns. The central intent is to reconcile aggregate occupational evidence, which points to little if any change over the decade, with a large literature that argues for significant economic change. Their linked database uncovered patterns of movement not visible from cross-sectional snapshots even if organized on a synthetic cohort basis. While the longitudinal data point to a degree of occupational stability, they also reveal significant movement by younger people out of farming and into commerce and industry, a very different pattern from that exhibited by older men. Ethnic differences are also uncovered. Continental Europeans chose agriculture more consistently than other ethnic groups. Those of Scottish origin led the way into industry. The linked data confirm, though, that farming remained the most attractive occupational choice and that relatively few left over the course of the decade. Younger men were more likely to change, presaging a different future within a broader context of continuity.

Baskerville employs a database of linked individuals to examine who was most likely to move residences over the decade of the 1870s. His unit of analysis – 555 household heads from one rural township, Logan, Perth County, Ontario – is smaller than that of Darroch and Antonie et al., but his data are hand linked to all of Canada and the United States, not just to the county or even the province as a whole. It is local in terms of the study group but international in terms of the linkage scope. The paper emphasizes that linkage decisions and the size of catchment areas are crucial determinants of valid conclusions. In contrast to many small area studies, he finds less movement across time, although the extent of such mobility is still striking. He also suggests that the dominant explanation for movement offered in the traditional literature, one that emphasizes economic reasons, needs qualification. Cultural issues were, arguably, for many settlers in Logan Township, more important determinants underlying decisions to move or stay put. Finally he shows that tenancy could be a multifaceted process, one that requires deconstruction if its impact on settlers' decisions is to be clearly understood.

Sylvester and Leonard employ a linked database of all farm households in twenty-five townships in the State of Kansas between 1875 and 1940 to examine the changing nature of landed inequality. They note that from the perspective of a single census "it has always been difficult to sort out the effect of period and generational change in understanding the patterns of American inequality." Their database, constructed from state agricultural censuses for every half decade, allow them to move beyond snapshots to uncover the dynamics of longitudinal change. They find that throughout most of their study area those families that came first controlled the destinies of later generations. As the authors note, even single census snapshots point to age stratified ownership rates, but their longitudinal approach casts a clearer light on the social processes at work overtime. In the early years, with a relative abundance of open land, farm sizes fell thus facilitating ownership at lower age levels. When available land became scarce the social process of farm growth changed little: the persistence of modest farm sizes, even in areas where wheat farming would have accommodated an expansion of farm size, permitted, at least for family members, continued, if somewhat delayed, access to ownership. These trends were most visible in the townships that exhibited the greatest degree of farm household persistence. That persistence was accompanied by a culture of familial entitlement, manifested by social parity in farm size. In the case of Kansas, cultural determinants mitigated inequalities in land ownership.

Most North Americans lived in rural communities, however we also examine city-dwellers in Part Three, "Mobility in the Urban World." Olson and Roberts trace the intracity spatial and social movements of residents of two of North America's major urban centres, Montreal and Chicago, in the late nineteenth and early twentieth centuries. Both authors carefully guide the reader through the process of constructing databases composed of individuals linked across space and time. The strengths and limits of these databases are clearly outlined. Readers are given a fascinating and in many ways an unprecedented moving picture of urban residents striving to succeed in conditions not totally of their own making.

Using a "dyadic" strategy – searching for people in pairs – Olson links 40,000 Montreal residents from the 1881 census to the 1901 census (one-third of estimated survivors); many of these are also linked to marriage and tax records. The resultant database allows her to trace spatial and social movements within the city over a generation. That in itself is a worthy achievement, but Olson desires to escape the census' rigid focus on the household as unit of analysis in order to explore links between census households. Previous studies of social movement within Montreal over a five-year time span have suggested that 25 per cent of the population moved every five years, but only 20 per cent seemed to have moved "up" in a social/economic sense. Her study of movement over nearly a generation confirms the high propensity to move to a different neighbourhood (five out of six did so over the twenty year period). In contrast to the short-term studies, Olson finds significant upward mobility of a social/economic sort over twenty years. Her principal evidence is that the large majority of moves were to streets of higher median rent. This finding also stands in contrast to many studies of mobility in the United States and Britain in the later years of the nineteenth century, studies which, as Roberts notes, have charted declining social mobility.

Perhaps most exciting is Olson's focus on "near-residence": who lived close to whom. Linking by pairs within individual households in 1881 allows her to see where these people lived in 1901. She finds that one-half of her 20,000 households were themselves linked to another household by a close relationship to two or more people. For half of these linked households the distance between them constituted a short six-minute walk. This desire for close kin to be close neighbours spanned the city and crossed the three cultural communities that made up Montreal: the French Catholics, Irish Catholics, and Protestants. Lastly, Olson notes that those individuals who were between the ages of fifteen and twenty-four in 1881 were the most difficult to find in 1901. Antonie et al. and many other projects have encountered the same problem. Rather than simply ignoring them, however, Olson makes the valuable point that this is a generation "at risk" and charts the many ways that that was the case. Olson's employment of a longitudinal perspective provides richly nuanced insights into the strategies and challenges that faced Montreal's residents as the nineteenth century came to a close and a new century commenced.

Roberts' study of a group of working-class men and their families in Chicago utilizes a 1925 survey questionnaire with some 477 respondents. The survey was one of many at the time undertaken to investigate the social conditions and living standards of working-class families. Again in common with other such surveys, the 1925 data exist as a snapshot at a point in time. Roberts enriches the survey considerably by linking 277 of these families to the 1930 census. The longitudinal data allow him to comment on residential and social change over time. Indeed his study is one of only a few that employ longitudinal analysis to uncover social mobility in the early twentieth century United States.

Roberts finds that the sample families compare well with similar families enumerated in the 1920 census and can be seen to be representative of other working-class families in Chicago at that time. He finds that spatial movement was extensive and almost totally within the city. Indeed median rent increased; one-third of the renters in 1825 owned their own homes in 1930. Both changes point to increased social mobility. But, Roberts cautions, most still rented in 1930. Moreover, occupational change although dramatic across the five years (80 per cent were in different occupations or industries by 1930) does not point to general social improvement. While many did move from unskilled to skilled jobs, just as many moved from skilled to unskilled positions. Wives and children continued to work over the five years, and boarding remained a significant source of income. These continuities point to the constrained nature of any upward social mobility in the later 1920s. Roberts' study is the first to employ longitudinal analysis at a micro urban level for the early twentieth century United States. It awaits other studies for comparative analysis.

The final part, "Ethnicity and War," examines ethnically defined groups who participated in the First World War. The first two papers, as with Roberts and Olson in the previous part, connect individuals in the census to another source, in this case military personnel records. Another methodological difference is that these two papers do not provide a narrative of people moving through their life courses. Rather, they bring together information collected at different points to provide a richer cross-sectional profile and evaluate select hypotheses about French Canadian and aboriginal soldiers in the Canadian Expeditionary Force. Neither paper could resolve the issues under examination without observing people at different points in their lives and in different sources. The final paper, by Bogaert, van Koeverden, and Herring, does follow people through time in a profoundly interesting narrative of the Polish Army in North America.

In the first paper Cranfield and Inwood demonstrate that for as long as we can measure, the French-origin population in Canada has been shorter than other North Americans. Towards the end of the twentieth century the difference diminishes greatly but is still visible. The authors believe that stature or height is not just an idiosyncratic personal circumstance; for a large enough group it can be an informative marker of standard of living. Cranfield and Inwood find no evidence of systematic genetic differences, so the most likely explanation is socioeconomic stratification and the inferior social position of French Canadians. The authors link military records for a set of soldiers to the 1901 census, which provides additional information needed to permit a sophisticated econometric test. Somewhat surprisingly, the socioeconomic factors explain only a small share of the difference in stature. This redirects attention to cultural factors and perhaps a reconsideration of the genetic hypothesis.

Aboriginal and mixed-race soldiers in the Canadian Expeditionary Force during World War One (WWI) are examined by Fryxell, Inwood, and van Tassell. The authors take advantage of the unusually thorough 1901 Canadian census and linking from census to WWI records to identify Aboriginal and mixed-race soldiers whether or not they self-identified as Indigenous at the time of enlistment.[1] Thus the authors are able to examine, for the time, Indian soldiers who did not have reserve status as well as those recognized officially as members of a treaty band. The new linked census-military data reveal similarities and differences between Aboriginal and other Canadian soldiers, as well as considerable diversity among the First Nations – regionally and between mixed race and pure bloods. The mixed-race men had a particularly high enlistment rate. Eighty-eight per cent of the pure blooded and one-third of the mixed-race Indians spoke an indigenous language as their mother tongue; collectively the Indigenous soldiers had thirty-one different native languages and five European languages as a mother tongue. The authors argue for the importance of recognizing the contribution of mixed-race soldiers and for the enormous diversity of Aboriginal contribution during the war.

The final paper, by Bogaert, van Koeverden, and Herring, tells the story of WWI Polish army troops who came from across North America to train at Niagara-on-the-Lake during 1917 and 1918. In a way this paper differs from the others in that it does not employ linked data from two or more large-scale quantitative data sets. It is based primarily on qualitative data supplemented with some quantitative data on the enlistment patterns of Polish Americans. Yet from another perspective the paper exists as a fitting finale to the cumulative process of mobility charted in this book. The three authors uncover a complex series of moves made by individuals with multiple identities and links to the Old World and the New, who were unwitting transporters of a fatal germ and who faced the ultimate risk of those who migrated – death.

The authors assemble their narrative of the Polish army training camp at Niagara-on-the-Lake from a variety of qualitative and quantitative sources. The story told by Bogaert, van Koeverden, and Herring has bittersweet resonance because the movement of Polish recruits helped to bring the deadly 1918 influenza epidemic to Canada. In their account, the authors intertwine the diffusion of influenza with recruitment and training during the latter stages of the war. At Niagara-on-the-Lake many hundreds of Polish soldiers were struck down by flu, and twenty-five died. Annual ceremonies to remember the camp and its casualties continue to commemorate the importance of these contributions to Polish identity and nationalism.

The story of the Polish Army Camp at Niagara-on-the-Lake reminds us that longitudinal history unfolds in days and weeks as well as decade by decade and cohort by cohort. The papers in this volume, each in a different way, illustrate the great diversity of longitudinal research from historical sources. Some of the papers use sources being examined for the first time and methodologies still being developed. All of the papers struggle one way or another with being able to link between sources only a subset of the population, and this subset may not be entirely typical of the entire population in either year. All of the papers, each in a different area, contribute to the frontiers of knowledge being generated for the first time. Like all pioneering work these papers will attract others; few of these authors will have the last word on their topics. The collective contribution of these papers to the development of the genre of longitudinal research from historical sources may turn out to be as important as the knowledge each of them generates on individual topics.

PART ONE

Transnational Migrations

2

A Test of Character: A Case Study of Male Convicts Transported to Van Diemen's Land, 1826–38[1]

REBECCA KIPPEN AND JANET MCCALMAN

INTRODUCTION

Convicts transported to the Australian colonies from 1788 to 1868 were among the most carefully observed populations of men, women, and children in the nineteenth-century world. Their records have provided rich data for the biological standard of living and the history of punishment and criminality.[2] Australian history abounds in stories of convicts who went on to make new lives after servitude, and the family history movement has revealed some remarkable lineages.[3] But until recent developments in information technology, in particular the explosion of genealogical information on the Internet and the digitization of vital and historical records, it has not been possible to study convicts at a population level outside the "paper panopticon" created by the various convict departments of the penal colonies. Now it is easier to reconstruct convicts' lives and social contexts both before and after transportation, providing richer data than the bare bones of date and place of birth, sentence, type of crime, and height. Will these change our understanding of transported people as subjects for wider economic, social, and demographic analysis?

Economic historians pioneered the use of convict records, in particular for height, geographic origin, and occupation, for both convict history and for the impact of economic change and dislocation on vulnerable populations in the Old World. For this purpose, it was important for convicts to be understood as representative of "ordinary" urban and rural poor people. This was the central claim of Stephen Nicholas et al.'s *Convict Workers* and Deborah Oxley's work on convict women.[4] Australian and labour historians have also sought to rescue transported people from the "contempt", even more than from the "condescension of posterity." Convicts as a "class" were more sinned against than sinning, and in popular history the catalogue of crimes for which they were often transported appear trivial to the ahistorical eye. Nicholas, Oxley, and Meredith created databases from the indents held in the Mitchell Library of New South Wales.[5] Haines and McDonald compared the convicts from their datasets with bounty immigrants who arrived in New South Wales in 1841 and found that free and bond had more similarities than differences in human capital. The "character" rather than the skills of the transported constituted the divide between them.[6] Therefore how important was "character" – temperament, behaviour, and moral quality – and how can we measure it?

Until recently such questions relied on inference and supposition, but with the digitization of the archive of the Van Diemen's Land Convict Department held in the Tasmanian Archives and the new online tools for tracing in vital registrations and historical records, we now have access to a wider range of data both in time and kind. We can investigate how well the potential convict workforce survived penal servitude and contributed to the colonial project after sentence. Did the difference in "character" matter in the final sum of things? Were convicts little different from assisted immigrants – which is the popular understanding of Australia's convict founders – or did their character and time under sentence make for a different outcome? This test case seeks to determine the significance of psychological characteristics – temperament and "character" – in the outcome of the lives of those transported.

A MORAL LABORATORY

We can conceive of the convict population as a "natural experiment" of people about whom we know quite a lot. They were subjected to a stress regime that ranged in intensity from benign to unspeakably cruel, with torments to both body and mind, all of which were meticulously recorded in time and place within a closed system. What were the characteristics of convicts who "survived" the system and those who became its victims? What were the effects of varying degrees of stress and extreme punishment on later health and longevity? What can we learn about resilience? What can we learn about ageing? And how important was "character" compared with biological characteristics in survival? The Founders and Survivors Life Course (FAS) project[7] seeks to answer these questions through a cradle-to-grave study of men, women, and children transported as convicts to Van Diemen's Land (modern Tasmania) between 1812 and 1853 and of their traceable descendants through to the early twentieth century.[8]

The project has been framed around two core questions: family formation as a test of biological and social "success," and length of life or "survival." The convict life course has three key stages: before, during, and after sentence. What factors in life before sentence might be protective or not while under sentence? To what degree were the convict's reactive behaviour and the accumulation of insults during sentence indicative of survival or failure after sentence? And what were the outcomes of these life courses: first in remaining a visible and discoverable member of colonial or British society, second in family formation, third in socioeconomic and geographic mobility, and finally in life span and end-of-life health?

The Founders and Survivors project has been able to mobilize crowdsourcing of volunteer historians to process the vast archive of records and extract and code detailed data.[9] This has significantly increased the number of variables available for analysis. The conduct records – kept meticulously throughout a convict's time in the system – register every instance that a convict was accused of offending against penal discipline, the outcome of the hearing before a police magistrate, and of any prosecution in the higher courts. Offences against convict discipline included many actions that can be understood as reactive behaviour: much of it justified resistance to bullying, insult, abuse, and cruelty. Other offences were moral: drunkenness, sexual relationships (both heterosexual and same sex), procuring, and visiting disorderly houses. Convicts continued to thieve, but their thefts were frequently of food and clothing because corrupt overseers were siphoning off their legitimate rations. They went absent without leave overnight, especially after they were paid, usually to drink or have a sexual liaison. They absconded. And there were convicts who were violent, savage, even homicidal.

Most infractions were understandable, but they were unquestionably imprudent because the British penal system in the Australian colonies was intended to rehabilitate. Convicts were promoted and demoted in a system – not unlike the game "snakes and ladders" – where good behaviour and good fortune could secure an early ticket of leave and even a pardon, while recalcitrance could spiral into an unremitting punishment of mind and body. The records minutely describe descents into hellish confrontations and madness. Survival depended fortuitously on the moral quality of masters, mistresses, and overseers and on the convict's capacity to remain docile, obedient, hard working, and deferential to one's superiors. Industrious, loyal, sober, and honest convict servants could be rewarded with significant patronage that transformed their life chances after sentence. The noncompliant could be destroyed by their servitude. Therefore the conduct records document intense interactions that provide indications of temperament and response to stress: insolence, refusal to work, and disobedience of rules, drunkenness, sexual misbehaviour, dishonesty, violence, flight. Persistent drunkenness, despite repeated punishment, might presage alcohol addiction in later life. Violence towards other prisoners might be matched by convictions later for domestic violence and fighting. Thieving often proved to be habitual. The frequenting of disorderly houses while under sentence sometimes prefigured a "career" as an emancipist. Above all, an unblemished or scarcely blemished conduct record, however frustrating for historians, might be predictive of a viable life after sentence.

The conduct records, therefore, provide the core data of this "natural experiment" of a stress regime inside a total institution. They provide a detailed record of insults – both physical and psychological – that can be quantified as strokes of the lash, days in solitary confinement, hours on the treadmill, weeks and months in chain gangs or in mines and then analysed against the human capital a convict brought with them into servitude and against the life they managed to lead on release. Penal discipline and convicts' reaction to its constraints and injustices were an intense test of character: the critical demarcation, according to Haines et al., between free and unfree labour brought to New South Wales by assisted immigration and transportation.[10] One way we can measure this is to use a control group of prisoners who were less morally culpable: political prisoners. The cohort of 332 machine breakers – known as the swing rioters – who were sent to Van Diemen's Land in 1831 provides a useful comparison with prisoners of similar social background and experience.

THE TEST CASE AND THE CONVICT POPULATION

The swing rioters were convicted of machine breaking, arson, and demanding monies in what was the last great agrarian revolt in English history. The riots began in mid-1830 in East Kent in protest at the introduction of threshing machines amidst the crisis of agrarian society driven by enclosures and the proletarianization of agricultural labour. Mechanized threshing threatened the rural workforce's main source of winter work.[11] As the disturbances quickly spread through the agricultural counties, the rioters sent letters signed by a symbolic "Captain Swing" to those in authority demanding removal of the machines and increased pay for labour. Groups of up to 400 moved around the countryside invading farms, menacing the inhabitants, and, when their demands were ignored, destroying the threshing machines and burning down barns and haystacks. Almost 2,000 were brought to trial and 252 were sentenced to death, but just as was to happen after the arrest of the Tolpuddle Martyrs in 1832, public outrage at their prosecution resulted in the commutation of most of those death sentences to transportation and merely nineteen were hanged. Local communities petitioned the courts for leniency on the grounds of previous good character, and the courts distinguished between those with no criminal record by sentencing the minority who were already known to police or who had committed thefts during the riots to fourteen instead of seven years transportation.[12] Four hundred and eighty-one were transported, 332 men and one woman to Van Diemen's Land, arriving in 1831. A small minority were criminals who had taken advantage of the riots to thieve and burn. The majority had no or few previous convictions, and the violence of the swing rioters was commensurate with the violence endemic in rural culture.[13]

The swing rioters were prisoners under what was known as the assignment period, which operated until 1840, through which convicts were assigned to work either for the government or for private masters. In 1841, assignment was replaced by a new philosophy of criminal punishment and redemption that operated with a probation period of two years on government work, often in a chain gang, before a convict could enter the labour market as a paid worker with a master.[14] Discipline shifted from punishment of the body to reformation of the soul through solitary confinement and the silent treatment for secondary offenders in the new Model Prison at Port Arthur. The assignment period was quite different. Employers took immediate responsibility for convict workers as master and servant but with the power to bring them before a magistrate who could order punishments including fines, flogging, the treadmill, hard labour, chains, or solitary confinement. Reconviction in the superior courts would result in servitude in a penal station. Convict discipline under the assignment system was more arbitrary and personal, between employer and bonded worker, but it was also possible for obedient, industrious convicts to be treated well and even be offered patronage as a continuing faithful servant upon freedom from servitude. Exemplary behaviour and hard work could be rewarded with early recommendations for tickets of leave, allowing them to work on their own account, a conditional pardon, or even a free pardon before their sentence was completed.

The broad male convict population was diverse, comprising men and boys born in every part of the British Isles, the overseas colonies, and non-British countries. Irish, Scottish, and English convicts each had their distinctive characteristics from their national and geographic origins in rural communities, towns, and port cities. The swing rioters, all coming from the agricultural counties across the southern half of England, are best compared with other English convicts of similar rural background, as well as with the wider population of city, town, and village, English, Scottish, and Irish. Irish convicts during the assignment period were largely born in Ireland but convicted in England or Scotland: it would not be until the 1840s that ship loads of Irish began arriving direct from Irish ports. This comparison therefore is between convicts and swing rioters who shared a similar background and passed through a similar penal regime.

Life before Sentence and the Convicts' Personal Characteristics

The other assignment convicts in the sample ("other convicts") totalling 1,802 arrived on ten ships between 1826 and 1838 (see table 2.1). Their crimes were overwhelmingly (95 per cent) ones of theft (table 2.2), with just 8 per cent convicted of crimes that involved violence. The thefts were largely of money or items that could be sold on or pawned: just 5 per cent were for food for consumption. Of the swing rioters, 92 per cent were convicted of machine breaking (political protest), 1 per cent of arson, and another 7 per cent of robbery with violence (rioters who took advantage of the disorder to obtain money or goods by threat or assault). Eighty-one per cent of the swing rioters received the minimum sentence of seven years, while 12 per cent received fourteen years,

Table 2.1
Ship and year of arrival

Ship and year of arrival	*Swing rioters*	*Other convicts*
Woodman 1826		152
Governor Ready 1827		162
Eliza 1831	225	
Proteus 1831	97	
Eleanor, Gilmore, Lord William Bentinck, Lotus, Mary, York 1831	10	
Strathfieldsay 1831		224
Atlas IV 1833		197
Enchantress 1833		201
Southworth 1834		192
George III 1835		80
Augusta Jessie 1835		209
Bardaster 1836		237
Royal Sovereign 1838		148
Total	332	1,802

and 7 per cent life. The longer sentences were for those who committed arson and crimes of violence and who had an existing criminal record before the riots. Quite different were the other convicts, where a third (34 per cent) were transported for life, 14 per cent for fourteen years, and just over half (52 per cent) for the minimum seven years (table 2.2).

All the ships came from English ports, so while all the swing rioters were born in England, 88 per cent of the other convicts were as well, with 4 per cent born in Ireland but convicted in England[15] and 5 per cent brought down from Scottish courts that were reluctant to transport offenders unless they had a bad record. The remaining 3 per cent were born in either British colonies or Europe. The swing rioters were different from the other convicts in key respects: first, they were older with an average age of 29.6 years compared to 26.1 years for the other convicts, many of whom were typical young male offenders rather than career criminals. The swing rioters were therefore taller (66.3 inches) at transportation compared with the other convicts who included many boys (64.6 inches). The heights of rural men by age 25, however, were similar. Over half the swing rioters were or had been married (50 per

Table 2.2
Sentence, crime, and background characteristics

	Swing rioters	*Other convicts*
CRIME	%	%
Theft from the person	0	10
Theft of money or valuables	0	60
Theft of food for consumption	0	5
Theft of animals or poultry	0	14
Robbery involving violence	7	6
Acts of political protest	92	0
Counterfeiting, coining, forgery, perjury	0	2
Arson	1	0
Sexual offences	0	0
Violent assault	0	1
Homicide	0	1
Desertion	0	1
Total	100	100
SENTENCE	%	%
7 years	81	52
14 years	12	14
Life	7	34
Total	100	100
AVERAGE AGE AT TRANSPORTATION	29.6 years	26.1 years
AVERAGE HEIGHT AT TRANSPORTATION	66.3 inches	64.6 inches
COUNTRY OF BIRTH	%	%
England	100	88
Ireland	0	4
Scotland	0	5
Other	0	3
Total	100	100
ECO-LOCATION	%	%
Rural	100	31
Market or semi-industrial town	0	28
Urban	0	41
Total	100	100
OCCUPATION	%	%
Unskilled	9	43
Semiskilled	64	36
Skilled	27	20
White-collar	0	2
Total	100	100

Table 2.2 (*continued*)

	Swing rioters	*Other convicts*
MARITAL STATUS	%	%
Single	46	71
Married	50	25
Widowed	4	4
Total	100	100

Adult swing rioters are not significantly taller than other adult rural English convicts.

cent married, 4 per cent widowers), whereas merely 25 per cent of the other convicts were married men with another 4 per cent widowers (table 2.2). Therefore the swing rioters were at a different life stage, defending their families and communities compared to the many, often impulsive, juvenile offenders among the other convicts.

The swing rioters were all rural men, but only 31 per cent of the other convicts shared their background and skills. Hunting and poaching skills had proved valuable in the early days of the colony when the Europeans, with their dogs, lived from game.[16] Almost 70 per cent of the other convicts came from the big cities or towns. The variable "economic location" seeks to break down the convicts' backgrounds into the "economy" in which they were operating at the time of offending. This is not always precise and depends on the level of detail about the bringing of charges provided in the indent. It is intended to separate those who were operating in rural settings from those who were in localities that may have been market towns or semi-industrial towns and from those who were operating in complex urban environments ranging from rapidly growing industrial cities to port cities. The place of conviction is not always a reliable guide to the convicts' economic locations, as they were brought to county capitals for the assizes and quarter sessions, so we have also coded for native place, which enables us to measure geographical mobility before transportation. Here we are going into greater detail about background than the coding used by Nicholas and Oxley and is closer to that employed by Richards and McDonald for the bounty immigrants.[17] The significance of these distinctions is highly historically specific. Convicts transported at the end of the 1830s who came from small towns and pre-industrial manufacturing communities, were often victims of rapid economic change overtaking cottage industry, and they found themselves transported to a colonial colony that had little use for their skills as weavers or stockingers. However, those with metalworking experience, even of a trade half learned, might, with further training within the convict system, be able to set up as a blacksmith after sentence. Agricultural labourers who could plough were to find themselves valued, and those who could grow fruit and vegetables could prosper. The street-smart denizens of the Great Wen, however, rarely possessed skills that were transferable to lawful employment, unless they were fully literate. Pickpockets often had no alternative but to continue their "trade" on release, but those who were street smart could scratch a living after sentence as a hawker or dealer, especially if they later crossed Bass Strait to the booming new city of Melbourne in the early 1850s.

Convicts were the primary source of labour in the colony, and the convict indent sought to identify convicts' economic potential. There were obvious places for men with good literacy and education who could become clerks and schoolmasters, for metalworkers who might become blacksmiths, former soldiers who might become constables, and wood workers and masons and manual workers who were needed as carpenters and brick makers and layers. Skilled drivers of horses and bullocks were essential workers, tailors and hatters might continue to ply their trade, and from 1834 at Point Puer, the juvenile reformatory on the Tasman Peninsula, young convicts were often trained as shoemakers. Artists, draftsmen and architects, fine metal workers, and jewellers all found needs for their skills and prospered if they could keep their fingers out of the till and their thirst for alcohol under control.

But the core of the Van Diemen's Land economy was agricultural: it needed men who could plough, sow, harvest, thresh, and manage stock. The colony particularly needed skilled horticulturalists. One of the quiet success stories among the swing rioters was Thomas Kimmer who won prizes for his vegetables in Launceston before moving with his new wife to Melbourne, starting a market garden, and finding £1,500 worth of alluvial gold in the first year of the gold rush. He purchased fifteen acres of good land near Melbourne where he established a very successful nursery business. Apart from his conviction and transportation for participating in the riot, his only setback was the reluctance of his master at the Van Diemen's Land Company, Edward Curr, to support his application for a ticket-of-leave because his gardening expertise was so valuable. The reputation of the swing rioters had preceded them to Van Diemen's Land, and on arrival at Hobart colonial farmers were waiting eagerly to hire them for their skills and steadier character.[18] By contrast, the majority of urban convicts had to learn their colonial work skills in the convict system. Weavers and pottery workers, city hawkers, and magsmen had less to offer the colonial economy. How did they fare once inside the system?

Time under Sentence: "Character" and the Accumulation of Insults

The conduct records contain, literally, a blow-by-blow account of the individual's moral career through the convict system. Every infringement of discipline was recorded and taken before a magistrate who made a judgement of guilt and appropriate punishment. This meant that during the assignment period to the end of 1839, convicts who were assigned to private employers were still subject to legal processes and not flogged on the spot at the whim of their masters and mistresses. Magistrates, of course, varied in their severity and were themselves usually masters of convicts and social associates of those bringing the charges. Under the probation period, convict discipline and management were centralized, convicts had to serve an initial probation period of hard labour, and punishment of the body was superseded by punishment and modification of the mind with solitary confinement.

Convict discipline was a complex system, with multiple punishments and insults to body and mind. To make sense of these data, offences, reactions, and punishments were coded in hierarchies of severity. Table 2.3 provides descriptive information on the behaviour and punishment of convicts under sentence using the following categories.

"Conduct offences" were coded to capture in five broad categories the number or intensity of offences while under sentence. The actual range in convicts' records is very wide and some offences were trivial and dealt with by admonishment. This coding is designed to give an indication of the frequency only, and whereas only 12 per cent of the other convicts passed through the system with no offences recorded against them, almost half the swing rioters (47 per cent) had an unblemished record. At the other extreme, just 8 per cent of the swing rioters committed six or more offences, compared with 49 per cent of the other convicts.

"Alcohol-related offences" gives the number of times that drunkenness was indicated in the conduct record. This can be significant for a convict's risk of alcoholism, and here 17 per cent of the other convicts

Table 2.3
Behaviour and punishment under sentence

	Swing rioters	*Other convicts*
CONDUCT OFFENCES	%	%
No offences	47	12
1–2 offences	31	18
3–5 offences	15	21
6+ offences	7	29
Constant offences	1	20
Total	100	100
ALCOHOL-RELATED OFFENCES	%	%
0	75	50
1	18	22
2	4	11
3+	2	17
Total	100	100
REACTIVE BEHAVIOUR	%	%
None	77	41
Insolence	16	29
Refusal to work	5	13
Tearing clothes	0	2
Threats or violence	2	16
Total	100	100
TIMES ABSCONDED	%	%
0	97	78
1	2	11
2	1	4
3+	0	6
Total	100	100
TOTAL STRIPES	%	%
0	83	55
1–29	4	11
30–49	2	6
50–99	8	16
100+	3	11
Total	100	100
TOTAL DAYS IN SOLITARY	%	%
0	89	63
1–13	9	19
14–27	2	8
28–41	0	4
42+	0	6
Total	100	100

Table 2.3 (*continued*)

	Swing rioters	*Other convicts*
INSULTS	%	%
None	50	17
Admonishment, fine, short solitary	19	16
Longer solitary, extension of probation	6	5
Multiple solitaries, flogging, treadmill, chains	20	32
Multiple floggings, mines, Port Arthur	6	30
Total	100	100

were punished more than three times for drunkenness compared with 2 per cent of the swing rioters. Alcohol was the greatest risk to civilian health and wellbeing in colonial Australia and would prove to be the undoing of many men and, especially, women after sentence. Within the convict system, only the most committed drinkers continued to reoffend in the face of punishment.

"Reactive behaviour" seeks to grade the level of psychological stress exhibited under convict discipline despite the severe penalties for resistance to authority. The coding is in increasing level of severity of response and the coders were asked to code for the most serious reaction from none, to insolence, to refusal to work, to tearing clothes and damaging government property (which was often a reaction of extreme distress under confinement), to threats or violence. The swing rioters had been treated differently from other convicts from the time they embarked. On board they had been excused the wearing of prison garb and chains, and their distinctiveness continued throughout their servitude. Fully 77 per cent recorded no instances of reactive behaviour against prison discipline, compared with 41 per cent of the other convicts. Insolence (16 per cent/29 per cent), refusal to work (5 per cent/13 per cent) and especially rage-induced violence or threats (2 per cent/16 per cent) were a fraction of the other convicts' behaviour. The swing rioters were ordinary rural men subjected to forced labour and exile from home and family – often at the peril of wives and children "left on the parish" – by a prosecution that they and many in the wider society considered a travesty of justice, and yet they restrained their frustration. The rates of violence and rage from other convicts point to the presence of many more psychologically disturbed individuals among their number and to the higher level of bullying and provocation inflicted on them.

"Times absconded" records the number of occasions the convict was reported to have absconded. The punishment for this offence was severe until late in the penal era when the colony of Victoria's prosperity was such a lure that labour shortages in Van Diemen's Land impelled the authorities to be more lenient. It does not include "absent without leave," which was a lesser offence and often indicated that convicts were drinking or conducting a sexual relationship, and here just 3 per cent of the swing rioters made a run for it, compared with 22 per cent of the other convicts.

"Total stripes" comprises the total number of stripes, either on the back or the breech, that a convict received during penal service and that were listed in the conduct record. The total number of lashes provides a clearer measure of the extent of insults suffered than does the number of occasions on which a convict was flogged. Here 83 per cent of the swing rioters avoided the lash compared to 55 per cent of the other convicts. Twenty-seven per cent of the other convicts received more than fifty stripes, compared with 11 per cent of the swing rioters.

"Total days in solitary" likewise provides a general measure of the extent to which the convict experienced solitary confinement. The degree of insult that this inflicted is reflected more in the length of confinement than the number of confinements. The time spent in total isolation and often darkness needed to be sufficient to induce disorientation – usually at least three days. Thirty days could be devastating, and those convicts who were incarcerated in the Model Prison or on Norfolk Island could be caught in a terrifying cycle of reaction and punishment that amounted to multiple events a day. As the emancipist John Mortlock wrote, "Of course, the brain is the seat of pain – very dreadful."[19] The swing rioters were even more successful in avoiding solitary confinement (89 per cent) compared with 63 per cent of the other convicts. None of the swing rioters spent more than twenty-seven days in solitary, whereas 10 per cent of the other convicts racked up large totals.

Finally, "Insults" seeks to grade the total measure of insults to body and mind suffered by the convict during servitude. It takes into consideration changes in punishment regimes that may not have been captured in the coding, in particular the lengths and frequency of time spent doing hard labour in chains, which was a most severe experience often leaving convicts debilitated or semicrippled. Similarly long or frequents periods on the treadmill could be just as damaging as flogging.

The code for insults often, but not invariably, matches that for "Conduct offences," because some convicts committed frequent offences, such as drunkenness, for which the punishment might be a fine or a short solitary. Others received terrible punishments for a relatively small number of offences. The insults coding is, therefore, a measure of intensity of stresses to body and mind both in severity and frequency. Here the reduced load of stress on the swing rioters is clear: 69 per cent of them passed through with nothing or the lightest punishment, compared with 33 per cent of the other convicts. At the far extreme of insults, just 6 per cent of the swing rioters suffered the maximum measure of insults compared with almost a third (30 per cent) of the other convicts. Of the other convicts, more than half (62 per cent) had a severe, potentially damaging time under sentence. Whether these insults translated into shortened life spans and marred life chances is the focus of the final section of the analysis.

Life after Sentence

The historical life course analysis is framed around two core questions: family formation as a test of biological and emotional "success," and length of life or "survival." These are not intended to be simple tests of biological fitness because the ability to form a family and sustain a household is also a test of the host society and economy in which individuals existed. If work is elusive, poorly paid, and insecure, households and the children they might produce are at risk. Emancipists faced significant hurdles in starting a new life after sentence: what work skills could they offer the economy, were they fit still in body and mind, and could they overcome the stigma of convictism, especially if the stigmata of servitude were inscribed on the body in marks of flagellation, broken noses, scars, or legs crippled by wearing irons? They rarely entered freedom with any capital; most had no "character" or references; many were troubled: irritable, touchy and quick to anger. The hardest cases were deeply embittered and considered themselves unbeholden to the norms of civilized behaviour because civilization had certainly failed them.[20] Many others could "pass," change their name, and hope that no one from the past might suddenly appear in the town, but some were forever blighted by the "Vandemonian cast" which aroused fear in their early years and amusement in their old age as they passed through the lower courts as pitiable objects – filthy, demented, and drunken.

Table 2.4
Life after sentence

	Swing rioters	*Other convicts*
EXIT FROM CONVICT SYSTEM	%	%
Not known	2	4
Ticket of leave	0	9
Conditional pardon	7	25
Cut free, certificate of freedom, free pardon	84	51
Absconded	0	1
Died under sentence	6	10
Total	100	100
TRACED	%	%
Traced to death	64	45
No sighting outside convict system/departures	28	35
No trace after marriage/children	2	3
Died in gaol?	0	2
Insufficient data to confirm sightings	2	3
Name too common	4	12
Total	100	100
MARRIAGE AFTER TRANSPORTATION	%	%
No evidence	66	76
Permission to marry failed	0	1
Permission to marry successful	10	15
Marriage/s outside system	24	8
Total	100	100
CHILDREN, GRANDCHILDREN	%	%
None found	70	80
Children, no grandchildren	3	9
Grandchildren	27	11
Total	100	100
AVERAGE AGE AT DEATH[a]	65.7 years	58.9 years
Rural English	65.7 years	62.5 years

a. Based on single-year-of-age mortality rates at age twenty-five years and over.

The reconstruction of lives after sentence has required intense genealogical and historical research by volunteers across many different sources. Some convicts returned home and they can now be followed through the United Kingdom censuses, and a tiny handful can be found in the United States censuses with Australian-born children.

Convicts who married under sentence were required to apply for governmental permission to marry and so can be found in the "Permission to Marry" registers and traced to marriage. Tasmania and Victoria were both early adopters of modern systems of vital registrations: in 1838 in the case of the former and 1853 in the latter. The Victorian vital registrations implemented William Farr's full program and remain among the best nineteenth-century birth, death, and marriage records in the Anglophone world. Institutional records, especially of those caring for the destitute aged, are a rich source of convicts' final years, and colonial police gazettes record recidivists. Finally, most of Australia's relevant historical newspapers have been digitized by the National Library of Australia and are text searchable through TROVE. Vital registrations in other colonies are less satisfactory in their coverage, detail, and accessibility; New Zealand, the destination of many Tasmanian emancipists, currently has limited access to digitized records. In addition, descendants have contributed their own family history research, fleshing out stories and recording families where name changes made them otherwise invisible.

Table 2.4 gives descriptive statistics on life after sentence of the two convict populations. The swing rioters were the most likely to exit the system with a free pardon: 84 per cent, with another 6 per cent dying under sentence. Deaths under sentence for the non-swing rioters were slightly higher even though they were younger than the swing rioters. The swing rioters were more likely to be traced to death (64 per cent) than were the other convicts (45 per cent). Swing rioters likewise remained more visible in later historical records and did better at making a new life independent of the government provisions for care in old age.

Male emancipists faced a marriage market in Van Diemen's Land where men outnumbered women seven to one. Convict marriages, however, were encouraged for the sake of building a community and for reformation, and both groups found wives while under sentence or soon after with a successful application for permission to marry. However, the swing rioters were three times more likely to find a wife outside the convict system and almost three times more likely to have grandchildren. Swing rioters were also more likely to return to the families left behind or to bring them to Australia. Some parishes raised the funds for wives and children to join their emancipist fathers. Finally, the swing rioters had an average age of death based on single-year-of-age mortality rates at age 25 years and over of 65.7 years, compared with

Table 2.5

Logistic regression: variables associated with behaviour and punishment under sentence

	Model 1: 6+ conduct offences		*Model 2: 3+ alcohol-related offences*		*Model 3: Any reactive behaviour*		*Model 4: Violent reactive behaviour*		*Model 5: Absconded*		*Model 6: Flogged*		*Model 7: Solitary confinement*		*Model 8: Insults*	
	OR	*p*	*OR*	*p*	*OR*	*p*	*OR*	*p*	*OR*	*p*	*OR*	*p*	*OR*	*p*	*OR*	*p*
Ref cat: Swing rioters																
Other convicts	4.72	0.000	5.54	0.000	3.34	0.000	4.89	0.001	5.00	0.000	2.48	0.000	2.70	0.000	2.75	0.000
Ref cat: 7 years																
14 years	1.77	0.000	2.27	0.000	1.42	0.025	1.04	0.863	1.48	0.029	1.30	0.085	1.61	0.002	1.74	0.004
Life	1.53	0.000	1.76	0.000	1.05	0.656	1.07	0.674	1.45	0.009	1.02	0.870	1.03	0.828	1.47	0.010
Age	0.94	0.000	1.02	0.068	0.94	0.000	0.93	0.000	0.96	0.000	0.93	0.000	0.94	0.000	0.96	0.000
Ref cat: England																
Ireland	1.31	0.371	1.64	0.170	0.98	0.943	2.25	0.013	1.39	0.318	1.06	0.847	1.66	0.091	1.07	0.870
Scotland	0.80	0.368	1.01	0.966	1.06	0.814	0.91	0.760	1.41	0.181	1.06	0.803	1.48	0.109	1.32	0.482
Other	1.85	0.070	2.49	0.011	1.27	0.491	1.88	0.117	1.20	0.634	1.28	0.456	1.30	0.434	0.87	0.714
Ref cat: Rural																
Market/semi-industrial	2.45	0.000	1.84	0.001	1.41	0.015	1.70	0.010	1.29	0.148	1.38	0.026	1.52	0.004	1.44	0.037
Urban	2.11	0.000	1.12	0.561	1.38	0.018	1.76	0.004	1.53	0.011	1.44	0.008	1.24	0.130	1.89	0.000
Ref cat: Unskilled																
Semiskilled	0.84	0.176	0.95	0.756	0.89	0.333	0.83	0.268	0.86	0.308	0.94	0.623	0.78	0.041	0.90	0.460
Skilled	1.34	0.052	2.13	0.000	0.96	0.800	0.78	0.220	1.03	0.885	1.07	0.647	0.83	0.219	1.33	0.119
White-collar	0.50	0.148	0.68	0.546	0.20	0.002	0.28	0.219	0.62	0.462	0.23	0.021	0.95	0.918	1.21	0.748

Ref cat: Single																
Married	0.75	0.051	0.85	0.394	0.71	0.010	0.90	0.647	0.84	0.368	0.89	0.435	0.92	0.597	0.80	0.142
Widowed	1.15	0.648	1.06	0.870	0.90	0.709	0.52	0.295	0.18	0.020	0.88	0.672	1.31	0.376	0.73	0.297

Ref cat: Reference category

OR: Odds ratio. Values greater than 1 mean that the convicts in this category are more likely to experience the event than convicts in the reference category. Values less than 1 mean that the convicts in this category are less likely to experience the event than convicts in the reference category.

p: p-value. p-values of less than 0.10 are considered to be significant. p-values of less than 0.05 are shaded dark grey. p-values between 0.05 and 0.10 are shaded light grey.

only 58.9 years for the other convicts. The rural English convicts, however, were more resilient – or less damaged by servitude – than their urban peers and had an average age of death just three years lower than the swing rioters (62.5 years)

ANALYSIS

The relevant significance of factors measured in life before sentence and experience under sentence, and the effects of both on the outcomes of life after sentence were the final test of the role of "character" as well as background in these convict experiences. Table 2.5 gives the results of eight logistic regressions, testing whether swing rioters had a different pattern of behaviour and punishment under sentence than did other convict cohorts, controlling for relevant factors. The eight factors tested for are (1) six or more conduct offences; (2) three or more alcohol-related offences; (3) reactive behaviour of any kind; (4) violent reactive behaviour; (5) absconded at least once; (6) flogged at least once; (7) kept in solitary confinement at least once; and (8) insults of any kind. Odds ratios greater than one mean that the convicts in the relevant category were more likely to experience the event than convicts in the reference category. Odds ratios less than one mean that convicts in the category were less likely to experience the event than convicts in the reference category. P-values of less than 0.05 are considered to be significant and are highlighted in dark grey. Levels between 0.05 and 0.010 are considered to be marginally significant and are highlighted in light grey.

The strongest effects across the eight regressions are seen for the swing rioters compared to the other male convicts. For all models the swing rioters stand out as behaving better and receiving less punishment. In terms of the control variables, the results are as follows: convicts with a seven-year sentence had fewer offences and less punishment than did those with a fourteen-year or life sentence – as expected – as they were exposed to the system for less time. The older a convict was at transportation, the less likely he was to offend and receive punishment under sentence. The exception was alcohol-related offences. Older convicts were more likely to have three or more alcohol-related offences under sentence. Irish convicts were more likely than the English to exhibit violent reactive behaviour. Convicts from outside England, Ireland, and Scotland were more likely to have six or more conduct offences and three or more alcohol-related offences.

Table 2.6
Logistic regression: variables associated with outcomes after sentence

	Model 9: Received free pardon[a]		*Model 10: Traced to death*		*Model 11: Marriage after transportation*		*Model 12: Grandchildren traced*	
	OR	*p*	*OR*	*p*	*OR*	*p*	*OR*	*p*
Ref cat: Swing rioters								
Other convicts	0.22	0.000	0.50	0.000	0.57	0.003	0.56	0.005
Ref cat: 7 years								
14 years	0.24	0.000	1.51	0.007	1.49	0.020	1.26	0.290
Life	0.02	0.000	1.67	0.000	1.92	0.000	1.46	0.030
Age	1.01	0.488	1.01	0.064	0.93	0.000	0.97	0.004
Ref cat: England								
Ireland	0.83	0.624	1.07	0.843	0.71	0.399	0.39	0.198
Scotland	1.12	0.738	0.79	0.363	0.81	0.491	0.62	0.320
Other	0.69	0.436	0.95	0.885	1.31	0.470	1.06	0.924
Ref cat: Rural								
Market/semi-industrial	1.10	0.636	1.07	0.648	0.73	0.067	0.61	0.027
Urban	1.18	0.366	0.98	0.913	0.95	0.728	0.66	0.048
Ref cat: Unskilled								
Semiskilled	1.14	0.429	0.91	0.455	1.58	0.001	1.27	0.182
Skilled	1.51	0.045	1.26	0.106	2.70	0.000	1.66	0.013
White-collar	0.80	0.691	0.73	0.484	1.07	0.916	0.58	0.606
Ref cat: Single								
Married	0.91	0.645	1.20	0.184	0.76	0.098	1.55	0.019
Widowed	0.93	0.852	1.24	0.441	1.07	0.843	0.66	0.373
Ref cat: No reactive behaviour								
Insolence	1.11	0.624	1.01	0.932	0.86	0.387	1.14	0.544
Refusal to work	1.39	0.228	0.90	0.611	0.78	0.264	0.97	0.917
Tearing clothes	2.00	0.193	1.53	0.244	0.94	0.884	1.22	0.735
Threats or violence	1.10	0.707	0.91	0.621	0.91	0.648	1.13	0.680
Ref cat: No insults								
Admonishment, fine, short solitary	1.10	0.697	0.71	0.044	0.85	0.398	0.96	0.858
Longer solitary, extension of probation	0.69	0.284	0.71	0.170	0.80	0.430	0.79	0.496
Multiple solitaries, flogging, treadmill, chains	1.12	0.651	0.64	0.010	0.78	0.190	0.56	0.015
Multiple floggings, mines, Port Arthur	0.89	0.671	0.54	0.002	0.54	0.007	0.51	0.021

Ref cat: Reference category
OR: Odds ratio. Values greater than 1 mean that the convicts in this category are more likely to experience the event than convicts in the reference category. Values less than 1 mean that the convicts in this category are less likely to experience the event than convicts in the reference category.
p: p-value. p-values of less than 0.10 are considered to be significant. p-values of less than 0.05 are shaded dark grey. p-values between 0.05 and 0.10 are shaded light grey.
a. Analysis excludes convicts who died under sentence.

Rural convicts were better behaved and received less punishment than those from towns or cities. Skilled convicts had more conduct offences and more alcohol-related offences than did the unskilled but were more likely to marry and establish a lineage. White-collar convicts had less reactive behaviour and were less likely to be flogged. Convicts who were married before transportation had fewer conduct offences and less reactive behaviour in the system.

These results confirm the finding that greater family support in being already married, living in one's native place (unlike the Irish), being older and more mature, coming from a quieter rural society than the complex criminal cultures of big port cities and industrial towns, and possessing more human capital in terms of skills were protective factors for survival through the penal system and for life after sentence. In these assignment records, literacy and birth family composition were too irregularly reported to be useful for analysis.

Table 2.6 gives the result of variables associated with success measured on four points: (9) gaining a free pardon; (10) able to be traced to death; (11) marriage after transportation; and (12) grandchildren traced. Variables considered are the background characteristics included in the previous models plus reactive behaviour and punishment under sentence. Again, controlling for other variables, the swing rioters had better outcomes than did other male convicts. They were more likely to gain a free pardon, to be traced to death, to marry after transportation, and to have grandchildren traced.

Results for the control variables are as follows. Those with a seven-year sentence were most likely to gain a free pardon. Those with a life sentence the least likely. Older convicts were more likely to be traced to death, less likely to marry after transportation, and less likely to have grandchildren traced. Rural convicts were more likely to marry and to have grandchildren traced. Skilled convicts were more likely to receive a free pardon, to marry, and to have grandchildren traced. Those married before transportation were less likely to marry after and more likely to have grandchildren traced.

Reactive behaviour under sentence did not correlate with successful outcomes, but the more insults a convict experienced, the less likely he was to be traced to death, less likely to marry, and less likely to have grandchildren traced. Finally, adult height was not a significant variable in any analysis (not shown).

CONCLUSION

The regression analysis revealed that "character" was the single most important characteristic that determined how a convict survived penal servitude. The exceptionalism of the swing rioters shows them to be closer to "ordinary working men and women" than to their fellow convicts for whom the impact of cascading insults reduced chances of remaining visible in the historical record, of finding a wife, raising children, and surviving well. The stress regime of penal servitude and convict discipline exacted a cumulative toll on the mind even more than the body, confirming John Mortlock's bitter words: "the brain is the seat of pain – very dreadful." There were remarkably resilient individuals, but the majority of the men transported for felonies rather than political offences during the assignment period had their lives wrecked and truncated by their penal servitude. Merely 11 per cent of this sample of other convicts in the assignment period left descendants in the growing colonial population (table 2.4). They did not make a contribution to the building of the colony beyond that of their own labour, and in old age they returned to the care of the state in the charitable institutions for the destitute aged that were little different from their convict barracks. Swing rioters were more likely to die in the arms of their families.

If convicts transported to Van Diemen's Land were "ordinary workers" except for their character, their character and experience as convicts severely compromised the effectiveness of the state's investment in their transportation. In other words, many were irredeemable. Most survived their servitude, but they had to compete for wives and livings against free immigrants who laboured under less stigma and had fewer traumatic memories. The stories of "winners" among the emancipists have distorted our understanding of the penal system. Most men transported before the reforms of the 1840s and the eventual breakdown of the penal system, died "without friends" as they termed it in the nineteenth century: far from kith and kin, perhaps with some mates made over the years of servitude and afterwards but largely remembered only in the historical record through their own voice as they gave their personal details to a clerk in a benevolent or lunatic asylum, a charity hospital, or a gaol, just as they had for the indent when they began their servitude. If details were recorded at the end of life it was a courtesy but not an administrative necessity. To die without friends, as Grace Karskens first noted, was their greatest dread lest they rest in "dishonoured graves" with no one to make them a coffin and no one to remember them.[21] It was still about "character" even in death.

3

Sickness and Death on Convict Voyages to Australia

HAMISH MAXWELL-STEWART AND REBECCA KIPPEN

The passage taken by convict vessels en route to Australia was one of the longest that any unfree migrants have been subjected to – an average of four months at sea. Only French prisoners shipped to New Caledonia (1864–97) and Russian convicts sent from Odessa to Sakhalin (1879–1905) were moved greater distances.[1] Despite the length of the voyage, monthly mortality on Australian-bound convict vessels was not excessive. In this chapter we put this experience into a wider context. As a number of historians have pointed out, ocean voyages in the eighteenth and nineteenth century became progressively less deadly, although there is some disagreement about the factors responsible for this change. Using the detailed records available for convict voyages, we explore the ways in which experiences on land and sea affected voyage outcomes for both male and female prisoners. Finally, the chapter will relate these findings to the wider debate on mortality decline in the age of sail.

Between 1788 and 1868 a total of 825 convict vessels sailed from British and Irish ports to the Australian colonies. In the first half of the nineteenth century the thought of spending four or more months at sea was a daunting prospect for most landlubbers. Even free migrants were warned that the distance of Van Diemen's Land and New South Wales from British and Irish ports rendered the voyage a "terrible undertaking."[2] It is thus commonly assumed that the 141,000 male and 26,000 female convicts shipped to Britain's Australian penal colonies suffered great hardships at sea.

Perhaps surprisingly, however, death rates on the First Fleet, which sailed in May 1787, were remarkably low given the scale of the operation. In all, the scheme involved shipping 736 male and female prisoners a distance of some 14,000 miles. Although the voyage lasted 252 days, the monthly death rate of less than seven convicts per 1,000 embarked was benign by late eighteenth-century standards.

To be sure, the death rate on the Second Fleet, which left Britain's shores for Australia in January 1790, was much higher than that of its predecessor (forty-nine per 1,000 per month). Moreover, arrival in New South Wales brought little relief. The survivors were landed in a very weakened condition, and a further 16 per cent died shortly after disembarkation. As the Rev. Johnson memorably put it, they arrived, "wretched, naked, filthy, dirty, lousy, and many of them utterly unable to stand, to creep, or even to stir hand or foot."[3]

Reports of inadequate provisions and the crowded conditions on board Second Fleet transports prompted greater government regulation. In the years 1792–5 a naval-trained surgeon was appointed to "superintend" every transport vessel. A further rise in death rates following the discontinuation of this experiment led to even tighter regulation. From 1800, bonus payments were made to masters for landing convicts in good health. Surgeons were reinstated and, after 1805, placed on the same ranking as army medical officers. As in the slave trade, ships' masters often pulled rank on surgeons countermanding their orders.[4] In order to solve this problem, surgeons were given authority over all disciplinary and medical matters in 1815, including the ventilation and cleaning of the vessel.[5]

Following the introduction of the tightened "surgeon-superintendent system" monthly death rates fell decisively, averaging just 2.4 per 1,000 in the period 1815–68.[6] To put this achievement into perspective, the equivalent rate for males aged between fifteen and forty-four on emigrant ships sailing from Europe to the United States between 1836 and 1853 was 4.4 per 1,000. The discrepancy is especially noteworthy when one considers that, as well as being free, the trans-Atlantic migrants were embarked on a voyage that took an average of forty-five days compared to 116 to Australia.[7]

While the low mortality rate on Australian-bound convict vessels is remarkable, a number of other studies have recorded falling death rates at sea in the period 1700–1850. Before convicts were shipped to Australia they had been lagged across the Atlantic to be sold in Britain's Caribbean and North American colonies. Well over 50,000

British and Irish felons were shipped in this manner between 1619 and 1775.[8] While losses of more than 70 per 1,000 per month were reported for the years 1718–36 these fell to just twelve in the period 1768–75.[9]

Improvements of a similar magnitude were observed on eighteenth-century slave vessels. Although the terrible conditions that prevailed on slavers were widely publicized by abolitionists, mortality had improved considerably by the 1790s. Ironically, while the Second Fleet's appalling death record has been attributed to the contractor's close involvement with slaving, its losses were noticeably higher than the mean for late eighteenth-century British slaving operations.[10] The crude monthly death rate on slaving vessels declined from a high of ninety per 1,000 in 1691–1700 to a low of thirty-two in 1791–1800.[11]

This trend reflects similar observations for terrestrial populations. British death rates started to fall in the eighteenth century before improving dramatically in the second half of the nineteenth. As Thomas McKeown pointed out, it is difficult to attribute improvements in life expectancy to increased medical intervention before the introduction of sulphonamides and other antibiotics from the 1920s onwards. With the notable exceptions of smallpox inoculation (later vaccination) and the use of antiscorbutics at sea, effective treatments for most disorders were not discovered until long after the onset of declining mortality rates. McKeown thought that the explanation for this could be found in rising levels of nutrition and an associated increase in the effectiveness of immune responses.[12]

Yet, the declining record of mortality at sea would seem to suggest that medical intervention might have played more of a role than McKeown allowed. Over the course of the eighteenth century it became increasingly common for surgeons to be employed on slaving vessels, and after the passing of the Dolben Act of 1788 their presence was mandated by law.[13] Just as on convict vessels, the introduction of medically trained professionals appears to have coincided with marked improvements in voyage outcomes.

In order to determine why this was so, it is necessary to explore the prevoyage experiences of passengers as well as those they encountered at sea. Surgeon-superintendents on convict vessels, for example, often argued that deaths and sickness at sea could be attributed to the dissolute lives their charges had led (alcohol and opiate abuse and indiscriminate sexual encounters were commonly ascribed as preexisting causes of death). In similar fashion, slavers maintained that they were powerless to prevent deaths on the Atlantic passage as the slaves they purchased had been so mistreated by their African captors that their chances of surviving while at sea were dramatically reduced. While abolitionists were quick to point out that such arguments conveniently shifted the onus of blame from Europeans to Africans, it stands to reason that the prevoyage nutritional and disease history of passengers could impact upon postembarkation death rates.

The reverse is true of the other end of the voyage. As the experience of the Second Fleet demonstrates, the impact that conditions on board had on death rates can only be adequately measured if postvoyage mortality is also taken into account. The difficulty here is that new disease environments and exploitative colonial work regimes might also impact the postdisembarkation experience of death.[14] While it is important to take such considerations into account the overall message is clear. In order to analyse what happens at sea it is necessary to place the experience of passengers within a shore-based context.

If this is true of passengers it is also true of the vessels that they sailed on. Some have argued that changes in ship design helped to improve conditions encountered at sea. Copper sheathing, first introduced in the 1750s, led to faster voyages and drier quarters since it protected the hulls of ships from marine boring worms, helping to keep timbers dry. Ship design could also impact ventilation and the amount of space allocated to each passenger – critics of the slave trade, for example, argued that "tight packing" was a principal cause of mortality.

Finally, if – as some have suggested – medical intervention made a decisive impact on eighteenth- and nineteenth-century voyage outcomes, then it is reasonable to suspect that some surgeons were better at ameliorating, or perhaps preventing, the onset of sickness at sea than others. One might think, therefore, that medical training, the degree of control vested in the surgeon, and prior experience of practicing medicine at sea might collectively shape voyage outcomes.

The probability that a convict would die during the voyage to Australia might be influenced by many factors. A history of poor prevoyage nutrition (perhaps exacerbated by a life of debauchery) might fatally weaken a passenger long before they were embarked. Experiences in prison could exacerbate these effects if punitive, but institutional diets, clothing, and heating might also ameliorate the worst effects of preexisting poverty. The use of appropriately trained medical professionals might improve the capacity for effective prevoyage screening, as well as facilitate the management of disease and hygiene regimes. There might be little, however, that a surgeon could do to mitigate the impact of poor rations (lack of vitamin C springs to mind here) or contaminated water – other than persuading the ship's master to stop off in order to resupply. On a fully loaded vessel the surgeon might well be overwhelmed by the number of patients or find himself powerless to stop infection spreading through crowded quarters. Poorly maintained vessels could also pose a threat. Poor ventilation and shipboard spaces contaminated by years of accumulated dirt might encourage the spread of infection. Failure to make good speed could put pressure on the available supplies (including drugs and other prophylactics), while weather could play havoc with the best laid medical plans. Tropical heat might exacerbate some disorders, while pitching seas and wave-soaked decks would cut down exercise time and make it impossible to keep bedding and clothing dry. Finally, the behaviour of the convicts themselves could affect voyage outcomes. There was a world of difference between treating compliant, as opposed to unruly, patients.

THE DATA

While not all of these issues can be explored through the examination of longitudinal data, many can. Fortunately, when it comes to convict voyages, there is no shortage of available information. As Australia operated as a gaol without walls, physical descriptions of every prisoner were placed on file. This enabled the colour of the eyes and hair, height, age, place of birth (and hence accent) of all absconders to be circulated – they were gazetted in colonial newspapers. It is thus possible to know the 160,000 convicts transported to Australia down to their tattoos, moles, scars, and inoculation marks.

Other information was required to manage the legal aspects of transportation. The court, length of sentence, and day of conviction were thus recorded, along with the nature of the offence that brought each offender to the Antipodes. This information was entered into what was colloquially known as the "black books." A note of every subsequent encounter with a colonial magistrates' bench was also transcribed into this voluminous series, including the number of strokes of the lash awarded as punishment and days spent labouring in irons or walled up in a solitary confinement.[15]

In contrast to prisons and other systems of incarceration, the purpose of transportation was to derive benefit from the bodies of the convicted by deploying them as cheap colonial labour. In order to facilitate this end, the colonial state also elicited information about the skills of convicts and their levels of literacy. Musters were taken in order to determine where each prisoner was deployed and lists collected of those who died under sentence so that they could be struck off the books.

The surgeon-superintendents charged with maintaining the health of convicts on the long voyage to Australia were required to keep medical journals. As well as entering information on every hospitalization, more detailed case notes were kept for serious cases. Observations of ailments might include the species of worm that infected a convict's gut, the signs of scurvy that erupted on their limbs and swelled their gums, and the state of their pulse.

These journals reveal as much about the surgeons as they do about their patients. Each diagnosis betrayed views on the nature of bodily disorders and modes of infection. The length of case notes might provide an indication of the state of sickness on board the vessel or, equally, the degree of attention that the surgeon paid to the task of maintaining a daily record of morbidity. Taken as a whole, the surgeons' journals can be read as a collective *curriculum vitae.* They help to identify voyages undertaken by greenhorns new to the business, as well as those superintended by old hands who had made several previous trips.

The vessels upon which surgeons and convicts sailed were themselves subject to regulation. For insurance purposes each was graded – receiving ratings that reflected age and general condition. The insurance registers also noted tonnage.[16] When each vessel completed its voyage, port officers recorded the number of individuals on board, including crew, military guard, and other passengers and their children who had been shipped in addition to each consignment of convicts.

Such records make two things possible. They enable historians to follow the experiences of individuals in detail. In the case of convicts it is possible to piece together much of their lives from cradle to grave as they passed through courtroom, prison, transport vessel, colonial farm, and punishment gang. Collectively, however, such a body of data can be used to place individual records of life and death within a wider context.

In order to do this we assembled data for 289 convict vessels that sailed from southern English or Irish ports to the British penal colony of Van Diemen's Land in the period 1818–53 (thirty-nine voyages for which surgeons' journals could not be located were omitted). Together the vessels in our study carried a total of 48,215 male and 12,396 female convicts. As well as information on the tonnage, insurance rating, and age of each vessel, we calculated the number of days spent at sea and the amount of time that elapsed between the start of the embarkation process and the point at which each vessel actually sailed. We used the list of cases treated recorded in each surgeon-superintendent's journal to determine the day each patient entered the ship's hospital, the day that they were discharged, the diagnosis, and the outcome.[17]

While the surgeons' journals are a rich source of information they vary greatly in terms of the number of cases covered. Charles Henry Fuller on the *Blenheim*, for example, recorded 356 separate morbidity episodes while, by contrast, William Henderson on the *Bussorah Merchant* recorded just six.[18] We found that the more experienced the surgeon (measured in terms of the number of times they had previously sailed to Australia on a convict vessel), the fewer the number of cases they were likely to record. There are two plausible explanations for this. First, it is possible that old hands were better at preventing and treating disease than greenhorns. If this was the case it might provide powerful evidence that medical expertise could make a dramatic difference at sea. Second, surgeons who had previously made the voyage to Australia felt that they knew the ropes and as a result were more blasé about keeping detailed paperwork, only noting the most serious cases. As we could find no relationship between the number of recorded cases of sickness and the number of deaths, we suspect that the second explanation is closer to the mark. In other words, there was nothing to suggest that experienced surgeons were more successful at keeping their convict charges alive.

We also found another underlying trend in the data. The number of cases entered onto the sick list increased over time. A previous study of morbidity on female convict vessels sailing to New South Wales uncovered a similar trend. R.V. Jackson attributed this to the tendency for larger numbers of female convicts to be shipped on later sailing vessels.[19] Thus, he reasoned that more crowded conditions at sea led to increased levels of sickness. We agree that there was a rise in reported morbidity over time but note that this was not matched by a similar rise in mortality. Once more we suspect that the increase in cases reflects record-keeping trends rather than deteriorating onboard conditions.

These findings raise uncomfortable questions. Was it possible that our data might tell us something about shifts in record-keeping practice but otherwise shed little light on the factors that impacted upon life and

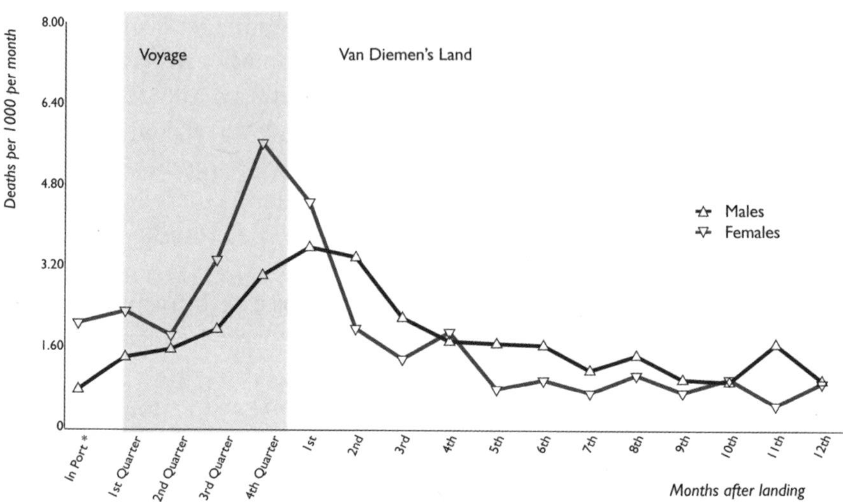

Figure 3.1 Death rates at sea and during the first year in the colony for male and female convicts arriving on voyages to VDL, 1830–53

death at sea? Reassuringly, however, we did find a relationship between the amount of sickness on board (measured in terms of the total number of days convicts were recorded as being sufficiently unwell to require treatment) and deaths. Intriguingly we also found an even stronger relationship between sickness at sea and postvoyage mortality. Convicts who arrived on sickly ships were less likely to survive their first year under sentence in Van Diemen's Land.

THE DEATH RATE IN PROFILE

Convict monthly mortality rates for the period between embarkation and sailing, the voyage, and the first twelve months of colonial servitude are provided in figure 3.1. These have been separated by sex. In all, 128 surgeon's journals recorded both the date when convicts were brought on board and the date of sailing. The embarkation process was slightly longer for female vessels, seventeen days compared to sixteen for male. The length of the voyage to Australia ranged from the eighty-day voyage of the *Rodney* in 1853 to the 190-day passage of the *Jane* in 1831. Mean sailing time for both male and female voyages was just less than four months (116 days for male, 118 for female). In order to examine the timing of death across the entire cohort, we split each voyage into quartiles.

Several trends are discernable, of which perhaps the most notable is the increase in mortality over the course of the voyage. This is in sharp contrast to the profile of deaths on free-migrant voyages sailing to South Australia in the second half of the nineteenth century. Migrants, particularly infants, died in their greatest numbers a third of the way into the passage.[20] Analysis of the timing of deaths in the Atlantic slave trade has also suggested that peak mortality occurred midvoyage, although there was much variation.[21] It is possible that the larger vessels and faster sailing routes to Australia introduced midcentury were more successful in combating mortality amongst free migrants in the second half of the voyage, as opposed to the first. The large number of infants on board migrant vessels may also have increased the risk of mortality from diarrhoeal diseases in the tropics (the equator was crossed a third of the way into the voyage).[22] Yet, the difference in the timing of deaths on convict and migrant vessels is striking and remains largely unexplained.

Other historians have argued that mortality on male vessels was likely to be higher than that for female ships as they were more crowded. We can find no evidence to support this.[23] Despite the greater numbers on board male vessels and the need for stricter levels of security that limited opportunities for exercise, female mortality was higher in port and remained high for the duration of the voyage. While the spike in the female death rate for the last quartile was accentuated by the peculiar experience of the *East London* (a vessel that had a particularly traumatic passage), the death rate remained significantly higher than that for male convicts even when data for this voyage were excluded.[24] Second, mortality rates for male convicts remained high in the period immediately following disembarkation. Third, the female mortality record postvoyage fell to below that of men and remained consistently lower for the twelve months after disembarkation. While the female death rate in the first two months after landing was elevated, the trend was far less accentuated than it was for males. Finally, female convicts also spent significantly longer in sickbay during the voyage.

As these results reveal, the morbidity and mortality outcomes for transported men and women were strikingly different. One possible explanation for this was that smaller and older vessels were disproportionately used to ship female convicts. Surgeon-superintendents certainly rated this as a risk factor. Morgan Price, for example, reported of a voyage he undertook in the sixteen-year-old vessel the *Hector* in 1835: "The ship was of a less Tonnage than usual[ly] taken up for the conveyance of Female Prisoners to the Colony – being only 338 Tons having on board including the ship's company upwards of Two hundred individuals and the unusual length of the voyage and the very indifferent manner the prison and between Decks was ventilated [it] is rather extraordinary that no illness of any consequence appeared on board on a voyage of one hundred and twenty nine days." This was Price's eighth voyage as surgeon-superintendent in charge of a convict vessel.[25] The result of our analysis suggests, however, that his fears were unjustified.

We found no evidence that the size of the vessel and the number of passengers on board had an impact on mortality rates. In all we were able to locate population data for 228 (79 per cent) of the voyages in our sample. We estimate that just over 10,000 seamen were employed to man the vessels that brought the 60,611 convicts in this study to Australia. While military detachments were not employed on female vessels, a guard was present on all male voyages. We estimate that just over 7,400 soldiers also made the voyage bringing with them 1,300 wives and just fewer than 1,800 children. A small number of free passengers were also present, most of who arrived on board female vessels (considered to provide a safer passage). Many of these were the wives and dependents of male convicts who had already been transported and were considered to have behaved well enough for the state to assist with family reunification.[26] They also included small numbers of cabin-class passengers, generally the wives and family of officials travelling to Australia. Together these amounted to 700 adults and around 750 children. Finally, the 12,396 female prisoners were accompanied into exile by 1,900 of their own children (a further eighty-one births occurred on the voyage to Australia). Thus, in total we estimate that in addition to convicts, the vessels in our sample carried a further 23,800 other passengers.

Our analysis reveals that male ships were more tightly packed than female. They carried 0.62 passengers per ton while female convict vessels carried 0.54. We failed to find evidence of a relationship between loading and mortality, and this remained true even when male and female ships were examined separately. Our results mirror findings for the slave trade and free-migrant voyages. Contrary to expectations, the density with which vessels were packed does not appear to have significantly affected mortality levels.[27] Comparative analysis with other voy-

Table 3.1
Loading and mortality

	Passengers per ton (excluding crew)			*Monthly death rate (per 1,000)*		
	All	*Male Vessels*	*Female Vessels*	*All*	*Males*[a]	*Females*[a]
Immigrant Vessels	0.369				4.4	6.2
Convict vessels	0.524	0.549	0.465		2.1	3.5
Slave ships	Over 2			32		

[a] Aged 25–34.

Source: Cohen, "Mortality on Immigrant Voyages" and "Determinants of Individual Immigrant Mortality"; Klein, *The Middle Passage*, 195–6.

ages serves to illustrate the point. Although convict vessels were more crowded than those employed to carry free passengers across the Atlantic, their record of age-specific mortality was noticeably better (see table 3.1).

There is little evidence that the vessels used to ship female convicts to Australia were in other ways deficient. The ships employed in the male trade were on average thirteen years old, while those used to transport female convicts had spent an average of just eleven years at sea. As this would imply, the latter were more likely to have better insurance ratings.

Neither was there a significant difference in voyage length. Female vessels took an average of 118 days to reach their destination compared to 116 for their male counterparts. In contrast to the slave trade where the monthly death rate was higher on longer voyages, we could find no such relationship.[28] This is because, unlike their trans-Atlantic counterparts, convict transports often put in to port en route in order to resupply. While vessels that stopped generally took longer to reach Australia, stopping reduced mortality rates. Thus, while putting into port carried the risk of exposing those on board to new sources of infection, these dangers appear to have been outweighed by reductions in deficiency diseases resulting from the opportunity to purchase fresh rations.[29]

We could also find no difference in the age structure of male and female convicts except that fewer female convicts were transported in their early teens. The mean age of male and female patients recorded on admission to hospital on the passage to Australia was nearly identical (26.25 for men compared to 26.92 for women). Although we did find that surgeons on female convict vessels were less likely to have sailed as a surgeon-superintendent to Australia before (they made on average 0.83 prior voyages compared to 1.63 for those on male ships), as noted earlier we found no evidence that prior experience was associated with a reduction in either morbidity or mortality.

That convict women were at greater risk of mortality at sea compared to men is in itself not surprising. Cohen's study of trans-Atlantic free migrants found a similar discrepancy in mortality outcomes for men and women.[30] A further study by Staniforth of assisted migrant voyages sailing to Australia in the years 1837–39 also suggested that women died at greater rates than men – a discrepancy he attributed to the comparatively poor prevoyage nutrition of women and deaths in childbirth at sea.[31] This is plausible.

If differences between the vessels used to ship male and female convicts to Australia, the number of passengers placed on board, and the relative experience of surgeon-superintendents cannot explain variations in shipboard mortality and morbidity, it is possible that differing prevoyage experiences might. Several surgeons on female vessels were concerned that the convicts they received were predisposed to sickness, especially deficiency diseases. Since the way in which male and female convicts were processed prior to embarkation differed, this is a distinct possibility. After they had been sentenced to transportation most male convicts were removed to hulks. These were dismasted vessels anchored in ports and used as mobile labour depots. The average amount of time that lapsed between sentencing and embarkation for Australia was seven months.[32] This was nearly twice as long as the voyage itself. By contrast female convicts were forwarded to the transport vessel from regional prisons. As these two types of institution were characterized by different work and dietary regimes it is possible that this had an impact on male and female convict experiences at sea.

Scurvy, the most prominent of the deficiency diseases recorded in the surgeons' journals, was more prevalent amongst convicts than soldiers and sailors despite the similarity in the shipboard diet supplied to all three. Thus, there is reason to suspect that prevoyage experiences did indeed predispose some convicts to deficiency diseases. The voyage of the *Emily* is particularly revealing. On 15 June 1842 this vessel embarked eighty male convicts from the *Justicia* hulk and a further eighty from the *Warrior*. It then left Woolwich to sail down the Thames to Sheerness where a further eighty convicts were taken on board from the *Fortitude* hulk. Shortly after the ship crossed the equator, scurvy appeared among the prisoners. The surgeon, Andrew Henderson, found that 28 per cent of those embarked from the *Justicia* had spongy gums or other symptoms of the disease compared to just 9 per cent from the *Warrior* and 5 per cent from the *Fortitude*. A month later he carried out a second inspection. By now 51 per cent of the *Justicia* convicts showed symptoms of the disease, many being badly affected (one had already died) compared to just 13 per cent of the convicts embarked from the *Warrior* and the *Fortitude*.[33] He concluded that differences in the diet aboard the three hulks had predisposed the *Justicia* convicts to scurvy.

Some British prisons had experienced problems with scurvy before. Many Millbank prisoners had been struck down by the disorder after potatoes were stripped out of the diet in 1823.[34] The problem amongst transported convicts seems to have been largely restricted to men who were more likely to be diagnosed with scurvy during the voyage than their female counterparts. Male risk of death from deficiency diseases at sea was also greater (see table 3.2). It is noticeable that the only source of vitamin C supplied in the hulk ration was derived from potatoes (soup with a vegetable content was served to female prisoners in a majority of county gaols). While potatoes are an effective antiscorbutic, their prophylactic value is considerably reduced if they are peeled. This, or reductions in the quantity and or quality supplied in the hulks, probably accounts for the elevated rates of scurvy experienced by male convicts during the voyage to Australia.

While the hulk diet may have at times been deficient in vitamin C, it was in other respects superior to the institutional diet supplied to women prior to sailing. Although there were many regional variations in British prison diets in the nineteenth century, all were designed to be punitive. A survey of sixteen English county gaols and houses of correction revealed that the diet supplied to women consisted of very small quantities of meat (an average of just under twelve ounces a week) supplemented by bread, gruel, soup, and potatoes. The estimated daily calorific value was around 2,000, less than an English workhouse diet (2,400).[35] The diet for women in Millbank undergoing longer sentences of detention was more generous (2,300). The hulk diet supplied to male convicts provided an estimated 3,000 calories per day, although unlike their female counterparts they were engaged in hard labour. This was more generous than the ration supplied on male

Table 3.2
Mortality and morbidity classified according to cause or symptom

	Monthly mortality rates per 1,000		*Monthly morbidity rate per 1,000*	
Cause or symptom	*Men*	*Women*	*Men*	*Women*
Diarrhoea and dysentery	0.51	1.43	118.88	221.41
Respiratory tuberculosis	0.36	0.19	30.89	25.29
Other diseases of the respiratory system	0.22	0.21	134.20	152.33
Fever	0.20	0.25	77.19	103.46
Diseases of the digestive system	0.14	0.29	70.35	237.52
Diseases of the nervous system	0.10	0.06	14.87	21.42
Debility and marasmus	0.10	0.08	10.03	27.06
Diseases of the circulatory system	0.09	0.17	7.28	8.28
Scurvy	0.09	0.04	110.63	31.93
Other infectious diseases	0.08	0.04	19.57	18.54
Diseases of the musculoskeletal system	0.04	0.00	35.61	63.12
Accident	0.03	0.02	38.87	54.98
Diseases of the genitourinary system	0.03	0.06	12.74	72.16
Diseases of the skin	0.02	0.04	108.00	95.13
Parasitic disease	0.02	0.00	5.71	3.86
Unclassifiable	0.02	0.02	10.27	13.47
Unknown	0.02	0.02	5.77	26.43
Diseases of the blood	0.01	0.04	1.67	1.85
Diseases of the eye and ear	0.01	0.06	72.06	47.51
Other tuberculosis	0.01	0.02	14.11	13.14
Mental and behavioural disorders	0.01	0.08	2.59	51.29
Nausea	0.01	0.06	3.31	13.45
Paralysis	0.01	0.00	1.06	7.38
Sexually transmitted diseases	0.01	0.10	7.55	63.71
Unspecified natural causes	0.01	0.00	0.28	0.00
Convulsions & teething	0.00	0.02	0.01	0.60
Neoplasm	0.00	0.04	1.63	3.14
Pregnancy, childbirth, and the puerperium	0.00	0.10	0.02	29.94
Suicide	0.00	0.02	0.04	0.15
Total	2.13	3.49	915.20	1,408.56

convict vessels that delivered approximately 2,700 calories a day. Nevertheless the voyage diet appears to have been adequate considering the reduction in energy requirements. The surgeon Andrew Henderson weighed his male charges on three voyages to Van Diemen's Land

and discovered that they put on an average of 9.5 lbs over the voyage as a whole, weight gain being more pronounced in the first half compared to the second.[36]

Mark Staniforth argued that female assisted-migrants were more at risk than their male counterparts because of their comparatively poor prevoyage record of nutrition. There are a growing number of studies that suggest that intrahousehold distribution of calories favoured men at the expense of women as working class families attempted to protect the wage earning potential of male breadwinners. There is evidence, for example, that female prisoners gained weight in gaol in contrast to men.[37] Thus, while women received significantly fewer calories while in prison awaiting transportation, it is possible that this represented an improvement in their recent nutritional circumstances. Institutional work regimes that subjected men to greater physical labour may have also served to effectively close the gap. While it is difficult to assess the impact that institutional diets had on voyage morbidity and mortality rates, we found no evidence of elevated mortality on male and female convict vessels departing Ireland after the outbreak of the Irish potato famine, a sharp contrast to the rate of "ship fever," probably typhus, recorded on postfamine migrant voyages to the United States.[38] This suggests that, while institutional prevoyage diets may have been meagre by modern standards, they were sufficiently high to mitigate the effects of chronic undernutrition.

Several surgeons commented on the fatigued state of their female charges. While those embarked from prisons in the greater London area appeared healthy, others who had travelled from county gaols were not as fit. David Thomson, on board the *Eliza*, expressed concern for the wellbeing of Elizabeth Fielding who fell seriously ill the day after she was embarked. He discovered from a companion that she had suffered from dysentery in Stafford gaol and had subsequently been moved to London on the outside of a coach "exposed to the weather."[39] Joseph Street on the *Edward* remarked that "the prisoners come on board in small numbers – at different times, and as some come from considerable distances (York, for example) they are often much fatigued and not infrequently have catarrhs." Nevertheless he added that these were rarely severe.[40] When diarrhoea accompanied by fever broke out amongst the women on board the *William Bryan* the surgeon, Thomas Robertson, reported that it appeared "chiefly amongst the country women."[41] Morgan Price on the *Hector* reported that the considerable number of women forwarded from Scotland "had suffered severely

Table 3.3
Morbidity rate and risk

Distance from London (miles)	*Morbidity rate per 1000*	*Relative morbidity risk compared to in London*
0–69	246	1.00
70–99	256	1.04
100–69	260	1.05
>170	280	1.14
Scotland	220	0.89

from a very tedious voyage ... in a small sloop and were consequently very crowded and their health had suffered greatly."[42]

We found that there was a relationship between the distance travelled prior to embarkation and female convict morbidity rates at sea. Women who travelled from prisons located in Northern England, Western Wales, and Devon and Cornwall spent longer in hospital than women who had been transferred from the Midlands. Those convicted in London and the South-East had an even lower morbidity record. Women convicted in Scotland were at the least risk, suggesting that a voyage on a mail packet was less demanding than being transferred overland or that institutional diets in Scotland were superior or possibly that Scottish women were in better shape prior to conviction than their English and Welsh counterparts. Nevertheless, the overall differences were small. The mortality risk for a woman convicted in northern England was only 1.14 times greater than that of a woman convicted in London (see table 3.3).

If the distance travelled to the convict vessel had an impact on morbidity and mortality at sea one would expect this to be particularly so during the winter months when temperatures were colder and travel by road more difficult. Like Jackson, we found that female convict vessels departing England and Ireland in December, January, and February had longer sick lists than those that departed in other months.[43] This difference was not statistically significant, however, nor did it result in a greater number of deaths.

The distance travelled to the vessel may have had an impact on voyage morbidity and mortality in other ways however. Female convicts were nearly four times more likely to die in port than their male counterparts. In part this reflects the differing embarkation procedures. Because their charges were loaded in divisions from hulks located near to the transport vessel, surgeons on male ships were able to conduct prevoyage screening checks, a task in which they were assisted by the hulk surgeon. The relatively low rate of death on male transports prior to embarkation suggests that these measures were at least partially successful.[44] It was more difficult for a surgeon on a female transport to reject a woman who had been transferred from a gaol outside of London, since returning her from whence she had come was logistically more complicated. This was especially the case if the woman was accompanied by one or more children. Indeed the presence of children almost certainly restricted the ability of the surgeon to prevent the introduction of pernicious disorders since it was logistically impossible to reject a sick child without also rejecting the mother, regardless of the latter's state of health. Under such circumstances it seems likely that surgeons were pressured into embarking passengers on female vessels whom they would have otherwise rejected.

MORBIDITY AND MORTALITY AT SEA

While differences in prevoyage experiences can explain some of the elevated risk that female convicts were exposed to on the voyage to Australia, it is noticeable that the risk of death increased as the vessel neared its destination. A feature of both male and female voyages was that some conditions were more likely to be diagnosed in the first half of the voyage and others in the second. Disorders that tended to decline over the course of the voyage included diseases of the digestive system (largely constipation), fevers, and headaches. Those that rose included scurvy, accidents, diarrhoea and dysentery, and diseases of the respiratory and musculoskeletal systems. Although deaths related to pregnancy, childbirth, and the puerperium accounted for less than 2 per cent of all female mortality, other disorders appear to have posed a significant risk. This was particularly true of diarrhoea and dysentery, listed as a cause in 47.6 per cent of female deaths but just 27.1 male (see table 3.2).

This discrepancy suggests that female convict vessels were less hygienic than male. This poses something of a puzzle since similar hygiene regimes were imposed on all vessels. Surgeons were able to ensure that their charges were regularly washed (usually twice a week), as were their clothes, while bedding was aired and decks dry scrubbed.[45] Indeed others have assumed that death rates on female vessels would be lower than those for men, not just because of the additional space allocated to each prisoner but because the ratio of surgeon to convict patient was lower thus leading to a better ordered voyage.[46] If the introduction of trained surgeons made an impact, it is natural to assume that this would be particularly noticeable on voyages where there were fewer potential patients. It was also the case that female convicts spent longer on deck since they were considered to present less of a security risk and that therefore there was little need to exercise them by division as was common practice on male ships.[47]

It is possible that the water placed on board the vessel at the start of the voyage was a source of contamination. Thames water was notoriously offensive. Waterborne infectious agents were not isolated until the second half of the nineteenth century – Dr John Snow published his famous map showing the relationship between London water sources and cholera rates in 1854, the year after the last vessel in our study sailed.[48] Despite this, the common assumption that "all smell is disease" undoubtedly provided some protection to convicts. River water was filtered (presumably by passing it through beds of sand or gravel) before it was placed in casks.[49] From the 1820s on, all convict vessels were also fitted with charcoal water filters.

Contamination is likely to have been a far worse problem during summer, although we could find no evidence that summer departures presented additional dangers for those on board. Neither could we find anything to suggest that female convict vessels were more likely to depart at a particular season compared to male nor any reason why the water supply on female vessels would be worse than that provided for male convicts.

While the evidence that season of departure could impact on voyage outcomes was weak, the same could not be said for season of arrival. Convict vessels that reached their destination during the Antipodean winter had a higher rate of onboard morbidity and postvoyage mortality. The Southern Ocean was a wild place. Indeed, it is noticeable that after convict vessels moved into the South Atlantic, the accident rate increased as wind speed and wave height picked up. Sailing vessels in these latitudes made rapid progress, but they did so at added risk to the wellbeing of their passengers. The impact on conditions on board is vividly illustrated through the rise in accidents. Convicts, crew, and passengers were hurled across decks and down companionways. As the accident rate increased so did the risk of infection on female convict ships.

Bad weather put excessive strain on the use of water closets. Men were encouraged to relieve themselves on deck using the heads that were also used to service the needs of the crew and military detachment. Tubs were provided for female convicts. On all convict vessels prisons were also fitted with water closets. It was not just that heavy seas put greater strain on these facilities. Pitching decks and poor light impeded cleaning, a problem which surgeons thought was particularly the case on female vessels.[50] One reason for this was the number of children who accompanied their convicted mothers on the journey to Australia.

While the military detachments placed on board male vessels were accompanied by significant numbers of wives and children, these were quartered in a separate section of the vessel away from the areas set aside for prisoners. Thus, there is no reason why male prisoners would have come into contact with young children. By contrast, children were present on every female convict vessel and were housed in the prison where their presence almost certainly increased the risk of faecal oral transmission particularly when rough seas compromised routine sanitation and messing arrangements.

POSTVOYAGE EXPERIENCE

Despite their greater record of mortality at sea, female death rates declined more quickly than male following disembarkation in Van Diemen's Land. Postvoyage mortality was undoubtedly influenced by the experience of being at sea for nearly four months. The number of deaths that occurred during the passage and the average number of days spent per convict in sickbay were both correlated with postvoyage mortality. The comparatively quick adjustment made by women to colonial conditions compared to men, however, suggests that factors other than voyage knock-on effects were also at play.

Upon disembarkation women were sent to the Cascades Female Factory while men were marched to the Penitentiary in Campbell Street. The principal use to which female convicts were put was as domestic servants, demand for their services often outstripping supply.[51] After landing, mothers were separated from children who had been weaned, and, while the children were institutionalized, the women were assigned to colonial settler households. Many of these households were located in Hobart, and therefore the distribution of women to their places of colonial employment did not take long to organize.[52] By contrast male convicts were either employed in road gangs or assigned to farms in the interior. The logistics of allocating male convict labour was thus more complicated, and delays were the inevitable consequence. As a result, it is likely that female convicts spent less time in institutions in the months immediately following disembarkation than their male counterparts and thus had a comparatively lower exposure to infection.

Colonial labour extraction processes also appear to have taken their toll. The labour that male convicts under sentence performed was dangerous. While the standard punishment reserved for female convicts, working at the washtubs, may have been physically demanding (and demeaning), it carried less risk of death than quarrying or stone breaking. While medical causes of death were only sporadically recorded in the records maintained by the convict department, accidents were always reported. Male convicts were run over by loaded carts, killed in quarry explosions and landslides, and even asphyxiated by carbonic gas. Many were employed in timber felling, and significant numbers were killed by falling trees. Others were drowned, often in rivers while attempting to cool off in the summer months. There were also a considerable number of violent deaths connected with other aspects of the convict system. Several male prisoners were shot attempting to abscond. The execution rate was also far higher than in England and Wales – a bloody code was certainly in operation in the penal colonies. In all, nearly 19 per cent of male convict deaths can be attributed to violent causes. This was 6.7 times more than that for their female counterparts.

It is often argued in a British context that the disproportionate number of violent deaths experienced by men more than offset the increased risk women were exposed to as a result of childbirth.[53] This was certainly the case in Van Diemen's Land where convict women's risk of childbirth-related death was reduced by state policy. In order to preserve the pool of single convict women, their right to marriage was curtailed. In all, 45 per cent of the female convicts in the 1822 muster were recorded as married. By the 1830s this had fallen to just 10 per cent. Colonial regulations increasingly tied the "indulgence" of marriage to dutiful service. Thus, from 1829 all applications to marry by convict women were rejected unless they had served a minimum of twelve months service assigned to a private settler without having an offence recorded against their name.[54] While there was a rise in the female convict marriage rate in the 1840s depression, most female convicts married late in their sentence.

The state also policed women in other ways. Pregnancy out of marriage was treated as an offence. Unmarried pregnant female convicts were sent to the factory to give birth. After weaning, mother and child were separated – mothers to undergo punishment before being returned to the domestic labour market and infants to take their chances in government-run nurseries and orphan schools.[55] This policy appears to have been successful in reducing the female convict birth rate.

From 1843 illegitimate births were recorded on every female convict's conduct record. We examined data for one in twenty-five female convicts arriving in Van Diemen's Land in the period 1844–53. Not one of these 267 women gave birth during their first year in the colony. This suggests that measures to separate crew and female convicts on the passage to Australia, another of the surgeon-superintendent's duties, were largely successful. Just over 1 per cent of our sample was punished for giving birth to an illegitimate child in year two and nearly 4 per cent in year three. Thereafter the rate declined, a reflection of the colonial state's increasing willingness to endorse petitions to marry as convict sentences started to come to a close.[56]

CONCLUSION

There was a significant reduction in mortality on Australia-bound convict vessels after the introduction of the surgeon-superintendent system. This phenomenon formed part of wider trend. Death rates started to fall on both slave and convict vessels in the mid-eighteenth century and these improvements coincided with increased medical regulation. On the face of things this is surprising. There is little evidence that the state of medical knowledge prior to the second half of the nineteenth century was sufficient to effect a change in morbidity and mortality outcomes – a point forcibly made by McKeown. Before the post-Crimean War Nightingale reforms, for examples, hospitals are generally considered to have done more harm than good.[57] Shipboard experience, however, suggests that this was not necessarily the case.

The majority of surgeon-superintendents were anticontagionists who attributed disease to a combination of "preexisting" and "exciting" causes. In their view the chief amongst the latter was exposure to "miasmas" (emissions emanating from damp environments and decaying and fetid matter). While their patients may have brought many "preexisting" causes on board – the effects of living life at the sharp end of the industrial revolution – surgeon-superintendents had one advantage not shared by their shore-based medical colleagues. As their charges were unfree they could impose their authority, punishing those who refused to obey medical instructions. For much of the nineteenth century, respect for privacy was seen as an English virtue and this meant that state attempts to regulate domestic environments remained unpopular.[58] By contrast all space on a convict vessel (apart from the officers' quarters) was public space.

Although miasma theory was based on a poor understanding of disease transmission processes, the authority vested in surgeon-superintendents meant that the measures they put in place were largely effective.[59] Such processes included deck scrubbing and scraping and regular washing of both convicts and their clothing and bedding. While, like slavers, surgeon-superintendents were quick to blame deaths at sea on preexisting causes outside of their control, longitudinal analysis suggests that the power that they exercised over both their charges and shipboard space was effective. The evidence from convict vessels is that medical intervention led to noticeable improvements in health at sea largely because of the emphasis that surgeon-superintendents placed on controlling exciting causes. The measures they adopted were used to regulate subsequent assisted-migrant and indentured voyages and informed wider public health debates.[60]

We could find no evidence that the density with which vessels were packed affected mortality outcomes. While more passengers were embarked per ton on some voyages than others, this did not jeopardize the welfare of convicts. Heavily loaded vessels would have kept the surgeon busy, yet, higher patient to medical practitioner ratios were unlikely to make any difference as – once patients fell sick – medical intervention did little to affect the outcome (with the notable exception of scurvy where an effective remedy was available). If medical intervention had made a difference we would have expected to find a relationship between the prior experience of the surgeon and reductions in shipboard mortality. We did not.

The other principal benefit of employing medically trained officials was that they were able to conduct prevoyage health checks. As on free passenger voyages, they were less effective, however, at reducing death rates amongst women. Longitudinal analysis suggests that some of the difference in these outcomes can be attributed to the ways in which male and female convicts were processed prior to embarkation. Women were supplied with fewer calories than their institutionalized male counterparts, and some were moved long distances in the days immediately proceeding embarkation.

It is also possible that the lives led by convict women prior to arrest were characterised by extreme disadvantage, putting them at greater long-term risk than their male counterparts. While working-class nineteenth-century women may have been nutritionally disadvantaged as a result of intrahousehold food distribution strategies, there is little evidence that this put them at risk during the voyage to Australia. If this had been the case we would have expected to see rising morbidity and mortality amongst postfamine convicts shipped from Ireland. That we did not suggests to us that prison and hulk diets were sufficient to offset the most pernicious effects of prearrest malnutrition.

Analysis of the diagnoses provided for female convicts en route to Australia indicates that they were at greater risk of diarrhoeal disorders. The most likely reason for this was the presence of infant children in the prison where female convicts were quartered. High seas in southern latitudes, particularly in winter, appear to have further compromised shipboard hygiene. The presence of children also impacted on the ability of the surgeon to conduct effective preboard screening.

In marked contrast to shipboard experience, female convicts were at less risk of death in the first year in the colony. Postdisembarkation death rates for both sexes were elevated as a result of the knock-on effects of a long voyage at sea. Women, however, were able to make a swifter transition to lower mortality rates because their experience of postvoyage institutionalization was benign compared to men and, perhaps ironically, because the coercive practices of the state separated them from their children.

The manner in which the colonial state policed the private lives of convict women also resulted in lower fertility, thereby reducing the risk of death in childbirth. By contrast, the work undertaken by male convicts carried significantly higher risk of accidental death, and this was especially true of those undergoing punishment labour. Thus, exploitive labour practices had diametrically opposed impacts on male and female death rates. In general, however, state surveillance (and the increased regulation that came with it) lowered rather than raised mortality rates. While transportation may have conferred physical benefits this does not mean, however, that it was psychologically beneficial. Indeed, it was precisely because the prisoners shipped to Australia were placed in a situation where they were relatively powerless that the state was able to improve morbidity and mortality outcomes.

STATISTICAL APPENDICES

The analyses in these tables test whether there is a relationship between each of the (independent) variables listed in the first column and each of the (dependent) variables listed in the first row.

"Annualized average days in voyage sickbay per convict" gives the average (mean) number of days each convict spent in sickbay on the voyage, standardized so that each voyage is assumed to take one year. For example, convicts on ships that left England had an average of 12.4 days each in sickbay per voyage-year, and 237 ships in the sample left England, out of a total sample of 284 ships.

"Annualized convict deaths on voyage per 1,000 convicts embarked" gives the average (mean) number of convict deaths per voyage per 1,000 convicts embarked, also standardized so that each voyage is assumed to take one year. For example, ships that left England had an average of 28.8 deaths per 1,000 convicts embarked per voyage year.

"Convict deaths in arrival year per 1,000 convicts disembarked" gives the average (mean) number of convict deaths per voyage in the first year after arrival in Tasmania per 1,000 convicts landed.

A significant relationship is considered to exist between an independent variable and a dependent variable if the test of the relationship results in a p-value of less than 0.05. These are highlighted in gray, with p-values of less than 0.05 starred and p-values of less than 0.01 double-starred.

Results – Appendix Table 3.4

1 Days in voyage sickbay and mortality on and after the voyage are not related to place of departure.
2 Convict deaths in arrival year are related to season of departure from the British Isles, with more deaths for ships departing in spring.
3 Days in voyage sickbay are related to season arrived in Tasmania, with more deaths for ships arriving in winter and fewer for ships arriving in spring and summer.
4 Deaths in arrival year are related to season arrived in Tasmania, with more deaths for ships arriving in winter.
5 Ships arriving in the earliest period 1818–24 have fewer average days in voyage sickbay per convict.

Table 3.4
Appendix: Statistical analyses of the relationship between convict voyage characteristics and days in voyage sickbay, voyage deaths, and deaths in arrival year

	Annualized average days in voyage sickbay per convict		*Annualized convict deaths on voyage per 1,000 convicts embarked*		*Convict deaths in arrival year per 1,000 convicts disembarked*	
	Mean	*# ships*	*Mean*	*# ships*	*Mean*	*# ships*
Place of departure[b]						
England	12.4	237	28.8	237	16.1	182
Ireland	14.3	47	40.5	47	18.8	49
TOTAL	12.7	284	30.8	284	16.7	231
Season vessel sailed from British Isles[b]					*	
Winter	14.0	47	34.4	47	16.0	36
Spring	14.1	86	31.2	86	20.7	69
Summer	11.3	76	27.6	76	14.0	61
Autumn	11.7	75	32.1	75	15.2	65
TOTAL	12.7	284	31.0	284	16.7	231
Season arrived in Tasmania[b]	*				*	
Summer	10.5	72	29.4	72	15.2	62
Autumn	13.2	57	28.2	57	15.0	45
Winter	15.2	78	32.4	78	20.5	64
Spring	11.9	76	33.5	76	14.9	61
TOTAL	12.7	283	31.1	283	16.5	232
Year of arrival[a]	*					
1818–24	6.1	19	22.6	19		
1825–29	13.6	33	35.3	33		
1830–34	10.4	46	37.6	46	14.9	46
1835–39	15.6	36	23.3	36	18.9	36
1840–44	12.4	76	30.7	76	18.4	76
1845–49	15.5	42	30.2	42	15.6	42
1850–53	12.8	33	33.1	33	13.5	33
TOTAL	12.7	285	31.1	285	16.6	233
Voyage length (days)[a]						
Under 106	13.7	70	26.3	70	17.0	66
106–13	12.3	69	32.6	69	16.8	59
114–25	12.1	69	31.6	69	15.1	52
126 and above	12.9	77	33.6	77	17.9	53
TOTAL	12.7	285	31.1	285	16.7	230

Table 3.4 (*continued*)

	Annualized average days in voyage sickbay per convict		*Annualized convict deaths on voyage per 1,000 convicts embarked*		*Convict deaths in arrival year per 1,000 convicts disembarked*	
	Mean	*# ships*	*Mean*	*# ships*	*Mean*	*# ships*
Vessel age (years)[a]						
0–4	12.8	60	36.5	60	13.9	52
5–10	13.3	70	28.9	70	17.0	56
11–17	13.6	70	35.1	70	15.6	50
18 and above	12.7	71	26.9	71	19.1	62
TOTAL	13.1	271	31.7	271	16.5	220
Route taken[b]	*					
Direct	15.2	45	33.4	45	14.9	35
Stopped enroute	11.1	71	29.2	71	15.3	49
TOTAL	12.7	116	30.8	116	15.1	84

[a] Test used: simple linear regression. Variables analysed as continuous.

[b] Test used: one-way ANOVA

Results with p-values (p) of less than 0.05 are considered significant and are highlighted.

* p<0.05

** p<0.01

6 Days in voyage sickbay and mortality on and after the voyage are not related to voyage length nor vessel age.

7 Days in voyage sickbay per convict were higher for ships that took a direct route rather than stopping en route.

Results – Appendix Table 3.5

8 Ships carrying female convicts had more sickbay days per convict and higher convict mortality than did ships carrying male convicts.

9 Ships carrying male convicts had higher convict mortality in the first year after arrival.

10 Ships with fewer than 240 people onboard had more sickbay days per convict and higher mortality than did ships with more people.

11 Ships with more people had higher mortality in the first year after arrival.

Table 3.5
Appendix: Statistical analyses of the relationship between convict voyage characteristics and days in voyage

	Annualized average days in voyage sickbay per convict		*Annualized convict deaths on voyage per 1,000 convicts embarked*		*Convict deaths in arrival year per 1,000 convicts disembarked*	
	Mean	*# ships*	*Mean*	*# ships*	*Mean*	*# ships*
Gender of vessel convict population[b]	**		**		**	
Male	11.2	205	25.6	205	18.9	166
Female	16.7	80	45.1	80	10.7	67
TOTAL	12.7	285	31.1	285	16.6	233
Total onboard population[a]	*		**		**	
Under 240	14.9	57	43.9	57	12.3	52
240–289	12.7	60	28.5	60	15.0	54
290–369	12.4	60	28.0	60	18.8	60
370 and above	12.3	55	22.1	55	18.0	55
TOTAL	13.0	232	30.6	232	16.1	221
Total onboard children (female ships only)[a]						
0–6	14.2	1	27.0	1		
7–11	8.4	2	9.2	2	11.9	2
12–24	16.8	28	35.9	28	8.3	25
25 and above	16.5	45	51.8	45	12.2	40
TOTAL	16.4	76	44.5	76	10.7	67
Total onboard population per tonnage[a]						
Under 0.45	12.0	68	31.4	68	18.6	27
0.45 to under 0.55	14.0	60	38.9	60	12.7	59
0.55 to under 0.65	12.5	88	28.8	88	16.3	79
0.65 and over	12.5	69	26.9	69	19.5	68
TOTAL	12.7	285	31.1	285	16.6	233
Number of previous voyages by surgeon[a]						
0	14.1	122	32.7	122	15.3	95
1	12.8	71	31.9	71	18.5	61
2–3	11.0	57	34.6	57	15.7	45
4 and above	10.8	35	17.8	35	17.9	32
TOTAL	12.7	285	31.1	285	16.6	233

Table 3.5 (*continued*)

	Annualized average days in voyage sickbay per convict		*Annualized convict deaths on voyage per 1,000 convicts embarked*		*Convict deaths in arrival year per 1,000 convicts disembarked*	
	Mean	*# ships*	*Mean*	*# ships*	*Mean*	*# ships*
Annualised average days in voyage sickbay per convict[a]			**			
0–4			20.5	70	19.3	48
5–9			30.3	57	13.6	48
10–14			35.2	66	15.3	57
15+			36.7	92	18.1	77
TOTAL			31.1	285	16.7	230
Annualised convict deaths on voyage per 1,000 convicts embarked[a]						
0					14.5	57
Under 20					15.5	53
20 to under 40					20.1	59
40 and above					16.6	61
TOTAL					16.7	230

[a] Test used: simple linear regression. Variables analysed as continuous.

[b] Test used: one-way ANOVA

Results with p-values (p) of less than 0.05 are considered significant and are highlighted.

* $p<0.05$

** $p<0.01$

12 There was no relationship between children onboard female convict ships and sickness and mortality.

13 There was no relationship between onboard population per tonnage and days in voyage sickbay and mortality on and after the voyage.

14 There was no relationship between previous voyages by the surgeon and days in voyage sickbay and mortality on and after the voyage.

15 Higher onboard mortality was related to higher onboard days in sickbay per convict.

16 Mortality in the year after arrival was not related to onboard mortality.

4

Wanderlust: The Multiple Migrations of New Zealand's Scots, 1840–1920

REBECCA LENIHAN

The history of Scottish wanderlust is a long and eventful one dating back to at least the middle ages and spanning the British Empire and beyond. The nineteenth and twentieth centuries are a particularly remarkable chapter in that history both for Scotland and for the overseas destinations Scots chose for their new homes. In New Zealand, for example, Scots numbered approximately one-fifth of all migrants who arrived between the beginning of formal colonization in 1840 and the end of world war one, leaving such a mark on the fledgling colony as to have it described by one twenty-first century historian as "*the* neo-Scotland."[1]

The voyage from Scotland to New Zealand took up to five months and was both costly and dangerous for the emigrants; deaths at sea were not uncommon, and, migration costs incurred aside, the loss of several months' wages was not inconsiderable. However, migrating from one end of the world to another was not simply a matter of boarding a ship and surviving until arrival. More often than not it was preceded by substantial preparation and travel to the port of departure as well as the recomposition of families and communities within Scotland, followed by a lengthy settling in period, reconstituting a sense of belonging as well as coming to terms with such further upheavals as occupational change after arrival in New Zealand. Beyond this transoceanic travel, and less visible in the historical record, were transitions made by many migrants within Scotland before departure and within New Zealand after arrival. In this paper I analyse a database of New Zealand's Scottish migrants to demonstrate the complexity of this process. While some Scottish migrants moved directly from their parish of birth to their final destination, quite often the voyage that brought them to New Zealand was only one step in a series of movements over their lifetime.

Scotland's migrants have received much scholarly attention over the past few decades. While studies regarding the development of Scottish settlements in Europe, the Caribbean, South Africa, and Australia are increasingly plentiful, the historiography is especially rich with regard to those migrants who made their way to North America and, in particular, those compelled by famine and the Highland clearances to flee Scotland.[2] New Zealand's Scots had received very little attention until publications within the past decade.[3]

While the literature pertaining to these long-distance Scottish migrations is increasingly abundant, other aspects of the Scottish migration story have yet received scant attention, primarily due to the poor visibility of these aspects within the historical record. Whereas settlers in overseas destinations have left behind numerous sources through which historians can study them in order to tell the story of international immigration, evidence of internal, step, and return migration is harder to come by. Until relatively recent technology advances, enumerated census data was of comparatively little value when attempting to trace internal migration. Projects such as "People in Motion," currently being carried out at the University of Guelph using sophisticated databases to trace people between Canadian censuses, promise to open up lines of enquiry into internal migration and emigration considerably. Without access to such extensive databases, scholars necessarily expound from relatively small samples, examine these trends in broad terms based on published statistics, or search for movement in qualitative sources.[4] Internal migration within Scotland has primarily been discussed with regard to the "four horsemen" of early nineteenth-century Scottish migration, namely the agricultural revolution, industrialization, famine, and clearance. Although modern database technology is enabling us to better examine internal migration within Scotland, investigation of step and return migration is still limited because these movements are seldom captured in contemporary sources. Scholars of Swedish migration who have fuller records at hand are more fortunate in this regard, though even they have their investigations hampered by such issues as the recording of last place of residence rather than place of birth on ship lists.[5]

Although return migration has a notable impact on the home countries in economic, labour market, and sociopolitical terms and has been a subject of interest to European migration scholars for some time,[6] it has only been examined by Scottish migration historians in any detail in the past decade.[7] Aside from studies of highly visible step migrants – for example the Reverend Norman McLeod and his followers journeying to Canada and Australia before making final landfall in New Zealand[8] – step migration has been very scantily examined due to the difficulty in tracing these movements on anything beyond the individual level. No study has yet been specifically dedicated to the subject, and little more than a passing mention of an individual making a stepwise move is usually made in volumes about migration more generally.

In examining the internal migration within Scotland and within New Zealand of New Zealand's Scots migrants, as well as the steps they took between Scotland and New Zealand and their return migration, the present study serves to extend and complement this previous scholarship. Besides simply adding the experiences of another group of migrants to our collective pool of knowledge, this Scotland–New Zealand migrant stream is particularly interesting in regard to step and return migration because the distances involved in these movements likely made the decision to migrate further, having already attempted settlement outside of Scotland, or to return home from New Zealand, more difficult. Further, by drawing upon information collected from a genealogical society register, this study demonstrates the value of such collections when other sources of information are scarce, advocating the use of such underutilized sources of crowd-sourced data in scholarly investigations.

The genealogical society register that forms the basis of the "NZSG data" analyzed below was a register of New Zealand immigrants of Scottish birth arriving before 1 January 1921 compiled by the New Zealand Society of Genealogists Scottish Interest Group. It was conceived as an aid to family historians in New Zealand and abroad researching their own Scottish family histories. Each entry has been created by a process of record linkage, the contributors of the information, often descendants of the migrants, individually linking various sources and records before submitting the information to the register. It is therefore a self-selected rather than a random sample of the migrants.

Because the register was not created with the intention that it become the foundation for a statistical database, fundamental difficulties arise from its use for such a purpose. For example, the data has an inherent bias towards men who arrived in New Zealand married because although the "guidelines for contributors" asked that "one entry form for each New Zealand immigrant born in Scotland" be completed, often forms were completed for only the father of a family of migrants, with information for the spouse and children filled in on the same form. Further, because many of the forms were filled in by descendants of the migrants the data also has a distinct bias with regards to men who arrived single; given the stark gender imbalance in New Zealand during the period investigated, many men who arrived single never married, producing no descendants to fill in registration forms about them in the twenty-first century. Descendants contributing the information means the data also favours those who remained in New Zealand over those who returned to Scotland or who migrated to another country after arrival.

Keeping the inherent biases of the data set firmly in mind, the NZSG data nevertheless allows aggregate statistics to be collated and many questions regarding the migrants to be addressed. Additionally, the nature of the database source is such that rich qualitative material is able to be drawn from the data from which patterns can be discerned when the quantitative data is insufficient. This has proven especially useful regarding questions of internal and return migration, however it has also allowed the stories of the migrants who make up the otherwise faceless aggregate statistics to be incorporated into analysis of New Zealand's Scots migration patterns.

ORIGINS WITHIN SCOTLAND

As previously noted, in the first few decades of the nineteenth century Scotland witnessed pulses of migration, internal and external, greater than had been seen before, stimulated primarily by the agricultural revolution, industrialization, famine, and clearance.[9] Each of these processes contributed in such a way as to ensure that by the time New Zealand was ready for formal colonization, in the 1840s, the majority of the population of Scotland lived in what may be termed Lowland Scotland. It should therefore come as no surprise that the majority (70 per cent) of New Zealand's Scotland-born emigrants between 1840 and 1920 were from Lowland Scotland.[10]

The indices in table 4.1 represent the difference between the distribution of the migrants' origins in the NZSG data over the full eighty-year period (as shown in the "whole period" column) and the distrib-

Table 4.1
Proportion of New Zealand immigrants from each region of Scotland, with indices of representation based on the Scottish population distribution in 1871

Region	*Whole period*	*Index*
Far North	5.46	1.79
Highlands	13.1	1.54
North East	11.43	0.97
Eastern Lowlands	32.77	0.98
Western Lowlands	27.92	0.79
Borders	9.32	1.15
n	6,243*	

*Figures exclude those in the data whose birth region is unknown.

Sources: NZSG data 1840–1920; Return Relating to the Population of Scotland at each Decennial Period, Table II, 1881 Census of Scotland, 2–3

ution of the population of Scotland as at 1871, the census chosen for this index as the most logical midpoint for comparison with the NZSG data. The closer the index number is to one, the less difference there is between the NZSG data and the census distribution. As may be inferred from table 4.1, in 1871 over three-quarters of the population of Scotland was living in the Eastern or Western Lowlands or the Borders Region, an increase of approximately 10 per cent on the figures for these regions combined in 1801.[11]

Refining this analysis of where in Scotland the migrants to New Zealand were from to county level, the six Scottish counties that sent the largest numbers of migrants to New Zealand were Lanarkshire (15.9 per cent), Midlothian (8.0 per cent), Aberdeenshire (7.0 per cent), Ayr (6.5 per cent), Perthshire (6.0 per cent), and Renfrew (5.6 per cent). With the caveat that although Aberdeenshire is not located in the Eastern or Western Lowlands or Borders Region it is nevertheless usually considered to be a "Lowland" county, the "top six" origin counties for migrants to New Zealand may therefore, more or less, all be considered "Lowland." These six counties alone supplied 49 per cent of the Scottish migrants arriving in New Zealand during the period 1840–1920, the same proportion as was living in those six counties at the 1841 Census. Whether the six counties also contributed nearly half of Scottish emigration is unknown, such county breakdowns of migration to other destinations not yet being available.

Further examination of the county-level origins of New Zealand's Scottish migration reveals that the number of migrants immigrating to New Zealand from each region and county of Scotland was approximately the same as the proportions of the total population of Scotland resident in these regions and counties. Few counties sent excessively disproportionate numbers of migrants; Ross and Cromarty, Angus, Aberdeen and Lanarkshire sent fewer migrants than was proportionate to their share of the population of Scotland, while Argyll, Nairn, and Moray sent more.[12] McClean first noted this "evenness of distribution" of the New Zealand Scots' origins in her 1990 thesis; the present findings therefore reinforce those of McClean and indicate that this trend of even distribution among New Zealand's Scots continued after 1880. The extent of the "evenness" of the migrant distribution among New Zealand's Scots is significant: although Scots migrants have been noted for the relative evenness of their origin distribution generally, studies of emigration from Scotland indicate clustering, especially from parishes in the Highlands, and consequently also a degree of clustering of migrant origins among Scots to other destinations.[13]

New Zealand is not, strictly speaking, unusual in its "evenness" of Scots migrants. Scottish emigration in general has been noted for this relatively even distribution in terms of migrant origins when compared to other European countries that were concurrently dispatching large numbers of migrants.[14] However, due to a relative lack of the cluster and chain migration commonly seen in other Scottish migrant destinations, the evenness in the distribution of New Zealand's Scottish migrants' origins is much easier to identify.[15] Coming later as a potential destination, New Zealand did not have the benefit of a long migration tradition to attract migrants. Partly as a result of this late start and the absence of tradition, as well as the additional distance it was necessary to travel and the costs entailed, chain migration may have been less common among Scots to New Zealand than elsewhere.

INTERNAL SCOTLAND MIGRATION

Place of birth is the only clear and consistent indicator of "origin" encompassing all of the migrants in the NZSG data. However basing "who New Zealand's Scots were" in terms of origins solely on place of birth is problematic. Many of those who eventually made their way to New Zealand first migrated internally within Scotland, making the move to New Zealand when these (relatively) short-distance migrations did not improve their prospects as much as they may have hoped for.

Just over 15 per cent of migrants in the NZSG database migrated within Scotland prior to their departure for New Zealand. For some this move was a short flit within their county of birth (36 per cent of the subsample), for others a moderate jaunt within the region of their birth (27 per cent), while the rest of these internal migrants moved to other parts of Scotland entirely (37 per cent). Given the previously noted population trends in Scotland at this time, it should come as no surprise that migrants born in the Western Lowlands were disproportionately likely to migrate within their county or region of birth and likewise disproportionately unlikely to leave their region of birth. Though that region contributed just 28 per cent of all NZSG migrants, Western Lowlanders made up 31 per cent and 31 per cent respectively of the "within county" and "within region" subsamples and just 20 per cent of those departing their region of birth for other parts of Scotland. Highland migrants, on the other hand, were much more likely to leave the Highlands altogether before migrating to New Zealand, Highland migrants making up just 11 per cent of the "within county," 15 per cent of the "within region" and 21 per cent of the "within Scotland, outside of region" subsamples, and contributing 13 per cent of all NZSG migrants.

The population of rural areas of Scotland, such as Argyll, fell into a gradual but steady decline over the early to mid-nineteenth century; while the population of Argyll was at its all-time peak of 100,973 in 1831, there were only 75,679 people residing in the county by 1871.[16] As the nature of farming changed, small plots being consolidated into larger farms and agriculture generally becoming more mechanized and less labour intensive, agricultural districts were increasingly unable to retain their populations. While clearance and evictions prompted many to emigrate, unemployment was often circumvented by temporary internal migration.[17] Temporary out-migration had been a feature in Argyll for decades, and it has been suggested that few Argyllshire families in the early nineteenth century could have survived without the income from seasonal work in the Lowlands.[18] These traditions of temporary migration were often a prompt to permanent migration, bringing familiarity with conditions outside of the home county and loosening bonds with home communities.[19] Familiarity with conditions outside the home county, coupled with "push" factors – including eviction – and the prospect of greater opportunities in the central Lowlands and abroad, underlay the gradual but steady decline in the population of Argyll post-

1831.[20] The county's already long-standing flow of migrants to nearby Glasgow increased over this period. By 1851, while Edinburgh was drawing most of its migrants of Highland birth from Inverness and Ross and Cromarty, between 61 and 87 per cent of Highland-born migrants residing in Glasgow parishes were from Argyll, 10,575 people from a total Glasgow population of approximately 329,495. This was at a time when the population of Argyll itself was just 89,298. Arguably this was largely due to the proximity of the county to Glasgow though, as Brock notes, Dumbarton (with a population of 45,103) was closer to Argyll and received far fewer Argyll migrants than Glasgow.[21]

Lanarkshire was one of the primary receiving counties for internal migration within Scotland generally, as was Midlothian – Glasgow and Edinburgh respectively being the primary draw cards. Donald McKenzie and his family were among those living in Glasgow in 1841 who had been born outside of Lanarkshire. Donald, wife Catherine, and their three children migrated to Glasgow in approximately 1840. All five of them had been born, and had subsequently resided, in Inverness up to that point in their lives, although Donald had travelled during his service with the 42nd Highland Regiment. The family remained in Glasgow until 1849, with three more children being born in the intervening years. Though family records give no indication as to why the family moved from Inverness to Glasgow, nor why Donald chose to migrate to New Zealand in 1849, the ship they departed on carried a number of other New Zealand Fencibles, and Donald served with that force for a time after his arrival.[22]

These interregional migrations were not a one-way phenomenon. Though it was much less common, it was not unheard of for those born in these lowland population hubs to migrate to the Highlands and Islands prior to departure for New Zealand. William Perston and his parents, born in Glasgow, were among those participating in this Lowland to Highland flow of internal migrants. Though William's family had resided in Glasgow for several generations, where William's father had been employed as a power loom operator, they migrated to Rothesay in Bute when William was just two years old. William's father was based in Rothesay as a carrier of goods between Bute and Glasgow. William's younger brother John was born in Rothesay shortly after the family's migration there. When the brothers migrated to New Zealand in the 1870s, separately, both had been residing in Bute until their departure.[23] Harriet Sydney Hogg was among those making many short-distance migrations across her lifetime, from the Borders to the

Lowland regions. Born in Selkirk in 1827, Harriet did not migrate to New Zealand until she was fifty-one years old. During that half-century she had lived in Yarrow (Selkirk), Linlithgow (West Lothian), Edinburgh (Midlothian), Glasgow (Lanarkshire) and Alloa (Clackmannan), before eventual departing from London on the *Forfarshire* in 1879. Her husband had been born in Renfrewshire but worked as a merchant in Glasgow, Lanark. It is unknown where the couple met, but they were married in Linlithgow in June 1855. All of their nine children were born in Glasgow between May 1856 and February 1869, and the family migrated to Alloa sometime in the following decade.[24]

Though the frequency of internal migration evidenced by Harriet Sydney Hogg, entailing residence in at least five different Scottish counties over her lifetime,[25] appears to have been unusual, at least among those Scots who later migrated to New Zealand, multiple moves within the county of birth were not uncommon.[26] Born in Barony parish (Lanarkshire) in 1829, Margaret McArthur married, had her first two children, and continued to reside in Barony until around 1854. Over the following two decades Margaret and her family moved first to Shettleston in Glasgow, then to the parish of Old Monkland, on to Hamilton parish, then back to Barony, all within Lanarkshire. The family left for New Zealand from London in 1874.[27] Born in Foveren parish, Aberdeenshire, George Brechin Coull moved within the county at least four times before migrating to New Zealand (via a one-year stay in Australia) at the age of thirty-three, shifting from Foveren to Logie Buchan, on to Waterton in Ellon, and then to Aberdeen City itself.[28] Given the information provided to the NZSG register and available for the present study, it is impossible to accurately assess just how common internal migration within Scotland was among later emigrants. Nevertheless, the genealogical evidence suggests that a significant number of people were migrating within their birth county, birth region, or within the whole of Scotland before immigrating to New Zealand.

George Brechin Coull was by no means alone in his experience of migrating to a country outside of Scotland on his way to New Zealand. In some instances this step in the migrant chain further complicates the issue of "origins." Elizabeth Connely is a very clear example of this. Born in Dunfermline, Fife to Scottish-born parents, Elizabeth resided in England for all thirty-seven of her years before migrating to New Zealand in 1892. Though her likely motivations for immigration almost certainly had very little to do with push factors in, or pull factors perceived from, Scotland at the time of immigration, her birth in Scotland necessitates her inclusion in the present work as one of New Zealand's Scots, a further illustration of one of the difficulties with using place of birth as a signifier of origin.[29]

STEP MIGRATION, COUNTRIES BETWEEN SCOTLAND AND NEW ZEALAND

The NZSG data suggests that Elizabeth was one of 12 per cent of New Zealand's Scots who spent time in another country between their departure from Scotland and arrival in New Zealand. Knowing simply that this step in the migration chain was made, we can only speculate as to what motivated these migrants to depart their first-choice destinations to continue their travels to the most far flung outpost of the British Empire, but this is nevertheless a question worth keeping in mind. Information in the NZSG data is insufficient to permit a detailed analysis of the immigration patterns of those Scots spending time in other countries on their way to New Zealand – information as to length of residences being especially scarce – but some basic statistics enable at least an indication of the flows.

Of the 764 NZSG migrants who had resided in a country other than Scotland prior to immigration to New Zealand, 720 had resided in one other country only. As Figure 4.1 shows, for the vast majority of these migrants that other country was Australia, 70 per cent having stopped there before travelling on to New Zealand. This pattern of immigration to New Zealand via Australia was relatively common (that is, common among those who did not immigrate directly to New Zealand) and by no means confined to Scottish migrants; numerous English and Irish migrants also gained experience of colonial life in Australia before travelling on to New Zealand.[30] England was the prior country of residence for 10 per cent of this subsample, Ireland 4 per cent, and Wales 0.5 per cent, a total of 14.5 per cent for other countries of the United Kingdom. Canada was not far behind England among the step-migration migrants, though nearly two-thirds of those recorded were followers of the Rev. Norman McLeod who took ship for Waipu, New Zealand direct from Nova Scotia. McLeod himself arrived at Waipu after exploratory travel through Australia and New Zealand.

Among those who first took passage to Australia then moved on to New Zealand, were John and Mary Edie. Both John and Mary came from coal mining backgrounds. Shortly after their marriage in July

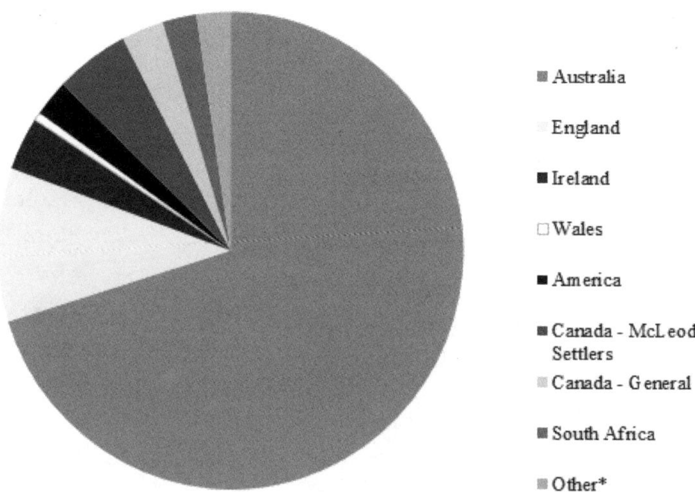

*Other = India (5), Germany, Russia, West Indies, Tonga, Samoa, Ceylon (3), Gibraltar, Brazil, Chile, Singapore

Figure 4.1 Proportions of Scots residing in only one country other than Scotland prior to migration to NZ

1854, the couple succumbed to the lure of the Victorian gold rush, setting sail for Sydney from Liverpool in November that year. Working to pay their way to the gold fields through 1855, John was mining in Bendigo from February 1856. The couple remained there until 1862, when they left for the Otago goldfields, joining Mary's sister Margaret in Dunedin, where she had arrived as an assisted migrant in 1861. Having learnt from his experience in Bendigo that supplying the diggings was a more steady and reliable source of income than mining itself, John worked as a carrier between Dunedin and the diggings at Dunstan.[31] This move, from the Victorian to the Otago goldfields, is a common experience in the stories of Scots arriving in New Zealand in the 1860s. Many of them – like John and Mary – remained in New Zealand after the gold rush had passed.[32]

Of the forty-four other NZSG migrants with a prior country of residence recorded, thirty-four had resided in two other countries, seven in three other countries, one in four, and another, a soldier, in six prior to arrival in New Zealand. As shown in figure 4.2 below, for more than 62 per cent of these forty-three migrants, the last stop before immigration to New Zealand was Australia, though a further four migrants

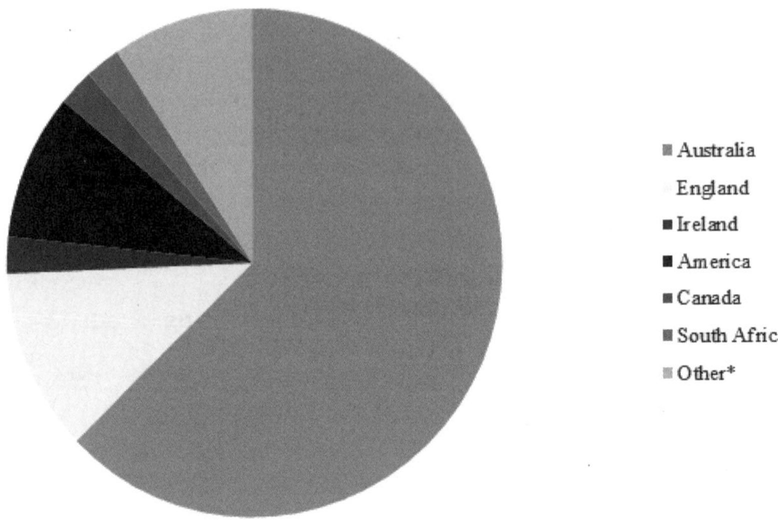

*Other = Ceylon, Malta, New Caledonia, and West Indies

Figure 4.2 Last country of residence for Scots with more than one country of residence prior to emigration to New Zealand

had also spent time in Australia: fourteen had stopped for a time in Canada, six of these being McLeod settlers who followed him to Australia before immigrating to New Zealand, and sixteen of the migrants had spent time in England or Ireland before coming to New Zealand.

The remaining migrant of the subsample of forty-four, Matthew Findlay, differs in an important respect from the others. He is the only individual in the database exhibiting a pattern of migration known to have been common among migrants to New Zealand – temporary migration to Australia postarrival in New Zealand. Because the relevant space on the NZSG registration forms queries "If resident in another country before N.Z., where & for how long," contributors omitted providing information regarding subsequent movements after arrival in New Zealand. Thus this further migration can only be deduced from place of death if the migrant died outside New Zealand. Matthew arrived in New Zealand on the *Ionic* in 1909, the day before his ninth birthday. In 1928 he, with his wife Isobel and son Robert James, left New Zealand for New South Wales. Isobel died in Australia in 1935 and Robert James in 1941. Matthew remarried in 1936, but his second wife, Helen Mary, died in 1943, and in 1944 he returned to New Zealand.

Table 4.2
Proportion of migrants from each region of Scotland who died outside of the New Zealand province in which they first arrived*

	%	n**
Far North	20.9	225
North East	26.9	412
Highlands	29.3	529
Western Lowlands	29.8	1,168
Eastern Lowlands	27.6	1,396
Borders	21.6	380
Scotland total	27.5	4,110

* Lyttelton has been included as being the same port of arrival as province of death for both the West Coast and for Canterbury Province.

** Figures exclude those for whom there is no port of arrival information, no province of death information, and/or no place of birth information.

Source: NZSG data

He married his third wife, Winnifred Annie, in Auckland in 1945.[33] Though he was in Australia for longer than most New Zealanders spending time across the Tasman Sea, and as such it might be argued that his intention may not have been temporary migration but permanent settlement, it is probable the experience of Matthew Findley of Neilston, Renfrewshire, was more common than the NZSG evidence suggests.[34]

INTERNAL NEW ZEALAND MIGRATION

Even for those who remained in New Zealand, however, arrival in New Zealand wasn't always the end of the line in terms of migration. Analysis of the NZSG data suggests that only 73 per cent of Scots settled near the port they arrived in – i.e. for just over 27 per cent of migrants, arrival was not the end of their migration experience (see table 4.2).

It is likely no coincidence that those from areas with higher levels of internal migration within Scotland – the Highlands and Western Lowlands regions – were also less likely to settle permanently in the area of New Zealand in which they arrived. Those who had migrated frequently within Scotland in order to improve their prospects were probably less likely than those with no previous migration experience to be content with whatever opportunities presented themselves in the area around their port of arrival. The enumerators' schedules for the New Zealand census prior to 1966 having been destroyed, leaving only the published statistics produced from the censuses, internal migration within New Zealand is even more difficult to quantify than within Scotland.[35] Fortunately the rich qualitative evidence the NZSG data offers gives some indication of this internal migration.

For William Berry, born in Edinburgh in 1861, it was job opportunities that prompted his further migrations through New Zealand. Arriving in Auckland on the *Royal Stuart* in 1863 with his parents and younger brother, William (junior) and his family remained in Auckland where his father, William, was employed by the *Daily Southern Cross* newspaper as a journalist. Later, when William (senior) was forced to resign from the paper in 1868, the family moved to Thames where William (senior) had been hired as the editor of the *Thames Advertiser*. The family moved again in 1875, returning to Auckland where William (senior) was then the editor of the *New Zealand Herald*.[36] William (junior) followed in his father's journalistic footsteps, working as a reporter, and ultimately as parliamentary reporter, for the *New Zealand Herald* under his father's editorship. In May 1886 William (junior) was appointed to a position on the Hansard staff and made a final and permanent move to Wellington in that year.[37]

Family was the motivating factor for both Robert Fordyce and Ann Ursula Petrie. When Robert settled in Auckland, having arrived in Wellington via England, he did so because of extended family already in Auckland.[38] Ann Ursula arrived in Napier on the Clarence in 1874 and shortly afterwards moved to Wellington. Her sister, Agnes Beatrice, had arrived in Wellington as an assisted passenger thirteen months earlier.[39]

The migrations of Robert Rose McKay Sutherland, born in Halkirk, Caithness in 1846, were likely for vocational reasons. Robert arrived in Lyttelton Harbour with his family in 1862, and he worked as a clerk in Christchurch for six years before returning to Scotland to attend university between 1868 and 1879. Returning to New Zealand at the end of his studies, Robert settled this time in Dunedin where he was a minister from 1879–1919. Upon his retirement he remained in Dunedin another ten years until, at the age of 83, he migrated north to Wellington.[40]

Given the "tyranny of distance" and the costs involved, Robert's return to Scotland to attend university seems, at face value, a strange decision but, as the following section will elaborate, he was by no means the only person making this move.

RETURN MIGRATION

Though hard statistics on return migration are notoriously difficult to gather, there is evidence in the NZSG data that at least some of those who migrated to New Zealand made the return journey. While figures indicate that approximately 18 per cent of Swedes in America between 1875 and 1930 returned home, estimates relating to the return migration of United Kingdom emigrants suggest that 40 per cent of those who emigrated from England and Wales between 1870 and 1914, and approximately one-third of Scottish emigrants over the same span, returned permanently to their countries of origin.[41] Whether these estimates are mirrored amongst those who had immigrated to Australia and New Zealand is as yet unknown. Considering the "tyranny of distance" faced by emigrants departing for New Zealand and Australia, and the costs involved, it seems unlikely. Broad estimates based on place of death suggest that around 10 per cent of Australian migrants may have returned.[42] As Richards has noted, "the real and psychic distances between Europe and Australia [and, it may be added, New Zealand] were much greater than those between Europe and America, and it seems unlikely that many migrants before the First World War ... would have regarded emigration to Australia as a temporary move."[43] Furthermore, the large numbers of migrants assisted to immigrate to Australasia as domestic servants or as agricultural labourers were unlikely to have "prospered so quickly that they could afford a double passage," having needed heavy subsidization to immigrate to the antipodes in the first place.[44] Nevertheless, whether or not the rate of return migration from Australasia was as high as amongst immigrants to, for example, the United States or Canada, there was undeniably a flow of return migration. What complicates the tracing of return migration is identifying the various streams making up the flow; not all of those returning, for instance, were intending to return permanently. Richards states the dilemma succinctly: there is no way of knowing whether migrants were "first time emigrants, reemigrants, holidaymakers ... 'transients' ... 'double migrants,' 'sojourners,' 'pensionados' ... or 'quasi-migrants.'" Return migrants, both temporary and permanent, "were part of the statistical awkward squad."[45]

In terms of the return migration of New Zealand immigrants of Scottish birth to their homeland, very little data is readily available. Though it is theoretically possible to track ships departing New Zealand bound for Scotland, it is almost impossible to establish whether those on board were returning temporarily or permanently, indeed whether they were from Scotland in the first place, without compiling life histories for each passenger. This is an instance in which genealogical material could potentially be of great value. Unfortunately, however, the NZSG data is not especially revealing. The majority of the contributors of information to the NZSG register were members of the New Zealand Society of Genealogists; thus the migrants included in the register were overwhelmingly those who remained in New Zealand. Further, the NZSG forms sought no information about travel outside of New Zealand postarrival. However, there is one variable in the NZSG data which may be used to indicate permanent return migration – twenty of the 6,612 NZSG migrants died in Scotland. Though this subsample of twenty migrants is obviously too small to draw any firm conclusions, it is nevertheless useful to consider briefly what is known about the individuals involved.[46]

Place of birth is known for nineteen of the migrants in the subsample; four were born in the Borders, four in the Western Lowlands, five in the Eastern Lowlands, four in the Highlands, and two in the North East. The subsample includes fourteen males and just six females. Age at arrival of the migrants is relatively even; four arrived under twenty years of age, five migrated aged twenty-one to thirty, and five were aged over forty.[47] The parents and siblings of the three migrants in the subsample who arrived in New Zealand as children all died in New Zealand, probably indicating return migration of these child immigrants in their adult years, rather than them being the only member of their family to return to Scotland and not remigrate to New Zealand.

Marital status upon arrival in New Zealand is unknown for five of the migrants; seven were already married while five were single. Only two of the migrants did not marry at some point before death: Septimus Leishman, born in Dollar, Clackmannan in 1848, was twenty-nine at arrival and has neither spouse nor children recorded on his registration form. He died in Edinburgh aged seventy-two; however, his registration form gives no indication as to when he returned to Scotland.[48] William Hannah arrived in New Zealand as a one-year-old and returned to Scotland at some point between his twenty-third birthday and his death in Glasgow three-and-a-half years later.[49] Of the migrants who were single at arrival, all but Septimus married in New Zealand – two, Donald McLennan and Jane McDonald, married each other. It is likely Donald and Jane knew each other prior to immigration to New Zealand; both were born in Fodderty, Ross and Cromarty. It is unknown when Donald arrived in New Zealand, but Jane arrived in June 1872, and they married four months later. The couple had one child in New Zealand, born in 1875. At some point in the following two years the young family returned to Strathpeffer, Ross and Cromarty, where three more children were born. All six members of the family appear to have subsequently lived and died in Scotland.[50] What motivated the couple to return to Scotland is unknown, but quitting the colony may have been prompted by economic factors – perhaps Donald's work as a publican was not sufficiently providing for his young family – or by a desire or need to raise their children nearer to kin and the support network a family can provide.

More revealing when considering who might be more likely to return permanently to Scotland is occupation. While those working in low-income occupations, for instance labourers and domestic servants, were always less likely to have the means to fund a return trip to home, they might nevertheless have had more incentive to return to Scotland if New Zealand was not providing them with the opportunities they had anticipated through immigration. Those who became very successful in New Zealand would have had the means to take passage to Scotland but were probably less likely to return permanently, already enjoying comfortable lifestyles. Without a much larger statistical base, speculations as to who was likely to permanently return to Scotland must be tentative.

Occupation is unknown or unclear for five of the females in the sample and one male. Agriculture had been the occupation for four of the migrants in New Zealand, only one of whom was recorded as having been a "farmer" rather than a "farm labourer." Of the remaining males, two were builders, one was a blacksmith, one a coal miner (William Hannah, who returned to Glasgow, as noted above, before his twenty-seventh birthday), and three were involved in "dealing" (a publican, a coal merchant, and a draper). The three other migrants were of independent means (Septimus Leishman) and medical practitioners.

One of the medical practitioners, and the one female in this subsample, is Isabella Carr. Born in Auchtermuchty, Fife in October 1867, it is unknown when Isabella migrated to New Zealand. It is therefore also unknown whether she migrated before returning to Scotland to study or if immigration came after she became a Licentiate at the Royal College of Physicians and Surgeons in Edinburgh. Whatever the case, when Dr Isabella Hardie Carr died in Auchtermuchty, Fife in October 1944, aged seventy-six years, her working life in New Zealand had been relatively short, she having been in charge of the McLeod Hospital in Ceylon for forty-two years.[51]

It would not be unreasonable to assume that migrants in professional occupations were more likely than others to be involved in return migration. At the higher end of the income scale, professionals were more likely to have the means to return to Scotland. Not being tied to the country, unlike business owners or runholders, they were also able to pick up and remigrate with their skills to Scotland or to any other part of the world. Analysis of the Rolls of Graduates of the University of Aberdeen to 1925 suggest that those who immigrated to New Zealand as teachers were more likely than their cohort in other professions to return to Scotland. Of the eighty-two Aberdeen University graduate immigrants to New Zealand, it is possible to establish for sixty-two of them whether they settled permanently or only temporarily in New Zealand. Sixteen of the graduate emigrants definitely returned to Scotland postmigration to New Zealand, and place of birth is known and identified as Scotland for eleven of them. Of the eleven Aberdeen University graduates born in Scotland who immigrated to New Zealand, then returned to Scotland, one was a nurse, one a missionary, and one a church minister. For two, occupation in New Zealand is unknown. Six were involved in education in New Zealand: two were schoolteachers, three were school principals, and one a lecturer in Classics at Otago University.[52]

The Aberdeen graduate rolls also reveal next-generation return migration for the purpose of tertiary education. Of the eighty-two Aberdeen University graduates who immigrated to New Zealand, three, in fact, had been born in New Zealand. Rae McRae, born in Otago in October 1882, was the son of John McRae, a woollen manufacturer. Between 1908 and 1910 Rae received his M.B.Ch.B., D.P.H., and M.D. from Aberdeen University. Postgraduation, Rae returned to New Zealand.[53] Gray Hassell, born in Oamaru in October 1860, also "returned" to Scotland for his university training. Hassell left New Zealand for Aberdeen in 1873 to complete studies begun in New Zealand, graduating from Aberdeen University with an M.B.C.M. in 1881 and an M.D. in 1890. He returned to New Zealand in 1882 and in 1895 became medical superintendent of the government lunatic asylum in Porirua, Wellington, a role he continued in until his retirement in 1920.[54] With Edinburgh University being considered the foremost medical training institute of its time – "the seat of the medical muses" – a survey of the graduates would likely exhibit similar next-generation "return" migration patterns. Otago University's medical school had a strong connection to Edinburgh University from its earliest days, due to this enviable reputation. Initially Otago taught only a partial course, two years in duration, after which students completed their studies in Edinburgh.[55] What is clear is that the migration and return migration of professional migrants in both the nineteenth and twentieth centuries merits further attention.

While the subsample of returnee NZSG migrants above consists of those who – purposefully or not – returned permanently to Scotland, as indicated by place of death, a qualitative sample of solely temporary migrants compiled by Tanja Bueltmann shows similar patterns. She notes that New Zealand Scots who returned temporarily to Scotland primarily returned for three reasons: for leisure, business, and education. "Leisure" returnees were returning to visit family and to "explore the country," often in a fashion that may be considered "early roots-tourism." Those travelling for "business" included ministers returning "to reeducate themselves by attending Church meetings and meeting former teachers," and may be compared with the likes of Dr Isabella Hardie Carr, returning in the course of her work. Bueltmann notes that "education" returnees especially included those returning to study medicine, as the examination of University of Aberdeen Rolls of Graduates above corroborates.[56]

CONCLUSION

Despite a significant increase in scholarship regarding migration and diaspora in the past decade, flows of internal, step, and return migration remain under examined. The importance of these movements to our understanding of the broader migration story cannot be denied. It has long been recognized that the experience of internal migration was often the impetus to migrate further afield, and both step and return migration brought knowledge of other destinations and the opportunities therein to friends and families of migrants, encouraging further migration among their communities. While technology is allowing us to trace migration through the historical record much more effectively than ever before (by, for example, linking individuals across censuses), the complexity of these movements is such that many slip through the scholars net of sources unrecorded. Should internal migration be tracked using census data alone, for example, the subtlety of intercensal movements made by individuals is lost. Further, as this paper has shown, the complexity of step and return migration patterns is such that to capture them at all requires record linking at the level of the individual. The NZSG data analyzed for the present study provides a compelling example of the benefit of crowd-sourced information when it comes to addressing these issues. The intricate record linkage process carried out by independent family historians for each of the 6,612 individuals in the data has enabled a collective biography that has illuminated the story of internal, step, and return migration of these individuals in a unique way.

Because it was not one of the major destinations during the age of mass migration in terms of total figures, migration to New Zealand has inevitably remained on the periphery of migration studies. As this study has shown, however, the Scotland–New Zealand migrant flow is remarkable in several respects. For one, the marked evenness of the migrants' origins within Scotland contrasts with the clustered patterns often emphasized by studies of Scottish migration. Secondly, though not one of Scotland's major migrant destinations, Scotland contributed upwards of one-fifth of all settlers in New Zealand to 1920, and Scots played an important role in the shaping of New Zealand society. Finally, and seldom before recognized, the Scotland–New Zealand flow is particularly interesting with regard to step and return migration. "The real and psychic distances" between Scotland and New Zealand were much greater than between Britain and North America and surely meant both step and return migration was a more difficult decision for individual migrants to make.[57] While this paper has only speculated at some of the motivations behind these movements of New Zealand's Scots, the figures presented suggest that this migrant stream is worthy of more detailed investigation. Beyond a deeper statistical investigation of these flows, an examination of qualitative sources that reveal what drove those in this Scotland–New Zealand migrant cohort to continue their travels beyond initial landfall would surely be telling of the motivations behind Scottish wanderlust more generally.

PART TWO

Mobility in the Rural World

5

Lives in Motion: Revisiting the "Agricultural Ladder" in 1860s Ontario, a Study of Linked Microdata[1]

GORDON DARROCH

INTRODUCTION

This study employs old data – in two senses – to reconsider an old topic, with the aim of shedding some new light. The data are old, first, as microdata drawn from the Ontario censuses of 1861 and 1871 and, second, because these linked samples were among the earliest of their kind. The topic, the so-called agricultural ladder, is also long in the tooth both among agricultural historians and among researchers of historical mobility more broadly. Some of the new light I hope to shed comes from placing the experiences of entry into farming in the 1860s into a broader context of a highly mobile population, socially and geographically. Beginning with an overview of occupational transitions in this decade, I focus on the questions of entry into farming: first considering age of entry, then assessing the significance of boarding, lodging, and apprenticing as steps on the agricultural ladder, turning to the role of intraregional migration in farm acquisition, and, finally, examining differences in farm size and improved acreage and, for 1871, tenancy and owner occupancy.

The image of the agricultural ladder has been central to the literature on mobility in the North American farm economy. Others have very ably summarized its central features, especially Allan Bogue, Donald Winters, and Jeremy Atack for the United States and William Marr for Ontario.[2] I confine myself to a brief account.

In the US literature the debate has taken several turns. Its most recent version largely returns to the original thesis that in the nineteenth century farm labourers aimed to attain farm ownership by mounting various steps, including farming with their fathers or labouring on other's farms or adopting tenant farming as a prelude to converting their accumulated experience and capital into ownership. This is a rather unadorned upward mobility thesis. By contrast, a downward thesis prevailed in the 1920s and 1930s, in particular, in which rates of tenancy were understood to mark accumulating farm failure.[3]

Closer scrutiny of the thesis readily reveals complexities. In a still largely agrarian economy such as Ontario in the 1860s, yeoman farming remained the much-aspired-to epitome of independence, self-reliance, and respectability. But how did mobility into farm ownership compare to mobility into nonfarm occupations in the same era? What do we know about the movement into farming not only of labourers but of artisans and skilled workers or, for that matter, of merchants and manufacturers and other white-collar workers? And what relationship did geographic mobility have either to farm or nonfarm occupational mobility? Finally, following Catharine Anne Wilson's detailed studies for Ontario we need to consider more carefully the prospect that tenancy served as more than a step on the agricultural ladder; perhaps for some farm families it was the preferred form of land occupancy.[4]

THE STUDY REGION AND DATA

The map in figure 5.1 shows the study area, which I call Central Ontario. The 1871 census reported a population for this region of about 730,000, approximately 45 per cent of the provincial population. For 1861 the figure was 650,000, about half the province. The region comprises more than 34,000 square kilometers (8.5 million acres), a sizeable landmass, larger than Belgium or the state of Maine. Although it excludes the early settled areas of eastern Ontario and of significant later settlement in Western Ontario, the region was the social, political, and economic core of the emerging province.

The data I use here are linked records from two samples of the 1861 and 1871 population census. The samples and the linkage procedures have been described in detail in a number of publications.[5] The samples are *randomly selected clusters* of surnames based on Soundex phonetic codes. For each sampled person, all the enumerated information on the members of their households was transcribed. Our procedure

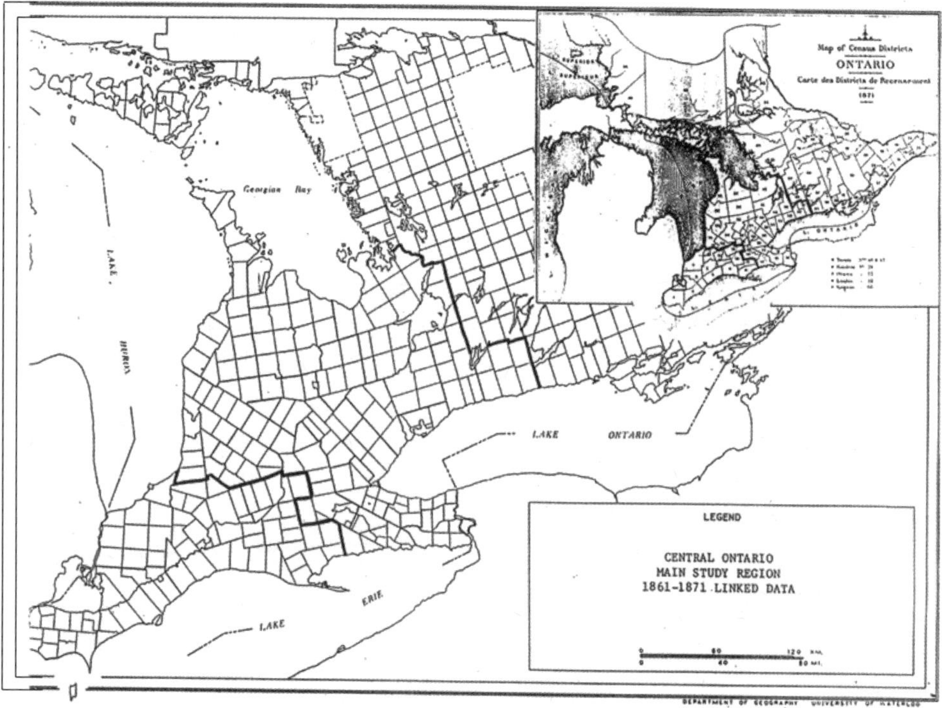

Figure 5.1 Central Ontario main study region, 1861–71 linked data

relied on random selection in order to ground statistical estimates in sampling theory. This differs from other surname samples of nominative historical data that are based on purposively selected but non-probability sampling.[6]

We developed a semi-automated linkage procedure that relied on computer sorts of names and ages and then on a fairly elaborate algorithm of visual matching within the sorted clusters. The linkage algorithm incorporated specific allowances for contingent variations in recorded names, ages, and a few other presumptively time-invariant characteristics. Subsequently many fully automated linkage systems have been developed. Were we to undertake the study today we would probably follow suit. Still, we know that linkage decisions are relatively straightforward for a large proportion of nominative records, perhaps 75 to 85 per cent; the difficulties arise in the residual 15 to 25 per cent of the least obvious cases.[7] Moreover, record linkage is above all a pattern recognition process, and humans are remarkably efficient at accomplishing it.

Table 5.1
Linkage, population turnover and adjusted out-migration estimates, South-Central Ontario, 1861–71

	N	*Per cent*		
Out-migrants and Other Losses	21,925	61.1		
Linked, 1861–71	13,973	38.9		
Total, 1861	35,898	100.0		
In-migrants and Population Growth	28,062	66.8		
Linked, 1861–71	13,973	33.2		
Total, 1871	42,035	100.0		
	Adjusted rates (Estimated losses due to mortality, marriage, linkage failure)			
	Low losses		*High losses*	
	N	*Per cent*	*N*	*Per cent*
Estimated out-migrants, 1861–71	9,836	41.3	4,701	25.2
Linked, 1861–71	13,973	58.7	13,973	74.8
Adjusted Totals	23,809	100.0	18,674	100.0

Definitions and samples given in the text.

In order to minimize selection bias, in addition to names and ages, only four variables least likely to be subject to reporting variations between censuses were considered (gender, marital status, birthplace, and religious affiliation). By today's standards, the files were of modest size, about 36,000 in 1861 and 42,000 in 1871. The number of record comparisons required for linkage decisions was greatly reduced by the need to make them only within the separate surname clusters. Table 5.1 provides the basic information on the linked samples; I only note a few key features as background to the analysis.[8]

The top panel divides each sample into two components, the linked individual records and unlinked residuals, which combine in 1861 the unknown failures of linkage with the out-migrants and in 1871 in-migrants and population growth. We confidently linked about 14,000 individuals (13,973), which is the first component reported in the table for 1861. The second component, the unlinked residual, is about 22,000 records out of a sample of 35,898 persons in 1861 and in 1871, about 28,000 of 42,035. One can estimate the main elements of the failures of linkage. The lower panel of table 5.1 presents these as the combinations of the lowest and highest estimates. Four main factors affect linkage rates: mortality in the 1860s, the loss of women to name linkage due to marriage, a combination of original enumeration errors, and failures of our linkage procedures. I made estimates of the losses due to mortality from life-tables, of women's age-specific marital rates from the samples themselves, and of the problems of nineteenth-century enumeration and linkage from a substantial literature.[9]

Table 5.1 shows that my lowest estimates suggest we linked about 60 per cent of the population at risk of linkage in 1861; a combination of highest estimates gives a linked proportion of three-quarters. They also yield adjusted estimates of regional out-migration, given in the lower panel of table 5.1. The range is wide, between 40 and 25 per cent. Given the assumptions required, a single, midrange estimate might be a rate of regional linkage success of 65–70 per cent, which accords with the fact that this is a large region, a single decade, and that historically much residential movement is local and short distance. That implies that some 30–5 per cent of the regional population left the region entirely, as we know, mostly through the porous, midcentury southern border.

OCCUPATIONAL MOBILITY IN 1860S ONTARIO

My first analysis focuses on occupational mobility, considered as changes in major labour force locations. Following convention, the analysis is restricted to males age fifteen and over due to the unfortunate limitations of recorded women's work.

Table 5.2 gives the occupational distributions in each year for the linked sample of men. For context, table 5.8 in the appendix compares them to the full, cross-sectional samples for each year and to the very limited occupational information in the published censuses for the same area. The appendix provides the details. In brief, farmers are somewhat overrepresented in the linked sample, with the differences mainly offset by the underrepresentation of labourers and those not in the labour force. For 1871 selective regional out-migration is the main source of the differences, since farmers are the most geographically stable group. For 1861, the smaller differences are due to some selection bias, which we have addressed elsewhere.[10] We have no reason to think the latter seriously affects our main analysis.

Table 5.2
Occupational distributions for men aged fifteen and over in 1861, linked in Central Ontario, 1861 and 1871.

	1861		*1871*	
Occupation	*Per cent*	*N*	*Per cent*	*N*
Merchants and manufacturers	4.2	170	6.5	265
Professionals	2.1	85	3.1	125
Other white-collar	1.2	50	1.2	50
Artisan and skilled	13.3	543	15.5	634
Semiskilled	2.2	90	3.3	136
Labourers	14.7	600	9.1	373
Farmers	35.9	1,467	50.0	2,044
Farmers' sons	10.1	413	5.8	239
Not in the labour force	16.4	670	5.4	222
Total	100.0	4,088	100.0	4,088

Table 5.2 reveals four main shifts in the labour force distributions among men who remained in Central Ontario through the 1860s. Very large numbers took up farming. Artisanal and skilled work increased very slightly, while many men left labouring. Lastly, the men not recorded as in the labour force declined by two thirds. We included the unusual, explicit category of farmers' sons because the two censuses enumerated such individuals as labourers in 1861 and farmers in 1871, so we inferred comparability from the occupations, surnames, ages, and positions in the household. This reclassification misses some sons of farmers who were not enumerated with an occupation; they are classified with others "not in the labour force."[11]

This last category is an especially complicated one and warrants additional comment. First, contrary to current, conventional expectations, the absence of a record for occupation in a nineteenth-century census is not a matter mainly of adolescents who were yet to enter the labour force. Only half of the group were under age twenty in 1861 and most would have had work experience in or outside of their family households. Moreover, some seven in ten of these young men were farmers' sons. The other half without enumerated occupations were prime-aged or older men, more than a fifth of whom were or had been married and another 12 or 13 per cent were single men boarding or lodging with nonfamily members. Some of these older, apparently unemployed men were surely among the disparate, vulnerable, "unwilling idlers" identified by Baskerville and Sager.[12] Moreover, more than 80 per cent of those over age twenty were immigrants, so a good many were recent arrivals. Their exclusion from the enumerated labour force might in part be witness to the idiosyncratic irregularities of the 1861 census.[13] We address the implications of this complex category throughout the following analysis.

Table 5.3 provides the male occupational mobility table using these categories. I emphasize two features of the distribution: the highly variable proportions of men who remained in the same occupations at both ends of the decade (a few likely left and reentered the category) and the significant numbers from all nonfarming origins who entered farming. The diagonal of the table reveals that occupational stability ranged from a high of more than 80 per cent among farmers to a low of just 9 per cent of those who were not in the labour force in 1861. The other occupational groups vary from a relatively settled artisanal and skilled group – with more than 60 per cent remaining in some similar work – through a little more than half of those reported as merchants, manufacturers, and other retailers, and of the professionals to between a quarter and a third of farmers' sons, labourers, semiskilled workers, and those in nonprofessional white-collar work (who were mostly retail and office clerks).

The off-diagonal figures are revealing: men from many occupational origins crowded onto the agricultural ladder or ladders in 1860s Central Ontario. Despite a growing core of commercial and industrial activity in the region, with a few exceptions the largest numbers of occupationally mobile nonfarmers in this decade moved into farming.

Specific figures are partly a product of the occupational classification, as they are of any, but the general movement is quite striking. In some cases the movement into farming represents a third or more of the men who stayed in the region and changed the way they made livings. For only three groups of those changing occupations (off-diagonal cells) do we observe more movement into alternative, nonfarm work than into farming. First, a few more merchants, manufacturers, and related men appeared to have become artisans in 1871 than farmers (16.5 versus 12.9 per cent). This transition is particularly affected by our classification, since distinguishing craftsmen from small makers and manufacturers by occupational title alone is an exercise in educated guesswork. The other two changes involved the small numbers of "other white-collar" workers: whereas only one in ten became farmers,

Table 5.3

Decadal occupational mobility of men, aged fifteen and over, 1861–71, Central Ontario.

	Percentage Distribution of 1861 Occupations in 1871										
Occupation in 1861	*Mercht& Maufact.*	*Profess-ional*	*Other Non-manual*	*Artisan-Skilled*	*Semi skilled*	*Labour*	*Farmer*	*Farmer Son*	*Not in L.F.*	*Total*	*N*
Merchants&Manuf	52.4	2.4	4.1	16.5	2.9	2.9	12.9	0.6	5.3	100.0	170
Professional	11.8	55.3	2.4	8.2	3.5	0.0	14.1	0.0	4.7	100.0	85
Other Non-Manual	26.0	16.0	28.0	2.0	8.0	0.0	10.0	2.0	8.0	100.0	50
Artisan & Skilled	7.9	1.7	1.3	64.1	2.0	5.3	13.4	1.1	3.1	100.0	543
Semi-Skilled	5.6	3.3	2.2	15.6	30.0	11.1	26.7	0.0	5.6	100.0	90
Labourer	4.2	0.8	0.7	11.0	7.7	27.7	40.7	2.3	5.0	100.0	600
Farmer	2.2	0.3	0.1	4.1	0.7	5.0	82.3	0.5	4.8	100.0	1,467
Farmer's Son	3.9	2.2	0.7	6.3	1.9	4.6	49.2	25.9	5.3	100.0	413
Not in L.F.	4.8	5.2	1.5	12.5	3.1	10.6	37.9	15.4	9.0	100.0	670
N	265	125	50	634	136	373	2,044	239	222	100.0	4,088

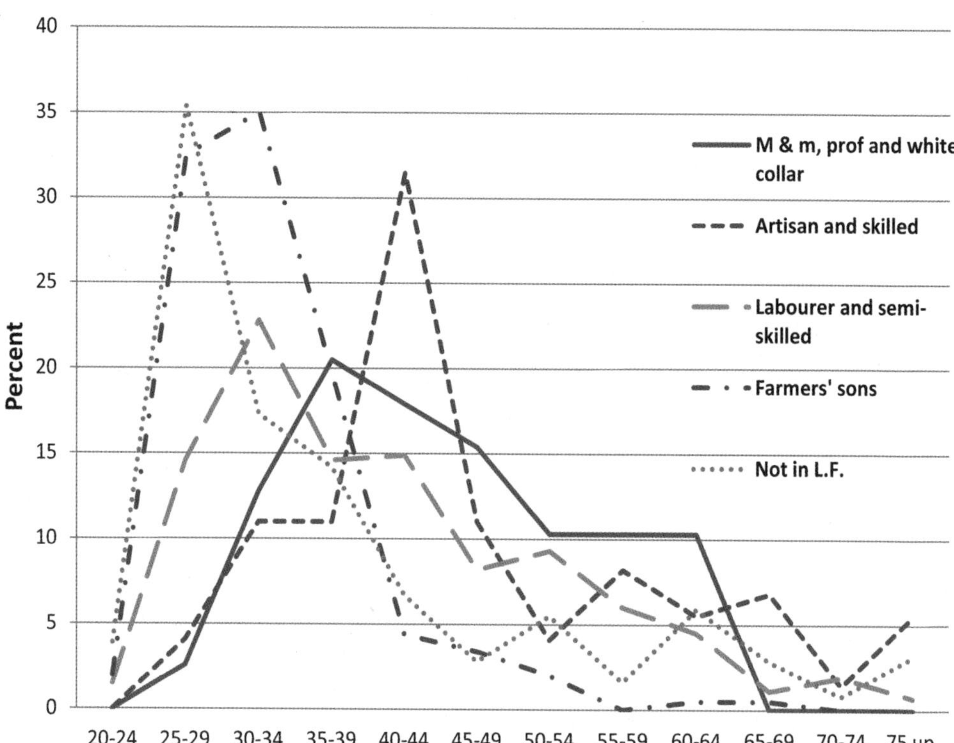

Figure 5.2 Distribution of new farmers by age in 1871, by 1861 occupational origins, for males aged fifteen and up.

nearly one in three moved "up," we might infer, into merchant and manufacturing and retail ownership. Another 16 per cent moved into the professional occupations – doctors, parsons, lawyers, and the like. But the really striking pattern is the flood into farming, with the main streams coming, obviously, from farmer's sons (about half in just ten years) and then from the two largest nonfarm groups, labourers and those entering and reentering the labour force. These two groups represented about 30 per cent of the region's 1861 male population over age fourteen; about four in ten took up farming within ten years.

TAKING UP THE LAND

What can one say about the conditions that fostered farm entry? Figure 5.2 first shows the age patterns of entry into farming by slightly reduced occupational origin categories for 1861, obviously excluding continuing farmers. We observe two early peaks, two lower and more extended patterns of age of entry, and one late entry pattern.

Farmers' sons and those whose first recorded occupation was farmer were much alike, with younger men entering farming in large numbers and entry dropping off quickly with age. Census-identified farmers' sons tended to delay entry a few years longer than men previously not recorded as working, matching them with well over one in three entering before age thirty, and another 35 per cent between ages thirty and thirty-five, compared to the latter, among whom about 17 per cent entered after age thirty. The delay probably reflects the fact that many farmers' sons waited to start new families and on various negotiations with their land-owning parents about inheritances, conditions of land transfer, and the sons' responsibilities to their parents as the latter aged.[14]

Labourers and semiskilled workers are plotted together here, with labourers the great majority. Like farmers' sons, a large number entered farming between ages thirty and thirty-four (a fifth), but quite a few entered later, even into their fifties, sixties and seventies. Initially this pattern is a puzzle. Closer scrutiny reveals that prime-aged and older immigrants accounted for most of the delayed farm entry. Presumably these immigrant farmers had arrived prior to 1861 while in their prime years or later. Only in the next decade it seems did they have the means and the knowledge to acquire landed titles or leaseholds.

Merchants, manufacturers, professionals, and other white-collar workers display an unsuspected pattern. As a group they tended toward quite delayed and extended entry, the largest proportion, a fifth, doing so between ages thirty-five and thirty-nine, with fully a third taking up farming between ages fifty and sixty-four.[15] And all of these older new farmers were immigrants. Finally, the transition for artisans and skilled workers was the most delayed on average, though less extended into their middle and later years. Just less than a third waited until they were between forty and forty-four years old, while others displayed late-in-life peaks (another third were over fifty years of age in 1871). Almost all of these formerly artisan and skilled workers were also immigrants, suggesting personal and family strategies of late, landed investments and perhaps retirement, possibly finally fulfilling their immigrant dream of title to their own land and its vaunted security.

Figure 5.3 displays these age-of-entry patterns for the Canadian-born and immigrant populations separately, which clearly reveal the contrast in the age patterns of farm entry.

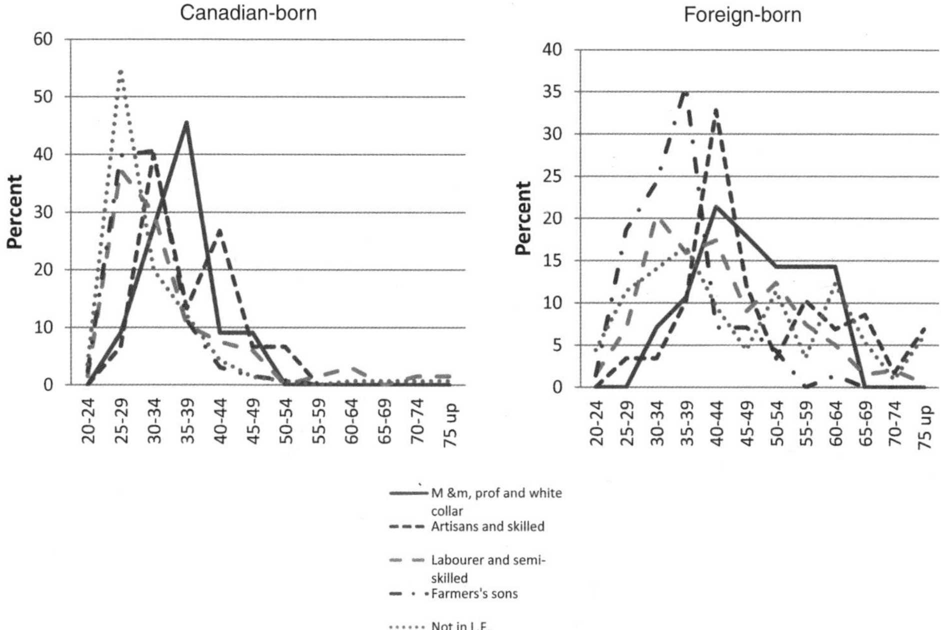

Figure 5.3 Age of new farmers, 1871, by occupational origins for Canadian-born and foreign-born males aged fifteen and over, 1861

A majority of the recent labour force entrants and farmers' sons were Canadian born (56 and 66 per cent). The men entering farming for the first time were predominantly immigrants, which is no surprise since Ontario's nineteenth-century labour force was largely immigrant: two-thirds of the linked, male population aged fifteen and older was foreign born. The relative success of these immigrants in entering farming testifies to their drive, adaptive capabilities, and their desire to achieve the promised land of a landed "competency." It also testifies to the varieties of access points into the Central Ontario land market of the era.

RUNGS ON THE AGRICULTURAL LADDER

Table 5.4 introduces another perspective on the life cycle in the transition into farming in nineteenth-century Ontario, distinguishing three basic household situations of individuals: whether they were children residing with a parent or parents; whether they were single, unrelated

Table 5.4
Household status transitions of new farmers (males aged fifteen up), 1871 by 1861 occupational origins.

	Household status of Individuals						
	Children with parent		*Boarder/lodger or resident kin (% kin)*		*Ever-married person*		
Origin occupations 1861	*1861*	*1871*	*1861*	*1871* (*row percent*)	*1861*	*1871*	*N*
Merchants–Manufs Prof & other white-collar	10.3	0.0	17.9 (0.0)	10.3 (2.6)	71.8	89.7	39
Artisan–skilled	6.8	0.0	15.1 (4.1)	2.8 (1.4)	78.1	97.3	73
Labouring–semiskilled	14.6	2.2	35.4 (6.3)	11.9 (1.1)	50.0	85.8	268
Farmer's sons	87.2	4.4	1.0 (0.5)	12.3 (1.0)	11.8	83.3	203
Not in L.F.	53.9	7.5	13.0 (2.0)	15.0	33.1	77.6	254
Total, these origins	43.2	4.1	17.7 (3.1)	12.1 (1.2)	39.1	83.9	873
BASE COMPARISONS							
Linked Population	24.7	10.2	12.2 (2.0)	7.6 (0.8)	63.1	82.8	4,088

men boarding and lodging (or single resident kin); or whether they were ever-married persons. Two simple questions are posed here. Did new farmers in 1871 tend to apprentice for their landed enterprise by living and working in the households of others ten years earlier? Were those labouring at the outset of the decade more likely to board and apprentice with farmers, compared to those with other occupational origins, as their foothold on the agricultural ladder? I focus on the proportions of the new farmers who were single boarders and lodgers in 1861 (and report in parentheses the small numbers classified as resident kin). Farmers at the outset of the decade are obviously excluded.

The answers to both questions are positive. The middle columns show that among those with nonfarm occupational origins, slightly higher proportions augmented others' households in 1861 than in the linked population as a whole – about 18 per cent overall.[16] But nearly twice that proportion of new farmers who were previously labourers and semi-skilled workers resided outside their natal homes in 1861 (35.4 per cent), compared to half or less of this proportion among those with other occupational origins. Looking more closely, I find that 70 per cent of boarding or lodging labourers lived in the homes of farming heads of households in 1861 (another 23 per cent were in households headed by labourers). This apprenticing in residence was matched by the men who were not recorded in the labour force in 1861 but farmed in 1871. For such new farmers living as a farm labourer in a farmer's household clearly served as a step on the rungs of the agricultural ladders, as Spillman suggested as early as 1919 for the United States.[17]

As a point of comparison with the new farmers, I replicated these distributions for those who changed occupations to any nonfarm pursuit, including farmers (not reported here). Boarding and lodging were only marginally lower among these occupationally mobile individuals, but they lived in homes headed by men with a much wider range of occupations than the new farmers and this was particularly so for labourers moving into nonfarm occupations. It is reasonable to think that the diversity of boarding and lodging locations among these mobile men was part of their exploration of wider occupational options to farming.

NONAGRICULTURAL LADDERS

What conditions might have fostered different occupational mobility transitions? The 1861 population and agricultural schedules allow one to consider, for example, if prior home ownership or recorded "business investments" might be clues to the material conditions engendering particular mobility paths. In fact, the historical clues reveal quite predictable life cycle and geographic conditions of mobility. On the one hand, along with the new farmers, men who did not change their main occupational locations were much more likely to own homes in 1861 than those entering nonfarm work (about two-thirds compared to a third). These differences reflected a combination of the relative youthfulness of those entering nonfarm occupations and their much more common town and city origins and destinations.[18] On the other hand, the intriguing 1861 records of business investments reveal only minor differences among the three groups, with men not changing occupations slightly more likely than the others to report some capital, in part a consequence of their age and labour force experience.[19]

Table 5.5
Intertownship (town) migration, men, aged fifteen and over in 1861, by occupational mobility, 1861–71, Central Ontario.

	Per cent migrant, 1861–71			
Origin occupations 1861	*Same occupation, 1871*	*New farmers, 1871*	*Other occupation, 1871*	*Total labour force*
Merchants–Manufs				
Prof & other white-collar	40.7	61.5	51.7	47.5
Artisan–skilled	31.9	57.5	47.5	38.9
Labouring–semiskilled	33.2	58.6	51.1	49.0
Farmers	17.3		45.8	22.4
Farmer's sons	7.5	36.5	44.7	30.5
Not in L.F.	21.7	31.9	36.8	33.6
Total	22.6	44.9	44.8	33.6
N	2,065	837	1,186	4,088

Other distinguishing background conditions were not apparent in these data, with one clear exception.[20] The exception is the familiar story about the historical relationship between residential mobility and occupational mobility. Table 5.5 provides the essential information. Figure 5.4 highlights the main features of the distributions.

SOCIAL AND SPATIAL MOBILITY

In this analysis, migration is assessed as intraregional movement, that is, relocation between townships or towns and cities, of which there were 216 areas geographically matched between the two censuses. This is a minimal measure of migration, since it is assessed as a single change of location between the two ends of the decade. A large international literature assures us that much more relocation was the order of the day in the mid-nineteenth century. Were we able to track, say, annual relocation, vastly more men and their families would certainly have been found on the move than is reflected in our measure, and some would even have relocated back to places they previously left.[21] The rates would be still higher if one added those who left the region entirely to take their chances in the labour markets of Ohio or New York State or to risk pioneering on the Canadian prairies or in the Canadian West beyond the West.[22] Our middle ground, single estimate

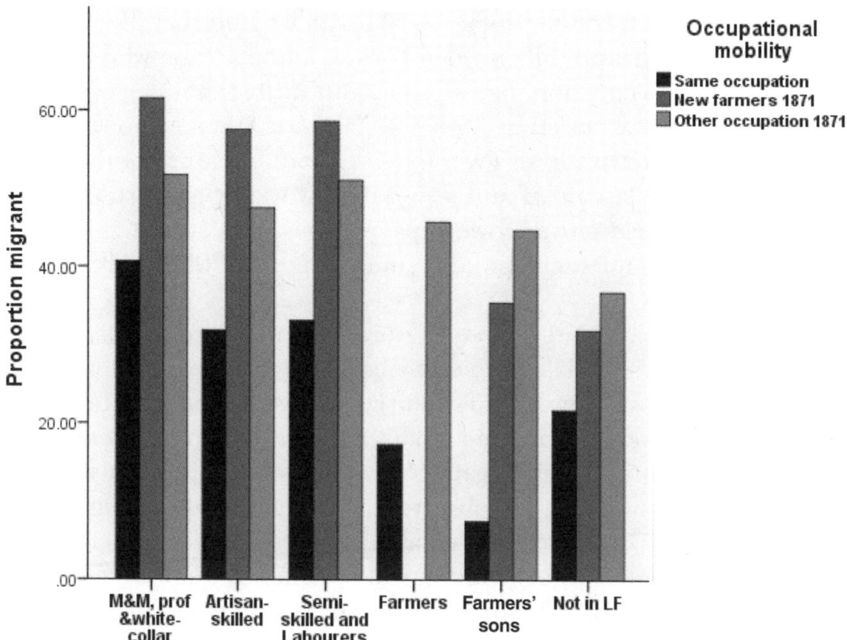

Figure 5.4 Intertownship (town) migration, men aged fifteen and up, by occupational mobility, 1861–71, central Ontario

of this out-migration was about another third of the entire 1861 population (table 5.1), a low estimate for men over age fourteen.

In table 5.5 the right-most column for the occupational origin groups of 1861 and the total row for the destination groups of 1871 provide the broad parameters of nineteenth-century Ontario's spatial mobility. One-third (33.6 per cent) of men aged fifteen and older in 1861 who remained in (or returned to) Central Ontario in this decade had relocated to a different township or town. Only two occupational groups had less than a third of the men on the move, farmers and farmers' sons. About a fifth of the former relocated townships and just less than a third of the latter did so. Almost half of the 1861 labourers and semiskilled were intraregional migrants and, more surprisingly, nearly as many of those with merchant, manufacturer, professional, or white-collar occupations at the outset of the decade. Nearly four in ten artisan and skilled workers were migrants. Those newly recorded in the labour force were among the least likely to move, matching the total rate of a third.

Considering the column totals of table 5.5 we find that the propensity to move geographically is notable even among those who did not change major occupational groups, about a fifth (22.6 per cent; column 1). The lowest rate was for stable farmers, among whom 17 per cent made intertownship or town moves. About one-third of the occupationally stable labourers and semiskilled workers, and artisans and skilled workers had moved townships or towns, and even higher rates prevailed among the merchant, manufacturing, and white-collar workers (four in ten).

Although farmers and their sons were least prone to migrate, their rates were hardly trivial given the obstacles faced by farm families including the costs of acquiring new land, investments in land clearance and improvement, and in animals and equipment, to say nothing of the uncertainties of establishing new farms and farm households. Some of the movement we observe very likely parallels that which Québec scholars have documented about the willingness of established farmers to move lock, stock, and barrel in order to help provide land for their children, although regional cultural differences played some role.[23] But much of it, I think, still remains quite beyond our current interpretive perspectives.

The column totals show that occupational mobility tended to entail geographic mobility: many of each group of occupationally mobile men could be found on the regional roads and waterways at some point in the decade. Considering the interior of the table, two groups shared the lowest rates of migration. Just over a third of farmers' sons moved township of residence in order to begin as independent farm occupiers (36.5 per cent), a relative stability that undoubtedly followed from their local experience and family-assisted landed settlement. Similarly the numbers of "hidden" farmers' sons among those without an occupation recorded in 1861 partially accounts for the somewhat lower migration rate among this composite group (31.9 per cent). But we observe unexpectedly high and similar rates of migration among the three main nonfarming occupational groups, with about six in ten migrating among those becoming farmers and about half of those moving into alternative, nonfarm occupations.

That labourers and their families moved about the region seeking other forms of work fits our conventional images of the peripatetic unskilled worker, but current interpretations are strained to account for the high propensity for migration among merchants, manufacturers, professionals and white-collar men, or among artisans and skilled tradesmen. Indeed, rather than inhibiting migration, the property, capital, and other resources of the better-off appear to have fostered movement, especially if they left one occupational category for some other and most of all if they had become farm occupiers.

ACQUISITION, IMPROVEMENT, AND LAND TENURE AMONG FARMERS

Other key questions we can initially address with the current evidence are about the acquisition of land, its improvement and about land tenure among farmers of 1871. Table 5.6 gives the distribution among the 1861 occupational origin groups of the size of farm land occupied, of improved acreage, and of owners and tenants among all 1871 farm occupiers. The farm size categories employed here were introduced by McInnis, and I have elsewhere followed his lead.[24]

In 1871 most Ontario farmers were middling farmers in terms of the size of landholdings and improved acreage, 53.5 per cent for the men reported here.[25] For an understanding of the character of nineteenth-century Ontario's agricultural ladders, the key observation is that, no matter their occupational origins, the differences among farmers in 1871 were modest both in terms of land occupied and land improved. Continuing farmers are our benchmark, working the largest acreages and averaging the most improved acreages, 56 per cent held middling acreages with 14 per cent occupying 170 or more. Farmers' sons followed with 55 per cent reporting middling acreages and over 9 per cent, 170 or more, which are impressive proportions given the demands of land clearance, purchase, planting, harvesting, and family maintenance in the 1860s. Again they witness Ontario's' active, mid-century land market, as well as the enterprise and resilience of the men and their families.[26] Even more striking, nearly half of the 1861 labourers new to farm occupancy held the same middling acreages (48.5 per cent): a testament to how relatively readily one could step up a nineteenth-century agricultural ladder. Even less expected was the nearly half (47.6 per cent) of those without a recorded occupation in 1861 who farmed middling acreages in 1871. The latter figure reflects the number in this category who went unrecorded as farmers' sons in 1861 but also, I suspect, the numbers of the seemingly unemployed who were prime-aged immigrants with some farm experience and some accumulated capital by 1871. Still, both these groups were less likely than continuing farmers to occupy the largest acreages, and labourers

Table 5.6

Farm acreage, improvement, and tenure among farmers (males, aged 15 and up) in 1871 by 1861 occupational origins, Central Ontario.

	Farm size (row percent)				*Improved acres*		*Tenure (row percent)*			
Origin occupations 1861	*Farmers w/out farms*	*1–69*	*70–169*	*170 up*	*Mean**	*S.D*	*Own*	*Tenant*	*DK*	*N*
Merchants–Manufs										
Prof & other white-collar	15.4	20.5	59.0	5.1	58.4	31.5	61.5	17.9	20.5	39
Artisan–skilled	12.3	38.3	41.1	8.2	50.1	43.6	60.3	16.4	23.3	73
Labouring–semiskilled	9.3	36.5	48.5	5.6	44.7	37.1	55.6	27.2	17.1	268
Farmers	8.0	21.9	56.1	14.1	66.5	40.1	79.8	9.1	11.1	1,207
Farmer's sons	12.3	23.2	55.2	9.4	60.9	35.2	65.5	17.7	16.7	303
Not in L.F.	16.9	26.8	47.6	8.7	56.9	42.0	66.1	14.2	19.7	254
Total	10.0	25.1	53.5	11.4	61.3	40.2	72.5	13.4	14.1	2,044

**Note:* The figures for improved acreage is based on the Ns for farmers reporting acreage. For the occupational groups in 1861 they were: 33, 64, 243, 1,111, 178, 211. Total = 1840.

just entering farming evinced the least capacity to acquire improved acreage and/or to improve it in the decade. These acquired acreages among new farmers at least imply considerable access to land and of land turnover, rather than increasing barriers to agricultural entry or widespread hierarchies of the soil.[27]

It also is intriguing that among new farm occupiers those who earlier had been merchants, manufacturers, professional, or other white-collar workers were the most likely to have acquired middling or larger land holdings: nearly six in ten were in the middling category by 1871, with just fewer than the continuing farmers occupying the largest acreages. Though relatively few (table 5.3) and highly mobile (table 5.5), these men and their families apparently had a level of material well-being and resources in 1861 that allowed them to ascend the agricultural ladders two or more steps at a time. Their ascension initially challenges our common notion that occupational status and relative well-being historically fostered both occupational and geographic stability. However, although difficult to explore either in documentary or microdata records to date, we have strong hints that many such men had farm experience, having spent a good portion of their lives in rural areas and having routinely juggled farming and other occupational pursuits. Our knowledge of this multiplicity of nineteenth-century occupations remains limited, but a few studies have reported that it was widespread, in some cases combining farming and small manufacturing or trades work, in others, practiced in seasonal series, as in farming and lumbering, and sometimes as a life cycle sequence of jobs, " ... cotton-mill piecer, peddler, porridge maker, weaver, cook, grocer, farmer." [28] This still largely unexplored question of the diversity of types of work and of working knowledge shared by nineteenth-century men and women seems likely to be key to our understanding of the relative fluidity of movement among occupations and, specifically, of movement into farming.

Turning to landed tenancy, the 1871, but unfortunately not the 1861, census provides a valuable record although one that is difficult to interpret due to the relatively large numbers of land occupiers for whom no information was provided. The rightmost columns of table 5.6 display the proportions reported as owners, as tenants, and as missing or illegible records. Overall, 14 per cent of the tenure records for the linked samples were blank or illegible, mostly the former. Taking the records at face value suggests wider differences among the several routes into farming than differences observed for land occupancy and improved acreage. Fewer than one in ten continuing farmers reported being tenants, but 27 per cent of the formerly labouring male population did so. Recorded farmers' sons turned farmers in 1871 were twice as likely as continuing farmers to have been tenants, presumably using leaseholding as another of their steps up the agricultural ladders. But they were nearly matched by the formerly artisan and skilled workers, as well as by the merchants and manufacturers, professional, and other white-collar workers who declared themselves farmers in 1871. This evidence accords with the recent literature in which tenancy is seen as a step into farming, rather than the fate of failed farmers, but also leaves open Catharine Anne Wilson's stronger interpretation in which tenant status was a preferred, especially flexible, sometimes inheritable, mode of farm occupancy for significant numbers of farmers.[29]

SEPARATING EFFECTS: MULTIVARIATE MODELS

Finally, by exploring several multivariate models, I try to separate the effects of key conditions on the likelihood of men entering farming in this decade and on the likelihood of tenancy versus ownership among farm occupiers. If farm entry was age related, as much evidence shows, and tenants were generally reported to be younger than owner-occupiers, how important were such life cycle effects in the context of other conditions of farm entry? [30] Did the Canadian-born have some sustained advantage over immigrants in climbing the agricultural ladders and in ownership of farm land? In light of these influences, we can also ask how salient were prior occupational origins in influencing farm acquisition or on the propensity to be a tenant rather than owner? Lastly, given the historical association between spatial and social mobility, did intraregional migration have an independent effect on farm entry or on tenancy in old Ontario?[31]

The first model assesses the odds of any nonfarmer in 1861 becoming a farmer in 1871 for men aged fifteen and over. The second is a specification of the first, considering only the occupationally mobile men, asking what were the relative chances of becoming a farmer rather than taking up some other nonfarm occupation? With the exception of migration, on which I comment further, the independent variables refer to conditions in 1861.

Table 5.7
Logistic regressions for the odds of entering farming or nonfarming among all 1861 nonfarmers, among all mobile 1861 nonfarmers, and of tenure among 1871 farmers, males, age 15 and over, Central Ontario, 1861–71

Characteristics (1861)	*Farm vs nonfarm: all 1861 nonfarmers Exp (B)*	*Farm vs nonfarm: mobile 1861 nonfarmers Exp (B)*	*Tenant vs owner: 1871 farmers Exp (B)*
Age	1.108***	1.129**	0.982**
Age sq.	0.999***	0.999**	
Nativity			
Canadian-born (ref)			
Foreign-born	0.816	0.839	1.408*
Occupational Origin			
Merch/manuf/white-collar:	0.095***	0.101***	1.702
Artisan/skilled	0.109***	0.201***	1.659
Labourer/semi-skilled	0.488***	0.463**	2.659***
Not in labour force	0.631**	0.369***	1.439
Farmer's sons (ref model 1& 2)			1.773*
Farmers (ref model 3)			
Intertownship/town migration:			
Stayer (ref)			
Mover	1.630***	1.152	2.111***
Constant	0.110***	0.100***	0.154***
N	2,621	1,763	1,755

Note: *p<.05; ** p<.01; *** p<.001

Since we can consider the three dependent variables as dichotomies, logistic regression models are employed. Table 5.7 provides the exponent of the coefficients, interpreted as odds ratios between the characteristic in question and a reference group, and their significance levels. The models are designed to take into account the effects of the surname clustering in the samples on the estimated statistical significance of the coefficients. Including in these models a labour force variable that has separate categories for men not in the recorded 1861 labour force and for farmers' sons might appear to risk some collinearity with age, since these two groups were on average young and certainly younger than the other occupational groups.[32] Statistical analysis indicates that there is no risk to the estimates reported here, partly because the relatively wide variation in age distributions within each group.[33]

The first and second models include two age terms, age and age squared, to try to portray an anticipated curvilinear relationship between age and occupational mobility. The age squared variable was not substantively or statistically significant in the third model and was dropped from it.

In the first model, we find a slightly curvilinear relationship between age and farm entry: the youngest nonfarmers in 1861 had lower odds of becoming farmers in 1871 than men in their prime years and the odds fell off somewhat in later years. This is a readily understood relationship, given the time needed to acquire the skills, capital, and, probably above all, the family labour needed by most men in moving into farming (the labour of wives certainly but of older children as well).

Although we expected the native-born to have experienced some advantage in entering the land market compared to immigrants, including nativity in the model indicates that, although the coefficients suggest some immigrant deficit, the differences between them may well have resulted from chance alone.

Considering position in the labour force in 1861, we take the farmers' sons as the reference group in this model and in model two given their obvious leg up on the agricultural ladders. In the first model, all the reported coefficients for occupations are less than one, reflecting farmers' sons' clear advantage in comparison to other origin groups, an advantage observed in table 5.3, but here independent of the effects of age, nativity, and migration. The 1861 labourers were about half as likely to have become farmers as the farmers' sons, and those not recorded in the 1861 labour force were even more likely to have moved into – or back into – farming, although still some 37 per cent less likely than farmer's sons. These are not trivial differences in the chances of clambering up Ontario's early agricultural ladders, but the comparison is with those who had a decidedly advantaged entre, adult sons living in farming households, themselves working land, and with prospects of landed inheritance and family assistance.

The model further shows that intraregional relocation among towns and townships significantly conditioned farm entry. Those who relocated within Central Ontario were some 60 per cent more likely to have become farmers than residentially stable men. The direction of this relationship has to be interpreted with caution, since occupational and geographic movement were simultaneous in the only way one can measure them in such short-term, longitudinal data. Nevertheless, a selection argument makes considerable sense: those who moved spatially did so in order to take advantage of farming opportunities thought or known to be located elsewhere in the region, just as those who moved beyond the region were largely in search of new work and lives.[34]

The second model considers agricultural ladders in a more specific sense, considering only men willing and able to alter the way they made livings in this decade. So the model compares the odds of entering farming in 1871 to the odds of taking up any nonfarm occupation. In this analysis, age had a significant and slightly stronger relationship to the relative chances of farm entry, rising slightly more steeply among prime-aged men, before declining with advancing age. But again, in pre-Confederation Ontario it mattered not to farm acquisition if one was native-born or an immigrant.

Regarding occupational origins, the results reveal one intriguing change from the first model. With known farmers' sons as the reference group, considering only those who changed labour force locations indicates it was the experience of labouring in a rural economy that was most commonly translated into subsequent farm acquisition even compared to men just entering or reentering the labour force, which again includes some "hidden" sons of farmers and some immigrants with prior farm experience.

It is also reasonable to think that the search for and acquisition of farmland by nonfarmers entailed a greater tendency to migrate than other occupational changes. But whereas moving geographically accompanied farm entry among all nonfarmers in 1861 (model 1), among the occupationally mobile men it did not significantly distinguish new farmers from others changing labour force locations. Locating a farm appears to have entailed no greater requirement for spatial relocation than locating other new ways of making livings: geographic and social mobility went hand in glove in this nineteenth-century world for farmers and nonfarmers alike.

Finally, in the third model of table 5.7 I examine the conditions fostering tenancy among all farm occupiers, noting that the limits of the reports of tenancy qualify any strong conclusions. First, like others we find that young aspiring farmers were most likely to use land leasing as their gateway into farm life.[35] Still, tenancy was not the preserve of the young, as other studies have also shown.[36] Among those for whom there is a record in our data, some 30 per cent of farming men aged fifteen to twenty-four were tenants but just less than a quarter of those aged twenty-five to fifty and even 14 or 15 per cent of farmers over age fifty.

Second, immigrants were more likely than the native-born to be leaseholders, as suggested in the early reports of William Marr for Ontario and by some US scholars, although in our evidence the relationship was just statistically significant by conventional standards.[37] Further, with farmers as the appropriate reference group, the model shows that, independent of the other variables, the 1861 labourers were over two-and-a-half times more likely than continuing farmers to have adopted tenant status as an entry to farming, although farmers' sons also had some greater propensity (just statistically significant in this model and with a coefficient not different from new farmers who had been merchants, manufacturers, and other white-collar workers or artisanal and skilled workers).

Finally, a farm occupier who relocated his township of residence within the region was more than twice as likely to have been a tenant as a nonmigrant.[38] The question remains open to what extent tenant farmers tended to move as part of a search strategy aiming to locate affordable, available, or optimal farm lands and to what extent farm tenancy was a preferred circumstance for those wishing to remain mobile and not locked into the responsibilities of mortgages and the full burdens of farm ownership and operation.[39] Being a willing migrant probably gave a lessee some negotiating advantage among landlords.

CONCLUSION

Life in motion was the leitmotif in 1860s Ontario. Both occupational change and residential relocation were so relatively frequent that one might assume they were taken for granted and, thus, not often remarked upon in the quotidian accounts of everyday worlds. Parkerson's description of New York State in the same period as a "culture of mobility" could well apply to nineteenth-century Central Ontario.[40] Men from all occupations changed their labour force positions over the decade, with large majorities of those in labouring and semiskilled work as well as those in clerical work on the move. Farming was the occupational destination for a great many of these mobile individuals, but even a fifth of farmers became nonfarmers in these ten years.

Reconsidering the notion of a nineteenth-century agricultural ladder, I reveal the distinctive age profiles of entry into farming depending on one's occupational origins, that living and apprenticing in farm households was a likely first step on the agricultural ladders, and that intraregional migration was especially likely among labourers entering farming but so too among merchants, manufacturers, artisans, and skilled workers who took up the land. I find, too, a surprising egalitarianism in terms of farm sizes and improved acreage between continuing farmers and new farmers of various occupational origins. Multivariate analysis revealed that entry into farming and farm tenancy were age related, but the life cycle patterns were less strong than expected. Moreover, the native-born had no clear advantage over immigrants in the chances of farm acquisition, although they were more likely than the native-born to become tenants. Farmers' sons had the expected advantages of farm experience, inheritance, and family assistance in becoming farmers within a decade, but entering farming was also common among the apparently unemployed in 1861, some of whom we found to be unrecorded farmers' sons and others mainly immigrants probably reentering the work force. Labourers were somewhat less, but still quite likely, to enter farming. Among men who changed labour force positions, labourers were only a little less than half as likely to do so as farmer's sons. In qualified evidence, tenant farming in 1871 appears rather more common among immigrants than among the native-born and among men who had been labourers and farmers' sons ten years earlier. Intraregional migration accompanied movement onto the agricultural ladders among all nonfarmers but was not more likely among new farmers than other mobile men, although tenant farmers tended to relocate more than owner occupiers.

Men faced undoubted barriers to farm entry, including relocation, land and implement costs, land clearance, and limited labour, but these appear to have been offset in the 1860s by the drive for a landed living, by the availability of land both in the land market and in some new settlements, and by the widespread farm experience attained by many men prior to entry. The pervasive geographic and occupational movement, especially into farming, invites some reconsideration of our conventional notions about how nineteenth-century men and women assessed obstacles to change and risk taking.

The evidence presented here also suggests we might usefully modify the metaphor of a singular agricultural ladder, which imposes a strong sense of hierarchy on our conception of the historical movement into farming.[41] Certainly we found that some specific steps enhanced a man's chances of farm entry, but nineteenth-century Central Ontario provided not one but a series of ladders allowing farm acquisition from different prior labour force circumstances and for men of varying life cycle stages, whether they were immigrant or native-born. Agricultural ladders were features of a wider network of paths for movement across labour and land markets, as well as up and down them.

APPENDIX A

Table 5.8 compares the distributions of occupations for men age fifteen and over in the linked sample to the same distributions for the full, cross-sectional samples for each year. Although the very limited occupational information in the published censuses does not allow us to make detailed comparisons with the occupational categories reported here, other comparisons for age, gender, marital status, birthplace, and the counties of central Ontario show that the cross-sectional samples closely match the published census results, giving us confidence in the samples' broad representativeness. For occupations the only comparisons we can make are for three large groups – farmers, labourers, and all others – as reported in the censuses. The regional samples overrepresent farmers in each year and labourers in 1861 by about 3 per cent. The discrepancies between the samples and the census reports for labourers and all others in 1871 are less than 2 per cent. In this study the more relevant comparisons are between the regional samples and the linked sample. Again the greatest discrepancies are the overrepresentation of farmers in the linked sample, 8 per cent in 1861 and 17 per cent in 1871 with a corresponding underrepresentation of two groups, labourers (3 per cent in 1861 and 2 per cent in 1871) and those not in the labour force (4 and 8 per cent respectively). The other, smaller occupational groups are more closely matched, with the exception of farmer's sons who are slightly overrepresented in the linked sample in 1861 but underrepresented by half in 1871 (6 per cent in the linked sample and 12 per cent in the regional sample in the latter year). The differences between the linked and cross-sectional samples result from a combination of sources, with linkage selection

Table 5.8
Occupational distributions for men aged fifteen and up, Central Ontario in 1861 and 1871, full samples for each year and linked sample across the decade

	Regional Samples		*Linked sample*	
Occupation	*1861 per cent*	*1871 per cent*	*1861 per cent*	*1871 per cent*
Merchants and manufacturers	3.9	4.9	4.2	6.5
Professionals	2.5	3.0	2.1	3.1
Other white collar	1.5	2.2	1.2	1.2
Artisan and skilled	14.1	16.4	13.3	15.5
Semiskilled	2.9	4.1	2.2	3.3
Labourers	18.2	11.2	14.7	9.1
Farmers	27.8	32.6	35.9	50.0
Farmers' sons	8.8	12.1	10.1	5.8
Not in the labour force	20.2	13.6	16.4	5.4
Total	10,981	12,232	4,088	4,088

bias and out-migration from the region the most salient. For 1871, selective regional out-migration is the main source of the differences, since farmers are the most geographically stable group. For 1861, the smaller differences are due to some selection bias, which we have addressed elsewhere.[42]

6

Change amid Continuity in Canadian Work Patterns during the 1870s

LUIZA ANTONIE, PETER BASKERVILLE, KRIS INWOOD, AND J. ANDREW ROSS

INTRODUCTION

The third quarter of the nineteenth century marks a significant turning point in the evolution of the north Atlantic societies. Technological advances, new management structures, and organizational change fuelled a second phase of industrialization that slowly but surely transformed work and everyday life in the United States, Britain, and, increasingly, the rest of Europe.[1] Within Britain the working classes finally began to share in some of the gains of the industrial revolution. Trade expanded enormously as transportation costs fell and the telegraph made long-distance communication routine.[2] Governments responded with industrial policies designed to take advantage of new opportunities and mitigate the more disruptive consequences of market realignment.[3] A steady growth of incomes contributed to fertility decline, greater longevity, and, increasingly, rural-urban and long-distance migration. Within the United States, settlement spread across the continent with lightning speed following the abolition of slavery and cessation of the Civil War.

In Canada as well, the economy appears to have been changing rapidly. Incomes rose, and the population expanded westward and northward. Fertility and mortality declined, emigration increased, and family reproduction strategies adapted to changing circumstance.[4] New national policies responded to powerful economic cycles of boom, bust, and recovery.[5] Farmers successfully reoriented their production as western farm products invaded eastern markets.[6] Entirely new manufacturing industries appeared, and output and productivity increased within established industries in a process of successful industrialization.[7]

And yet, the aggregate evidence of economic and demographic transformation is muted. National income estimates suggest an image of balanced rather than revolutionary growth, with modest structural change.[8] Most puzzling of all is the structure of the labour force, which at first glance appears to have changed very little. Our goal in this paper is to reconcile the conflicting evidence of continuity and change with a particular focus on the labour market. We do this through a reexamination of changes in work patterns during a pivotal decade, the 1870s. By following a large number of individuals from census to census we can identify slow moving but powerful processes of change consistent with the macro vision of structural change and industrialization.

THE 1870S: A PARADOXICAL DECADE

The 1870s was the first full decade for the new Canadian Confederation. Over the decade Canada's population grew 17 per cent, spilling into three new provinces and a territory, to reach 4.3 million in 1881. There has been some uncertainty about how to interpret change in the agriculture sector, the single largest economic area, at this time. Regional and community microstudies have pointed to "a genuine crisis" in 1860s agriculture, especially in Ontario, and with it substantial economic instability and social mobility.[9] In contrast, Drummond argues that there were significant economic changes, that farmers adapted well to new pressures by moving into mixed farming, and that this freed up labour for other sectors such as manufacturing, which in Ontario grew by one-third in the 1870s.[10] Crowley also questions the severity of the rural crisis and explains apparent mobility by the continuous opening up of land in the Canadian and American Wests. In his interpretation, agriculture retained its importance and in Ontario "the movement into farming remained the predominant agricultural occupational trend ... during the third quarter of the nineteenth century."[11] Contemporaries also saw the changes and felt the uncertainty. After midcentury, many observers worried that farming and the mechanic arts were declining in opportunity and status, an anxiety enhanced by the vicissitudes of the business cycle, a tendency for young people to leave their farm families, and, of course, change within individual occupations.[12]

Table 6.1
Distribution of occupations from published tabulations, Canada, 1871 and 1881

	Agricultural	*Industrial*	*Other*	*N*
1871				
Ontario	.49	.20	.31	463,424
Quebec	.47	.19	.34	341,291
New Brunswick	.47	.22	.31	86,488
Nova Scotia	.42	.29	.29	118,645
Total	.475	.211	.314	1,009,848
1881				
Ontario	.48	.21	.31	630,762
Quebec	.47	.19	.34	433,264
New Brunswick	.52	.18	.30	105,459
Nova Scotia	.45	.28	.27	141,695
Total (old Canada)	*.477*	*.207*	*.316*	1,311,180
Prince Edward Island	.60	.19	.21	34,132
British Columbia	.15	.38	.47	18,027
Manitoba	.58	.11	.31	23,261
Northwest Territories	.26	.07	.67	4,004
Total (all Canada)	.477	.207	.316	1,390,604

Source: Census of Canada, 1870–71, Vol. II, table XIII (Occupations of the People), p. 245 and *1880–81,* Vol. IV, table J (Occupations of the People and their Ratios), p. 72

And yet, surprisingly, national indicators show little evidence of structural change. Agriculture's contribution to GDP fell only slightly (35.2 per cent to 34.6 per cent) and the manufacturing share remained steady at 21 per cent during the 1870s.[13] The census reports of occupations present a similar paradox. Nearly half (47.5 per cent) of those reporting an occupation in 1871 were in the agricultural class; one-fifth (21.1 per cent) were in the industrial class. Ten years later the picture is remarkably similar: 47.7 per cent of the reported occupations were agricultural and 20.7 per cent were in industry (table 6.1). Change was limited even within individual provinces, with the exception of New Brunswick (which lost much of its manufacturing sector in the devastating Saint John fire of 1871). Inclusion of the three new provinces and one territory that joined Canada in the 1870s makes little difference to the national total although individually they do show greater variation of economic structure.

This picture of aggregate stability is at odds with the evidence of numerous community and institutional case studies, the severity of the business cycle, and the general sense of political and economic transformation. At a local, or disaggregate, level scholars see evidence of considerable change and transformation, but at the aggregate level we see continuity and very limited change. Admittedly, we are using very broad occupation categories that conceal any shifting within each category. Nevertheless, the overall impression of the national experience suggests limited change.

One way to reconcile divergent impressions is to imagine that recent immigrants took up occupations in a way that exactly offset any transformation among the native-born. In fact, there was relatively little immigration to Canada during the 1870s (and net emigration was still at modest levels).[14] Of course it is still possible that individual subgroups within the population changed in ways that happened to offset each other. In order to consider this option we need more refined evidence. Ideally, we would like information on how individuals changed or did not change jobs during the decade.

We attempt to provide this detail with databases of individual-level information (microdata) from the 1871 and 1881 census enumerations. The easiest way to do this is to compare select subgroups within each census. For example, we can learn about the decadal trajectory of fifteen-year-old Presbyterians in 1871 by comparing them with twenty-five-year-old Presbyterians in 1881.[15] This approach, which is to compare the same kinds of people rather than exactly the same people, has been used very widely by social scientists. And yet, knowing the characteristics of a group and knowing the characteristics of individuals within a group are two different things. In our example, some people may have changed churches, while others may have emigrated and been replaced by Presbyterian immigrants of the same age. These changes remain invisible to the extent that they offset each other, which of course limits the quality of our analysis. In order to bring greater precision we need to examine exactly the same people in both years and to do so for large numbers of people in order to develop generalization. A method for doing this with North American census data was developed in the 1980s, refined in the 1990s, and then implemented on very large databases more recently.[16]

This method, in its most recent incarnation, relies on data mining techniques borrowed from computing science in order to identify pairs of records with exactly the same characteristics in two different bodies of data. The method remains experimental, but, if successful, will generate in a near-automatic way large representative samples of longitudinal data and even multigenerational data for historical populations.

We report in this chapter the first use of this method for Canada and use the data to provide new perspectives on the question of change versus continuity in work patterns during the 1870s.[17]

THE CONSTRUCTION OF LONGITUDINAL DATA FROM HISTORICAL SOURCES

Modern longitudinal data are collected either in repeated social surveys with adjustments for attrition or through synchronic surveys that rely on the recollection of earlier experiences and circumstances. Neither option is available to us. Our approach is to construct longitudinal data with custom-built data-mining software that allows us to track individuals and families through time.[18] We do this by comparing every possible 1871 record with every possible 1881 record and then classifying each comparison as a match or nonmatch. If we think a particular pair of records (one from 1871 and one from 1881) point to the same person, we accept them as a match. The process requires us to compare, literally, millions of records in 1871 with millions of records in 1881 in order to establish which pairs are identical, i.e. that describe the same persons. The comparison is made using four personal attributes that should not change over time (last name, first name, gender, and birthplace) and two others that change in a predictable way (age and marital status). We do *not* use information about occupation, location, and household composition in order to avoid any bias to people who persist in the same area, in the same job, or in the same family.

The process has two computationally demanding steps. The first is to calculate how similar each 1871 record is to each 1881 record on each of the six characteristics. Then the system classifies each possible pair of records as a match or nonmatch based on a score for their overall similarity.[19] The classification software is able to do this because it "learns" from a number of matches already confirmed as reliable on a case-by-case basis by expert genealogists. Without these training data, the software would not know how to classify new pairs of records. The individually prepared matches can also be used to assess the accuracy of the classification system.

We use the high-performance computing grid SHARCNET because of the computational demands of comparing the features (name, age, birthplace, etc.) of so many pairs of records and then classifying each pair as a match or nonmatch based on the patterns of similarity. The process involves many hundreds of millions of calculations. The use of parallel processors on SHARCNET is the key to calculating efficiently; we are able to compare first and last name at a rate of 104 million pairs of records per second. Even at this rate, a single run of the linkage system would be impractical without multiple processors operating in parallel, blocking to reduce the complexity of the system, and code efficiently written in C.[20]

The classification system connects pairs of records drawn from a systematic sample of 205,000 records from the 1871 census (www.census1871.ca) and a database of 4.3 million records from the 1881 created by The Church of Jesus Christ of Latter-day Saints and now housed at the Université de Montréal (www.genealogie.umontreal.ca/en/). Of course, many 1871 records cannot be matched because the individual died before 1881, left the country, or reported information differently in the two years. The most common reason for failing to identify a match is *not* an inability to find someone with the same characteristics ten years later. Rather, the biggest problem is that too many 1881 records have more or less the same characteristics as an 1871 record and so produce multiple links. In such cases we cannot identify which of the multiple links is correct.

Overall, we are able to link, uniquely, ~16 per cent of the 1871 records to an 1881 record. This allows us to observe 32,699 people at two points in their lives, ten years apart. Twenty-eight per cent of these people reported an occupation in both years and therefore are of interest for the analysis of occupational change. We summarize in table 6.2 the linked microdata with occupations in both years and the summary reported above in table 6.1, which was originally published by the nineteenth-century Census Bureau. The two tabulations are not directly comparable because we examine only a subset of the 1871 and 1881 populations and because our definition of the three broad classes differs from that of the Bureau.[21] Thus, it is not possible to interpret or ascribe meaning to differences between the relative size of occupational classes in published tables and in our summary of the microdata. Nevertheless, we observe that both sources describe the same broad pattern of *no change* in the broad distribution of occupations. In this respect the microdata replicate the feature of published tables that we wish to investigate: the impression that the Canadian labour market did not change over the decade of the 1870s.

Table 6.2
Distribution of occupations from published tabulations and from linked microdata, old Canada, 1871 and 1881

	Agricultural	*Industrial*	*Other*
Published tabulations			
1871	.50	.14	.37
1881	.50	.14	.36
Linked microdata			
1871	.48	.21	.32
1881	.48	.21	.32

Source: Table 1 and the People in Motion record linking system http://www.people-in-motion.ca as described in the text and in Antonie et al.

CHARACTERISTICS OF LINKED RECORDS

We assess the quality of our microdata links, first, by examining how well the automated system linked people who have been identified as correct by expert genealogists. It turns out that one-eighth of the expert-evaluated links returned by the system were incorrect.[22] Such mistakes occur most commonly because the correct person in 1881 reported characteristics with some imprecision. This does not mislead the genealogical expert, but the automated process was unable to select the right person and instead identified someone else who happened to have characteristics closer to the anticipated configuration.

This kind of error is inevitable because of the widespread repetition of names, even among people with the same age, birthplace, and marital status. Multiple people who share a common set of characteristics are challenging for several reasons. First, if a number of people have roughly similar characteristics (i.e. similar name, age, and birthplace), the system cannot distinguish among them, since a link cannot be accepted unless it is unique. Second, if the correct person reports age or name imprecisely, or if a woman changes her name because of marriage, an incorrect person with similar characteristics might be selected in place of the correct one. In the first case no link is identified; in the second, an incorrect link is made. A related problem arises if the correct person dies or emigrates before the next census and, therefore,

Table 6.3
Age distribution of 1871 population and linked women and men

	Women		*Men*	
Age in 1871	*Population*	*Linked records*	*Population*	*Linked records*
0 to 14	.38	.42	.39	.40
15 to 25	.24	.16	.22	.19
26 to 55	.31	.36	.30	.34
56 and over	.08	.07	.09	.07
All ages	1.0	1.0	1.0	1.0
Number of records	99,060	14,594	99,582	18,105

Source: The population proportions are estimated from Canada, census, 1871, 5 per cent microdata sample constructed at the University of Guelph http://census1871.ca (ignoring records for which age is missing). The linked records are generated by the People in Motion record linking system http://www.people-in-motion.ca as described in the text and in Antonie et al.

is not present in 1881. In this case we are at risk of mistakenly selecting someone else with a similar combination of characteristics.

Problems of this nature are more severe to the extent that some names are common especially if people report their characteristics imprecisely.[23] Unfortunately, North American census data are notoriously imprecise. Many people did not remember their age correctly, and the spelling of names varied a great deal. Currently we are refining the classification system with various strategies to address this problem and reduce the incidence of false links. For the moment, though, we proceed on the assumption that, although some proportion of the links are incorrect, there are enough correct links to permit generalizations at the level of the entire population.

Another way to assess our linked or matched data is to consider if they were broadly representative of the broader population. From the outset, we can anticipate reasons why the ~16 per cent of people who are linked may be slightly atypical. We are more likely to link people with less common names and people who report their personal details with greater precision and consistency because there will be less duplication of characteristics. In order to assess the strength of these and other biases in tables 6.3 and 6.4 we compare the age and ethnicity of the linked records with the entire population in 1871.

In table 6.3 we see one difference between linked records and base population in 1871: we link a much lower proportion of adolescents

Table 6.4
Distribution by nativity and ethnicity in the 1871 population and in linked records

	Population	*Linked records*
BIRTHPLACE		
Foreign-born	.19	.19
England	.04	.06
Scotland	.04	.04
Ireland	.06	.06
Germany	.01	.01
US	.02	.02
Canadian-born	.81	.81
Ontario	.33	.33
Quebec	.29	.28
ORIGIN OR ETHNICITY		
French	.32	.25
English and Welsh	.20	.27
Irish	.25	.24
Scottish	.14	.13
Continental European	.06	.09
North American	.01	.003
African	.01	.004
Other	.01	.01
All ethnicities	1.00	1.00

Source: Canada, census, 1871, 5 per cent microdata sample constructed at the University of Guelph http://census1871.ca and the People in Motion record linking system http://www.people-in-motion.ca as described in the text and in Antonie et al.

and young adults (fifteen to twenty-five years) than other groups. Young people are harder to link because they were of an age to move away from the family home, to start a new life, and to some extent reinvent themselves by reporting different characteristics. We are unable to link their records if characteristics are reported differently in 1881. A propensity for women to change their surname as they marry, of course, is an extreme example that leaves us with a noticeably smaller number of linked records for women (bottom line of table 6.3). The record linking process is most successful for young children and the middle-aged, presumably because their information was reported more consistently from 1871 to 1881. Of course, people over the age of fifty-five in 1871 are more difficult to identify in 1881 because they were less likely to be alive in the latter year.

Interestingly, there is no bias to a more effective linking of the native-born than of immigrants (table 6.4). The foreign-born share of linked records is exactly the same as the foreign-born share of the population in 1871. This implies the linkage rate for immigrants is comparable to that of Canadian-born.

There is some variance, however, with different ethnicities. Here we use the census category of "origin" as a measure of ethnicity. The information in table 6.4 indicates that fewer French-origin people are linked while the English-origin are linked more successfully, both by a considerable margin. One possible explanation, since the two groups had different dominant languages, is that the quality of enumeration was influenced by the choice of language. Lower-quality enumeration might imply less precise or less consistent information that, in turn, would be more difficult to link. There is no reason, however, to think the census was undertaken less carefully in Francophone districts. Quebec intellectuals headed the Census Bureau in 1871, and most enumerators in French-speaking areas were themselves Francophone. A more likely influence is that the relatively small pool of French names makes it harder to isolate a unique match. The lower level of literacy in Quebec may also have had an effect because of reduced precision with which characteristics are reported. Moreover, emigration during the 1870s was greater from heavily Francophone districts; anyone who left Canada would not be found in the 1881 census. Unfortunately there is no easy way to disentangle the relative importance of these effects. Each of them is potentially significant.

Overall, it seems that the linked records are roughly representative of the 1871 population, with two important exceptions. The linked records contain a smaller proportion of young people and of the French-descended population. A third difference, the lower proportion of women in linked records, largely reflects a gender difference in the difficulty of linking young people. We view name changing at marriage as part of a broader tendency for adolescents and young adults to modify their identity as they leave home.

THE PATTERNS OF OCCUPATIONAL CHANGE

We are unable to use all linked records for the analysis of occupational change because not everyone reported an occupation in both years. The

Table 6.5
Share of linked records with occupation, by age and sex

	Men		*Women*	
1871 Age cohort	*1871*	*1881*	*1871*	*1881*
0 to 14	.02	.47	.01	.09
15 to 25	.77	.92	.12	.12
26 to 55	.96	.94	.07	.07
56 and over	.91	.75	.08	.05

summary in table 6.5 shows very different patterns for men and women. Most men aged fifteen to fifty-five years in 1871 reported an occupation in both years. The youngest males did not have an occupation in 1871 although many moved into an occupation during the following decade. By 1881 some older men ceased to work. In this paper we examine only those who reported an occupation in both years. We are interested in occupational changes and not the choice of occupation for those entering the labour market for the first time or the age at which people retire in different occupations.[24] Consequently, we lose a few of the records for linked males and a large majority of the linked records for females.

Occupational reporting by women reflects both the extent to which women worked outside the home and a well-known gender bias in occupational reporting.[25] Many women, even if they worked outside the home, did not report an occupation. The bias was most extreme for married women. Those women who did report an occupation in both years, and are linked from 1871 to 1881, are summarized in table 6.5. We organize the occupations into six broad categories: farming, manufacturing (all industrial occupations), commerce (merchants, retail, and wholesale), labour and construction (labour and trades), and other services (professionals and miscellaneous).[26]

Most women reporting an occupation in 1871 identified themselves in a service job of some kind (largely servants, members of religious orders, and teachers), and they remained in the service sector ten years later. For example, in 1871 Margaret Boutilier was working as a servant in the household of William Gammell, a retired merchant in Sydney Mines, Nova Scotia. Ten years later she had moved out to the local farm of Peter Jackson in Ball's Creek, again being employed as a servant. A relatively smaller number of women clustered in manufacturing, (primarily dressmaking and sewing, but also food preparation and other

Table 6.6
Occupational transitions 1871–81 of linked women with occupations, by age

		Occupation in 1881				
	N	*Farming*	*Industry*	*Commerce*	*Labour and Construction*	*Other Services*
Occupation in 1871						
Farmer	8	6	1	0	0	1
Manufacturer	40	3	27	3	2	5
Merchant	5	0	1	3	0	1
Labour/Construction	5	0	0	0	2	2
Other Service	147	8	8	1	6	124
Total	211	17	38	7	10	139

industries).[27] One married woman, Catherine Brennan of Tyendinaga Township, in Hastings Country, Ontario, was listed as a cheesemaker in 1871 and also in 1881, by which time she was widowed and supporting her seven children. However, she was an exception insofar as the information in table 6.6 mainly describes the subset of women who did *not* marry since most women who married would have ceased to report an occupation and therefore drop out of our analysis. It might be tempting to look for additional patterns, but the number of records is not large enough to permit further meaningful observations. An analysis of occupational change for women must wait for improvements to our linking methodology that would increase sample size (and even then our analysis will be complicated by biased enumeration).

We are able to say more about men since a much higher proportion reported occupations.[28] In table 6.7 we report men by province of residence in 1871. The provincial comparison points to distinctive and offsetting regional patterns of change. Ontario saw a net movement of men out of farming and into commerce. Quebec men also moved into commerce and, importantly, into manufacturing. New Brunswick and Nova Scotia, in contrast, saw a sizeable net movement *into* farming. Divergent regional trends in occupations are consistent with the long-run pattern of structural change in which the Atlantic region, apart from its small coal belt, conspicuously failed to industrialize.[29]

We organize the same data in table 6.8 to highlight differences by birth cohort rather than province. We distinguish younger from older men using their age in 1871; the two cohorts were born 1816–45 and

Table 6.7
Occupational sectors of linked men in 1881 by province of residence in 1871, with change from 1871

	N	*Farming*	*Industry*	*Commerce*	*Labour and Construction*	*Other Services*
Ontario	4,415	.56	.13	.06	.16	.09
Change from 1871		*-1.3%*	*0.0%*	*2.0%*	*-0.6%*	*-0.1%*
Quebec	2,786	.49	.13	.06	.19	.14
		1.4%	*1.1%*	*1.4%*	*0.6%*	*-4.5%*
New Brunswick	865	.60	.12	.02	.15	.11
		5.7%	*-0.7%*	*0.0%*	*-3.4%*	*-1.5%*
Nova Scotia	1,175	.46	.16	.03	.12	.24
		3.3%	*-1.6%*	*0.6%*	*-1.7%*	*-0.6%*

1846–55. A desire to maintain a sufficient number of observations in cells throughout the table recommends that we drop the provincial distinctions. At the level of the entire country, the younger group, adolescents and young adults, had a net movement into commerce and manufacturing and out of farming and other sectors (comparing the shaded bands in the table). The reverse is true for middle-aged and older men: there was a net movement into farming. There was *no* net movement of older men into commerce or manufacturing.

Admittedly, the interior diagonal of the table for each age group (in bold face) indicates substantial occupational persistence. Most men, even the younger ones, stayed in their occupational classes. Labour and construction occupations showed a strong preference for turning to farming, a reflection of the large component of farm labourers in this group. Farming itself shows the highest degree of persistence, although age was a significant factor: 86 per cent of farmers aged twenty-six to fifty-five who farmed in 1871 continued to do so in 1881, compared to 74 per cent of those aged fifteen to twenty-five. Figure 6.1, which includes both age groups, shows the relative size of the transitions in proportion, as well as the continued dominance of farming.

The younger men switched out of farming at double the rate of the older generation: either into manufacturing (7 per cent of young men compared to 3 per cent of older men), commerce (3 per cent compared to 2 per cent), or labour/construction (12 per cent to 6 per cent). Among the labour/construction occupations, which often served as transitional jobs for younger men, we see that the younger

Table 6.8
Occupational transitions 1871–81 of linked men with occupations, by age, Canada

		Distribution of occupations in 1881, by 1871 occupation					
		Farming	*Industry*	*Commerce*	*Labour and Construction*	*Other Services*	
Age 15 to 25 years in 1871 (n=2,499)							
	Share in 1871						
Share in 1881		.46	.16	.06	.18	.14	
Farming	.47	**.74**	.07	.03	.12	.05	1.00
Industry	.14	.15	**.57**	.05	.12	.11	1.00
Commerce	.02	.09	.14	**.54**	.12	.12	1.00
Labour/Const.	.20	.31	.15	.04	**.40**	.10	1.00
Other Service	.17	.17	.10	.12	.15	**.46**	1.00
Age 26 to 55 years in 1871 (n=5,690)							
	Share in 1871						
Share in 1881		.54	.13	.05	.16	.13	
Farming	*.52*	**.86**	.03	.02	.06	.03	1.00
Industry	*.13*	.18	**.61**	.05	.09	.07	1.00
Commerce	*.05*	.15	.11	**.50**	.09	.02	1.00
Labour/Const.	*.16*	.24	.09	.03	**.56**	.08	1.00
Other Service	*.14*	.16	.06	.06	.12	**.60**	1.00

cohort was more likely than the older to enter manufacturing (15 per cent to 9 per cent). Nonetheless, persistence of almost three-quarters of young men in farming attests to its pull, as does the significant numbers of young men entering farming from other sectors over the decade. The most important feature of table 6.8 is the shift towards commerce and industrial work and away from agricultural work for younger men. Yet the change should not be exaggerated. Farming declined from 47 per cent to 46 per cent for young men, and it increased from 52 per cent to 54 per cent for older men.

In Ontario, at least, it has been argued that farming was largely the preserve of the Canadian-born.[30] Our data in table 6.9 confirms this pattern for the country as a whole. In both cohorts more than half the Canadian-born are farmers; the foreign-born were more likely to be involved in industrial or labour/construction pursuits. Yet we do see an uptick in the number of younger and older foreign-born men entering

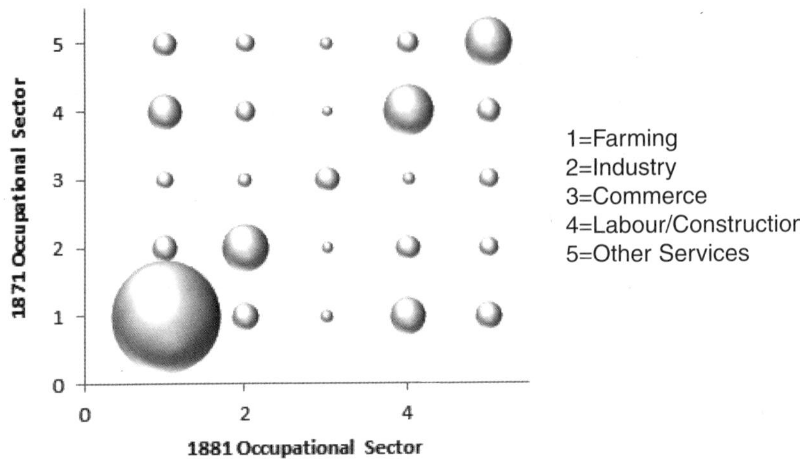

Figure 6.1 Occupational transitions of linked men (aged fifteen to fifty-five) from 1871 to 1881

the agricultural sector across the decade, suggesting farming still had an attraction for foreigners.

Information on ethnic origin sharpens the picture. In table 6.10 we show the proportions by ethnicity in each occupational sector in 1881 and the change from 1871 (in italics). While there is stability across the sectors, there is also some intriguing variation. Fewer than half of the younger men in each group were likely to choose farming, except for those of European heritage (mostly German descendants, many of them born in Canada), who showed a marked preference for farming in both cohorts. Over the decade, all groups of young men except those of Irish ethnicity shifted out of farming, labour/construction, and other services and moved increasingly to commercial and industrial pursuits. Those of Scottish origin led the way in these trends (especially the shift to industry). The occupational shifts are even subtler among older men; farming retained its allure especially for continental Europeans.

There was also a marked generational divergence within the French and Irish origin groups. In 1881, 8.9 per cent of the older French cohort but 14.6 per cent of the younger men were involved in manufacturing. The gap was similar for Irish descendants: 10.5 per cent and 16.5 per cent. The younger French also had the highest proportion of commercial workers. These transitions highlight the role of young

Table 6.9
Occupations of linked men in 1881 by birthplace and age, with change from 1871 to 1881

		Farming	*Industry*	*Commerce*	*Labour and Construction*	*Other Services*
15 to 25 years	Canadian-born	47.9% *-2.3%*	15.3% *-2.0%*	5.5% *-3.7%*	17.9% *–1.4%*	13.3% *–2.2%*
	Foreign-born	36.1% *-5.7%*	21.3% *-0.8%*	6.2% *-4.6%*	20.0% *–4.4%*	16.4% *–6.7%*
26 to 55 years	Canadian-born	58.0% *-1.1%*	10.7% *–0.3%*	4.2% *-0.1%*	14.0% *–0.6%*	13.0% *–0.4%*
	Foreign-born	45.6% *-2.1%*	16.4% *–1.1%*	6.9% *-1.4%*	18.7% *-0.2%*	12.4% *–2.6%*

French-origin and Irish-origin men in powering industrial growth, both in Quebec and in Ontario.[31]

The existing literature on the Irish and their descendants in Canada points to the importance of church or denomination; Darroch and Ornstein, and Akenson report that Roman Catholics of Irish descent were significantly less likely to be farmers than the Protestants.[32] We replicate this pattern in table 6.11. Irish-origin Protestants were more likely to farm, although there was a movement of older Roman Catholics of Irish descent into farming over the decade. Protestants were more active in industry at a younger age (though losing some ground over the decade), and yet the reverse was true in the older cohort, where Roman Catholics had a greater proportion in industry. Our longitudinal profile is broadly consistent with Akenson's suggestion that denominational differences among the Irish and their descendants arise in part from the timing of immigration; the Irish Protestant advantage of early arrival in Canada diminished as Roman Catholics were catching up during the 1870s.[33]

DISCUSSION AND CONCLUSION

The large-scale linking of census data allows us to follow a large number of Canadians from 1871 to 1881 and to generate a number of insights that would not otherwise be available. Unfortunately the num-

Table 6.10
Occupational sectors of linked men in 1881 by ethnic origin and age cohort, with change from 1871 to 1881

	Origin	*N*	*Farming*	*Industry*	*Commerce*	*Labour/ Construction*	*Other Service*
Age 15 to 25 years	French	671	44.4	14.6	6.9	22.4	11.8
			–1.7%	*1.6%*	*4.7%*	*2.1%*	*–6.7%*
	English/Welsh	675	45.5	18.7	4.6	16.3	15
			–0.6%	*2.7%*	*3.3%*	*–2.5%*	*–2.8%*
	Irish	583	45.3	16.5	5	18	15.3
			1.6%	*–0.1%*	*3.5%*	*–4.8%*	*0.0%*
	Scottish	320	44.4	18.1	6.6	16.9	14.1
			–3.4%	*5.0%*	*4.4%*	*–3.4%*	*–2.5%*
	Continental European (excluding French)	226	56.2	11.5	5.3	15.5	11.5
			–4.4%	*0.4%*	*4.0%*	*0.0%*	*0.0%*
Age 26 to 55 years	French	1,353	52.8	8.9	4.4	19.2	14.8
			0.7%	*–0.4%*	*0.4%*	*0.2%*	*–0.8%*
	English/Welsh	1,680	48	16.1	5.6	15.5	14.7
			0.4%	*–0.3%*	*0.6%*	*0.5%*	*–1.3%*
	Irish	1,311	56.6	10.5	5	17.3	10.6
			4.0%	*–1.3%*	*0.6%*	*–0.5%*	*–2.7%*
	Scottish	790	56.8	15.2	7.3	9.9	10.8
			1.9%	*–0.6%*	*1.1%*	*–2.1%*	*–0.2%*
	Continental European (excluding French)	494	65.8	11.9	1.8	10.1	10.3
			–0.4%	*–0.2%*	*–0.2%*	*–0.8%*	*1.6%*

Table 6.11

Occupational sectors of linked Irish-origin men in 1881 by birthplace and age cohort, with change from 1871

	Religion	*N*	*Farming*	*Industry*	*Commerce*	*Labour/ Construction*	*Other Service*
Age 15 to 25 years	Roman Catholic	227	38.8%	13.7%	3.5%	24.7%	19.4%
			0.9%	*–2.2%*	*2.2%*	*–3.1%*	*2.2%*
	Protestant	352	49.4%	18.5%	5.7%	13.9%	12.5%
			1.7%	*1.2%*	*4.0%*	*–5.4%*	*–1.4%*
Age 26 to 55 years	Roman Catholic	437	43.5%	12.6%	5.3%	24.7%	14.0%
			5.5%	*–0.2%*	*1.4%*	*–0.2%*	*–6.4%*
	Protestant	855	62.9%	9.4%	5.0%	13.6%	9.1%
			3.1%	*–2.1%*	*0.3%*	*–0.7%*	*–0.7%*

ber of women with occupations is not yet sufficient for meaningful analysis (table 6.5). For men, though, we see clearly that the impression of a stasis in occupational choice and patterns of work, suggested by table 6.1 and table 6.2, is incorrect. Patterns of work did change, and the changes are broadly consistent with previous literatures.

To a very large extent young people were the agents of change, but even older men contributed to the structural transformation of the economy. Adolescents and young adults were more likely to change occupation than older workers; the younger men increasingly entered the growing manufacturing, merchant, and service sectors. And yet there was considerable continuity insofar as a significant proportion of people moved into farming during the 1870s, and relatively few left. Farming remained the preferred alternative choice for all occupation groups (suggesting it was a default occupation), although individual trajectories provide evidence of a decline in appeal for the young. And when the linked data are viewed in combination with cohort data in 1881 for the youngest and oldest males, we can anticipate the longer-term shift out of agricultural occupations that took place over ensuing decades.

Our findings are consistent with the experience of the 1860s as interpreted by Darroch and Ornstein.[34] There were no radical breaks in the relative importance of agricultural employment during the 1860s or in the 1870s. While agriculture remained attractive, our linked individuals moved in and out of the sector more frequently in the 1870s. Darroch and Ornstein found ~90 per cent of farmers remained in the occupation from 1861 to 1871. In contrast, we find that only 86 per cent of the older farmers and a still smaller proportion (74 per cent) of the young farmers remained in the sector.[35] Significant numbers of young workers entered industry and commerce, which together expanded during the 1870s from 16 per cent to 22 per cent of all young workers (table 6.7). Some differences by province and ethnic origin are visible. There was a net movement into farming by workers in Nova Scotia and New Brunswick and a net movement out of farming by workers in Ontario (table 6.6). Men of central European origin (largely German ethnicity) continued to cluster in farming, while the Irish and their descendants (especially Roman Catholic Irish) stand out for a net movement into farming. Those of Scottish origin and, to a lesser extent, the English shifted into manufacturing and commerce (table 6.10 and table 6.11). Immigrants in general were more likely to enter farming (table 6.9).

An identification of broad patterns does not deny the diversity of individual trajectories. We have examined the experience of a small set of men who were eighteen years old in 1871. Some of them followed the pattern of Daniel Lank of Colchester County, Nova Scotia, who was a labourer in 1871 but ten years later was farming in his own right. Samuel Hiltz, a young farmer of German origin from Lunenburg, was able to stay on the family farm a decade later, but many others moved from farming to other occupational classes, particularly manufacturing: Nathaniel Haverstock moved into cooperage, Peter Frayne into harness-making, and Paul Belisle into shoemaking. In Ontario, Thomas Ripley and Swan Dean turned from farming to cheesemaking, and James Woodland became a butcher; all three left farming although they still contributed to the reorientation of Ontario agriculture towards mixed farming and animal products.[36]

In this paper we have not sought to analyze the patterns of residential continuity and change, even though relocation or migration was important for many individuals. For example, Jean Baptiste Robert was enumerated in 1871 as a farmer in Maskinongé, Quebec, on the north shore of the St Lawrence, but by 1881 he had moved one hundred kilometres upstream to work as a clerk in Montreal. Eighteen-year-old Julius Galbraith was enumerated as a printer in Orangeville, Ontario in 1871; ten years later he was a publisher in a small town on the Manitoba frontier and was married with two small children. Another small-town printer, Elias Saunders from Goderich, Ontario, also stayed in the trade; he moved to the nearby, regional centre of London. His upward mobility appears to have been less rapid: on enumeration day in 1881 he was still living in a rooming house. Additional examples add to the diversity. Joseph Allan of Portland, New Brunswick went from being a clerk to an umbrella mender and moved into Saint John proper. George Scarlett in 1871 was an eighteen-year-old teacher in Cramahe Township, but ten years later was a travelling salesman in nearby Cobourg.

These individual trajectories are part of the broader collective experience revealed by the linked data. In this paper we report on the construction of longitudinal data and use them to refine our understanding of economic and demographic change in Canada during the 1870s. The dominant impression created by the new source is one of change amid continuity. There was considerable occupational persistence and, yet, some weakening in the case of agriculture and a tendency for younger men to switch into manufacturing and commerce. Admittedly, change was slow and gradual and for that reason difficult to see in the aggregate published tabulations which until recently comprised our only evidence. The longitudinal microdata, however, document complex patterns of subtle change that cumulatively, over several decades, would transform Canada profoundly. The new evidence reveals that, initial impressions notwithstanding, Canada participated in the same processes of industrialization and structural change that swept through the north Atlantic societies in the second half of the nineteenth century.[37]

7

Wilson Benson Revisited: Movement and Persistence in Rural Perth County, Ontario, 1871–81[1]

PETER BASKERVILLE

Born in Belfast in 1821, Wilson Benson and his fourteen-year-old wife, Jemima, arrived in Upper Canada in 1841. Over the next eight years he worked at more than twenty different occupations and moved more than a dozen times. Historians often portray Benson as a representative figure for his time and class. Nineteenth-century North America is characterized as an era of extraordinary movement. "Upper Canadians, like most nineteenth-century populations, were people on the move," David Gagan asserted more than three decades ago.[2] While not disagreeing with this general characterization, this paper offers a cautionary perspective and stands apart from many mobility studies by focussing on a later time period and linking individuals and families over a much wider geographical span.

The paper emerges from the confluence of two separate projects: the People in Motion project, which is constructing a computerized linkage program for historical census data and the Perth County Project, a study of credit and community in an Ontario County between 1860 and 1921. The first project is linking nominal-level census data from the 1871 Canadian census to the 1881 Canadian census and the 1880 US census. The second is constructing and utilizing linked files from the 1871 through 1911 Canadian censuses (and other files) with special focus on Perth County. The whole of Logan Township (population 3,196) in Perth County in 1871 has been entered into a machine-readable file, and that population has been linked to an unusually large catchment area: the whole of Canada in 1881 and the United States in 1880. The

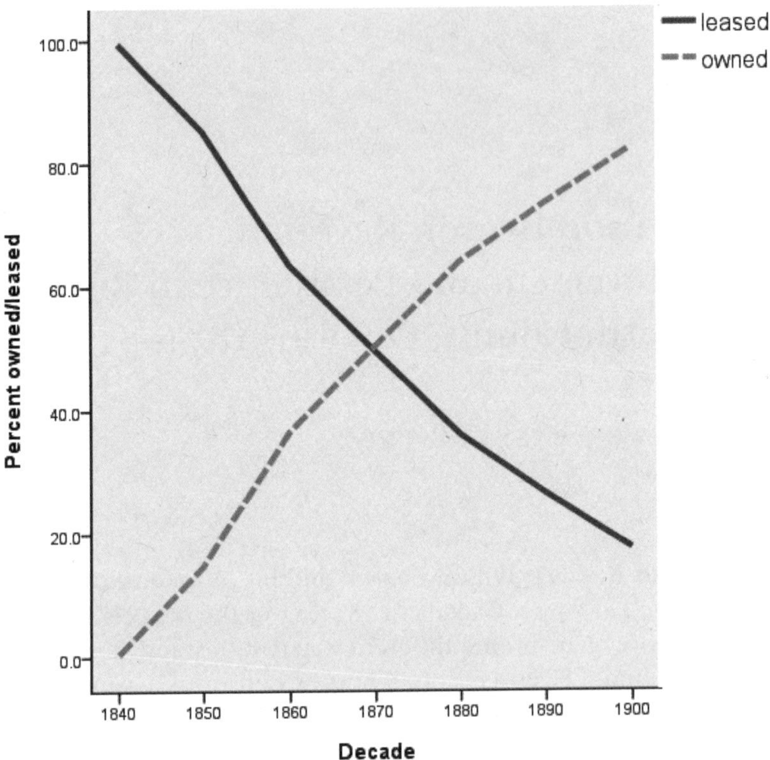

Figure 7.1 Tenancy rates: Logan Township, Perth County, 1840–1911

linkage was done by hand in accordance with rigorous rules to provide a set of true links both for use in training and testing the computer-generated linkage program for People in Motion (see Antonie et al., this book) and to further the general ends of the Perth County Project. The analysis focuses on a subset of Logan's 1871 population, all household heads, and seeks to establish the factors affecting the probability of Loganites persisting in the township or moving elsewhere in the decade of the 1870s.

Measuring persistence and movement in small areas is a venerable historical pursuit. The literature is characterized by three broad approaches. Several studies have used census data that contain information on where people had lived at some point in the past to examine mobility patterns. While significant, these studies were also extraordinary in that extremely few nineteenth-century censuses provide retrospective information.[3] The second and standard early attempt at such measurement assumed that if a person could not be found in the study

Table 7.1
Birthplace and origin: household heads, Logan Township, 1871

Place	*Birthplace*	*Origin*
Ontario	12.5	–
Elsewhere Canada	4.9	–
England/English	15.5	19.2
Scotland/Scottish	6.0	8.1
Ireland/Irish	29.6	36.7
Germany/German	28.6	32.4
Total Number	521	521

community at a designated point in the future then that person was classified as a mover.[4] A few studies controlled for death rates. But all of these studies were limited to the area they studied; thus little was known about where movers went and what movers did after leaving and, indeed, whether those they could not find actually moved. More recently longitudinal historical studies are employing sophisticated computer-assisted methods and broadening their geographical and chronological scope, tracing people within and between whole nations.[5] In a sense this study of Logan falls between the second and third approaches noted above. It is local in terms of the study group but international in terms of the linkage scope.

Can Logan Township be seen as representative of anything other than itself? Given the present state of historical knowledge, any declarative answer to this question would be quite presumptuous. I can, however, suggest some of the reasons why I chose to study this township. In the context of Ontario, Perth County was one of the last agricultural regions to be settled, largely because it did not abut any of the Great Lakes. Yet it was a relatively rich agricultural area. Wheat, barley, oats, and peas were the main field crops, and the sale of horses, cows, and pigs to the United States, Manitoba, and England provided good returns.[6] Importantly Logan also offered the opportunity to study a relatively large group of tenants and to compare their geographical and social mobility with that of owners over time. In this respect the township had one of the highest rates of tenancy anywhere in Ontario in 1871 (48.5 per cent of household heads in Logan were tenants in 1871 compared to a provincial average of 15.3 per cent)[7] (figure 7.1). Finally, Logan Township had a potentially interesting ethnic mix, which allows for an exploration of the effect of origin/ethnicity on geographical mobility (table 7.1).

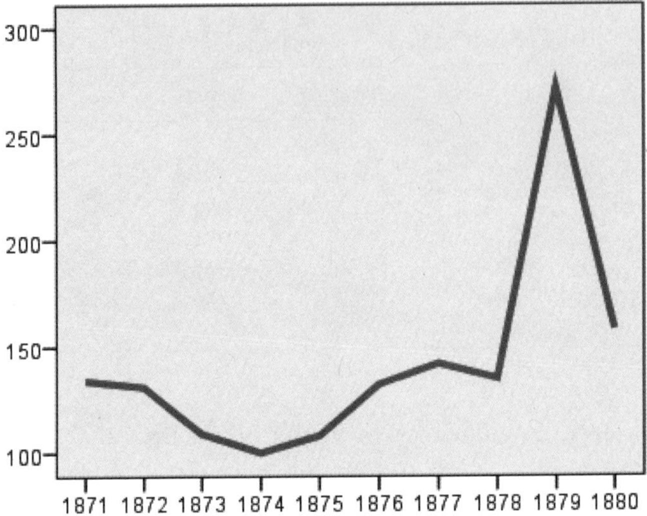

Figure 7.2 Number of chattel mortgages, Perth County, 1871–80

For North America in general, a downward spiralling business cycle, increased bankruptcies, and declining prices for goods characterized the decade of the 1870s. Perth County and Logan Township residents did not escape these unsettling forces. The annual reports of the Canada Company, a major landowner in the county, testify to the economic and financial pressures that beset the community.[8] Back to back poor harvests in 1869 and 1870 set the tone for the decade. Land sales and leases declined in 1872, 1873, and 1874. Low prices for produce in 1875 caused farmers to keep "their wheat from the market." In 1876 the company informed its shareholders that a "severe commercial depression" accounted for the falling off of profits. Depression and stagnation continued in 1877, 1878, and 1879. George Allan, the Company's local commissioner wrote in May 1879 that "true land sales" were few and "receipts very small." He referred to the last two years as a time of "great depression." Local papers corroborated the Canada Company's reports. Farmers must adapt to "continued and prospective dullness," the Stratford *Beacon* warned in July 1878. "Many of the farmers," the writer continued, "were hoping against hope that the prices would rally again but we presume from present appearances that the more intelligent of them have concluded to accept the inevitable and not be so foolish again."[9]

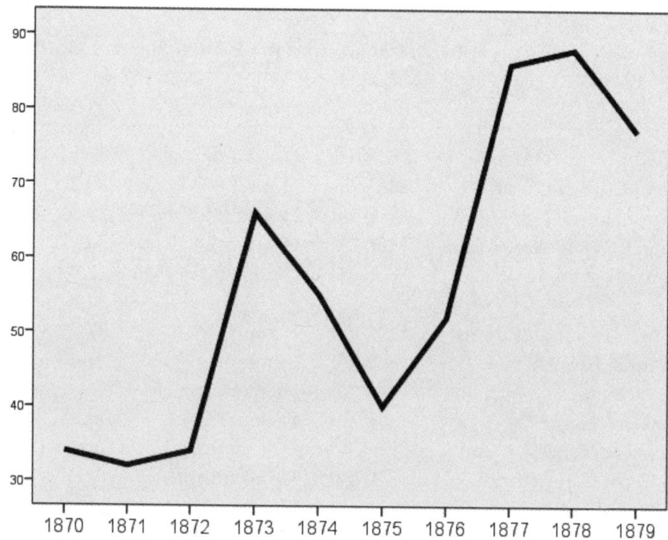

Figure 7.3 Number of mortgages, Logan Township, 1870–79

Two financial indicators point to increased indebtedness for many in Perth over the course of the decade. As figure 7.2 shows,[10] chattel mortgages, which one commentator believed "shows the poverty of the people of any country," reached a high for the decade in 1879.[11] Figure 7.3 shows that the number of mortgages on land for Logan increased significantly, peaking in 1878.

Yet not all was doom and gloom. Perth's population increased by nearly 18 per cent over the decade, although Logan's only increased by five. Even the Canada Company admitted that prices for land remained stable and that in June 1878 demand for land was also strong. While wages paid to mechanics and labourers in cities were down, farmers, Allan felt, were better able to prosper, "having a comfortable subsistence." Finally, in Allan's view, while the depression was bad, it was never on the scale of the troubled times in the late 1850s.[12]

There were 555 household heads in Logan in 1871 and we know that thirty-four of them died before the 1880s leaving 521 for analysis. Four hundred and fifteen heads were successfully linked to either the Canadian 1881 census or the US 1880 census, a linkage rate of less than 80 per cent. It is important to emphasize here that our linkage process does not require that we conflate persistency with successful linkages as is the case for most historical longitudinal studies focusing on small

Table 7.2
Some community studies of mobility: Canada and the United States, 1850–80

Number	*Community*	*Dates*	*Unit of analysis*	*Persistence rate (%)*
1a	Peel County Ontario	1852–61	Household head	37.5
1b	Peel County Ontario	1861–71	Household head	30.2
2a	Appanoose County Iowa	1850–60	Household head	28.6
2b	Appanoose County Iowa	1860–70	Household head	34.4
3	Wapello County Iowa	1850–60	Gainfully employed men	30.6
4	Bureau County Illinois	1850–60	Farmers	37.7
5	4 Iowa Townships	1860–70	Farmers	37–56
6a	Eastern Kansas	1860–70	Farmers	26
6b	Eastern Kansas	1870–80	Farmers	44
6c	Kansas, Nebraska, and Dakota Territory	1870–80	Household head	36
7	63 community studies	Various decades	Various units	Mean rate = 38 Span:14–74

areas. Because of the broader catchment area, our linkage rate is higher than that reported in most studies, and more importantly we can distinguish between persisters and movers with greater clarity and confidence. Thus, of the 415 linked heads 72 per cent (299) stayed in Logan and 28 per cent (116) moved.

At first glance these figures seem to indicate a relatively stable community; relative, that is, to the persistence rates generated by many other studies of mobility on the North American farming frontier. While these studies report a variety of persistence rates, some in the 50 per cent range, most, as table 7.2 indicates, reported far lower persistence. However, most of these studies have focussed on earlier decades, assumed that those who could not be found moved, ignored mortality rates, and focussed on small catchment areas. Table 7.2 provides a summary of many of the studies.[13]

It is difficult to compare the rates found for Logan with the studies listed in table 7.2 given the variety of methods employed, places selected, and decades covered. As Parkerson noted three decades ago "(T)he validity of ... hypotheses concerning persistence depends on the methodology of record linkage."[14] The method employed for the linkage in this paper privileges the systematic creation of relatively unbiased links on the basis of a few presumed constant characteristics. Whenever more than one possible link exhibited similar characteristics

Table 7.3
Logistic regression with linked/not linked as the dependent variable: all household heads, Logan Township, 1871

Variables	*Log odds of being linked*
Precedent years	*
0	0.26*
1–5	0.59
6–10	1.4
11–15	1.1
Reference category: 16+	
Farmer/not	**
Reference category:	0.48**
Farmer	
Age	**
20–29	3.1**
30–39	3.9*
40–49	1.5
50–59	2.5
Reference category: 60+	
Ratio dependants to Earners	1.03*
Owner/tenant	ns
Literate/not	ns
Gender	ns
Ethnicity	ns
Marital Status	ns

* sig is <.02

** sig is between .02 and .05

no * sig is >.05

ns: not significant, removed from the equation by the backward stepwise likelihood ratio procedure

that case was thrown out.[15] Moreover the catchment area is North America, not simply the township or county of initial residence. One result of this procedure is accurate links. A second result is a lower rate of movement than is reported in many other studies. Parkerson long ago warned that the linkage methods employed in earlier studies dramatically under estimated persistence rates, perhaps by as much as 20 to 30 per cent. Indeed, when the persistence rates found for Logan are compared to the few studies using methods like those employed in this paper, the persistence rates are remarkably similar.[16] Given that the linkage method employed here avoids many of the past problems with false links, mortality rates, and small catchment areas, the persistence level of 72 per cent for Logan is quite plausible.[17]

It is worth examining in more detail just how one's method can lead to varying persistence rates. Table 7.3 reports the results of a logistic regression with linked/not linked as the dependent variable. On the basis of existing studies of linkage rates we would expect that age would matter, with the elderly in 1871 less likely to be linked than those who were younger due to mortality risks. The logistic regression (LR) confirms that for Logan heads. The two younger age groups were the most likely to be linked, with those over forty the least likely. We would also assume that land owners, and most especially farmers, would be more likely to be linked than tenants and nonfarmers although that assumption should be somewhat qualified by the fact that we are able to link beyond the boundaries of the study region and thus we should catch some of those movers who might be tenants and/or nonfarmers and who, in other studies, would be unlinkable. The LR finds that farmers were more likely to be linked, but being an owner had no effect on the chances of a successful linkage. Current literature stresses the difficulty of linking those who were single and especially single women (due to name change at marriage). We would expect that our data might not be as challenged by these demographic characteristics because we are focussing only on household heads, and only a minority were single and even fewer were single women. The LR indicates that one's gender and marital status did not significantly affect the chances of linkage. Length of time in Logan had some effect on the chances of being linked: those who had been in the township less than one year were the least likely to be linked. Finally our data, drawn mainly from the 1871 nominal census, allows us to explore the effect of ethnicity on the chances of being linked. Given the results of past studies we would expect that those born in Canada would be most likely to be linked. The LR, however, demonstrates that ethnicity and/or birthplace is of no help in predicting a successful linkage, a finding different from that of other studies and probably due to the fact that our linkage compass or potential for linkage exceeds that of many past studies.[18]

Were the odds of being linked governed by a different set of characteristics than the odds of moving? Four characteristics influenced the probability of linkage: years in Logan, age, farmer or not, and the ratio of dependants to earners. Would these characteristics also be strong indicators of the probability of persistence? The results of a logistic

Table 7.4
Logistic regression with move/stay as the dependent variable

	Log odds of moving	
	All household heads	*Farm household heads*
OWNER/TENANT	**	*
Tenant	2.1**	2.2*
Reference Category: Owner		
ethnicity	*	*
Irish Catholics	2.7**	2.5**
Other Catholics	1.4	0.67
Irish Protestants	5.8*	5.1*
English Anglicans	3.8**	3.6**
English/Scotch Protestants	4.0*	3.5*
Reference Category: German Lutherans/Protestants		
FARMERS/NONFARMERS	**	
Nonfarmers	2.7**	——
Reference Category: Farmers		
IMPROVED ACRES AS A PER CENT OF OCCUPIED ACRES	——	*
>= 61 per cent		2.5*
Reference Category: <=60 per cent		
PRECEDENT YEARS	**	
0	3.0**	2.3
1–5	4.0*	3.5*
6–10	1.8	1.7
11–15	1.5	1.4
Reference Category: 16+		
RATIO DEPENDENTS TO EARNERS	ns	ns
MARITAL STATUS	ns	ns
LITERATE	ns	ns
GENDER	ns	ns
AGE	ns	ns
SOIL TYPE	——	ns

* sig is <.01

** sig is between .02 and .05

no * sig is >.05

ns: not significant, removed from the equation by the backward stepwise likelihood ratio procedure

Table 7.5
Variables compared between logistic regressions on odds of being linked and odds of moving: Logan household heads, 1871

Variable	*Significant log odds of being linked*	*Significant log odds of moving*	*Same/ Different*
Age	yes	no	different
Ratio dependents to earners	yes	no	different
Ethno/religion	no	yes	different
Owner/tenant	no	yes	different
Literate	no	no	same
Gender	no	no	same
Marital status	no	no	same
Farmer/not	yes	yes	same
Precedent years	yes	yes	same

regression with stay/move as the dependant variable reported in table 7.4 demonstrate that the answer is no for half of them. The logistic regression with stay/move as the dependent variable run with all linked heads and then with linked farm heads found there was no statistical relationship between the odds of moving and age, or dependants to earners. These findings are quite suggestive since many past studies of persistence have highlighted one or more of these characteristics as important predictors pointing to continued residency when in fact all they might be indicating is the odds of being linked.

Table 7.5 presents a comparison of the characteristics that affect the odds of being linked and those that affect the odds of moving. Just under half of the nine variables indicated different relationships. Many past local area studies have understandably concluded that a link was equivalent to a persister and given their limited catchment area such an assumption was true. The problem, however, arises when one then uses the characteristics of the linked persisters as evidence for explaining who persisted and who did not. The easy assumption is that the characteristics that led to a successful link also account for, or to some degree help explain, why a person persisted. Conflating persistence with linkage as has been done in the past is wrong in principle and misleading in practice.

By comparing the results of the logistic regressions reported in tables 7.3 and 7.4, we have provided a clearer understanding of the importance of method in accounting for movement and persistence in the nineteenth century and in the process underlined Parkerson's warning about possibly inflated rates of movement put forward in many past studies. This is not to suggest, however, that rates of movement were trivial. Far from it. In this paper we are only able to track movement at ten-year intervals, yet many people would have arrived and left between the years 1872 and 1880. In effect we are able to uncover only a small proportion of the numbers who actually moved in and out of Logan over the decade of the 1870s and even then almost one in three household heads in 1871 had left Logan by 1881. It is very worthwhile then to see what light we can shed on who moved and who stayed in this rural Ontario township and to offer some suggestions as to why some people moved and others stayed.

A closer look at the logistic regressions reported in table 7.4 provides a good starting point. That table reports regressions on all household heads and all farm household heads with move/stay as the dependant variable. The table contains five independent variables that relate to the individual's economic condition – owner/tenant, occupation (farmer or other occupation), improved acres as a per cent of occupied acres, soil type, ratio of dependents to earners, and six independent variables that relate to the individual's social characteristics – age, ethnicity, marital status, literacy, years in Logan, and gender. The standard explanation for mobility emphasizes economic conditions.[19] Troubled economic conditions push migrants to look for better prospects and/or seemingly more attractive conditions pull people to move in quest of greater returns.

Given the economic pressures of the decade it is no surprise to observe that three of the five economic indicators were significant predictors of who would move. In the context of a farming community, land ownership went hand in hand with persistence. Those household heads who leased, whether farmers or not, were more than two times more likely to move than land owners. Being in an occupation other than farming, led to increased odds of moving. More surprising is the finding relating to per cent of improved acres as reported for farm heads in table 7.3.[20] One might have thought that as the per cent of acres improved increased, the odds of one's chances of remaining in Perth would also increase. The assumption is that a great deal of time and effort had gone into developing the farm and, relatedly, the assumption is that that effort had led to a profitable venture. Yet the logistic regression indicates that those with more than 60 per cent of their occupied acres improved were 2.5 times more likely to move.

Indeed if the regression is run as in table 7.3 but with the independent variable per cent improved acres having five categories, (divided into twenty percentiles) farmers with between 60 and 80 per cent of their occupied acres improved were four times more likely to move than the those in the reference category, 21–40 per cent, and those with more than 80 per cent improved were 3.4 times more likely to move.[21] One possible explanation is that those with more than 60 per cent improved acres were older and perhaps approaching retirement, but a cross tabulation of acres improved and age yielded insignificant results. Perhaps there was a market for farms with a high per cent of improved acres and that this led to more movement in the 60 per cent-plus category. Or, looked at from the perspective of those with less than 60 per cent acres improved and especially those in the 21–40 per cent category, one might surmise that these farmers and their families were heavily involved in and committed to improving their landed assets, and thoughts of moving and starting over had little place in their minds. They were, perhaps, part of an aspiring community with their future before them. Another possibility is that Logan, a fairly small township, was simply an anomaly. At this stage in the research a satisfying explanation remains elusive.

Two economic variables proved to be poor predictors of movement. Soil type derived from a 1950s analysis shed no light on odds of moving perhaps because more modern assessments of soil qualities might have only a marginal relationship to the nature of soils close to one hundred years previously.[22] Certainly in the case of Logan much drainage awaited the decade of the 1880s, so conditions in the 1870s were probably quite different from the situation following those extensive drainage projects. The ratio of dependents to earners also proved to be a poor predictor of the odds of moving, perhaps because if a family had a large number of dependents moving might have been difficult and if they had a small number of dependents the incentive to move might be less compelling.[23]

Clearly one's economic position was directly related to whether one was more or less likely to move. Those who owned land tended to stay put as did those who farmed as opposed to engaging in other occupations. Those who were tenants were far more likely to leave. To the extent that this finding has been mentioned in the literature, it has also often been qualified by reference to a presumed agricultural ladder.[24] The assumption is that tenants were younger and on a bottom rung of the ladder and that, controlled for age, the increased tendency to move would dissolve. But it should be emphasized that, as the regression on farm heads in table 7.4 shows, age had no effect on the probability of tenants moving or staying.[25] The fact of tenancy itself was the operative influence.

Of all the cultural variables included in the regression for all heads and for farm heads only one's ethno-religious background proved to be a strong indicator of one's likelihood to move. We have noted that one's ethnicity (defined as a combination of origin and religion) was no help in predicting a successful linkage. By contrast, one's ethnicity was a most powerful predictor of the odds of moving from or staying in Logan. German Lutherans were by far the most likely of all ethnic groups to persist in the township. This finding is intriguing since many, but, as we shall see, not all, past studies have found the reverse: a number of studies have found that Germans in general (i.e., not controlled for religion) in both urban and rural areas in the United States in the nineteenth century were more, not less, apt to move when compared to other immigrant groups.[26] Yet a regression run with the dependent variable move/stay and all independent variables the same as in table 7.3 except for the substitution of place of birth for ethnicity yielded results virtually identical to the regression with ethnicity. People born in Canada, England, Scotland, and Ireland were all far more likely than those born in Germany to leave Perth County sometime in the 1870s.

Who, then, were the German Lutherans, and how do we explain their persistence? A study of nineteenth-century German Lutheran settlements in the Southern Riverina area of Australia noted the strong clustering tendency of these immigrants and their persistence on the land often through times of significant adversity. The authors offered two explanations: the German Lutheran's strong allegiance to church and community and their tendency to engage in a balanced form of mixed farming more than other ethnic groups thus allowing more flexibility to meet adverse challenges.[27]

As figure 7.4 clearly depicts, German Lutherans lived side by side to a greater degree than any other ethnic community in Logan in the 1870s. Language differences from the wider community encouraged such proximity. Religion, too, was definitely important to Logan's German Lutherans. Yet in the early years religious issues divided as much as united that population. Two groups split over a number of issues: where to establish a central church, the naming of the congregation, ownership of the Protocol Books and communion ware, synodical affiliation (Pittsburgh or Missouri), and the appropriate pastor. The min-

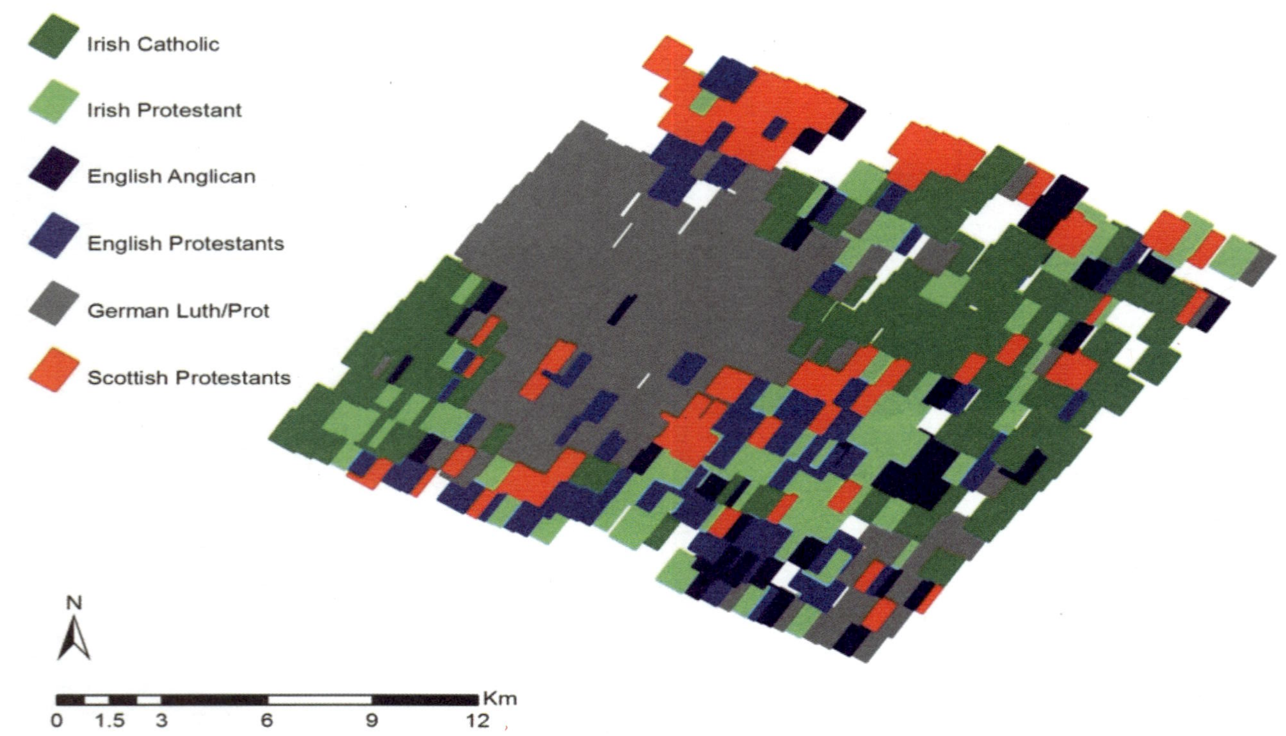

Figure 7.4 Ethnic Concentration, Logan Township, 1879

Table 7.6
Stockholding: German Lutheran farms compared to all other farms, Logan Township, 1871

	Per cent farms with stock		*Average stockholding for farms with stock*	
Stock	*German Lutheran farms*	*Other farms*	*German Lutheran farms*	*Other farms*
Horses	69.8	69.0	2.8	3.0
Working oxen	21.4*	8.4*	2.0	2.0
Milk cows	93.7*	84.0*	2.5	2.8
Other cows	83.3*	70.0*	4.3	4.6
Sheep	75.4	66.6	5.9	8.1
Swine	88.1*	77.7*	4.2	4.1

* Significance level of the chi-square <.05

utes of a congregational meeting held on 1 January 1867 declared that, "nearly the whole congregation dissolved into chaos." Church fences were torn down and apple trees left to foraging cows. After several years of strife, a truce was declared and a number of separate and fervently supported parishes were established in Logan around which German communities conducted their lives.[28] One might suggest that the intense investment of time, energy, and emotion expended on these early factional disputes cemented local attachments and contributed to long-term persistence.

It is quite possible, too, that environmental factors further contributed to German Lutheran persistence. Logan, like much of Perth County, was mainly comprised of subaqueous soil that demanded skills in wetland farming.[29] Many of the Germans in Logan came to Canada with those skills honed over generations in the northern provinces of Germany – Mecklenburg and Saxony – where wetland farming was common.[30] As well, by 1871 Logan's Germans had acquired about one-half of the township's best farming land.

Tables 7.6 and 7.7 suggest that the German farmers did adopt a balanced approach to stock raising and crop production.[31] A higher number of German-run farms grew peas, wheat, and oats and kept cattle, pigs, and working oxen. The affinity for pigs is consistent with behaviour in the "old country." Their tendency to utilize oxen, often instead of horses, for farming, was also a strategy consistent with traditional

Table 7.7
Crop cultivation: German Lutheran farms compared to all other farms, Logan Township, 1871

	Per cent farms with crop/acres		*Average crop production/ acres for farms with crop*	
Stock	*German Lutheran farms*	*Other farms*	*German Lutheran farms*	*Other farms*
Spring wheat (bushels)	83.8*	61.3*	54.3	41.4
Fall wheat (bushels)	20.6	23.7	51.6	57.9
Wheat (acres)	86.5*	65.5*	10.8	10.2
Barley (bushels)	38.9	48.8	39.4	87.5
Oat (bushels)	85.7*	69.0*	119.8	156.5
Pea (bushels)	82.5*	57.8*	64.0	61.4
Potato (acres)	90.5	82.9	1.5	4.3
Potato (bushels)	90.5	81.2	61.4	68.9
Hay (acres)	83.3*	73.9*	9.0	11.3
Hay (tons/bundles)	84.1*	71.1*	10.1	13.0

* Significance level of the chi-square <.05

practice in Germany.[32] Oxen were much more efficient than horses for working wetland environments. The fact that the average stock holding and crop production figures were smaller for German Lutheran run farms probably points to a balanced approach to agriculture. Indeed over time the German settlers attained a reputation for excellent farming skills throughout much of Perth County.[33]

Many studies of German farmers have pointed to the fact that their rates of ownership were high and that this further contributed to their high persistence rates.[34] We have already noted that being an owner did increase one's odds of staying in Logan. One might assume, then, that German Lutherans were the most apt to be owners and that that would help explain their high persistence tendencies. Yet, as table 7.8 demonstrates, the reverse is the case: German Lutherans were by far the most likely to be tenants; indeed, in 1871, they were the only ethnic group comprised of more tenants than owners. Among all tenants they were the strongest persisters. How is it that an ethnic group defies odds by being most likely to be tenants and least likely to move?

Conzen has shown that family strategies played a large part in accounting for the persistence of German Catholics in a Minnesota township.[35]

Table 7.8
Ethno/religion by tenant/owner: household heads, Logan Township, 1871, nominal level census

Ethno/Religion	*Per cent tenant*	*Per cent owner*	*Number*
Irish Catholics	42.9	57.1	84
Irish Protestants	43.2	56.8	74
English/Anglicans	46.7	53.3	30
English/Scotch Protestants	25.3	74.7	95
German Lutherans/Protestants	61.7	38.3	128

What strategy might have underlain the behaviour of German Lutherans? A good part of the answer to that question lies in the manner in which land was made available in Logan Township and much of Perth County. The Canada Company, a private company chartered in England in 1824, was granted rights to a huge area that included Logan Township in return for which the Company was expected to promote immigration and settlement.[36] As part of a developing strategy, the Canada Company advertised in Germany and hired agents there to promote the Company and encourage immigration to Canada.[37] "The character of these people [Germans] have for industry and good conduct," the Company's directors informed their Canada commissioners, "renders it very desirable to obtain them as settlers."[38] To sweeten the incentives, the Canada Company, in the early 1840s, instituted a long-term lease program (five to ten years) whereby new settlers could take up residence at a low annual rental fee. After fulfilling some requirements – erecting a house, fencing, and clearing land – the family had the right to purchase the land at the end of the lease period at an upset price established at the commencement of the lease. In effect the Company instituted a two-tiered system: the upset price was to be higher "than that paid by men of capital" to continue to "induce" such men to purchase; the leasing system was left for men of no capital "and little but their labour and industry to rely upon."[39] This campaign had some success, and German families, increasingly challenged by political and economic change in their homeland and generally without much ready cash, moved to Perth County and surrounding areas. Those who arrived first encouraged others to follow, and a form of chain migration was set in motion.[40]

Two snapshots in time (figures 7.5 and 7.6) provide an indication of the extent of the Canada Company's leasing business, and table 7.8 provides an indication of the degree to which German Lutherans were the

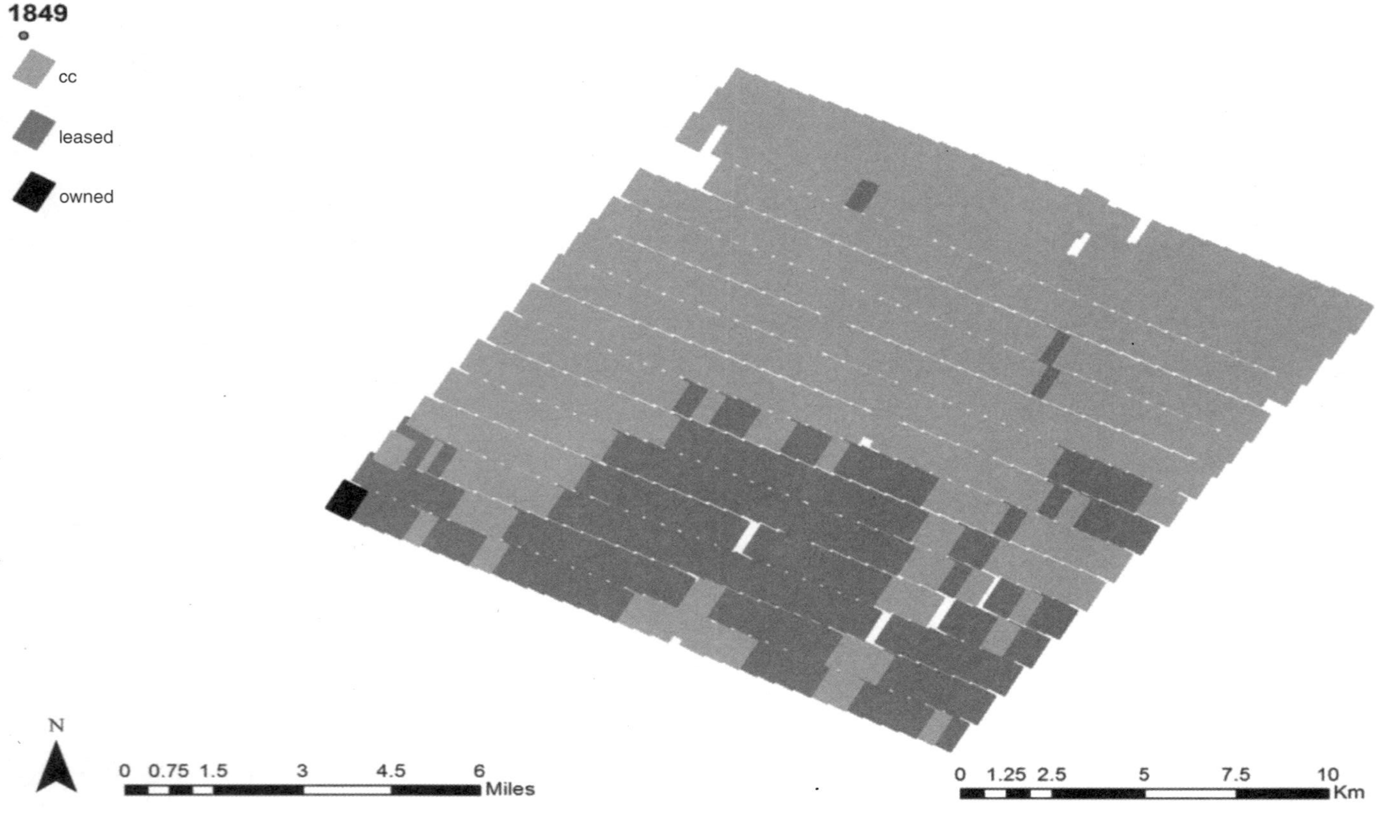

Figure 7.5 Leasing Logan, the Canada Company as land owner/lessor, Logan Township 1849

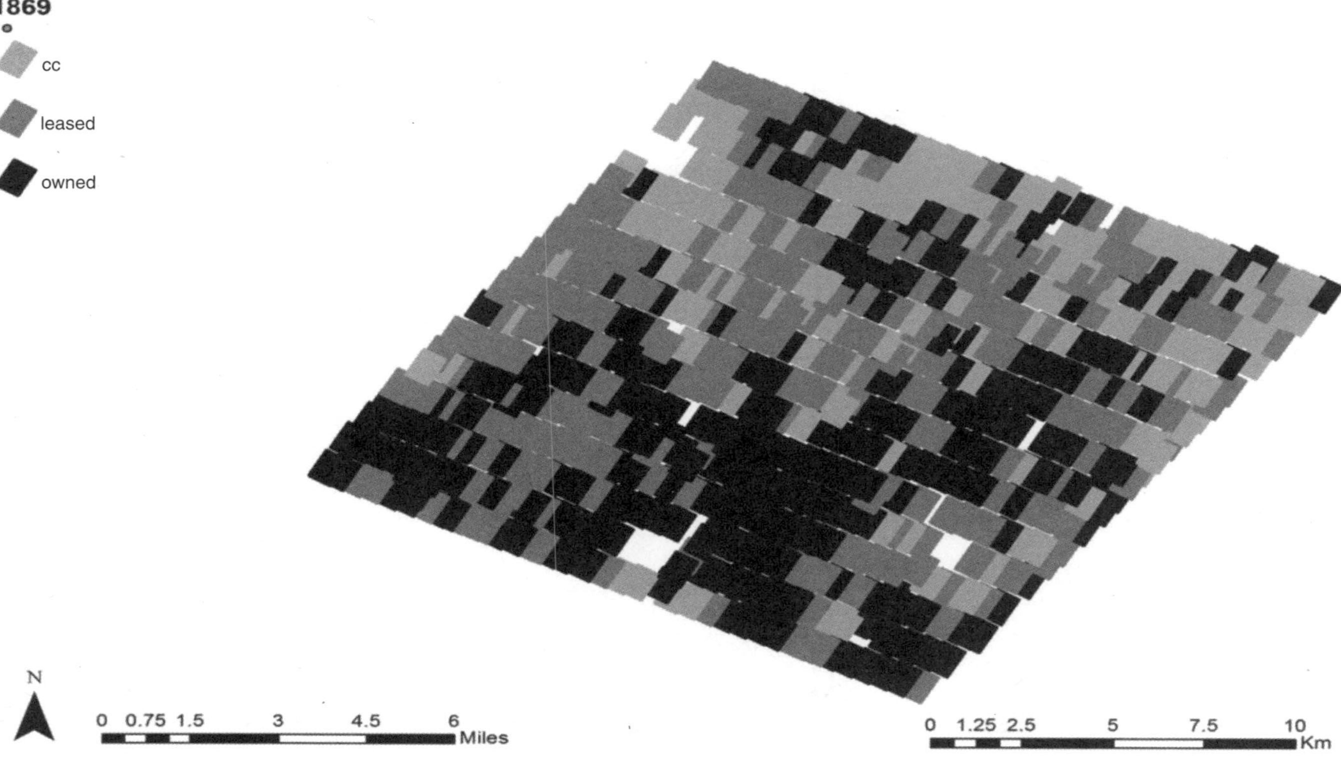

Figure 7.6 Leasing Logan, the Canada Company as land owner/lessor, Logan Township 1869

Table 7.9
Tenants and landlords: Logan Township, Perth County, 1871

Landlord	*Ethnicity of leaseholder (%)* Irish Catholic	Irish Protestant	English Anglican	German Lutheran/ Protestant	English/ Scots Presbyterian	Total Number
Canada Company	56.6	48.6	26.7	61.6	32.1	135
Other	43.4	51.4	73.3	38.4	67.9	120
Total Number leaseholders	54	37	17	116	31	255

Company's major customers. Between 1840 and 1876, the Canada Company leased 1,231 properties in Logan Township. By 1871, although leasing had fallen off from peak years, the Canada Company was by far the largest landlord in Logan, and German Lutherans were its favourite clients, followed by Irish Catholics.

It may well be the case that leasing appealed to settlers with relatively little start-up capital, in this case the German Lutherans and the Irish Catholics. Both these groups were the most apt to lease and the most apt to lease from the Canada Company (table 7.9).[41] By contrast, the English Anglicans and the English Scots Presbyterians leased less, and those who did lease in 1871 preferred landlords other than the Canada Company.

Who one leased from mattered in terms of the probabilities of living in Logan for the whole of the 1870s. No matter their ethnicity, those who leased from the Canada Company were more likely to stay in Logan than were those who leased from another landlord. Only 21 per cent of those who leased from the Canada Company in 1871 moved from the Township compared to 46 per cent of those who leased from another owner. Indeed for the Irish Catholics and German Lutherans those who leased from the Canada Company were more likely to persist than those who owned land. For the Irish Catholics 88 per cent of the Canada Company leaseholders persisted compared to 79 per cent of the owners. For the German Lutherans 89 per cent of the Canada Company leaseholders persisted compared to 84 per cent of the owners. The combined relevant percentages for the other ethnic groups were 51.9 per cent persistence rate for Canada Company leaseholders and 69.4 per cent persistence rate for owners.

Table 7.10
Landholding patterns by ethnicity: Logan Township, 1840–1911, (household heads, 1871 census cohort)

	Ownership patterns (%)			
Ethnicity	*Leased only*	*Leased then owned*	*Owned only*	*Number of cases*
Irish Catholics	13.3	57.4	28.0	75
Irish Protestants	8.2	55.7	36.1	61
English Anglicans	12.5	41.7	45.8	24
German Lutherans/Protestants	18.0	56.8	25.2	111
English/Scotch Protestants	10.1	35.4	54.4	79

Different types of leases were the result of different settlement strategies and led to different persistence rates. To test this conclusion further I ran two additional logistic regressions for Logan on farmer household heads with move/stay as the dependent variable. All independent variables remained the same as in table 7.4 for farm heads except leaseholders were differentiated by Canada Company leaseholders and non-Canada Company leaseholders. The regression with non-Canada Company leaseholders compared to owners resulted in the non-Canada Company leaseholders being 2.5 times more likely to move than the owners (sig .013). Ethnicity had no statistically important effect on the odds of moving. Very different results were attained for the regression with Canada Company leaseholders compared to owners. The ownership variable was discarded as insignificant. In other words, it did not matter whether one was an owner or a Canada Company leaseholder in terms of the odds of moving. The ethnicity variable, however, while indicating that Irish Roman Catholics and German Lutherans could not be distinguished in terms of their odds of moving, reported that all other ethnic groups were far more likely to move (sig .01). Those Irish Catholics and German Lutherans who leased from the Canada Company were far more likely to stay in Perth over the decade of the 1870s than were Canada Company leaseholders of Scottish or Irish Protestant background or English Anglican origin. They were also more likely to lease from the Canada Company than the other ethnic groups (table 7.9). By contrast, those German Lutherans and Irish Catholics who leased from non-Canada Company land owners could not be distinguished from other ethnic groups in terms of their odds of moving. The regressions clearly confirm that whom one leased from mattered in terms of the likelihood of moving or staying in Logan in the decade of the 1870s.

The data presented in tables 7.8 and 7.9 reflect the leasing patterns of household heads in Logan on enumeration day in 1871 and thus represent a snapshot at one point in time. Broader context of a longitudinal sort is provided by data in a rather unique local history that has compiled all land transactions for each lot in Logan Township from the date of first settlement to 2000.[42]

I have entered all transactions up to 1911 into a machine-readable database, called here the Logan Land Database (LLD). Using first and last name and land coordinates, I linked the LLD to the 1871 census thereby creating a longitudinal file of land transactions for household heads in 1871.[43]

In other words, I now have a file which shows the extent to which a head in 1871 owned/leased land in Logan before and after that date as well as at that date. To make sense of the data, I constructed three ownership categories: those who only leased, those who leased and then owned, and those who only owned.

Perhaps the first observation to be made is that the longer time frame depicted in table 7.10 compared to the one-year snapshot presented in table 7.8 points to the importance of using longitudinal data whenever possible. Over the course of the late nineteenth century, German Lutherans remained the most apt to lease and the least likely simply to own property in Logan. But the difference for the long period was somewhat less dramatic than for the single year, 1871, because German Lutherans leased to stay. Many more German Lutherans were leasing in 1871 than was the case for all other ethnic groups, but this was simply one point in time and did not necessarily reflect ultimate goals. Those goals only really become clear when we change our perspective from that of one year to that of seventy-one years. The broader time frame allows us to see the results of a process that was far from complete in 1871. Yet the perspective provided by the snapshot is also of great value. It shed a sharp light on the different strategies employed by different ethnic groups during the process of settling in Logan Township. The broader time perspective offers only a relatively blurred picture of the different means employed to achieve a somewhat common end.

Moreover, knowing the relationship to the means of production of Logan's household heads in 1871 with such clarity allows us to understand better why some stayed and others moved during that decade. While German Lutherans and Irish Catholics exhibited similar land tenure profiles (about 71 per cent of Irish Catholics leased at some time in Logan compared to about 75 per cent of German Lutherans, see table 7.10), they differed in one important respect: those Irish Catholics, and indeed all other ethnic groups, who leased in 1871 were more likely to move than German Lutheran leaseholders (table 7.4). Table 7.10 also hints at the possibility that more German Lutherans were content to lease only throughout their time in Logan than was the case for people in many other ethnic groups. Leasing land led to different outcomes for different cultural groups.

This study of movement and persistence of rural household heads in Logan Township during the economically troubled decade of the 1870s has underlined how one's method can condition the results obtained. The study finds that, although movement in this rural township was significant, it was significantly less than that reported by many previous studies of movement and persistence in nineteenth-century North American rural communities. The reasons for the different findings are directly related to methodological decisions. The size of the catchment area and the linkage processes employed are two crucial determinants of plausible conclusions. The study has also suggested how a combination of snapshot and longitudinal perspectives can lead to richer insights into settlement strategies over the short and longer terms. Moreover, the study points to the importance of nuanced microstudies for understanding human behaviour. Had one simply left leasing as an undifferentiated category, one of the central dynamics underlying settlement patterns and persistence rates would have been missed.

On a general level the study supports a somewhat standard interpretation found in the literature, one that privileges economic explanations for movement. But here, too, a cautionary note is suggested. Cultural issues also played a significant role in decisions to move or not. Yes, German Lutherans and Irish Catholics were probably the poorest of the settler groups in Logan in 1871 and that probable fact goes far to accounting for their strong tendency to lease and to lease from the Canada Company. And clearly the Company's leasing system was designed to attract and keep relatively poor settlers. Yet German Lutherans leased and persisted to a greater degree than any other ethnic group. This observation fits well with an emerging literature that stresses the variety of motivations that underlay lease holding in nineteenth-century North

America.[44] In October 1843, Frederick Widder, the Company's local Canadian commissioner, wrote a *Memorandum upon German Settlers and Emigrants.* In it he predicted that "where they [Germans] are once located, there they will remain, and be contented and prosperous."[45] How right he was. The Canada Company and their German settlers were a match made in heaven. The Canada Company sought settlers who would stay and take advantage of their leasehold arrangement. More than all other ethnic groups, German Lutherans came to Logan and leased to stay, in the process legitimating the Company's land lease program and complicating what leasing might mean for our understanding of rural strategies relating to movement and persistence in nineteenth-century Ontario.

8

Revisiting Wealth on the American Frontier: Farm Growth, Inequality, and Social Persistence in Kansas, 1875–1940

KENNETH M. SYLVESTER AND
SUSAN HAUTANIEMI LEONARD

The story of the United States has been shaped by small farmers and their access to land. From colonial times to the twentieth century, the drive to acquire and settle new territory was underwritten by early access to land ownership and the growing class of freeholders it created. By the time of the American Revolution, two-thirds of colonial families owned land, and as late as 1840, two-thirds of the population still lived on farms.[1] In 1862, absent persistent southern opposition, Congress took the ideology of territorial expansion and free soil even further, offering free land in the western plains. Although homestead grants of 160 acres did not reverse the growth of urban society or commercial agriculture, they provided another land frontier for the small holder, the poor, and the ambitious. The pace of American development depended in large measure on the fortunes of this class of independent farmers. Growth swung between commercial exuberance and self-sufficiency, riding the good and bad times. Nevertheless, for all of the technological and commercial change that settler families faced on the western plains, the American model of family farms negotiated the transition to modern agriculture quite well.[2] Egalitarian norms continued to shape the practice of how farms were made and remade well into the twentieth century.[3]

As the farm frontier was closing at the end of the nineteenth century and arable public lands were less available to ordinary families, concern grew that the yeoman ideal was out of reach for many rural youth. Writing in the 1930s and 1940s, the historian Paul Wallace Gates was among the first to sound the alarm about the status of owner-occupiers.[4] The issue was taken up by succeeding generations of historians interested in answering the question of whether upward mobility was blocked in the late nineteenth and early twentieth centuries. The metaphor, as Jeremy Atack summarized the discussion, was that farm tenancy represented a rung on an occupational ladder.[5] The belief that in normal times the farm labourer could advance up the rungs of the agricultural ladder helped sustain faith in the openness of economic life. Gates questioned that belief – that the various stages of tenancy still led to full ownership – during the hard times of the 1930s. The response of researchers from the 1950s through the 1980s, during more optimistic times, was that upward mobility continued to be a feature of American agriculture into the early twentieth century.[6] Darroch discusses this kind of mobility in the Canadian context in his earlier work and in a new contribution in this volume.

In spite of the more optimistic tone, most authors acknowledge a narrower achievement of full ownership in North America over time. When the US census first asked about tenancy in 1880, the proportion of those who rented was about one-quarter of all farmers across the whole country. By 1930, the published census reported that the proportion of American farmers who were classified as sharecroppers and tenants had risen to more than 40 per cent.[7] Over time, the young steadily lost the kind of access that existed while the public land frontier was expanding. Yet in spite of the growth of farm tenancy in the United States, Jeremy Atack's view was that movement up the rungs of the agricultural ladder was still a very real social process – most farmers still became owners by midlife, and this was not an artefact of the expanding frontier. Early in their careers farmers might rent land from their fathers or neighbours, while waiting to inherit or buy land. By the 1930s, this form of mobility was narrower and slower, but ownership was still the norm in midlife, as many contemporaries tried to point out to concerned policy makers.

We revisit this interest in social mobility and the life cycle from a slightly different vantage point: a longitudinal study of farm communities. From the lens of a single census, it has always been difficult to sort out the effect of period and generational change in understanding the patterns of American inequality. Even though the acquisition of farmland is well recognized as a life-cycle process, the dynamics clearly are very different in an expanding agricultural frontier.[8] For young farmers facing choices about whether to stay in their home community, the degree of landed inequality was a crucial factor in the decision about whether or not to build a future near their immediate kin. A great deal of the decision depended on the availability of land and the timing of succession. Yet we still know very little about whether social processes or structural conditions (redistribution or territorial expansion) were more decisive. The analysis that follows offers, we argue, an important clue. Though the paper focuses less exclusively on land tenure, the analysis suggests that social processes were vital through both eras. Social persistence constrained the growth of farms and inequality in the early settlement era and then set the pace of individual growth after agricultural lands were in private hands.

CENSUS DATA

Studies of agriculture based on individual-level information have been limited to the nineteenth century because the United States Commerce Department (which was responsible for conducting the agricultural census until 1997) destroyed the manuscript federal censuses of agriculture.[9] In many parts of the United States, therefore, the early social surveys conducted by sociologists and economists in the 1920s and 1930s are among the few studies that will ever reach beyond the aggregates reported in the published census. The situation was different in Kansas, where the state government conducted its own full-count census of agriculture and population in a conscious effort to boost and document internal growth. Unlike its federal counterpart, the agricultural census in Kansas has received less attention because it operated more as a prospective survey of the crop year. Instead of being asked about the previous crop year, farmers were asked what was already sown or about to be planted for the coming season. The lack of information on yields has been seen as a major shortcoming – particularly for economists interested in understanding rising productivity. However, for scholars interested in land use, farm practice, environmental impacts, and demographic change, the state returns offer enormous potential for new forms of microanalysis.

While ownership information can be reconstructed from other sources (like deed and tax records),[10] manuscript censuses of agriculture are the most readily available information on land distribution in the late nineteenth and early twentieth centuries. In Kansas, these documents have been preserved for the period from 1875 to 1940, and

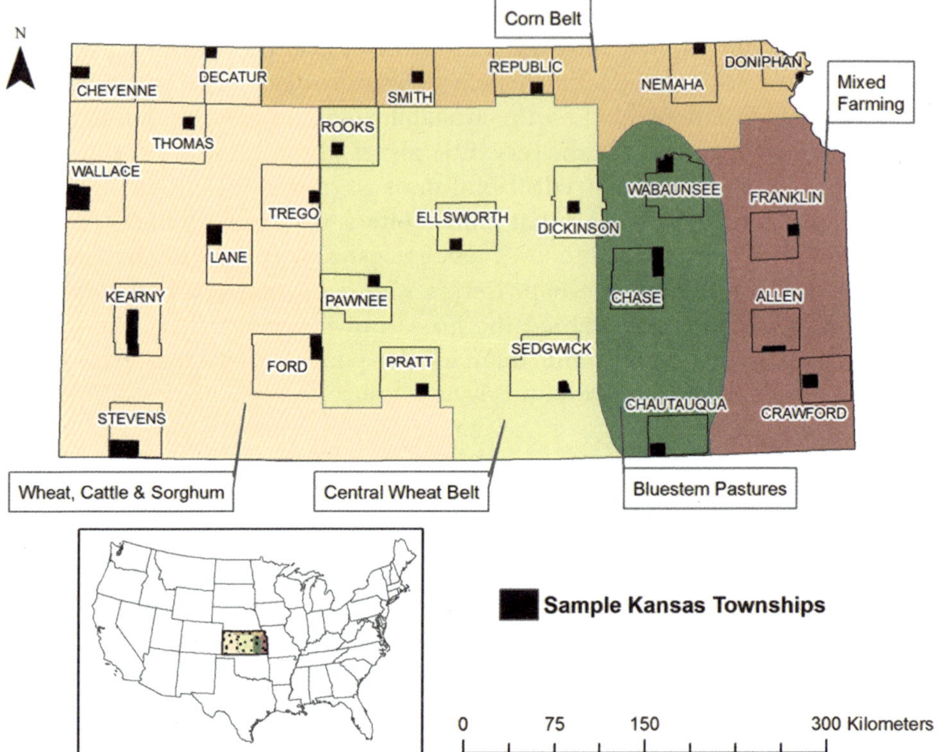

Figure 8.1 Sample townships by county and land-use region

the state agency that conducted the agricultural census also reported its tabulations in a long-running series of *Biennial Reports* from 1873 to 1976.[11] Unfortunately, levels of tenancy were only tracked in two census years, 1885 and 1920, as discussed below. Nevertheless, reported farm sizes are available in complete count returns for all enumerated farm operators in every organized township across the state. The manuscript censuses are particularly valuable for understanding the relationship between land use and demographic change, with consistent series on principal crops, livestock, farm size, and household characteristics.

Our paper uses a sample designed to link farm operators and their households over time.[12] Rather than a random sample of individual farms (without locational information), we selected twenty-five townships based on broad differences in the environmental settings across the state. From the selected communities we entered every person and every farm reported in the agricultural and population censuses. This multilevel design has several advantages. It allows us to control for the clustering of observations and to introduce contextual or higher-level covariates. In our case, farm-level change is nested within townships, across varied environmental contexts that can be specified explicitly at the township level in multilevel estimation models.[13] Therefore, the nested and repeated design of the dataset permits us to move beyond the snapshots offered by individual censuses to explore the dynamics of longitudinal change.

The geographic distribution of the sample townships is illustrated in figure 8.1. The study areas were selected based on the highest rural population densities in 1910 (as reported in the summary tables in the State Board of Agriculture's *Biennial Reports*, Kansas). This was done in order to capture more densely settled but predominantly agricultural townships, without towns or villages within their boundaries. The intention in using this criterion was to include areas best suited to arable agriculture, to track agricultural (as opposed to urban) change over time, and to create a place-based sample evenly distributed across the key environmental contexts in the state.

Most land in the central plains consists of level and open terrain, but the prairie is punctuated by numerous escarpments and river valleys. In the east, the most distinct uplands are known as the Flint Hills, where the soil is generally heavy clay braided with bands of chert or flint. Less land is arable on these thin upland soils.[14] Patterns of use were well documented by the early 1930s. In his discussion of adaptation to the semiarid environment, James Malin identified five major land-use regions in his synoptic work *Winter Wheat*,[15] following the guidance of US Department of Agriculture Cooperative Extension staff. Because of higher precipitation in the eastern half of the state, where rainfall averages forty to forty-four inches annually, strategies of mixed farming were common. In a tier of counties along the northern boundary with Nebraska, corn quickly became the predominant cash crop. East of the Flint Hills and south of the Kansas River, corn was combined more with wheat, oats, and other small grains and livestock on small farms. West of the Flint Hills, where the treeless terrain expands into an enormous high plain, Malin noted the transition away from winter wheat in the center of the state to farm production based on a combination of wheat, cattle, and sorghum in the west. Near the Colorado border annual rainfall is typically no more than fifteen inches.[16]

Farms grew larger in the far west to raise cattle and tended to combine livestock and arable production.

Because the sample is based on entire townships, boundary changes complicate our story in some areas. Although county formation was mostly complete by the late 1880s, some township boundaries were not finalized in the western part of the state until the 1910s. In Stevens County, for instance, the study township did not have a set boundary until the 1920 census. Our strategy in these cases was to gather all the data for each prior time point, even if the boundary was much larger, in order to maximize the observations that might link forward to the next observation time. This sampling strategy inflates early population and farm counts in some locations, where entire county populations were entered into the dataset. The occupational universe is also more diverse in the early years when the entire population of newly formed counties was entered. Later on, when the sample concentrates on the targeted agricultural townships, it focuses more on the farm population. Nevertheless, the sample is intended as a full count for each of the study areas, subject to the usual limitations of historical census enumerations, with well-demonstrated tendencies to undercount the poor.[17]

The population data are derived from the decennial federal census (conducted every ten years beginning in 1790) and a quenquennial population census conducted by the State of Kansas beginning in 1865. Virtually all of the agricultural data were taken from the Kansas state census, or the agricultural statistics rolls, as they are known in the Kansas State Historical Society archives in Topeka.[18] The only years for which federal agricultural census manuscripts were available were 1860, 1870, and 1880. The chief difference between the federal and state agricultural questionnaires is that the federal census asked retrospective questions about the prior crop year, in order to gather information on yields. The Kansas census served more as a survey of land use, of the acres sown to various crops, pasture, and grassland use, livestock inventories, machinery, and fencing. Questions were asked in spring about the winter crops already sown the previous fall and the intended plantings for the coming season. Overall, the sample design reached maximum counts of just over 13,000 persons and about 2,300 to 2,500 farms, per census year, sometime between 1895 and 1905.[19]

Occupations reported in the population censuses confirm the overwhelmingly agricultural nature of these communities. During most of the period, the proportion in agriculture is 70 per cent or more, most of them farmers. It is only in the very early years that the sample captures significant occupational groups outside of agriculture. The figures reported below in table 8.1 are for persons aged twenty and older with declared occupations in the population census. In the handful of counties that existed in eastern Kansas prior to 1880, the proportion of adults who identified their occupation as falling within the manufacturing or mechanical trades (builders, carpenters, coopers, meat packers, millers, potters, printers, railway workers, tailors, wheelwrights, etc.) reached as high as 10 per cent. But once the administrative boundaries of the target agricultural communities were better defined, we see that the service economy supporting agricultural communities formed a larger share of the nonagricultural population, with small but stable roles for trade and transportation and manufacturing. Fluctuations in domestic servants and in farm labourers reflect differing practices in the federal and state censuses, particularly in how wives and working-aged children's occupations were reported.

Because of the tendency in the United States for farmers to declare coresident adult sons as "agricultural labourers" and the timing of census enumeration, the scale of paid agricultural labour force is notoriously difficult to assess from manuscript sources. Enumerations of farm hands, hired for wages, are often missing from population schedules because of the seasonal nature of agricultural employment. Censuses are typically conducted in the spring and farm hands needed most during the late summer and fall harvesting season. In our dataset, because of the combination of federal and state population censuses, clear differences in occupational reporting are evident. Prior to 1910, the state population census consistently underreports persons (in 1865, 1875, 1885, and 1905) who might be classified as agricultural labourers. The federal census provides a better sense of the high-water mark for persons in agriculture who were not farm operators at the time of the census. Kansas census takers were more likely to grant farm sons "farmers in waiting" status, listing them in their fathers' households as farmers.[20] Those listed in the Kansas census as farm labourers more clearly reflect a lower rung on the agricultural ladder, men with no access to land. After 1910, state practices were more consistent with federal enumerations, and the swings between agricultural labourer and domestic labour categories were noticeably smaller between the federal (1910, 1920, and 1930) and state (1915 and 1925) enumerations (see table 8.1). The occupational data offer some sense of the changing composition of these largely agricultural communities. They are an important backdrop for the discussion of farm tenancy and farm sizes.

Table 8.1

Number and per cent of occupations reported by persons age twenty and older, 1860 to 1930, Kansas townships

	1860	*1865*	*1870*	*1875*	*1880*	*1885*	*1895*	*1900*	*1905*	*1910*	*1915*	*1920*	*1925*	*1930*
Farmer	1,365	437	2,122	2,220	3,219	2,922	2,471	2,567	2,276	3,116	3,343	2,892	2,564	2,528
Farm laborer	163	8	349	8	291	58	138	579	23	575	437	487	195	565
Other agriculture	1	4	40	56	73	109	11	63	56	24	124	27	17	38
Laborer nonspecific	62	40	219	216	252	55	61	67	163	160	153	80	158	167
Domestic servants	63	36	63	471	315	469	269	68	317	81	420	45	45	72
Clergy teachers	8	3	10	16	19	13	11	16	15	23	11	18	15	16
Other professional	68	42	376	191	125	66	142	171	145	224	153	202	167	243
Trade transport	34	22	416	352	96	54	123	189	156	324	125	337	172	364
Manufacturing mechanical	178	48	336	397	198	192	187	132	143	211	87	197	138	153
Total declared occupations	1,942	640	3,931	3,927	4,588	3,938	3,413	3,852	3,294	4,738	4,853	4,285	3,471	4,146
Farmer	70.3	68.3	54.0	56.5	70.2	74.2	72.4	66.6	69.1	65.8	68.9	67.5	73.9	61.0
Farm laborer	8.4	1.3	8.9	0.2	6.3	1.5	4.0	15.0	0.7	12.1	9.0	11.4	5.6	13.6
Other agriculture	0.1	0.6	1.0	1.4	1.6	2.8	0.3	1.6	1.7	0.5	2.6	0.6	0.5	0.9
Laborer nonspecific	3.2	6.3	5.6	5.5	5.5	1.4	1.8	1.7	4.9	3.4	3.2	1.9	4.6	4.0
Domestic servants	3.2	5.6	1.6	12.0	6.9	11.9	7.9	1.8	9.6	1.7	8.7	1.1	1.3	1.7
Clergy teachers	0.4	0.5	0.3	0.4	0.4	0.3	0.3	0.4	0.5	0.5	0.2	0.4	0.4	0.4
Other professional	3.5	6.6	9.6	4.9	2.7	1.7	4.2	4.4	4.4	4.7	3.2	4.7	4.8	5.9
Trade transport	1.8	3.4	10.6	9.0	2.1	1.4	3.6	4.9	4.7	6.8	2.6	7.9	5.0	8.8
Manufacturing mechanical	9.2	7.5	8.5	10.1	4.3	4.9	5.5	3.4	4.3	4.5	1.8	4.6	4.0	3.7
Total declared occupations	100.0	100.0	100.0	100.0	100.0	100.0	100.0	100.0	100.0	100.0	100.0	100.0	100.0	100.0

Source: Kansas township sample

TENANCY

Studies that look at the openness of the agricultural ladder have sometimes failed to address the size of the agricultural labour force. In fact, they have tried to make a rather indirect argument that growing tenancy was evidence of continued upward mobility in the United States.[21] Because agricultural populations were no longer growing in the early twentieth century and the proportion of agricultural labourers had peaked, an argument was often made that the growth of tenancy actually represented a route to ownership for agricultural wage labourers. The proportion of ownership might be declining, but the pool of agricultural labourers was not increasing. Therefore some labourers must be graduating to the ranks of farm tenants.

The belief that tenants would go on to some form of ownership was not just a product of this indirect logic. New Deal economist L.C. Gray presented the most convincing evidence, based on data collected from the 1920 federal census, that at least half of all new tenant farmers in the northern half of the United States between 1915 and 1920 had once been farm labourers.[22] Tenants were just as likely, Gray found, to rise to the ranks of farm ownership in the Midwest, where 50 per cent or more of the persons who became farm owners had once been tenants. Elsewhere in the north, ownership was harder to attain, with only 30 per cent of tenants rising to ownership status. There were also signs of downward mobility, with an average of 20 per cent of farmers in the northern states losing their ownership status and becoming farm tenants. We find evidence of both upward and downward mobility in Kansas, with farm sons having the best chance of becoming farm operators.[23]

The study of the life cycles of farm labourers by contemporary social scientists began in the 1930s. Harvard economists John D. Black and R.H. Allen constructed an age-stratified series to dispute the pessimism of the President's Committee on Farm Tenancy. The committee's findings alarmed FDR and other policy makers about declining rates of ownership in the United States. In spite of the worsening national averages, Black and Allen were able to show that tenancy rates remained stratified by age.[24] In his own work with census data, Atack has used cross-sectional data to tabulate rates of tenancy, according to age groups. Working with a large representative sample of US farm households in the northern states in 1860, Atack has detailed the consistent increase in ownership over the course of the life cycle.[25]

Table 8.2
Proportion of farmers who were tenants by age group, 1850–1930, expressed in rates per thousand, contiguous United States

Age group	*1860 North*	*1850 South*	*1860 South*	*1890*	*1900*	*1910*	*1920*	*1930*
Under 25	234	334	398	562	718	756	758	865
25–34	162	247	289	421	543	550	565	670
35–44	108	160	170	301	353	373	397	463
45–54	74	123	132	230	290	268	302	346
55–64	54	117	68	167	207	211	207	247
65 & over	46	108	83	118	149	151	165	164

Source: Atack (1989), Table 3.

In that sense, even the information reported in a single federal census still held out the prospect of ownership by the time farmers reached midlife (either between thirty-five and forty-four or forty-five and fifty-four years of age). Whereas more than three-quarters of farmers under twenty-five in the northern states were owners in 1860, that proportion had fallen to less than 15 per cent in all the states, north and south, by 1930 (table 8.2). But the decline in ownership among farmers in midlife was not as dramatic. Although circumstances had changed dramatically since the close of public land distribution in the 1890s, better than half of all farmers between thirty-five and forty-four owned their land in 1930 and nearly two-thirds could expect to own their farm by age fifty-four, across the entire United States. In effect, while questions remained about social renewal in rural America, the work of Black and Allen and of Atack emphasizes that most farmers were still owners by midlife.

Unfortunately, tenancy cannot be tracked as consistently over time in the state census of agriculture conducted in Kansas. In only two years, 1885 and 1920, is a land-tenure question posed of farm households. The relative disinterest in tenancy stands in stark contrast to the federal census, which intensified its gaze in response to the growth of tenant farming and sharecropping in the South following the Civil War. Labour-intensive crops like cotton were ill-suited to the drier and cooler climate of Kansas and never entered into the state in significant ways.[26] Recent settlement, access to public land into the 1890s, and the predominance of grain farming and family organization made tenancy

Table 8.3
Proportion of farmers who were owners and renters, rates per thousand, by age group, Kansas, 1885 and 1920

	1885		*1920*		
	Owner	*Renter*	*Owner*	*Part renter*	*Renter*
Under 25	704	296	155	86	759
25–34	783	217	287	109	604
35–44	901	99	537	128	335
45–54	934	66	659	134	207
55–64	954	46	813	80	107
65 & over	924	76	812	94	94

Source: Kansas township sample, number of responses: n=1,800 in 1885, n=2,166 in 1920.

less important and assured that the issue was addressed only intermittently in Kansas enumerations. The picture that can be reconstructed from our sample data in 1885 and 1920 illustrates that ownership was very high in Kansas during the settlement period but that by 1920 the rates were comparable to national trends.[27]

In frontier Kansas, rates of ownership for young farmers in 1885 were quite similar to rates across the Northern states fifteen years earlier, in the federal census of 1860 (table 8.2), and much higher than the post-frontier North 1890 rates, at every age. By 1920, as Kansas matured, its young farmers faced tenancy in almost identical proportions to the national rates. The only distinct difference from national rates in 1920 is found in the rates reported in midlife in the Kansas state returns, with fewer farmers listed exclusively as renters in the state than in the country as a whole, especially between ages forty-five and fifty-four, when only one-fifth were still renters compared to nearly one-third nationally. But if part-renters are added, the rates in Kansas are indistinguishable from the national figures.

The progressive access to land over the life course in 1885 is reflected in the difference in average age between renters (n=226) and owners (n=1,700), who were 35.3 and 43.5 years of age respectively. By 1920, the tenancy categories reported in the Kansas state census still fit the life course model. The average age, respectively, of renters (n=923), part-renters (n=269), and owners (n=1,299) was 35.1, 41.3, and 47.3. Farmers who stayed in agriculture had a reasonable expectation of ownership as they reached middle age. But the opportunities for young farmers had dramatically narrowed by the 1920s, and renting was firmly fixed as a part of the life cycle of farmers in Kansas.

FARM SCALE AND STRUCTURE

While opportunity for the young was narrowing, part of the reason that ownership remained within reach was that farm sizes did not grow dramatically in the era before 1940. This point is worth emphasizing because the microdata do not support the widespread view in the literature that large commercial farms were pushing smallholders off the land.[28] Rather than a pattern of land use fully immersed in technological change, the portrait that emerges from the microdata highlights generally conservative mixed farming practices and modest increases in average farm size. Instead of tractors, harvesters, monoculture, and corporate farming, family farms took advantage of the wider availability of land in the early stages of settlement to retain control of the lion's share of landed property throughout the period.[29] This limited the scope for outsiders or newcomers to disrupt an internally regulated process of land redistribution and social renewal. The interplay between individual growth and local property distributions is more evident in a place-based sample (like this one) where individual trajectories are traced over time and community conditions measured at similar time-varying intervals. Rather than an age-stratified contrast at a single point in time, repeated measures of individuals offer a reading of trajectories of change, in the context of changing opportunity structures.

In other words, the signs of life cycle growth visible at a single time point come into even stronger relief when farm households are observed over time. When the degree of social persistence – measured as the proportion of households linked from one population census to the next – remained high, the local demand for land added to the social and economic pressure for redistribution. Young farmers could still expand during a typical farm career, without displacing their neighbours from the land or increasing the proportion of landless labour, but as the pool of locally available land was increasingly fixed, opportunities for growth were even more dependent on local property distributions. The most striking aspect of this interplay between availability and life chances is the strong association between social persistence and parity between farms. This was actually most pronounced in the region of the state where the soil and climate might have supported much larger commercial wheat farms.

Opportunities for acquisition by big proprietors tended to happen in areas where environmental conditions were more challenging, either because the soil was of varying quality or the climate more arid. In these settings, the higher turnover is visible in the proportion of persons and households who did not link forward in time from one census to the next.[30] As the results in table 8.4 suggest, this kind of high turnover was more common during the early settlement process. But as farm households adjusted to the new environments and found land use regimes that worked best, the levels of household persistence grew and stabilized. The main exception is the far western part of the state where high turnover did not go away.

The higher turnover in population mirrored the unequal distribution of farmland in these far western communities. There was a core of midsized producers in each, but the churn in population also created opportunities for large commercial farms to take shape. Nearly all of the large proprietors in the microdata are in the far western part of the state. For example, only twenty-six out of 22,540 farms in the dataset report farm operations above 5,000 acres in size. Only one of these was located in the eastern half of the state. In the western part of the state, farms over 5,000 acres were all located in Kearny, Lane, Stevens, and Wallace Counties – the places that experienced the greatest population turnover – and most of these operations focused on raising beef. However, most of these corporate entities did not exist for longer than five years. And, in January of 1931 Kansas passed legislation banning corporate farming of certain crops, including wheat, arguing that "it is contrary to public policy to permit a corporation to acquire large blocks of land."[31]

Regional differences are striking when we compare the levels of inequality that emerged over time. Disparities in reported farm size are summarized here using a common statistical method known as the Gini coefficient. The measure has found wide application in the study of inequality because it is a ratio rather than a mean. The coefficient ranges from 0 to 1, with values at the low end of the scale indicating a more even distribution and values at the high end representing distributions close to perfect inequality. Gini coefficients of 0.40 are considered to be quite high.[32] The Gini coefficients for the reported farm sizes were calculated for each of the study communities and are plotted over time in figure 8.2. Townships are reported separately within each land-use region to give a sense of the variation. The comparisons suggest that the within-region variation was rather muted but that the

Table 8.4

Social persistence, measured as the proportion of household heads in the population censuses linking forward over time, 1860–1930

Region	*County*	*1860*	*1865*	*1870*	*1875*	*1880*	*1885*	*1895*	*1900*	*1905*	*1910*	*1915*	*1920*	*1925*	*1930*
Corn	Doniphan		24	47	47	51	62	41	53	65	50	59	52	54	55
Belt	Nemaha		20	38	38	47	43	28	55	53	58	60	43	57	44
	Republic				7	34	47	41	56	54	51	68	47	76	42
	Smith					22	55	40	51	54	50	55	62	62	60
Mixed	Allen		38	4	34	38		20	47	48	45	46	55	54	61
farming	Crawford				34	49		33	56	57	47	52	54	62	65
	Franklin		28	25	32	41	45	29	37	56	51	49	46	61	59
Bluestem	Chase		11	22	34	31	42	38	46	45	51	57	60	58	56
pastures	Chautauqua				5	42	29	33	43	49	52	52	47	46	59
	Wabaunsee		58	30	48	43	42	44	59	61	44	57	56	59	69
Central	Dickinson		33	12	31	34	51	53	59	51	43	51	48	69	57
wheat	Ellsworth				20		60	52	57	59	50	63	42	70	45
belt	Sedgwick				5	38	40	39	55	47	52	50	57	62	46
	PAawnee				1	9	51	43	57	53	52	48	53	54	70
	Pratt							20	41	36	22	38	46	47	68
	Rooks							56	64	58	48	59	51	57	57
Wheat	Cheyenne						7	2	57	53	47	74	48	68	74
cattle	Decatur						26	40	43	52	49	64	47	50	65
sorghum	Ford							52	62	59	50	63	55	63	70
	Kearny								35	42	7	59	43	35	32
	Lane						30			30	38	53	43	48	60
	Stevens								54	27	9	55	32	52	58
	Thomas							3	52		21	40	36	46	31
	Trego							4	30	35	56	60	51	78	80
	Wallace							0	45	40	20	49	53	46	54
	Average		30	25	26	37	42	32	51	49	42	55	49	57	57

Source: Kansas township sample.

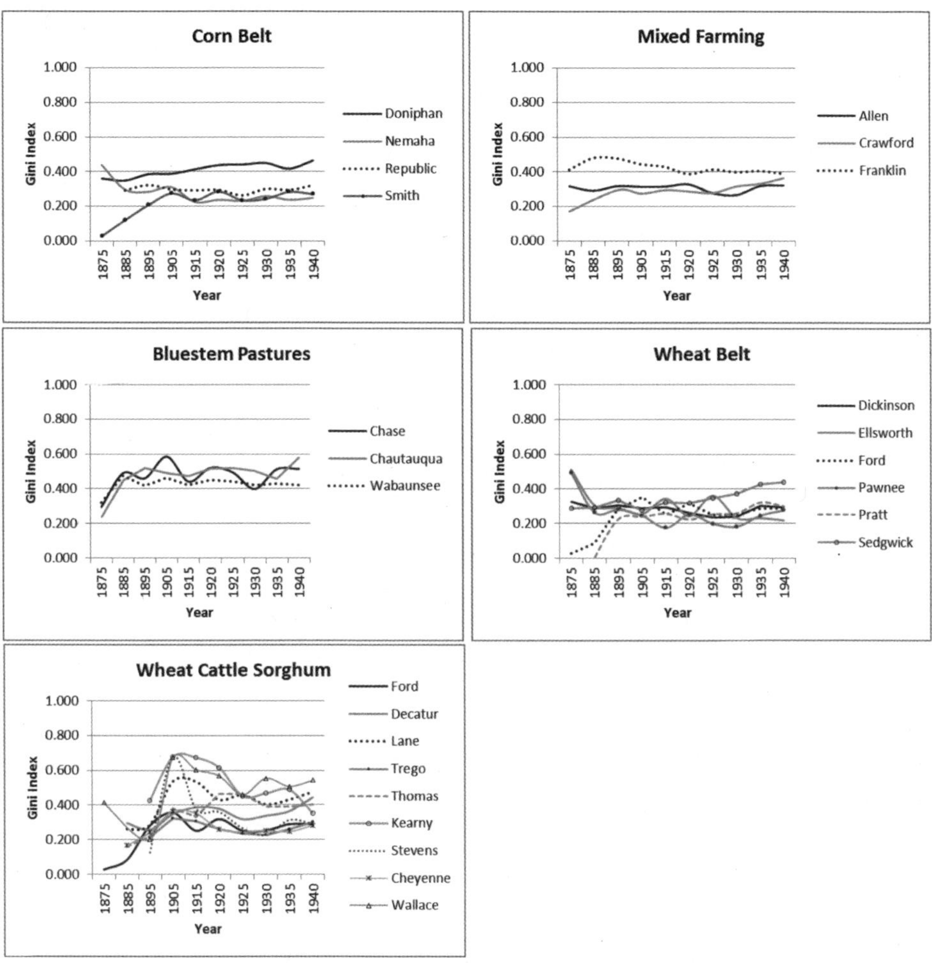

Figure 8.2 Township Gini coefficients, by region and year

far western part of the state is quite different with dramatic fluctuations in land distribution and a much higher range of Gini coefficients for a few townships. Perhaps equally striking is the relatively narrow range of the Gini coefficients in the big wheat-growing region in the center of the state. The parity of farm sizes among the wheat-growing farms bears some relation to the lower levels of population turnover.[33]

Two-way scatter plots also illustrate how different circumstances were in the far western region of the state. Figure 8.3 segments or pools the data into two periods and plots reported farm sizes according to the

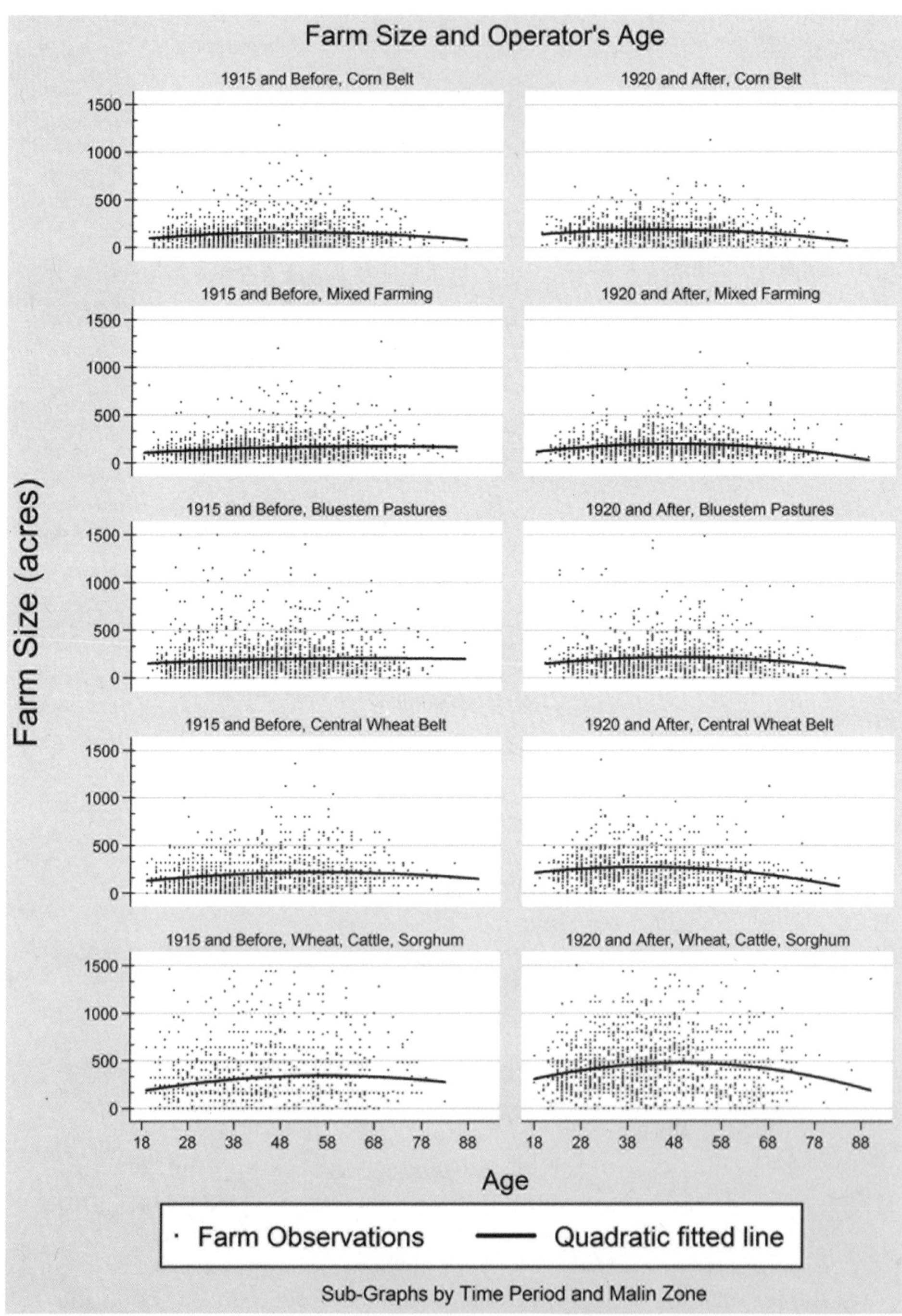

Figure 8.3 Two-way scatter of farm sizes by age, segmented by region and time period, fitted with quadratic curves: Kansas sample township farms 1,500 acres or smaller

age of the farm operator. Excluding values above 1,500 acres, the scattergrams reveal how tightly farms in the eastern half of the state clustered around the farm sizes framed by public land policy. The basic quarter-section land grant was 160 acres, and few farms in the Corn Belt or mixed farming regions were much larger than two quarter sections, in either period. The dispersion of farm sizes further west was quite different. Not only was the range of farm sizes greater but the dispersion visibly shifted higher after 1920, especially in the far west. The dispersion in the bluestem and Wheat Belt regions was higher, as well, but did not increase as much by the second era.

The broadest similarity between all the regions, on the other hand, is the more pronounced and age-specific pattern – the more curvilinear relationship between farm size and age – in the period after WWI. Farm size appeared less dependent on age-specific access in the settlement era, when distributions were uniformly flatter across the life course. Whether a farmer was eighteen or eighty-eight seems to have made little difference no matter where one lived in Kansas. But after WWI, the pattern is shaped by life-course dynamics. Farms were noticeably larger in midlife and the quadratic lines fit through the data points are more distinctly curvilinear. Ironically, this life-course pattern was more pronounced in the far west, where an eighteen-year-old farmer had a much stronger expectation of growing their farm into midlife after, rather than before, WWI. Another reading of the difference is simply that there was less access across the life course in the later period. And with lower chances of gaining entry to farming, those with access to land had a strong expectation of growth across the life cycle.

PREDICTING FARM SIZE GROWTH

In this final section, we disentangle the relative impacts of inequality and social renewal a little further. By pooling data in a slightly different way, we try to identify the relative impacts of period and social process on individual growth trajectories. As we have seen, age-stratified comparisons of single censuses offer strong evidence that opportunity was narrowing for young farmers, but signs of social renewal and life cycle process are still visible well after the closing of the frontier. Access to public land generated enormous opportunity in different places and times, but we still can say very little about how inequality and social renewal fed into the prospects for growth. Rather than treat the life circumstances as discrete, our approach here tries to evaluate the relative contributions of inequality and social persistence by examining repeated observations of individuals and the contexts in which growth occurred.

Our data are appropriate for multilevel or repeated measures modeling because they represent a clustered longitudinal sample. Multiple years of farm observations are linked over time, farms are nested within townships that have specific characteristics, and the changing conditions in the townships can be summarized in time-varying covariates. Each township has a different number of units of analysis and a different number of time points at which the outcome is measured. Therefore the dataset is considered unbalanced. Farms do not enter and exit at the same time because the townships were settled at different times, but because observations are linked over time, the estimates of growth trajectories "borrow strength" from all the observed values and the repetition of observations.[34] We use a mixed-effects model (the xtmixed procedure in Stata) to fit estimates of the determinants of farm-size growth, using individual-level predictors like land use and livestock, because land-use choices are distinct from farm size and township-level covariates, which measure changing levels of inequality and social persistence.

In the panel design, the model estimates the relationship of farm size, FS_{ijt}, for farm *i* in township *j* in year *t*. In the full model, the model estimates $FS_{ijt} = b1\ X_{ijt} + b2\ R_j + b3\ P_{jt} + b4\ G_{jt} + f_j + T_t + e_{ijt}$ where X_{ijt} is a vector of variables describing land-use practices chosen by farm *i* in township *j* in year *t*, including crop choices and the presence of livestock; R_j is a zero-one dummy for whether the farm was located in the wheat, cattle, sorghum region; P_{jt} is a time-varying vector of the level of social persistence in each township; and G_{jt} is a time-varying vector of the farm-size inequality in each township. We also estimate several fixed effects, including a vector f_j of effects for each farm, a vector of time T_t, and an error term e_{ijt}.

The model estimates presented in table 8.5 are also segmented by three time periods. The first model is for the period 1875 to 1895, the second 1905 to 1920, and the third 1925 to 1940. The maximum number of times a farm can be observed in each panel is three times in the first two periods and four in the last period. Readers should note as well that average number of repeated observations increases over time. By the last period 9,025 farms are observed and 4,930 farms are observed at least twice. The township covariates are listed at the top of the predicted results, followed by the coefficient for time, the coefficients for the farm-level covariates, and the regional effect of being located in the far west.

Table 8.5
Multilevel panel estimates of farm size growth, segmented by period, 1875–1940

		1875–95	*1905–20*	*1925–40*
Farm Size		*Coef.*	*Coef.*	*Coef*
Persistence		–41.030***	–108.468**	90.127***
Gini		0.063	3.476***	1.895***
Year		–0.649**	1.464**	3.200***
Wheat Acres		0.839***	0.931***	1.167***
Corn Acres		1.176***	0.946***	1.277***
Pasture Acres		0.609***	0.608***	0.817***
Milk Cattle		1.906***	0.485	1.858***
Beef Cattle		1.674***	3.292***	1.140***
Wheat Cattle Sorghum Region (dummy)		93.682***	107.967***	61.217***
Number of Obs		5,308	7,080	9,025
Number of Groups	Farms	4,315	5,138	4,930
Number of Groups	Townships	25	25	25
Obs per Group	Farm Level – min	1	1	1
	avg	1.2	1.4	1.8
	max	3	3	4
Obs per Group	Township Level – min	12	104	116
	avg	212.3	283.2	361.0
	max	431	528	676
		Random-effects Parameter Estimates		
Township Std Dev(cons)		32.465	36.694	43.754
Farm Std Dev(cons)		35.693	0.0002	42.982
Standard Dev(residual)		101.084	278.236	155.382
$chi^2(2)$=		220.820***	398.230***	420.54***

Significance Levels ***< 0.01 **< 0.05 *< 0.10

In spite of the very flat time trends suggested above, the pooling of the data into three time periods does reveal more dynamic shifts over time: From a negative estimate for every year under observation in the earliest period, to a predicted increase of 1.5 acres between 1905 and 1920, and 3.2 acres between 1925 and 1940, the average time trend in the data accelerated over time. Land use also contributed to farm-size growth in different ways across the three periods. Wheat, for instance, continued to grow in importance while corn was less important during the boom years leading up to the First World War. Pasture acres were a consistently significant predictor and a slightly stronger predictor in the period after 1920. Livestock also played a varied role depending on the era, with milk cattle more important to the prospects for growth during the early settlement era and again in the 1920s and 1930s and beef cattle being more strongly associated with farm size growth during the boom and war years from 1905 to 1920.

More compelling, perhaps, are the estimates for the contributions of the community levels measures of social persistence and inequality. In a sense, these are measures not just of distributions at a given moment in time but statistics that summarize longer processes that have taken place over the preceding interval of time. Broken into distinct periods, the most striking result is the large shift in direction in the effect of social persistence. We have measured this as the proportion of households in the population census that remain in the community at the next census. It is a good proxy for the local demand for land, of the population "in waiting," and the estimates clearly suggest that during the first two periods the higher the level of social persistence, the smaller the growth in farm size. For every point increase in social persistence from one census to the next, farm size is predicted to drop by forty-one acres in the period from 1875–95 and by 108 acres in the period from 1905–20. In the 1920s and 1930s there was a reversal; growth was more strongly associated with communities in which persistence edged higher. Every point higher on the social persistence scale added a predicted ninety acres to farm size.

In effect, the very flat growth trajectories that we saw in the scatterplots above in the period before 1920 reflected a pattern of more equal access to land across the life course. With more public land available, long-resident farmers and newcomers took advantage of greater access to expand the distribution of land and to redistribute land, and average farm sizes declined as a result. But when this set of structural circumstances changed, when access to land was determined more by long-resident families themselves, the route to growth was increasingly shaped by being a member of the persistent population. When family farms closed off access to new entrants by remaining on the land, they continued to promote a kind of parity between neighbours but also to reinforce the importance of life-cycle processes. This made it difficult for young farmers to own land at the beginning of their careers but kept farm acquisition within reach. The estimates for Gini scores in table 8.5, for instance, suggest that social persistence loomed larger in the transition between these eras. The association of inequality with growth was very modest and lower in the 1920s and 1930s than in the boom years before and during World War I.

CONCLUSIONS

The Kansas farms encountered here are not really the stuff of regional legend. Most grew too modestly to be forerunners of agricultural revolution. The growth in farm scale and inequality occurred mainly in more challenging environmental settings in western Kansas. Geography was not destiny in every case. Some communities were able to make the best of the drier climate and the uneven distribution of arable soils. The combination of population turnover and environmental challenge did generally lead to dramatic growth in landed inequality. In the far west, where combined cattle and grain farms were best suited to make use of an expansive and varied landscape, the less stable fortunes of the large western ranches and farms created opportunities for newcomers and like-sized and like-minded enterprises. Although their numbers were never overwhelming, the presence of large farm operations made it more difficult at times for young farmers to enter into agriculture.

Elsewhere families that took advantage of the wide availability of land during early settlement remained in control of patterns of land redistribution. Often the opportunities of subsequent generations were in the hands of the frontier generations. The patterns of mobility were always visible in single censuses stratified by age and ownership. But examined from a longitudinal perspective, the social processes loom larger. The impact of social renewal on prospects for growth is amplified when the actors' fortunes are examined over time and the periods segmented more clearly. The norms of wide access and redistribution were boosted by the availability of public land. Farm sizes fell during the settlement era. Yet the norms of redistribution were renewed by successor generations, and individual prospects for growth depended even more on social continuity into the 1920s. As long as family farms grew modestly in size, without pushing their neighbours off the land or increasing the proportion of landless labour, ownership remained within reach. Although the door was certainly less open for the rural youth that came to maturity once land was in private hands, the social parity created by settler families and by public land policy had enormous inertia. Rather than a departure from earlier American norms, Kansas agriculture in the early twentieth century fits comfortably within a larger story of making and remaking family-sized farms in the American experience.

PART THREE

Mobility in the Urban World

9

Ladders of Mobility in a Fast-Growing Industrial City: Two by Two and Twenty Years Later

SHERRY OLSON

To twenty-year-old students still living in the city where they were born, the challenges of finding work and starting a family appear novel, different from what their parents encountered at that age, and social networking seems to them a new technique for seizing opportunities. Yet this was already the case in Montreal a century ago. The twenty-year clip 1881–1901, approaching the perspective of a generation, brackets a spectacular surge of city building and a deep crisis of unemployment. To explore the social networks of the city and personal trajectories, we have to find new ways of interrogating our promising new digital resources. From the suite of census "snapshots," can we generate a "moving picture"?[1]

With that concern in mind, I took the census population recorded in Montreal and its suburbs in April 1881 and searched for each person in the nominative census of 1901. The 40,000 individuals retrieved (24 per cent), amount to one-third of estimated survivors. This chapter reports the methods, the survival rates we applied, and the implications of our findings for an understanding of the dynamics of residential choice and personal risk in a metropolis characterized by fast growth, cultural encounter, and extremes of wealth and poverty. Moves within the city, as well as migration into the city, were strategies for getting ahead, and the matching exercise yields evidence for access to property and access to kin as particular ladders of social mobility in the city.

Since "greater Montreal" nearly doubled in size in the twenty-year span (from 180,000 to 325,000 population), it was a "sink" like Chica-

Table 9.1
Retrieval of persons fifteen to twenty-four versus all other ages, by gender and cultural community

	Percentage retrieved in the census of 1901 of expected survivors							
	French Catholic		*Irish Catholic*		*Protestant*		*Entire population*	
Age 1881	*Male*	*Female*	*Male*	*Female*	*Male*	*Female*	*Male*	*Female*
15–24	27.6	28.5	23.6	21.0	16.9	19.5	24.6	25.0
Other	40.0	33.8	39.3	31.0	34.7	32.0	38.6	32.9
All	37.1	32.4	35.5	28.1	30.9	28.9	35.3	30.8

Sources: Census of Canada 1881 and 1901 for Montreal and suburbs

go, with heavy arrivals, especially of young women. The cultural balance was unusual: French Canadian (54 per cent rising to two-thirds), Irish Catholic (28 per cent, falling), and Protestant (18 per cent). The "tricultural" Montreal, based on bivariate assignment by religion and language, covers 99 per cent of the population of the city and its suburbs in 1881, 96 per cent in 1901. The mix contributed to a volatile cultural politics, since Irish Catholics shared their religion with the French-speaking and their language with the Protestant community. One-third of Protestants reported Irish origins, and Irish Catholic women accounted for a majority of mixed marriages.[2]

On a simple age criterion, we distinguish two populations both of which, I shall argue, have potential uses. As shown in table 9.1, those in the fifteen to twenty-four age group in 1881 are, as we might expect from studies elsewhere, hard to find: I retrieved fewer than one-quarter of those presumed to have survived. They are a large group (22 per cent of the entire population), heterogeneous, and we cannot assume that those retrieved are fully representative. For all other age groups – 78 per cent of the population – we shall see that those retrieved are reasonably representative and constitute a sample large and reliable enough to uncover parameters of household formation and dissolution, the trends of intraurban geographic moves, and a net upward social mobility.

The richness of nominative sources and improved digital access to census data are, as this volume demonstrates, magnificent attractions, but they tempt the scholar to narrow the sphere of research to a census profile, much like the proverbial drunk searching for the house key under the streetlamp. The case of Montreal suggests ways to extend the limits of what in the past seemed feasible, and each of the two age sets points to a research frontier beyond analysis of the "census family" and its internal structure. First, the intercensal linkages grounded in the "good sample" identify relationships *between* census households and offer evidence that such relationships mattered: they affected the way the city was organized. Second, the hard-to-match youth who escaped the net, merit more sustained attention. In transit between a family of origin and a family of destination, many of them were living as boarders on the fringes of a census family or were attached to uncommon types of census households, and their choices open up dimensions of risk. The paper is therefore organized in three parts. The first reports the methods employed, the second presents observations based on the "good sample," and the third discusses what we can discover from the hard-to-find set and how we might pursue them.

METHODS

The prime sources are a full digital set of 1881 census records for Montreal and its suburbs and, for the census of 1901, a full digital index that lists first and last names, age, birthdate, marital status, and relation to a designated head of household.[3] The method involves attention to dyadic cues (two by two), attention to addresses, and an attempt to partition the losses. To evaluate the extent to which the identifiable survivors were representative of the 1881 population, we must assess the losses to deaths, departures, name changes, census skips, and unrecognized identities.

Two by Two

In the matching process I depended primarily on names, using a dyadic strategy, that is, searching for people in pairs. The reference to a second person overcomes the problems of homonyms. Identifiable pairs in 1881, some of whom turn up in a 1901 household as well, include the 25,000 married couples, 37,000 mother-and-daughter dyads, and all the imaginable pairings of siblings, in the order of a million pairs among 73,757 offspring, of those mothers. We observe, in fact, scores of dyads whose relationship was unsuspected and remains unspecified although the two people shared a dwelling at both dates. Confirmation of identities for any dyad that recurs is nearly always reliable if we have the sur-

Table 9.2
Retrieval rates by characteristics of the individual and household in 1881: ethnicity, sex, age, relatedness, marital status, residential, and occupational status

	Population	*Percentage retrieved*		*Percentage*
	N	*of sought*	*of survivors*	*unrelated*
Ethnicity				
French Catholic	100,750	24.8	34.6	10.7
Irish Catholic	28,148	21.0	29.7	14.5
Protestant	40,341	21.7	29.8	12.5
Jewish	832	19.8		
Other	1,090	15.8		
Sex				
Female	91,174	22.3	30.8	14.8
Male	79,985	24.5	35.4	8.2
Age groups				
a <5 years	23,246	29.9	39.8	1.6
b 5–14	35,198	29.9	35.6	3.1
c 15–24	37,469	19.9	25.1	18.7
d 25–44	48,616	24.0	33.4	14.2
e 45–59	17,281	16.8	33.1	13.5
f >60	9,296	4.5	53.8	25.7
All	171,106	23.3	32.9	11.7
Relatedness				
Related *	151,064	25.9		
Unrelated	20,094	4.2		
Marital status				
Single	105,227	23.5	30.2	15.3
Married	57,322	25.0	39.9	1.5
Widowed	8,611	10.0	25.3	36.4
Residential status				
5 high	8,188	20.4	30.3	
4	8,121	20.6	24.3	
3	22,131	22.2	16.0	
2	49,026	24.8	8.3	
1 low	29,832	27.9	5.2	
Unspecified	53,863	20.8	12.0	
Occupational status .				
ab High	43,484	23.4	14.8	
cd Mid	31,133	25.7	6.8	
ef Low	75,562	24.0	11.7	
Unspecified	20,982	17.1	12.7	

Sources: Census of Canada 1881 and 1901 for Montreal and suburbs

name, first name, sex, and age of the two persons, with considerable tolerance for age. For analytic purposes, we use the variables of personal identity available in 1881 to distinguish the three cultural communities and sort them by sex and marital status into five-year age groups. Table 9.2 shows summary characteristics for the 1881 population targeted for search and for the individuals retrieved in the 1901 records.

In view of the bilingual nature of the city and its documents, matching called for experience, complementary source material, and manual detail.[4] I used FoxPro for DOS to set up numerous indexing variables, screen displays that triggered visual pattern recognition, and queries variously age-specific, sex-specific, and specific to widowers or servants. Computer queries tested for incongruities of age that might arise from confusion of father and son or mother and daughter who bore the same names.

A long series of record-matching exercises had allowed us to make numerous corrections to the 1881 digital file such as confirmation of maiden names for married women from parish registers.[5] A small sample (based on a selection of twelve surnames), matched to a wider variety of sources from 1840 to 1920, had shown how cultural variables such as religion, language, and national origin affected the comparability of sources as well as the chances that an individual would survive twenty years, marry, conceive, or make a move. Within the regional pool of records, the chief worry was never the mismatch. The problem is the no-match and the incidence of missing persons.

The Significance of an Address

Because the assessed rental value of a dwelling is an excellent indicator of household purchasing power, recovery of addresses is central to my appraisal of social status. The census of 1901 records a street address for the household but on a separate schedule, cross-referenced by page and line number.[6] For 1881, I assigned address from the municipal tax roll, which specifies the run of addresses on each property and associates with it a cadastral lot number and the array of householders on the premises.[7] For each occupant household, whether owner or tenant, the tax roll records the trade or profession of the householder and the annual rental value. The matching of census and tax roll, achieved for 70 per cent of census households within the city limits, allows us to evaluate the income selectivity of a set of data: Have we captured as large a proportion of low-rent households as high-rent households?[8]

Table 9.3
Street segments rated and standardized by median rent level, 1881 and 1901

Rent level	*Median rent $/year*		*Census households (%)*	
	1881	*1901*	*1881*	*1901*
5 High	300–710	350–800	7.0	8.1
4	170–299	181–349	6.9	8.3
3	80–169	101–180	18.9	14.8
2	50–79	66–100	41.8	41.3
1 Low	20–49	24–65	25.4	27.4
All			100.0	100.0
Mean level			2.3	2.3

Sources : Municipal tax rolls of June 1880 and June 1900

Table 9.4
Rent level indicators of social status for household heads of selected occupations

	Household heads by occupation group			
	Median rent $ per year		*Mean rent level street of residence*	
	1881	*1901*	*1881*	*1901*
Merchants	220	300	3.2	3.2
Accountants	200	160	3.6	3.1
Bookkeepers	120	140	2.8	3.3
Printers	60	90	2.3	2.2
Machinists	60	80	2.0	1.9
Moulders	50	70	1.7	1.7
Carpenters	50	80	1.8	1.8
Carters	50	70	1.5	1.6
Labourers	40	60	1.6	1.6

Sources: Census of 1881 and 1901, tax roll of 1880 and 1900

For household heads of a particular occupation or profession, the median of their rents is a convenient yardstick of occupational status. Neighbourhoods, too, can be classed by the median rent of resident households. In this paper I employ the median rent of small, rather homogeneous aggregates, microneighbourhoods we call "street segments."[9] As a next step, I class the segments into five intervals of median

Table 9.5
Rent level indicators of social status by cultural community

	Mean rent level, street of residence	
Cultural community	*1881*	*1901*
French Catholic	1.8	1.9
Irish Catholic	2.1	2.2
Protestant	2.9	3.0
Jewish		2.6
Italian		2.1
All households	2.2	2.3

Sources: Census of 1881 and 1901, tax roll of 1880 and 1900

rent (table 9.3) and employ the categories as an indicator of socioeconomic status of a person or a household living in that street. In this way we can characterize populations (e.g. an ethnic community) by mean rent level (weighted from one for the lowest to five for the highest rents). In view of a general modest trend to larger dwellings at higher rents, I calibrated the categories of residential status to obtain the same proportional distribution at either date.

The sensitivity of these categories can be seen in table 9.4 for a selection of occupations and in table 9.5 for the several cultural communities. The measure reflects the fine grain of residential segregation by ethnicity and status. Although the original geographic boundaries of the census tracts of 1881 and 1901 are hopelessly incongruent, precision of assignment to lots or street segments allows us, using GIS (computerized geographic information systems), to reaggregate the 1901 addresses for comparison with 1881 tracts and to estimate distances between households with greater precision.[10]

Relative to 1881, the city of 1901 shows a somewhat larger share of French Canadians, fewer married people under age twenty-one, fewer children under age five, in the reported work force a smaller share of labourers and many more young women, and among waged women a smaller proportion of domestic servants. There is little change in distribution of sizes of domestic households (mean of five persons), the share headed by women, or the very large share (85 per cent) of "simple" households consisting of parents and their children, the couple without children, or a surviving parent with children.[11] Commercial boardinghouses (three or more boarders) increased in mean size, and institutions expanded, several to more than a thousand inmates. Except for the greater numbers institutionalized (3 per cent in 1901), none of the changes should have a noticeable effect on the prospects for recognizing an 1881 individual.

Expectations

Across the twenty-year gap, what would be realistic expectations of match rates? Of the five prime reasons for a no-match, we can assert some control over three. The individual may have died, may have moved away from the city, may have taken a new "married" name, or may have been missed by census-takers of 1901. The fifth, of greatest import, is a well-known array of misapprehensions of spelling, handwriting, and transcription such as Gordon Darroch describes in chapter 5. Let us focus briefly on each problem in turn.

Studies half a century ago inferred enormous rates of departure from North American industrial cities because they did not take mortality into account.[12] In Montreal, deaths account for overall losses of 30 per cent. Patricia Thornton's Montreal life tables for 1881 show that survival rates by age and sex differed in important ways among the three cultural communities. From her tables we estimated expected numbers of survivors for each cell in the partition by sex, ethnicity, and five-year age group. Among Montrealers born in the nineteenth century, only half survived twenty years. Of couples newly married in 1881, 60 per cent would survive intact to century's end. Heavy as the losses are, they do not explain the failure to capture fifteen to twenty-four-year-olds, since their chances of survival were best, above 80 per cent.[13]

For departures from the city, I used the small surname samples for the decades of the 1860s and 1890s to estimate a rate of 10 per cent per decade or 19 per cent over twenty years. Out-migrants were concentrated in the same range of ages (fifteen to twenty-four) as in-migrants and missing persons, a little higher for men than women. In-migration was indeed high (fewer than half of young adults were born in Montreal), but departures from the urban "sink" were low.

Most of the women still single at twenty in 1881 would marry and change their names before 1901, and of girls under ten, half. To enhance recovery of females who married in the interval, I took advantage of digital marriage records – excellent for Catholics, not so good for Protestants.[14] From 39,052 marriages celebrated in Catholic parishes of Montreal 1881–1901, I matched 12,000 first-married brides to their families of origin in the 1881 census (31 per cent), 10,000 first-married grooms to their families of origin in 1881 (26 per cent), and 12,000 of the newly married couples (18 per cent) to couples or widowed parties named in the 1901 census index. Using the double or triple link to a marriage record, I could then (automatically) link a set of people who were single in 1881 to the census record of 1901. That rather tedious detour – linking 34,000 census records to a marriage record – produced only 4,000 automated matches of an individual between the two censuses. I then selected 8,500 cases I had set aside of a second (or third) marriage between 1881 and 1901 (2,500 women and 6,000 men). Tracking these people retrieved 750 more women and 2,000 more men who in 1881 were living with the earlier spouse or who were widowed and not yet remarried. The many changes of marital status disclose the mobility suggested by Kippen and McCalman (chapter 2) and were often associated with changes of employment or occupational status.

Census takers missed 10 per cent of the lowest-rent households in 1861, fewer in 1881.[15] However small the risk of missing a household, matching two censuses constitutes double jeopardy, and missing or inaccurate information in either census makes the individual harder to recognize. Age heaping, for example, severe in the 1881 data but much reduced in 1901, forces us to tolerate age differences as great as seven years.

All our earlier experience had demonstrated that we were not likely to achieve matches for more than two-thirds, as a result of illegible microfilm, mistaken handwriting, bizarre spellings, and homonyms – the John Smiths and Mary Ryans.[16] In all our matching ventures, even among records of the same year, we repeatedly reached a point of diminishing returns at 68 to 70 per cent.[17] The familiar array of problems is aggravated in Montreal as a result of bilingual records, linguistic mismatches between census taker and respondent, and (a century later) errors of transcription from the handwritten documents.[18]

Having established death rates, exit rates, and limits to matching, I set the targets for acceptable retrieval at half the number of expected survivors. To my disappointment, I achieved only one-third (32.9 per cent). Finding rates vary with ethnicity and sex, as well as age, as we saw in table 9.1, with further detail for marital and economic status in table 9.2. In most age groups retrieval rates are between 30 and 40 per cent of expected survivors, at ages fifteen to twenty-four they are closer to 20 per cent. What is more encouraging is the rather close fit of the

Table 9.6
Characteristics of populations sought and recovered, split by ages

	Age in 1881 under 15 or over 24				*Age in 1881 15–24 years*			
	Population 1881		*Retrieved 1901*		*Population 1881*		*Retrieved 1901*	
	N	*Col. %*	*N*	*%*	*N*	*Col. %*	*N*	*Col. %*
Ethnicity								
French Catholic	78,681	58.9	19,913	61.3	22,069	58.9	5,030	67.3
Irish Catholic	21,610	16.2	4,814	14.8	6,538	17.4	1,105	14.8
Protestant	31,853	23.8	7,479	23.0	8,488	22.7	1,265	16.9
Jewish	690	0.5	136	0.4	142	0.4	29	0.4
Other	858	0.6	129	0.4	232	0.6	43	0.6
Total	133,692	100.0	32,471	100.0	37,469	100.0	7,472	100.0
Sex								
Female	69,865	52.3	16,009	49.3	21,309	56.9	4,308	57.7
Male	63,825	47.7	16,462	50.7	16,160	43.1	3,164	42.3
Age groups								
a <5 years	23,246	17.4	6,942	21.4				
b 5–14	35,198	26.3	10,536	32.4				
d 25–44	48,616	36.4	11,670	35.9				
e 45–59	17,281	12.9	2,900	8.9				
f >60	9,296	7.0	416	1.3				
Unknown	55	0.0	7	0.0				
Relatedness								
Related	120,583	90.2	31,921	98.3	30,481	81.3	7,176	96.0
Unrelated	13,106	9.8	549	1.7	6,988	18.7	296	4.0
Marital status								
Single	73,884	55.3	18,909	58.2	31,343	83.7	5,855	78.4
Married	51,322	38.4	12,713	39.2	6,000	16.0	1,603	21.5
Widowed	8,485	6.3	849	2.6	126	0.3	14	0.2
Residential status								
5 High	6,104	4.6	1,396	4.3	2,084	5.6	278	3.7
4	6,109	4.6	1,401	4.3	2,012	5.4	270	3.6
3	17,060	12.8	4,083	12.6	5,071	13.5	834	11.2
2	38,895	29.1	9,964	30.7	10,131	27.0	2,173	29.1
1 Low	23,974	17.9	6,769	20.8	5,858	15.6	1,548	20.7
Unspecified	41,550	31.1	8,858	27.3	12,313	32.9	2,369	31.7
Occupational status								
ab High	37,193	27.8	8,766	27.0	8,302	22.2	1,496	20.0
cd Mid	25,384	19.0	6,639	20.4	6,137	16.4	1,394	18.7
ef Low	54,935	41.1	14,417	44.4	17,482	46.7	3,588	48.0
Unspecified	16,174	12.1	2,649	8.2	5,548	14.8	994	13.3
Household size								
1–4 persons	38,240	28.6	7,116	21.9	10,439	27.9	2,155	28.8
5–19 persons	90,177	67.5	25,221	77.7	25,753	68.7	5,269	70.5
Institutions	5,275	3.9	134	0.4	1,277	3.4	48	0.6

large pool of individuals retrieved at ages *other* than fifteen to twenty-four, when we compare their characteristics with the population from which they are drawn – the entire census population of the same ages. As shown in table 9.6, "the good sample" closely resembles the target population in ethnic composition and in the distribution of households by both residential and occupational status. There is a slight underrepresentation of females and singles, and the age distribution is what we expect from higher mortality of those over forty-five. The principal departure from a "representative" sample is the very poor showing for individuals with no reported relationship to other members of the household in which they were living in 1881.

As Lisa Dillon has pointed out, it is difficult to compare the results of various intercensal-matching exercises. All studies show rather similar selection effects of age and sex. For the ten-year span 1871–81, Dillon linked two-thirds of married persons in Quebec, as compared with our retrieval of 40 per cent over a twenty-year span. Darroch reports linkage of 36 per cent of married couples; of all individuals, he linked 40 per cent over the decade 1861–71 as compared with our 23 per cent over two decades. By tracking the Perth County household heads to the rest of Canada and the US, Baskerville achieved 80 per cent over a decade (chapter 7), and Avery Guest reports 39 per cent of male youth over two decades (US 1880–1900), greater than our 26 per cent.[19]

Can we do better? This kind of "hand-matching" is often treated as a gold standard for appraising computerized procedures.[20] Since we have employed manual linkage, let us instead refer to it as a mere "silver standard" and treat the miniature Montreal (twelve surnames) as our gold standard. Reconstituted and tracked year by year for sixty years through a wide range of sources including rural registers, they yield substantially higher retrieval rates: 28.8 per cent of the 1881 individuals sought, 41.1 per cent of the number presumed to have survived (table 9.7). But the biases are the same: low retrieval for the fifteen to twenty-four-year-olds, very low recovery of the unrelated (below 5 per cent), and some underrepresentation of Protestants, females, and those in the lowest-rent category. Although relatively low rates of retrieval for young adults and high rates for the elderly are consistent with normal assumptions about the propensity to migrate, we cannot assume that most of the unretrieved have moved away. Montreal was the grand attractor, and our gold standard reinforces the argument that the majority of missing persons, even among fifteen to twenty-four-year-olds, are simply people we cannot identify, affected by record-matching limitations.

Table 9.7
Rates of retrieval in 1901 of census populations of 1881 by age and ethnicity, surname samples compared with entire population of Montreal, both sexes combined

Persons retrieved as percentage of persons sought

Entire population 1881					*Surname samples 1881*				
Age group	*FC*	*IC*	*PR*	*All*	*Age group*	*FC*	*IC*	*PR*	*All*
a <5	28.5	32.4	33.0	29.9	a <5	26.8	41.0	44.7	35.1
b 5–14	32.8	28.5	24.4	29.9	b 5–14	34.3	35.5	39.5	36.3
c 15–24	22.8	16.9	14.9	19.9	c 15–24	32.5	18.1	24.1	25.9
d 25–44	24.9	21.1	24.1	24.0	d 25–44	34.1	22.1	28.0	28.8
e 45–59	17.1	13.5	18.3	16.8	e 45–59	30.9	13.2	34.3	26.6
f >60	4.4	3.6	5.3	4.5	f >60	8.0	0.0	11.1	6.0
Total	24.8	21.0	21.7	23.3	Total	31.0	23.2	31.0	28.8

Persons retrieved as percentage of expected survivors

Entire population 1881					*Surname samples 1881*				
Age group	*FC*	*IC*	*PR*	*All*	*Age group*	*FC*	*IC*	*PR*	*All*
a <5	38.5	41.9	40.5	39.8	a <5	36.2	53.3	54.8	45.8
b 5–14	38.4	34.3	28.3	35.6	b 5–14	40.2	42.7	45.6	42.6
c 15–24	28.1	22.0	18.4	25.2	c 15–24	40.1	23.6	29.8	32.4
d 25–44	33.7	31.8	32.7	33.4	d 25–44	46.2	33.9	38.0	40.3
e 45–59	37.6	18.1	37.6	33.1	e 45–59	71.1	35.4	78.2	63.7
f >60	59.2	34.5	59.4	53.8	f >60	92.9	0.0	152.7	62.5
Total	34.6	29.7	29.8	32.9	Total	43.5	35.3	42.6	41.1

Sources: Census of 1881 and 1901, surname samples Olson and Thornton, *Peopling*

PATHWAYS THROUGH THE CITY

If we set aside the fifteen to twenty-four age group for discussion in section three and accept the retrieved as promising samples of the remaining 80 per cent of the urban population, what do they tell us of social pathways? As Gordon Darroch has demonstrated again and again, any patient experimentation of an untested source, a neglected variable, an ambiguous term, or a new method will yield some validation or critique of the intended target. Such experiments often yield an incidental harvest of new questions and new hypotheses such as we see in his queries about domestic privacy and his observations of adolescents living away from home.[21] For our Montreal exercise, as for Darroch and the Princes of Serendip, the investment offered a bonus that outflanked the initial strategy by affording a glimpse of human connectivity as intricate as the wiring that in the twenty years 1881–1901 had crept over the housetops and draped the city streets.

Five out of six of the individuals I was able to retrieve had moved to a new neighbourhood. How far did they move? How were they resituated in the urban space? How were they repositioned in terms of social status or in relation to parents, children, or siblings with whom they were living in 1881? These are questions Evan Roberts asks of his Chicago residents for a five-year span (chapter 10), and Peter Baskerville asks of his Perth County families for a span of a decade (chapter 7). For the Montrealers, we will first take note of some life course transitions and then explore geographic moves through the city as evidence of social status trajectories and a preference for living near kinfolk.

Life Course Transitions

If we class people, male or female, as having made certain life transitions, moving into and out of marriages at certain ages, we may be able to make some observations about the extent to which those shifts undermine matching and consider how they might affect social or geographic mobility.

Married couples recovered in the same relationship in 1901 are most readily retrieved. Of widows and widowers of 1881 – an older group – small numbers are retrieved (but more than anticipated), and more women than men are retrieved. Of people who were single in 1881 and still single twenty years later, most were small children in 1881, still living with their parents in 1901 and, therefore, more easily found. They were more often young men who tended to marry two or three years later in life than their sisters. Men and women who embarked on a first marriage between 1881 and 1901 constitute a youthful distribution (dominant ages five to nineteen in 1881), and we know from earlier analyses that French Canadians were marrying younger than the others.[22] Inferences from recovery of a widowed or remarried spouse confirm more deaths of women at ages twenty-five to thirty-four, of men thirty-five to forty-four.

What about those whose trajectories were more complex? Persons married since 1881 and widowed before 1901 (two transitions) come from the same age groups as the couples surviving to 1901. Those who have married, lost a spouse, and remarried by 1901 (three transitions) are a little older and more are men (peak ages fifteen to twenty-four in 1881). Men and women already married in 1881 and widowed since are an older distribution for whom retrieval rates are reduced by a high probability of death of the second party. The women who remarried (far fewer) constitute a much younger distribution (peak ages twenty-five to thirty-four in 1881) as compared with the men (thirty to forty-four). Among those widowed and remarried, ages of women peak at forty to fifty-four and men at forty to forty-nine. Some of them have entered into recomposition of complex households, while others have exited as resimplified households – the new couple alone.

Those observations are unsurprising, useful chiefly in highlighting the large number of complex transitions. Moves into and out of marriages, by inducing rearrangements of households, compound the difficulties of tracking the fifteen to twenty-four age set, so many of whom were "in transit."

Pathways of Advancement

Montrealers of all social classes participated in the May Day move when the annual leases came to an end. Gilliland has estimated that in a given year, one household in six moved, making short term, short-distance adjustments. Within a five-year span, one-quarter had made a move, but of the movers only one in five seemed to be moving "up."[23] The new links across a twenty-year span offer insight into the changes from one generation to the next. Of the 40,000 people I recognized in the 1901 census, five out of six had moved to a different census tract from where they were living in 1881. A decided centrifugal tendency can be interpreted as a consequence of the attraction of newer housing on the periphery. Only in the small central business district (already thought of in 1901 as "Old Montreal"), and to some degree in flanking zones of Griffintown (southwest) and Saint-Jacques (northeast), did expansion of railways, office buildings, and industry produce net losses of residents. Everywhere else, density increased substantially over the twenty years.

Protestants were moving to areas they had already preempted (e.g. the "Golden Square Mile" and Côte Saint-Antoine, now Westmount), French Canadians to industrial suburbs of high French Canadian concentration, Irish Catholics to newly built Saint-Gabriel (Point St Charles) and to newer and better-off areas of Protestant occupancy.

Between the zones of ethnic concentration, a distinctive belt of diversity along "main streets" like St Lawrence and St Antoine functioned as a springboard, with higher rates of outbound moves as departing residents were replaced by newcomers from rural Quebec, Eastern Europe, or Italy.

The geographic moves demonstrate a net upward social mobility. The majority are moves to streets of higher status, but no differences are discernible as a function of the number of life transitions or changes of civil status in the interval. If we class the sixty-seven census tracts of 1881 by rent levels of their populations they will rank in the same order in 1901, and the overall distribution of residents in a tract shows little change, since the categories are adjusted to take into account the modest general increase of floor area occupied. The patterns reflect the stubborn persistence of high residential segregation as measured with respect to rent levels, language, the prime religious split, and the three largest cultural communities.[24] If, however, we limit the observation to people we know were residents of the city in 1881 (the 40,000 retrieved), from every tract the preponderance of moves is to streets of higher median rent.

The evidence suggests intergenerational advance was more important than the advance of a lifetime at work. These findings are consistent with observations based on occupational status: an earlier paper based on the same census files demonstrated net upward mobility among 5,000 city-raised sons relative to their fathers.[25] The degree to which the retrieved are representative of the original population (table 9.6) militates against the hypothesis that "losers" tended to leave the city, and I would hesitate to employ Thernstrom's term "the urban escalator" which suggests an automatic lift.[26] As we shall now see, the ladders of upward mobility observed in Montreal were diverse, and the climb, often arduous, entailed considerable risk.

Kinship Pathways

From the population retrieved, it would be possible to explore the extent to which sibling dyads persist or reemerge as coresidential arrangements and to consider the related problem of kin density. As Steven Ruggles has repeatedly pointed out, there were limits to the opportunity for elderly people to live with relatives because many of them had no relatives left.[27] Hazards of migration and high mortality created risks late in life of a shrinking web, sometimes stretched to

Table 9.8
Distance from nearest related household 1901, by cultural community and rent level

	Household pairs by cultural community				
	French	*Irish*	*Protestant*	*All*	
Distance (meters)					
<500	50.7	39.9	31.4	47.6	
500–1999	33.1	37.6	40.5	34.4	
>2000	16.1	22.5	28.0	18.0	
All	100.0	100.0	100.0	100.0	
Sample size	7,361	1,150	849	9,385	
	Household pairs by residential status				
	Low (1)	*(2)*	*(3)*	*(4)*	*High (5)*
Distance (meters)					
<500	55.6	48.3	40.1	33.1	24.0
500–1999	28.1	34.0	42.1	45.6	49.4
>2000	16.3	17.7	17.9	21.3	26.6

Sources: Census of 1881 and 1901, Montreal and suburbs

Relatedness is inferred from cues of coresidence in 1881. Ethnicity and status are based on census of 1881. Distances are calculated from addresses in census of 1901.

"fictitious kinship." In Montreal, the English-speaking populations were more often kin-poor as a result of long-distance moves, later marriage, and lower nuptiality.

Rather than coresidence, I sought to estimate "near-residence" or the neighbouring behaviour of kin. Our 40,000 personae of 1881 reappear in 1901 as residents of 20,000 different households, and this pool can be rearranged as 10,000 pairs such that household A and household B are linked by a close relationship between two (or more) persons – a parent and a married child or siblings who have married since 1880. The relationship is apparent from their coresidence in 1881: in the interval, the parties have established separate households. The 10,000 pairs are scattered across the city, but for half of them distances are very short. As shown in table 9.8, nearly half lived within 500 meters of each other – a six-minute walk. This is a tighter leash than the journey to work, where 1,000 meters seems to be the range observed among 1880 workers at the glass factory, the rubber factory, the Grand Trunk railway shops, or the city markets. The preference for close kin to be close neighbours is expressed in all three cultural communities, and their thickets of near-residence crisscross the entire city, densest in areas of high density and interrupted only by a few gross physical features like the canal right of way, railway corridor, or embankment.

Of the related households, about 7 per cent lived in an upstairs-downstairs context, in flats in the same building or on the same lot, with an additional 8 per cent in the same street segment, together 15 per cent at very close range. What appears to be a cultural preference (strongest among French Canadians) may be better explained by rent levels (lower panel of table 9.8), since occupants of a single-family house were less likely to occupy the same building or lot than the people who lived in three or four-room flats (three-quarters of the population). The design of duplex or triplex dwellings (double or triple-deckers) facilitated adaptation to larger kinships, so the Montreal yard often included four to six times what Peter Laslett referred to as a "houseful."

Could the observed degree of neighbouring of kin occur by chance? If, from the pool of 20,000 households of 1901, we generate the 10,000 pairs at random and map the distribution, only 1 per cent would be living within 500 meters. In a more realistic experiment, where random pairing is stratified consistent with the social status of the families in 1881 (five levels) and their religious and linguistic affiliations (three communities), 11 per cent would be living within 500 meters and fewer than 1 per cent as immediate neighbours. This test indicates that living near kin was a conscious strategy, and the priority was as compelling as the need to live near the workplace. On Moving Day, a family was reoptimizing in accord with its own multiobjective location model. Year after year over twenty years, families were maintaining the crochet of kinship from house to house and block to block.

The option for neighbouring seems to be a complement to the preference for living in small "nuclear" households. By living in such households, at a calculated distance from their relatives, five out of six families obtained a degree of everyday autonomy and privacy, while securing the potential of nearby kin available in an emergency or a more prolonged crisis.[28] The dense network of kinship overlapped with neighbour-relations and the everyday relationships involved in making a living. All three types of relationships – kinship, neighbouring, and localized communities of exchange – are primary forms of sociability, still important today but understated in the historiography of the industrial city.

HARD TO FIND BUT WORTH THE EFFORT

For tracing moves, it is tempting to exclude categories of greatest uncertainty such as the young unmarried women likely to change their names or young bachelors presumed footloose.[29] As a group, however, the hard-to-find fifteen to twenty-four-year-olds of 1881 demand attention. Who were they? We shall see that they were living in a great variety of household structures, but they shared a context of risk. As observed by Darroch in an earlier paper,[30] and in poignant detail by Bogaert et al. (chapter 13), Kippen, McCalman, and Maxwell-Stewart (chapters 2 and 3), the risks these young adults faced – by accident or by choice – make them a research target of great interest.

As we would expect, a large share of the missing young people (18.7 per cent) belong to a category of "unrelated individuals," a population of 20,000 who from their surnames, occupations, and origins seem not to be related to any other person in the household where the census taker recorded them.[31] They therefore fall outside the reach of the dyadic search strategy. As we have seen, most were not dying off or moving away; rather, they were moving into and out of marriages, making as many as two or three transitions. We need to know more about the time lapse before remarriage of the widowed, the fecundity of second marriages, ages of children at deaths of their parents, rates of turnover in institutions and boardinghouses, and the process of household formation as distinct from family formation.[32]

As shown in table 9.9, the living arrangements of the fifteen to twenty-four-year-olds are diverse. Youth fifteen to twenty-four account for half of the city's domestic servants (92 per cent female); a third of those living as boarders; a quarter of the nuns, novices, teaching brothers, and clergy; one-fifth of the protégés of institutions; and a tenth of the live-alones. The uneven coverage of these distinct lifestyles undermines representativity. While the fifteen to twenty-four-year-old population of 1881 resembled the other 80 per cent of Montrealers in ethnic origins, rent levels, and household sizes, recovery rates diverge and are somewhat erratic: more singles and women, more residents of small households, fewer Protestants or high-rent households (see table 9.6). The unusual "complex households" (around 15 per cent) harboured many of the "unrelated," and the heterogeneity, as well as low retrieval, suggests the likelihood of bias. Because their situations are so diverse, each group needs attention as a distinct problem.[33]

Table 9.9
Living arrangements of persons fifteen to twenty-four in 1881 versus other age groups

	Number of persons				
	All ages	*15–24*	*Other*	*Col. % All ages*	*15–24 as % of all ages*
Family (a)	151,034	30,475	120,559	88.3	20.2
Unrelated (b)	20,094	6,988	13,106	11.7	34.8
Entire population (c)	171,131	37,463	133,668	100.0	21.9
Types of unrelated					
Lone-dweller	1,625	238	1,387	0.9	14.6
Live-in help	5,704	2,999	2,705	3.3	52.6
Religious	1,816	492	1,324	1.1	27.1
Institutionalized	4,895	1,022	3,873	2.9	20.9
Boarders/lodgers	19,865	6,955	12,910	11.6	35.0

a Related to at least one other person in the household

b No apparent relation to other members of the household

c There are overlaps among religious, live-in help, boarders, and others in institutions

Sources: Census of Canada 1881 and 1901

What the fifteen to twenty-four-year-olds had in common was a situation of risk. They were embarked on a process of insertion or reinsertion into society – newly arrived in the city, in a new job or a new line of work, or temporarily lodged in anticipation of family formation or reformation after dissolution of a household or disengagement from the family of origin. The fifteen to twenty-four-year-olds were moving, some faster, some more slowly or by stages, toward greater integration or marginalization. Although there seems to be no unique pathway or universal norm, virtually everybody in that life span was facing a fork in the road, and this leads us to consider risk. In the fast-paced, high-risk urban economy, what were their strategies and their networks of support?

As newcomers to the job market, youth were "shock absorbers" for industrial reorganizations, cyclical and structural unemployment, and population pressure in the rural economy.[34] Risks were severely gendered, with young women at risk of unwed motherhood and complications of childbirth, young men at risk of industrial accidents.[35] Their vulnerability was heightened by legal constraints on minors (under twenty-one), inexperience, and personal challenges such as limited schooling or early loss of a parent.[36] Not every hazard had an instantaneous outcome; in some cases, it would handicap insertion much later, as a result of loss of hearing or vision as sequelae of measles or scarlet fever, loss of an eye or a thumb in factory work, growth stunted by recurrent intestinal episodes in early childhood, or latent infection with tuberculosis. Of all deaths at ages fifteen to twenty-four, 45 per cent were attributed to tuberculosis, a rate higher than for any other ages.[37]

A large literature of risk is confined to a few sectors. Economists of entrepreneurship and innovation have called attention to the range of personal preference for risk-taking or risk-avoidance; present day "environmental" hazards have elicited a new sensitivity to locations,[38] and demographers have observed with care the time–space variations in the odds of mortality. Lenihan's reconstruction of the trajectories of Scots colonists to New Zealand (chapter 4) reveals multiple moves, and the histories of transported convicts (chapters 2 and 3) confirm the complexity of relocation and reintegration into job markets. To appreciate the special role of the fifteen to twenty-four age group, we need to expand the notion to "social risks" to consider, as we do with mortality, the sequence over the course of a life and to inquire into strategies economists have identified for dealing with uncertainty such as flexibility, liquidity, networking, hedging, and diversification of assets. In Montreal, the one-year lease and frequent moves facilitated reassembly of households in response to variability of income and family size.[39] In the persistence of small firms alongside the new corporate scale of enterprise, Robert Lewis identified complementarities advantageous under conditions of uncertainty, and in Chicago Richard Sennett documented greater upward mobility in families that had incorporated relatives and boarders, thereby extending their antennae of information and trust.[40]

The principle of diversification of assets is familiar in management of a financial portfolio or the farmer's year-to-year adjustment of the mix of crops (chapter 8). The strategy can be applied by an individual, a household, a kin group, an enterprise, or an ethnic community. But we need to include social assets and alliances such as Peter Baskerville describes among the German settlers in Logan Township (chapter 7). Giovanni Levi, for a fourteenth-century Italian village, treats the diverse assets of a kin group such as well-placed relatives, political patronage, opportune acts of generosity, and a dispersion of occupations in the kindred. The social assets are especially intricate in the creation of reputation, locally embedded as a transactional history of debts and credits incurred year after year, even generation after generation, to accumulate and preserve a portfolio of social capital.[41]

In Montreal, access to property was facilitated by kinship strategies. Only 15 per cent of householders were property owners. This is unusually low, exceeded even among the working-class Chicago families of chapter 10. But the value of land tended to increase with the growth of the city, and access to property was therefore an important urban ladder, still in service today. Our case study of Notre Dame Street East, part of that backbone of "main street" diversity in Montreal, identified kinship networks among property owners. Over the course of a century, each kinship added ownership of property to its repertory, diversified its holdings of real estate, simultaneously enlarged the range of its commercial activities, and invested in the professional education of a son as a notary or doctor. They weathered severe blows (conflagration 1852 and municipal expropriation 1891), established a large progeny, and achieved a measurable upward mobility. Their strategies for spreading risk involved careful grooming of relations with neighbouring owners and intermarriage with other property-owning families in the street. Despite the risks of early death, families framed their ambitions with a distant horizon and, for assets yet to be acquired, organized transmission to grandchildren and great-grandchildren "born or to be born" – a practice that extended oversight of the property to relatives beyond the nuclear family.[42] Here we reconnect with the evidence from the 10,000 pairs, for the significance of social assets of near-residence of kin and an effective information network.

CONCLUSION

Attention to addresses makes it possible to ground census samples in the urban space and dwelling stock, to exercise greater control over geographic coverage of a sample, and to offer new ways to sample the social space. The digital data we used for 1881 and the digital index for 1901 were created and initially used by people seeking an individual or personal family history, as were resources used by other authors.[43] These digital collaborations now offer extraordinary tools for exploration by historians and historical sociologists and for construction of future samples by demographers and geographers who are rarely satisfied with a random 5 per cent.

Both the matchables and the unmatchables direct us along new lines of inquiry. The matchables invite study of kinship, neighbouring, and property as advantageous ladders of social advancement, while the unmatchables invite inquiry into risk, its incidence, and the strategies young people were employing to reduce uncertainty at critical junctures of family formation and family dissolution.

While kinship in the first degree is the acknowledged basis for organization of most households in nineteenth-century cities, its extension beyond the coresident census household has been neglected because of our dependence on the structure of the census document and the census maker's absentmindedness with respect to urban morphology. The census-linking exercise in Montreal offers a handle for identifying related households and their proximities. The wish to enjoy, extend, reciprocate, exploit, groom, and protect these relationships intervened in residential choices, providing evidence of kinship as a strategic component of the social organization of the industrial metropolis.

ACKNOWLEDGMENTS

Much of the research was carried out in collaboration with Patricia Thornton and Danielle Gauvreau. We are grateful to all the other contributors to digital databases: for the 1901 census samples, Peter Baskerville, Peter Gossage, Mary MacKinnon, Chris Minns, Eric Sager, the Canadian Families Project (Sager et al.); for the census of 1881, Lisa Dillon and the Latter Day Saints; for Catholic marriages 1881–1901, Michèle Jomphe at Projet Balsac, Université du Québec à Chicoutimi; for Protestant marriages, the Quebec Family History Society; for tax rolls and electronic base maps, Ville de Montréal, Service des archives and Service de géomatique, McGill University Libraries, and Bibliothèque et Archives nationales du Québec. Instrumental in construction of lots and map links were Robert C.H. Sweeny, Rosalyn Trigger, and others in the team MAP Montréal l'avenir du passé. All of those projects were funded at various times by the Social Sciences and Humanities Research Council of Canada.

10

Moving around the City: Residential and Economic Mobility in Chicago, 1925–30[1]

EVAN ROBERTS

INTRODUCTION

Academic studies of social mobility in North America and Europe have largely concentrated on the late nineteenth century and the late twentieth century. In the late nineteenth century the study of social mobility in North America and Britain has largely relied on linking individuals across different censuses. By contrast, in Scandinavia and the Netherlands prospectively recorded church and population registers explicitly recorded lives in transition, making historical longitudinal research slightly more feasible. In the late twentieth century, social scientists have relied on prospectively collected longitudinal samples that make repeated interviews of the same individuals or families. By comparison, social mobility from the turn of the twentieth century to World War II is somewhat under-studied. Studies of social mobility in United States in the late nineteenth century and late twentieth century suggest social mobility declined in both eras. Thus, unless social mobility has been continuously declining since the 1850s, the early twentieth century should have seen social mobility increase. It is clear, however, that the social structure of mobility and opportunity changed in the first half of the twentieth century.

Opportunities for social mobility in nineteenth-century North America were connected to the availability of cheap land. By the early twentieth century there was much less of the cheap land that had enabled men with little schooling to make rapid social progress by dint of their own labour and that of their family. Thus, the "opportunity structure" became more urbanized.[2] Residents of urban areas had a greater variety of jobs they could enter or move to if they were not satisfied with their current position. Olson's chapter in this volume shows a high degree of mobility in both jobs and residences in late-nineteenth-century Montréal. The concern of American corporations at the high turnover of workers in manufacturing jobs suggests that many workers exercised their options.[3] These factors suggest a basis for increasing social mobility. But at the same time, the returns to formal education expanded, and, at least partly in response to high labour turnover, large corporations developed extensive internal labour markets.[4] This chapter explores these issues by examining the residential and occupational mobility of a group of Chicago families in the late 1920s. The families persisted in Chicago, but the male heads of households shifted jobs at a high rate, confirming the impressions of contemporary observers about the turnover of urban workers between jobs. There is only limited evidence, however, that occupational mobility led to significant social or economic mobility for the group. While some men moved up the occupational ladder, their gains were nearly all offset by a slightly smaller group of men who moved down the occupational ladder.

BACKGROUND

Comparing the studies of late nineteenth and late twentieth century American social mobility suggest that social mobility may have increased between 1900 and World War II. The current consensus in the scholarly literature is that social mobility decreased up to 1900 and also decreased in the late twentieth century. For example, Joseph Ferrie and Jason Long have argued that the United States had high levels of social mobility between 1850 and 1880 but that social mobility declined towards British levels across the turn of the twentieth century.[5] Scholars analyzing the late-twentieth-century United States have drawn qualitatively similar conclusions to a century earlier. Social mobility may have increased in the immediate aftermath of World War II, but since the 1970s mobility has decreased. Viewed across a half-century American social mobility has at best been static.[6] Many other scholars argue that social mobility has decreased in the United States, both compared to its own past and compared to other industrialized countries such as Canada, Britain, or Australia.[7]

Thus, the emerging consensus that American social mobility declined in the late nineteenth century and at best was static in the late twentieth century begs the question of what happened in the first half of the twentieth century. The early twentieth century provides further data possibilities for researching social mobility than the late nineteenth century. Beginning in the late nineteenth century, American governments, academics, and advocates for social-policy reform carried out many social surveys. The surveys' focus on urban social conditions and living standards reveals a concern that recent migrants to the city – domestic or international – were, at best, at risk of not making enough money to support themselves or their families. At worst, urban migrants were seen as potential vectors of ill health and social disorder that would spread through neighbourhoods and even infect the middle and upper classes.[8]

Thus many of the surveys were concerned with understanding the ecology of urban life. Some prominent early examples include Charles Booth's multivolume study of the London poor, W.E.B. Du Bois' survey of African Americans in Philadelphia, and a multivolume study of Pittsburgh supported by the Russell Sage Foundation.[9] The majority of the surveys would be classified today as "mixed methods" research. They drew on multiple disciplines from the academy and relied on a synthesis of quantitative data from samples of households, with qualitative data collected from interviews with local elites (such as politicians and employers) and the study of relevant documents.[10] Social surveys of households and individuals often asked more questions than the contemporary census, such as income and hours of work.

Similarly, because social surveys were interested in assessing the inadequacy of low incomes they often asked about rents and expenditures on necessities such as clothing, heating fuel, and food.[11] Thus, when these social survey manuscripts survive for reanalysis by modern scholars they offer tremendous potential for understanding social conditions in the early twentieth century. Moreover, many of the surveys of individuals and households from the early twentieth century include identifying information about the respondents and their families. Privacy was a concern for scholars in the early twentieth century, but it appears to have been less of a concern than in the late twentieth century. Where manuscript surveys survive from this era they often include identifying information on the survey itself, or the "key" that links unique identification numbers and personally identifying information elsewhere in the archival record.

CHICAGO AS A SITE FOR SOCIAL RESEARCH

The lives of the urban working class in Chicago are well known to social scientists and historians. Between the 1880s and World War II, Chicago was the site of multiple social surveys by urban reformers and social workers, academics, and government agencies from the city to the federal level. In the earliest years the surveys were collected atheoretically or to document the case for progressive reforms. While the University of Chicago sociologists from the 1920s tried to separate themselves from the cause of social reform and the pragmatic needs of social workers, their theories of human ecology in the city owed a great debt to the masses of data collected about Chicago in the previous forty years.[12] Despite a growing interest in longitudinal research in other areas of social science in the 1920s, few of the Chicago studies returned to the same individuals or families to see how they had fared. Yet it was a mark of Chicago-area urban research that scholars returned to the same neighbourhoods and tracked how they had changed. The Chicago sociologists made it easy for other scholars to return to the same neighbourhoods by defining seventy-five (now seventy-seven) community areas that continue to be used in research.[13] In the 1920s as Chicago continued to grow rapidly, "residential stability" was a concern to the Chicago sociologists. In particular, they were concerned with how low levels of residential stability contributed to poverty, delinquency, and poor health.[14] The persistence of place, not people, was a defining element of the early years of Chicago social science. This generalization carries across in large part to the work done by the women scholars at the Chicago School of Social Service Administration.[15] Continuing more directly the line of work started by Jane Addams and the researchers who contributed to *Hull House Maps and Papers*, the emblematic works were largely done by the Abbott sisters, Grace and Edith, and Sophonisba Breckinridge.[16] Yet even though social work, compared to sociology, involved a greater continuing focus on the family and the individual, the research done by the (largely) female faculty and associates of the School of Social Service Administration also neglected longitudinal studies. The most prominent Chicago scholar to study subjects longitudinally before World War II was Ernest Burgess, whose interests in criminal recidivism and marital "success" led him to return to the same subjects for reinterview several years later.[17] But for the most part, social surveys in pre-World War II Chicago were social snapshots.

DATA AND METHODOLOGY

The preservation of many of the manuscript materials that underlie Chicago social research allows us to revisit some of the Chicago families and trace them through time. This paper uses a survey of working-class families by Leila Houghteling from 1924–25. Houghteling was an "heiress" who surveyed 477 families in Chicago and its immediately adjacent suburbs for her PhD dissertation research in the School of Social Service Administration.[18]

Houghteling aimed to measure the income and standard of living of families in Chicago. The dissertation and the monograph are both sparse on details of the sample collection. In common with other social surveys collected during the infancy of statistical sampling theory, there was no explicit probabilistic scheme for choosing a set of respondents. The sampling frame was derived from payroll records of large employers. But Houghteling compared her sample with the 1920 census and other surveys of Chicago workers, and the implicit ideal of a representative sample underlies the data collection.[19]

Working-class families – a husband, wife, and ideally some children – were the subjects of the study. The target population was consistent with other social surveys of the time, including those collected by federal and state agencies. For example, the Bureau of Labor Statistics 1917–19 Cost of Living Survey that collected the original weights for the Consumer Price Index had a similar definition.[20] Many of these surveys restricted the number of boarders or roomers a family could have if they were accepted into the sample. The moral concept was that intact families – who maintained a safe environment for their children by not having too many extra-familial boarders or roomers – were the families about whom governments and social service agencies should be concerned. Moreover, there were analytical reasons to restrict the numbers of nonfamily members in surveyed families. Household well-being is subject to significant economies of scale that come from sharing resources between household members. Nonfamily members may well have a different "sharing rule" with the household than the family. Working out how families pooled resources was a practical and analytical challenge given the technology of the time for analyzing quantitative data. The challenge would only be greater by including households with greater and more variable numbers of nonfamily members. Making the household composition of the sample more homogeneous thus had both moral and practical supports.

After Houghteling's 1927 death, the University of Chicago Press published a revised manuscript as a monograph.[21] The original survey manuscripts were bound in three volumes and are held in the Special Collections Research Center of the University of Chicago Library.[22] Like other social surveyors of the era, Houghteling relied on social workers to help with data collection. The sometimes-tense interactions between middle class, educated social workers and their working-class subjects are evident in many of the surveys.[23]

The judgments of the social workers are copious because, in comparison to other social surveys of this era and earlier, the Houghteling surveys have unusually detailed qualitative notes about the families. In part this was because the surveys included a question on "indications of poverty" and "indications of comfort" that invited the social worker to make subjective assessments of well-being. The instructions to investigators suggested "indications of comfort" could be "unusually good furniture, expensive rugs or lamps, etc."[24] Cleanliness dominated their concerns.[25] More than one hundred of the 477 surveys note that the house was clean and categorize cleanliness as an indication of well-being.[26] One interviewer noted positively that "the laundry had just come up from the hot wash ... and the underwear looked very new and well cared for."[27] Another commented favorably that she was offered wine while taking the survey.[28] Musical instruments, particularly pianos and organs, were noted as an indication of comfort. Often the notes explain the circumstances behind the numbers, such as a son-in-law not working because he had been gassed in the war or a husband who had to switch jobs after being burned at work.[29] Houghteling seemed to be planning a follow-up study of the same families because the social workers had to ask whether the wife and mother of the family was interested in the study, assess whether she kept good accounts, and ask if she might be contacted again. Houghteling's own untimely death meant that the follow-up study was never completed. Thus, in part, this chapter pays homage to the work of Houghteling and her collaborators on the original study, completing in some fashion what they could not by linking the surveys to the 1920 and 1930 censuses.

Like many social surveys of the era – especially in Chicago where there were many large employers – Houghteling collected her sample by approaching large employers and asking their employment office to suggest workers who might be approached to be interviewed. Thus a number of large employers dominate the list of where husbands in the 1925 survey were employed, including International Harvester, Swift,

Sears & Roebuck, Ryerson Steel, Wisconsin Steel, Chicago Surface Lines, Commonwealth Edison, and Pullman.[30]

The black families included a small number of "old settlers" and new migrants who had arrived during the Great Migration.[31] Black migrants turned out to be some of the hardest families to link from the Houghteling surveys to the 1920 and 1930 censuses. Although it is impossible to know why we could not link a particular family, we suspect that the black families were hard to find in the census because they were recently migrated or migrating at the time of the census. The enumeration of black households in the South appeared to be of low quality. Where we could identify a family there were often frequent small errors in the enumeration, either from lack of care or difficulty in communicating with the household. This pattern is consistent with evidence that the censuses of 1920, 1930, and 1940 had the highest under-enumeration of the black population in the century following the Civil War. In 1920, 15 per cent of the black population was uncounted and 1930 improved only marginally to 12 per cent.[32] Black under-enumeration was more than twice as great as the net under-enumeration rate.[33]

Because the Houghteling surveys were of families, we concentrated on linking families between the survey manuscripts from 1925 and the population censuses of 1920 and 1930. The primary objective was to link the married couple in the family to their household in 1920 and 1930. Going forward to 1930 we ignored the destination of young adults or other family members who had left the household. In common with other modern projects to link individuals or families between sources, we identified families with characteristics that should not change or should change predictably. In the Houghteling survey we knew

First and last names of all family members
Age of family members in 1925
Race of the husband and wife, defined as Black or White
Nativity of the husband and wife, defined as Foreign or US born
Ethnicity of the husband and wife

In both 1920 and 1930 the census provided similar information, allowing a relatively high rate of accurate linkages. Overall we linked 55 per cent of families to the 1920 census and 69 per cent (332 of 477) to the 1930 census. With the release of the 1940 census in April 2012, it has been possible to start extending the research forward another decade with one-third of the families currently linked to that census. This chapter analyzes the initial 277 families that were linked to the 1930 census.

The goal of the project was to link families both forward and backward, and searches in the Ancestry.com indices to the United States census were made jointly, trying to locate both 1920 and 1930 enumerations in one search. We began searching by trying for an exact match between the first and last name of the husband, his birth year calculated from his age in 1925, his spouse remaining the same, and his race. We prioritized searching for the husband because, in the rare cases where couples were not married at the 1920 census, we should at least be able to find the husband before marriage because his name would not have changed.[34] This did not always produce the right potential candidates for linking, so the next step was to try the characteristics of the wife. Finally, we tried including the characteristics of children. When we included children's characteristics, we began by adding the youngest child alive in 1920 and progressively adding more children's names and characteristics. The youngest child alive in 1920 (typically aged zero to five) was often still in the household in 1930, and this made it easier to find the correct household on an initial search that included children's characteristics. Younger children's names were often spelt more consistently in the two sources – census and survey.

The small (forty-eight of 477) number of native-born whites were the most straightforward to find, and we found two-thirds of these families going forward to 1930. Native-born families were harder to link in the first instance because the Houghteling sample did not record the state of birth. Once the family was found in one census we then had the state of birth for further searching. The most challenging couples to link were American-born blacks and descendants of European immigrants. There was substantial name homogeneity for both European immigrants and black migrants to the North. Names became more Anglicized over time for European migrants or descendants with a non-English name. For example, it was common for Stanislaus to become Stanley. The enumeration of blacks in the South appeared to vary more often from the Houghteling spellings and (especially) ages than the enumeration of native-born whites. Because of these challenges, we more often used information about children's names and birthplaces to find black and European immigrant families. Because the target population was families with children, this strategy should not produce large biases with 75 per cent of the families having a child aged between five and ten with a high likelihood of being present in both 1925 and 1930.

CHARACTERISTICS OF THE HOUGHTELING FAMILIES IN 1925 AND 1930

Despite the nonrandom sampling used in collecting the original Houghteling sample, the characteristics of the families match up well with similar families from the 1920 census. Taking the broad Houghteling target population to be Chicago families where the husband was a semiskilled or unskilled worker and comparing the distribution of other characteristics allows us to see how large any differences between the census and the Houghteling families actually are (table 10.1). One major difference is that the Houghteling sample is blacker and more foreign than the average family in Chicago with a semiskilled or unskilled father. The Houghteling families had more coresident children than similar census families, and wives were more likely to be working. The definition of women's work was much more inclusive in the budget studies than in the census. The higher prevalence of foreign and black families in the Houghteling sample probably accounts for the higher rate of boarding and lodging. Another factor inflating the rate of boarding and lodging in the Houghteling sample is that as a budget study it asked about boarders and lodgers in the household in the past year. To make the concept match more closely to the census enumeration, we would need to compute a rate of boarding at the time of enumeration. But the average earnings of the husbands/fathers in the Houghteling sample match up nearly exactly with the contemporary average earnings for manufacturing and transportation workers. The heads of the Houghteling households reported average earnings of $1,246, compared to the national average of $1,240 for manufacturing and transportation workers in the same year.[35] Thus we can be reasonably sure that in 1925 the Houghteling families were representative of other working-class families in Chicago.

Before we can discuss the transitions that the families made, we need to compare the 1925 characteristics of the families we linked to 1930. It is nearly a given in longitudinal research that the people who are "lost to follow up" are different in some way from the people who can be traced over time. Remarkably there are few differences between the

Table 10.1
Comparison of Houghteling families with 1920 census and 1925 Department of Public Welfare Survey

	1920 census	*Houghteling sample*	*Houghteling families linked to 1930*	*1925 public welfare survey*
DEMOGRAPHIC AND ETHNIC				
Age of father	40	39	40	
Number of children in primary family	2	3.6	3.7	
Foreign born white	0.59	0.72	0.75	
Native born white	0.06	0.10	0.11	
Black	0.35	0.18	0.14	
Speaks English (if foreign born)	0.87	0.76	0.75	
HOUSING				
≤ 1 person per room		0.34	0.35	0.52
Owned home	0.28	0.29	0.32	0.14
EARNINGS				
Total family earnings less than $100 per month		0.19	0.16	0.47
Mother/wife at work, or boarders kept	0.23	0.48	0.49	0.47
Father's earnings in past year		$1246.75 ($313)	$1257.15 ($329)	
Mother's earnings in past year		$166.56 ($296)	$160.71 ($289)	

Standard errors in parentheses

linked and nonlinked sample. But even the happy situation that we have here, where the two groups look alike at initial measurement, cannot obscure the likelihood that the groups differ on some unobservable characteristics (such as "persistence") or that the two groups develop differently after the initial survey.

RESIDENTIAL TRANSITIONS OF THE HOUGHTELING FAMILIES FROM 1925 TO 1930

The transitions of the linked families are nested within a very high degree of persistence in the city of Chicago and the surrounding area. Of the 277 families initially linked between 1925 and 1930, just ten

(3.6 per cent) moved out of Chicago. Most families that moved did not go far. Two families went as far as Michigan (Detroit and Hamtrack City), others as close by as Berwyn, East Chicago (Illinois), and Waukesha (Wisconsin). While few families moved out of Chicago, there was a high degree of movement within the city.

Two-thirds of the families lived in a different residence after five years. Yet this understates mobility by measuring it over a five-year period. Because some people move multiple times, annual mobility rates are not simply five-year mobility rates divided by five. Comparing annual and five-year mobility rates in the United States after 1950 suggests that five-year mobility rates are about three times annual rates.[36] If the same relationship held in interwar Chicago, one in five households would have moved annually. Even this estimate might be too low. Post-World War II surveys in the United States show around 35 to 40 per cent of renters moving at least once in the previous year.[37] While these five-year mobility rates appear high, they are comparable with other pre-World War II estimates of intraurban mobility rates.[38] For example, in the 1940 census, just 37 per cent of twenty-five to sixty-four-year-old men in Chicago employed in similar occupations to the Houghteling sample were living in the same house as five years earlier.

The high mobility rates in the Houghteling sample are consistent with evidence from other studies showing that before widespread car ownership people often moved when they changed jobs. In 1925 just six of the 477 families owned a car. With lengthy hours in working-class jobs, residential moves that reduced the daily journey to work economized on commuting costs. Moving closer to a job made more sense when people were more certain of remaining in a job. In 1925, at least, there was a clear relationship for many of the families between the duration of current employment and residential proximity to the workplace. A sample of men from two large companies with one main factory – Ryerson Steel and International Harvester – were selected to examine this question in more detail by geocoding addresses and measuring the distance to work. The longer a man had worked at either employer, the closer he lived to his workplace. Unfortunately the 1930 census only includes information on industry, and it is not possible to tell definitively whether a man had changed firms within the same industry or continued to work at the exact same firm.

The Houghteling families made a significant move into home ownership over the five years they were followed (table 10.2). In 1925, 33 per cent of the linked sample owned their own homes, while by 1930 45 per

Table 10.2
Home ownership in 1925 and 1930

Ownership in 1925	*Ownership in 1930*		
	Owned	*Renting*	*Total*
Owned	80 (89% persistence)	10 (11% move to renting)	*90 (33%)*
Renting	46 (25% move to owning)	137 (75% persistence)	*183 (67%)*
Total	*126 (46%)*	*147 (54%)*	*273*

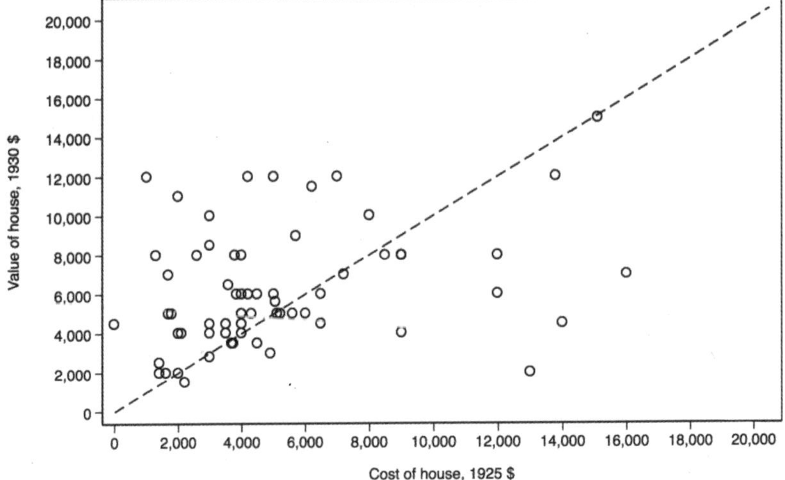

Figure 10.1 Cost of houses in 1925 versus value of house in 1930 (all families)

cent of the families owned their own home. Thus, by 1930 one-third of the families renting in 1925 had made a transition to home ownership, while just ten families had reverted to renting. While the sample that was successfully linked had a higher rate of home-ownership (33 per cent) than the nonlinked group (24 per cent) in 1925, the other characteristics of owning and renting families were similar in the linked and nonlinked groups. In both linked and nonlinked groups, the home-owning families were slightly older. Men who owned their own home were on average forty-two, compared to thirty-eight among renters.

Both the 1925 survey and the 1930 census asked about the "cost of the house" if owned and the value of the home. In both sources there is

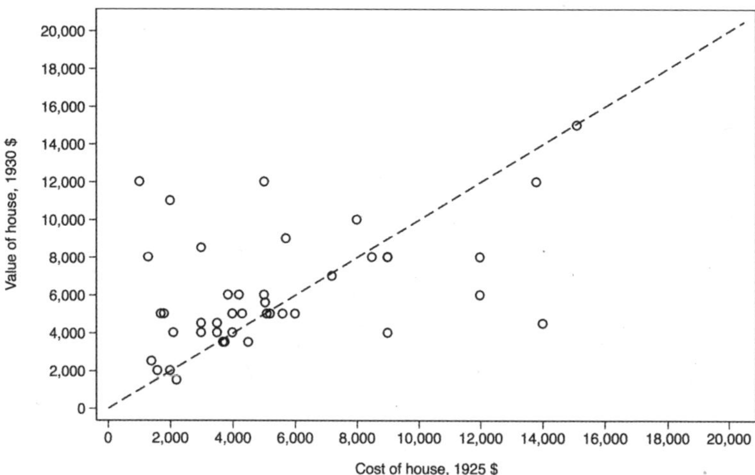

Figure 10.2 Cost of houses in 1925 and 1930 for families in the same house

some missing data so that of the eighty linked families owning homes in both years we only have sixty-five families who supplied the home value in both years. The values given in both years are highly correlated. For the forty-three families who lived at the same address in both years, the mean increase in value was $730 (figure 10.2). However, there were few families who reported the same cost in 1925 as house value in 1930, suggesting that respondents were trying to estimate current value in the 1930 census.

The transition to home ownership among a quarter of the 1925 renters is suggestive of the ambition for home ownership in Chicago families of the era that has been documented by other authors.[39] However, in both years a majority of families continued to rent. Concern with the rental market and the high proportion of income spent on rent by African American families was a major part of Houghteling's original report on her work.[40] The Houghteling study collected the total amount of rent paid in the previous twelve months, whereas the census in 1930 reported on the contracted monthly amount for rent. Although inflation was moderate between 1925 and 1930 (and in some measures negative), the average rents paid by the families increased significantly between 1925 and 1930 (figure 10.3). In 1925 the average renting family paid $23.27 per month in rent ($23.32 for the linked families). In 1930 the average rent had moved up to $32 per month. The increase in rents is visible all across the distribution (figure 10.4).

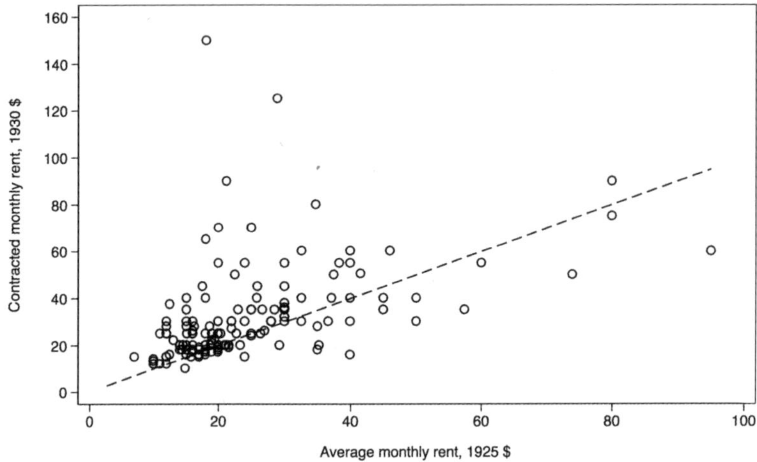

Figure 10.3 Monthly rents in 1925 and 1930

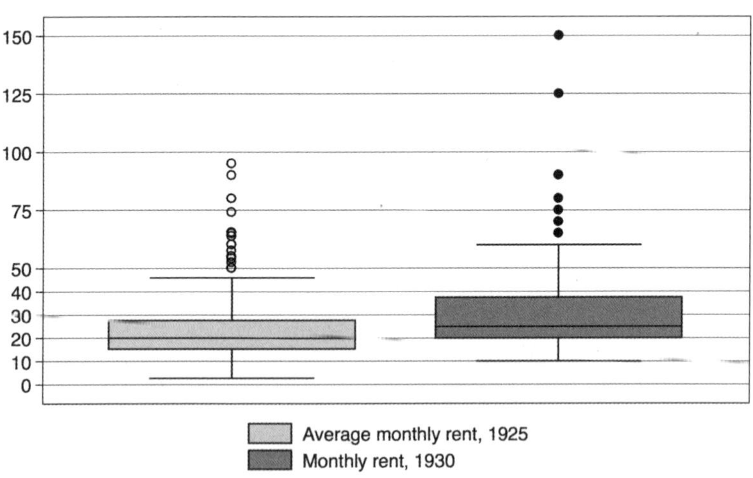

Figure 10.4. Distribution of rents in 1925 and 1930

At the twenty-fifth and seventy-fifth percentiles of the rent distribution, the increase was similar to the increase in the average rent. Without measures of housing quality in 1930 we do not know whether families were trading up to better houses. However, a pattern of more general rental increases is suggested by the fact that rents for families who remained in the same house also appeared to increase. Among the twenty-five families renting the same house in both years, the average rent increased from $20 per month to $25 per month – very similar to the movement in rentals overall.

While the move to home ownership suggests that these families improved their economic status, other indicators suggest fewer economic gains for the families. Both the Houghteling study and the 1930 census enquired about radio ownership. In 1925 only 8 per cent (36 of 477) of the Houghteling sample owned a radio (25 of 277 or 9 per cent in the linked sample). For comparison, 21 per cent of the families owned a piano, 40 per cent a "Victrola" record player, and 20 per cent a telephone. As has been well documented by many historians, radio ownership grew rapidly in Eastern and Midwestern cities in the 1920s and 1930s, and the 1930 census found that 40 per cent of households nationwide had a radio.[41] In large cities the rate of radio ownership was higher: in cities like Chicago, with a population of more than one million people, 59 per cent of the population and 56 per cent of households had radios. Thus the rate of radio ownership in the Houghteling sample in 1930 (125 of 277) of 45 per cent is actually well below the overall rate of radio ownership in New York, Chicago, Philadelphia, Detroit, and Los Angeles. Indeed in Chicago in 1930 63 per cent of the population lived in a home with a radio. But again, by comparing the Houghteling sample with a similar population from the 1930 census we see that the rate of radio ownership in the Houghteling families was commensurate with the level in similar families. The Houghteling surveys confirm that radio ownership diffused quite rapidly in American cities in the 1920s but that occupation and class stratified diffusion.

LABOUR FORCE AND OCCUPATIONAL TRANSITIONS

Despite the persistence in Chicago of the Houghteling families, there was a considerable extent of occupational and industrial movement by the husbands who were, by sample construction, all in full-time employment with large employers in 1925. Of the 277 linked husbands, only one-third (93 of 277) remained in the same major occupation and industry. Less than 20 per cent (54 of 277) were in the exact same occupation and industry as in 1925 (tables 10.3 and 10.4). Occupational and industrial change was measured by comparing the coded occupation, with occupations coded into the IPUMS 1950 coding

Table 10.3
Changes in exact occupation and industry

	Did not change exact industry	*Changed industry*	*Total*
Did not change exact occupation	54 (19%)	51 (18%)	105 (38%)
Changed exact occupation	58 (21%)	114 (41%)	172 (62%)
Total	112 (40%)	165 (60%)	277

Table 10.4
Changes in major group occupation and industry

	Did not change major group industry	*Changed major group industry*	*Total*
Did not change major group occupation	93 (34%)	55 (20%)	148 (54%)
Changed major group occupation	67 (24%)	62 (22%)	129 (46%)
Total	160 (58%)	117 (42%)	277

scheme.[42] In the 1925 survey some men reported multiple jobs over the year the survey enquired about. For these men, the job they held for the longest part of the year was designated as the occupation for comparison with 1930. Remaining in the same "exact occupation" meant that the occupational code was identical in both years, although the literal response given to the enumerator may have changed. Some of the occupational categories that were frequently given by the Houghteling sample were quite broad, so even this measure understates change. For example, a "packer" and a "box maker" both receive the same occupational code in this coding system, and a person switching between these jobs would be recorded as remaining in the same occupation. A more literal coding of some common occupations may reveal even more movement. People remaining in the same industry (meat packing or steel) could have changed employers. Thus we have a conservative measure of occupational and industrial transitions, so it is striking how much movement there was between jobs in just five years. Less than one in five of the linked sample could have still been in the same job five years later.

Table 10.5
Occupational transitions of head of household

	1930 occupation					
1925 occupation	*White-collar*	*Skilled*	*Semiskilled*	*Service*	*Unskilled*	*Total*
White-collar	3	1	2	0	2	8
Skilled trades	2	12	1	1	7	23
Semiskilled trades	4	8	15	4	31	62
Service	1	3	6	20	12	42
Unskilled	9	4	23	8	98	142
Total	19	28	47	33	150	277

Definitions of occupational categories: All occupations are coded into the IPUMS OCC1950 classification system.

White-collar: Major groups 0, 2, 3, 4

Skilled trades: Major group 5. Carpenters and other "named" trades.

Semiskilled trades: Major group 6. Apprentices, operatives, stationary engineers, and "makers"

Service: Major group 7. Janitors, waiters, watchmen, and guards

Unskilled. Major group 9. Labourers

The pattern of job transitions (tables 10.5 and 10.6) does not suggest major movements up the occupational scale. But it does suggest some degree of movement. Broadly speaking the IPUMS "major groups" correspond to levels of perceived occupational status. A quarter of the 277 linked men moved up the occupational scale between 1925 and 1930 (equivalent to a move to the left in table 10.5). A man who was a "labourer" in 1925 and a "maker" or "operator" in 1930 would be regarded as moving up the occupational scale. Indeed, one in six (23 of 142) unskilled workers in 1925 had moved up to a semiskilled occupation by 1930. Some had even become clerical workers or sales workers, and one solitary person had been promoted to the position of supervisor. More than half the skilled workers in 1930 had moved up from semiskilled, unskilled, and service jobs five years earlier. The specific occupations show a move into more skilled employment rather than a move into supervisory positions or lower-level management. None of the Houghteling heads of household reported being a foreman, though several of their adult sons still living at home in 1930 were foremen.

While some moved up, others moved down. Nearly as many men moved from a skilled or semiskilled occupation in 1925 to an unskilled occupation in 1930 (61 of 277) as moved up the occupational hierar-

Table 10.6
Industrial transitions of heads of household, 1925–30, industry in 1930

			Manufacturing			*Services*				
Industry in 1925	*Farming*	*Construction*	*Durable*	*Nondurable*	*Utilities & Transport*	*Trade*	*Commercial*	*Consumer*	*Public admin.*	*Total*
Durable goods manufacturing	3	1	88	14	10	5	1	4	13	139
Nondurable manufacturing	1	0	8	37	2	4	1	1	6	60
Utilities and transport	0	4	7	3	27	1	0	1	5	48
Wholesale and retail trade	0	0	1	7	1	6	1	1	5	22
Public administration	0	0	4	1	0	0	0	1	2	8
Total	4	5	108	62	40	16	3	8	31	277

chy. We should not make too much of these changes because it is difficult to tell from the limited descriptions in each source what exactly a person was doing. The skill and status difference between a semiskilled "maker" and a "labourer" may just reflect the differing terms used within different firms and not any real difference in what a person was doing. No matter how one interprets the differences between jobs, there is considerable evidence that these men were very mobile in the local labour market. Relatively few remained with the same employer five years later, and occupational changes were likely for those that remained in the same industry and thus potentially with the same employer.

CONCLUSION

Leila Houghteling's original research has been widely cited by historians because of her sensitive portrayal of the lives of the industrial working class in the mid-1920s. The very questions on her survey about automobile and piano ownership, and the frequent notes by the interviewers of sewing machine ownership, indicate that consumer culture and material comfort was within reach for the low skilled and immigrants in America. Yet as Susan Porter Benson has shown recently, working-class lives could also be ones of struggle and work.[43]

While longitudinal studies often focus on change, the involvement of older children and wives in earning was an important continuity for working-class families in Chicago. These families purchased their homes and consumer durables by relying on the labour of many family members. Husbands' wages were important but on average made up only two-thirds of family earnings in 1925. Just seventy-six of 477 families in 1925 relied solely on the earnings of the father. This pattern persisted in the 1930 census. Only 15 per cent of families relied solely on the husbands' earnings in both 1925 and 1930. For the remaining 85 per cent of families, taking in boarders and lodgers and the earnings of wives and children remained a visible source of income. The continuing involvement of wives and young adult children in the labour market suggests that the occupational mobility of male household heads did not bring a high degree of security.

The focus on this chapter on transitions over just five years serves to emphasize the high degree of occupational circulation among the male household heads. At most, only 20 percent of the male household heads could have been in the same exact job in 1925 and 1930.

A further 15 per cent of the men appeared to be working in a closely related job, remaining in the same broad occupational or industrial category. Thus, at least two-thirds of these men made a significant change in their job in the space of five years, consistent with other historical evidence that labour turnover rates were high, though declining, in the 1920s.[44]

At the same time, these men and their families circulated around the Chicago area with 97 per cent of the linked families remaining in the metropolitan area. The high degree of persistence in one area is also consistent with other historical evidence that American geographic mobility rates declined in the early twentieth century. Taken together, the high occupational mobility within a large metropolitan area suggests a new pattern of looking for opportunity within the city. In this volume, Olson's chapter on Montréal shows that these patterns of intraurban mobility emerged in North American cities in the late nineteenth century. The qualitative picture of urban life is similar – frequent occupational transitions led to frequent residential moves as families balanced proximity to kin and industry. The experience of urban families thus differs significantly from the interstate and long-distance moves for agricultural land that were common in the nineteenth century. While a significant minority of the families made a successful transition to home ownership by 1930, the aggregate pattern of only slight upward occupational mobility points to the continuing limits on social mobility for unskilled workers.

PART FOUR

Ethnicity and War

11

Genes, Class, or Culture? French-English Height Differences in Canada

JOHN CRANFIELD AND KRIS INWOOD

INTRODUCTION: THE RESEARCH PROBLEM

Why some people are taller than others is a long-standing curiosity. Genetic inheritance clearly matters. Scientists estimate that individual genetic composition accounts for as much as 80 per cent of the variation in height in any population.[1] However there are other influences. Environmental factors (broadly defined to include socioeconomic characteristics and context) account for the remaining 20 per cent of stature variation within a population as well as changes over time and differences between large populations. One example of socioeconomic influence is the slight decline of stature during nineteenth-century industrialization because of deteriorating health and nutrition while, in contrast, during the twentieth century people became taller because of improvements in medical knowledge, public health, income, and food availability.[2] Socioeconomic influences on nutrition and health also explain why white-collar workers and farmers in an earlier period were, on average, 1.5 to 2.5 centimetres taller than labourers even in the food-abundant breadbasket colonies of the British Empire.[3] Regional differences in stature are understood similarly. Spatial variation in stature within the nineteenth century United States has been shown to reflect population densities, disease prevalence, proximity to transportation corridors, and food supply.[4]

The spatial pattern of stature in Canada is harder to explain. Adult

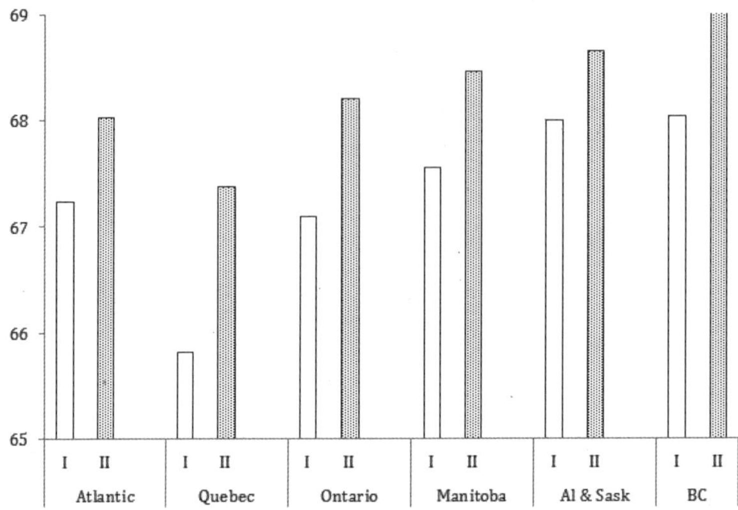

Note: I World War One; II World War Two
Source: Library and Archives Canada, First World War Records, B-surnames and Second World War personnel records, B and M-surnames, Killed In Action

Figure 11.1 Mean stature (inches) of Canadian-born WWI and WWII soldiers, by region of birth

stature circa 1900 generally increased from east to west although within the east those born in the Atlantic region were slightly taller and those born in Quebec were shorter.[5] Population densities, proximity to food supply, and isolation from transportation corridors can account for much of this pattern, with one striking exception. There is no easy explanation for mean stature in Quebec being markedly less than that of nearby Ontario and Atlantic Canada.

The Quebec differential reappears in a number of historical sources. Figure 11.1 reports the unconditional mean stature by birth cohort and province for Canadian men who served in World War One (WWI) and World War Two (WWII). During WWI those born in Quebec were more than an inch shorter than those born in Ontario and the Atlantic region; the gap was smaller but still substantial in WWII. United States authorities also reported that French Canadians were among the shortest soldiers in that country's WWI army.[6] The Quebec differential in Kingston Penitentiary inmates during the nineteenth century even survives multivariate analysis to remove the influence of confounding social influences.[7] The pattern is visible again in the nationally representative 1953 Height-Weight Survey (figure 11.2).

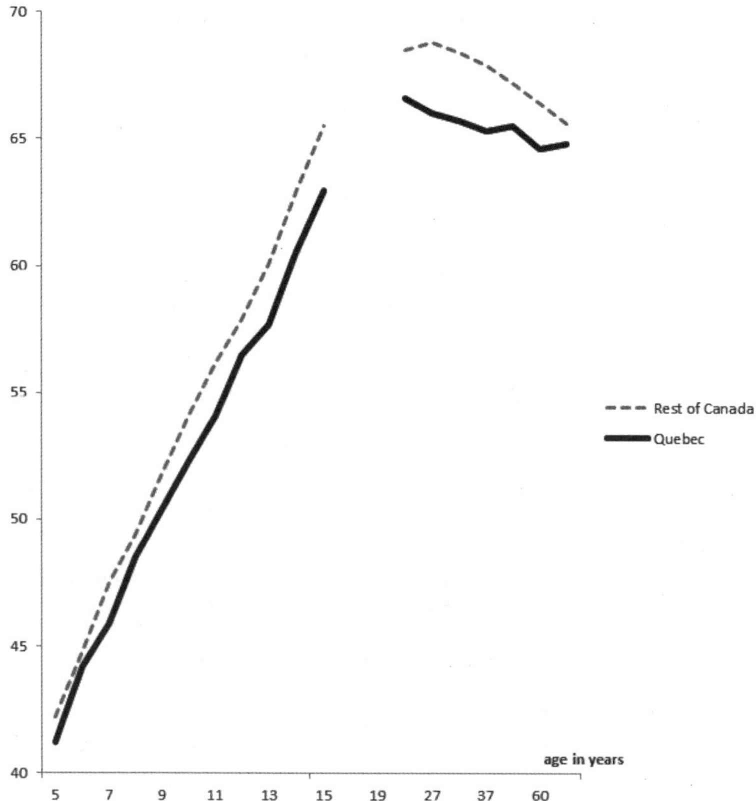

Figure 11.2 Mean height (inches) of men aged five to sixty-seven years, resident Quebec and in the rest of Canada, 1953 Survey

Even the late twentieth and early twenty-first-century social and health surveys indicate that the Quebec-born and, when that is unavailable, Quebec residents were significantly shorter (appendix: table 11.5). The differential appears to have diminished during the later twentieth century; moving from earlier to later surveys and the cohort comparisons within each survey point to a diminution of effects over time. The modern data also report French ancestry and/or the use of French language alone and alongside other languages (appendix: table 11.6). Neither language nor the Statistics Canada concept of ethnicity is an ideal indicator of ancestry, but the data suffice to persuade us that the French-descended population was shorter and that the patterns of relative shortness largely mirror that of the Quebec effect – not surprisingly given the considerable concentration of French-descended population in Quebec. In this paper we explore various explanations for the Quebec and French effects, beginning with the potential for genetic explanations.

IS THERE A GENETIC EXPLANATION?

The scientific understanding of human height has advanced considerably in recent years. The large-scale observational analysis of siblings and, more recently, the identification of individual genes allow geneticists to estimate that heritable genetic composition accounts for as much as 80 per cent of the variation in adult stature. Genetic influences on stature are complex, but all large populations are thought to have a similar *potential* mean stature.[8] Whether or not a population realizes its potential is attributed to "environmental" factors (broadly defined to include socioeconomic influences) and gene-environment interactions, which also account for the remaining 20 per cent or more of variation within the population.

We understand the environmental influences on height as a consequence of childhood "net nutrition," a convenient summary of socioeconomic status and public health influences such as food consumption, disease exposure, and energy expenditure.[9] Because of this relationship, stature provides valuable clues about health and the physical standard of living in the past. Admittedly, the identification of net nutritional effects for population subgroups is challenging because of the intervening influence of genetic inheritance. Large samples are needed in order to disentangle genetic from environmental effects.

A genetic explanation for the apparent tendency to shortness among the French and their descendants in North America is possible. The ancestors of Quebec's Francophone population migrated almost entirely from France between 1680 and 1760. There was little subsequent immigration especially to rural Quebec, and intermarriage with other ethnicities was limited except in the cities. If the genetic composition of the founding French population differed systematically from that of British and other immigrants, we would have a possible explanation for the Quebec effect in later centuries. This is a possibility, but corroborating evidence is needed.

Neither is there any reason to think that within Europe the French gene pool is predisposed to exceptional shortness. The mixing of populations across northwest Europe during the last three millennia makes it unlikely that France, or even northwest France which provided most of the migrants to Quebec, had a genetic composition substantially different than that of the British. The French invaded and occupied Britain in 1066, and in turn British armies invaded more than once and occupied parts of France for extended periods in subsequent centuries. The intermingling of the British and French people, especially in western France, from the eleventh to fifteenth centuries, makes it likely that their genetic inheritance is broadly similar.

The historical record of comparative height is itself unclear. Hatton and Bray report mean stature to be similar in France and Britain during the mid-nineteenth century.[10] Komlos argues the same for an earlier period: the mid-eighteenth-century French were slightly taller than the English and Scots.[11] Floud et al. present a different portrait of substantial French disadvantage during the late eighteenth and mid-nineteenth centuries.[12] The mixed record arises from different sources used in the three studies. As yet there has been no definitive resolution.

Another complication is that stature fluctuated over time in both countries, and these changes are understood by all of the researchers as having environmental rather than genetic origins. Even Floud et al., who identify a large gap, invoke standard net nutritional influences to understand stature among the French; they do not suggest a different genetically defined potential height in France and Britain. Moreover, the subsequent rise in French stature during the later nineteenth and twentieth centuries itself argues against a genetic constraint. If the French in Europe could grow substantially, and the only issue is genetic composition, surely this growth would have been possible for the French in North America.

Further research can be expected, both to reconcile the disparate historical sources and to identify more precisely genome-level differences among European populations. At present, however, the European record provides no evidence of a French-English difference in genetic endowment that would have implications for stature. If genetic analysis does not provide a satisfactory explanation, can we explain the differential with socioeconomic correlates?

THE QUEST FOR SOCIOECONOMIC EXPLANATIONS

For most of the last two centuries wages and per capita income have been lower in Quebec than in Ontario, food has been more expensive, and population densities have been higher than in Atlantic Canada. And, until relatively recently, the French-descended population clustered in the lower rungs of the Quebec and Canadian social order. Thus it is entirely plausible that Francophones in Quebec were shorter because of inferior net nutrition, which arose from social and economic circumstances of the kind familiar in the anthropometric literature. The problem here is to obtain data with which to evaluate the hypothesis.

The modern data are, surprisingly, of limited value. Only the General Social Surveys of 1985 and 1991 collected birthplace, stature, and ethnicity or language. Sample size for these data is small. The long-term reduction in size of the Quebec/French effect also makes the recent data less interesting. Fortunately we can turn to historical sources, which for this purpose are more helpful.

The absence of confidentiality restrictions for historical data allows us to link two large record series: the personnel records of the Canadian Expeditionary Force 1914–18 and the 1901 Canada census. Neither source by itself provides sufficient information, but a combination of the two provides a rich database of personal and anthropometric information. We begin with more than 64,259 records or roughly 10 per cent of the Canadian Expeditionary Force (CEF) for soldiers whose surname begins with the letter B. Thornton and Olson argue that B surnames are ethnically representative of the Canadian population and that B is seldom misheard by enumerators or misread by data entry operators. Elimination of duplicate records and records lacking detail leaves us with 53,960 records.[13] Removing the foreign-born drops the number to 26,990 records for men born in Canada before the 1901 enumeration. We link roughly 8 per cent of these records to the census with an intensive manual process, and then use the linked records to guide the development of an algorithm that expands the linked sample to 28 per cent of the available CEF records. Details of the method are reported in Kirk-Elleker.[14] Combining the manual and automatic links gives us 9,000 soldiers for whom family circumstances in 1901 are known.

The military records reasonably represent the Canadian male population. WWI enlistment was widespread among Canadian men.[15] Of course military-derived records overrepresent young adult males.[16] In table 11.1 we compare the Canadian male population of military age, all Canadian-born CEF enlistees with B-surnames, and records linked to 1901. These data indicate that enlistment drew disproportionately

Table 11.1
Percentage distribution of characteristics of the linked sample, all soldiers, and all Canadian men in the 1901 census

	Cdn-born men	*CEF records*	*Linked records*
DECADE OF BIRTH			
1860s	23.0	0.4	0.1
1870s	10.6	6.7	2.3
1880s	23.1	20.5	18.9
1890s	39.2	71.3	78.1
1900s	4.1	0.8	0.6
MARITAL STATUS			
Married	25.1	13.9	11.2
Not married	74.9	84.1	88.8
OCCUPATION			
Farmers	25.3	24.7	27.3
White-collar	15.4	21.4	24.7
Skilled	12.6	18.5	17.2
Unskilled	20.6	20.3	17.6
Labourer	12.1	11.1	8.1
Other	13.9	3.9	5.0
REGION OF BIRTH			
Atlantic	20.1	18.8	19.0
Quebec	26.7	25.7	22.5
Ontario	47.8	45.1	50.4
West	5.0	10.4	8.1
RELIGION			
Baptist	6.2	6.8	7.9
Church of England	15.4	18.2	18.4
Methodist	12.6	16.0	19.1
Presbyterian	16.1	17.2	20.6
Roman Catholic	45.0	35.3	28.2
Other	4.4	6.3	5.7
N	48,939	26,833	8,201

Source: Canada, 1901 census sample (Canadian Families Project); Canada, Canadian Expeditionary Force database

from the West, white-collar occupations, English-origin churches, and the unmarried men but in other respects was reasonably representative. A modest underrepresentation from Quebec Francophones and those of Irish ethnicity contributes to the smaller share of Roman Catholics in the CEF.

The linked records differ slightly again. We are somewhat more successful linking the 1890s cohort, farmers, white-collar workers, and the Ontario-born. Lower linkage rates for the 1870s cohort and general labourers undoubtedly reflect the greater imprecision of descriptions of older men and of occupations with higher rates of illiteracy and poverty.[17] Those born in Quebec were more difficult to link because of the homogeneity of the French Canadian name stock and a pattern of migration to English-speaking communities in which (a) some Francophones adopted English name equivalents and (b) many enumerators were unfamiliar with French spelling.[18] These differences between the military and the overall male population, and between linked records and the entire army, do not threaten the usefulness of the linked data, but they are large enough to suggest the value of specifying demographic categories in a multivariate analysis in order to adjust for compositional effects.

EMPIRICAL ANALYSIS OF STATURE

The simple medical exam undertaken at enlistment provides evidence of height. One complication arises from the CEF standards of physical fitness, which were intended to exclude men shorter than sixty-three inches.[19] Admittedly the requirement was not enforced systematically: "in the scramble for men, many battalions had not been fussy about whom they accepted. Doctors ignored physical defects and passed men as fit because their colonel needed them."[20] We use a standard multivariate technique to identify the various different influences on height in a way that recognizes the possible truncation at sixty-three inches.[21]

Measures of potential influences on stature are taken from both the census and the military record. Because physical growth prospects are determined early in life, we consider the effect of province, date of birth, and other indicators of childhood circumstance. The census also provides information on the mother tongue of the soldier, rural versus urban birthplace, the income reported by members of his family, the size of family, and birth order of children. The military record reports the soldier's own occupation at enlistment while the census provides the father's occupation during the soldier's childhood. The latter is preferable, but we report estimations with both measures because the soldier's own occupation is more commonly used in the anthropometric literature under an assumption of intergenerational persistence.

Of course any occupational mobility undermines the use of a son's occupation as a proxy for the father. We find in table 11.2 that at the

Table 11.2
Comparison of CEF soldier's occupation to head's occupation in 1901

Recruit's occupation code (from CEF records)	*Head's occupation code (from census records)*					
	Farmer	*White-collar*	*Skilled*	*Unskilled*	*Labour*	*Other*
Farmer	1634	82	122	104	158	20
	0.77	0.04	0.06	0.05	0.07	0.01
White-collar	367	603	357	255	86	67
	0.21	**0.35**	0.21	0.15	0.05	0.04
Skilled	327	166	335	213	144	30
	0.27	0.14	**0.28**	0.18	0.12	0.02
Unskilled	335	144	237	346	206	32
	0.26	0.11	0.18	**0.27**	0.16	0.02
Labour	188	38	89	125	132	9
	0.32	0.07	0.15	0.22	**0.23**	0.02
Other	75	150	52	47	18	14
	0.21	0.42	0.15	0.13	0.05	**0.04**

time of enlistment three-quarters of farmers but only one-third of those with white-collar occupations and even lower proportions of other groups were following their father's 1901 occupation. Overall, 58 per cent of the soldiers were in a different occupational class than their fathers. Of course, we are seeing father and son at different points in their lives. Therefore we also divide the soldiers in two broad age groups for older and younger soldiers (not reported). The men reporting white-collar occupations were more likely to follow their fathers as they grew older, and the older unskilled labourers were less likely to do so. In other respects, however, the patterns do not differ by age classes. Fifty-six per cent of the older soldiers were still in a different occupational class than their father. This evidence of considerable intergenerational mobility (apart from farmers) confirms the potential importance of taking socio-economic status from the father's occupation if possible.

We do this with a standard equation that explains height as a function of birth cohort, birth location, and alternate measures of socioeconomic status (appendix: table 11.7). Estimation with the soldier's occupation at enlistment is reported on the left while the right column uses occupation of household head in 1901. Surprisingly, given the extent of occupational change from father to son, a comparison of the two columns reveals no important differences in the pattern of estimated coefficients. From an inferential perspective the assumption of occupational persistence appears to have limited impact. One possible explanation is that occupational designations are sufficiently imprecise indicators of socioeconomic influences that the degradation of information from use of the proxy is of limited marginal consequence.

We wish to make use of additional information that is available from the census linkage. The census reports mother tongue and whether the birthplace was rural or urban. We do not know exactly how the rural and urban categories were defined. The census provided no instructions, except that individuals were asked to say if their birthplace was rural or urban. Whatever its definition, the greater disease exposure and higher food cost of urban life makes this a potentially important influence. The evidence of mother tongue is likely to have been defined more precisely although, admittedly, it too was self-reported. The language variable interests us because of the possibility that the Quebec effect arises entirely or in part from the Francophone majority in that province.

An estimation capturing these effects is reported in the column labeled "Mother Tongue and Rural" in table 11.3. The coefficient on rural birth has the expected positive correlation with height although it is not statistically significant. The introduction of mother tongue, however, markedly reduces the Quebec height disadvantage. It also increases the stature superiority of the Maritime or Atlantic coastal region, which had a substantial Francophone minority. It is clear that French-speakers who were largely of Francophone descent were systematically shorter. Separate regional regressions (not shown) confirm that the Francophone disadvantage was largest in Quebec (–2.0 inches against –1.6 inches in Ontario and –1.1 inches in the Atlantic region). It is clear that much, although not all, of the Quebec height penalty originates with its Francophone community and that, while being Francophone was disadvantageous outside of Quebec, stature inequality by language/ethnic group was greatest in that province.

Of course, other influences such as economic status may have overlapped with and be mistaken for the effect of being Francophone. Our standard measure of socioeconomic status (SES), occupation, is so crude that it may fail to capture variation in net nutrition and leave the Francophone variable to capture both inferior SES and any other consequence of being Francophone. We are fortunate, therefore, that the 1901 census enumerated individual earnings. This class of evidence has been used to demonstrate that Francophone families typically earned less than other ethnicities even within occupational groups.[22] With lower earnings, Francophone households might not have had the capability to provide comparable net nutrition for their children. Since there were more mouths to feed in larger households we use this information as income per person and assume income was pooled by all family members. We define the household to include immediate and extended family.

Another influence of potential importance is birth order.[23] Only the first child has the attention of parents without competition from siblings. With each additional child the mother is older and potentially weaker. Limitations of time and other resources can make it difficult for parents to give each additional child the same level of care. We cannot discriminate among these effects, but if any of them imply later-born children were weaker or received less care and other support, and Francophone families were larger, then the burden of weak net nutrition among high parity children may have fallen disproportionately on Francophones. The per capita measure of income provides a control for any effects of family size (positive or negative) that permit higher levels of parity, but a measure of birth order is needed to assess the additional effect of arriving late into an already large family. The 1901 census snapshot of the family misses those who have left home or are about to arrive, but it may suffice for our purposes.

The middle column of table 11.3 contains truncated regression results of the stature model with earnings and birth order effects. Both earnings per capita and birth order have significant effects. The occupational differentials on average do not change, but now earnings variation can capture intracategory variation. As earnings per household member increase so too does stature. As expected, birth order is inversely related to stature. The Quebec and French mother tongue effects remain significant. Indeed, the Quebec effect is more negative compared to the model without earnings and birth cohort effects.[24]

The results reported in table 11.3 also confirm that the rural-born were taller as adults although, again, the effect is not statistically significant. Enumerators were given no guidelines as to what constituted urban and rural, implying that the "rural" influence captured by this variable may not have been consistently specified.[25] Nevertheless, in spite of this imprecision, the potential importance of urban ill-health and the possibility that it varied across the country recommends another independent estimation for men born in urban and rural environments. This experiment (reported in appendix: table 11.8) demon-

Table 11.3
Truncated regression results for linked records with all census variables

		Mother tongue and rural			*With earnings and birth-order effects*			*With nonzero earnings and birth-order effects*		
		Coefficient	*z*	*P>z*	*Coefficient*	*z*	*P>z*	*Coefficient*	*z*	*P>z*
Density	Rural	0.123	1.34	0.18	0.116	1.246	0.213	0.089	0.801	0.423
	Urban	Omitted			Omitted			Omitted		
Cohort	Born pre-1880	Omitted			Omitted			Omitted		
	Born 1880–85	–0.094	–0.299	0.765	–0.073	–0.226	0.821	0.502	1.252	0.21
	Born 1885–89	–0.363	–1.294	0.196	–0.299	–1.031	0.302	0.038	0.107	0.915
	Born 1890–95	–0.35	–1.285	0.199	–0.27	–0.954	0.34	0.164	0.476	0.634
	Born 1895+	–0.638	–2.319	0.02	–0.526	–1.842	0.066	0.015	0.042	0.967
Birthplace	Maritimes	0.356	3.787	0	0.384	4.034	0	0.457	3.575	0
	Quebec	–0.294	–2.265	0.023	–0.315	–2.404	0.016	–0.563	–3.307	0.001
	Ontario	Omitted			Omitted			Omitted		
	West	0.612	4.859	0	0.6	4.731	0	0.734	3.996	0
Head's Occupation	Farmer	Omitted			Omitted			Omitted		
	White-collar	–0.085	–0.707	0.48	–0.202	–1.576	0.115	–0.381	–1.995	0.046
	Skilled	–0.502	–4.271	0	–0.596	–4.887	0	–0.643	–3.74	0
	Unskilled	–0.473	–4.054	0	–0.556	–4.618	0	–0.71	–4.163	0
	Labourer	–0.825	–6.264	0	–0.891	–6.638	0	–0.924	–5.212	0
	Other	–0.182	–0.731	0.465	–0.314	–1.245	0.213	–0.507	–1.6	0.11
Mother Tongue	English	Omitted			Omitted			Omitted		
	French	–1.583	–11.524	0	–1.562	–11.303	0	–1.446	–7.87	0
	Other	–0.368	–1.612	0.107	–0.357	–1.555	0.12	–0.485	–1.519	0.129

Age	Under19	–0.337	–2.464	0.014	–0.377	–2.713	0.007	–0.552	–2.919	0.004
	Age 19	0.163	1.134	0.257	0.143	0.987	0.324	–0.216	–1.094	0.274
	Age 20	0.064	0.497	0.619	0.045	0.351	0.726	–0.023	–0.126	0.9
	21 and over	Omitted			Omitted			Omitted		
Earnings p.c.					0.001	1.698	0.089	0.001	2.344	0.019
Birth order					–0.084	–2.95	0.003	–0.154	–3.947	0
	Constant	67.862	240.758	0	67.982	229.778	0	67.748	180.779	0
	Sigma	2.506	81.969	0	2.499	81.208	0	2.518	59.462	0
N		6459			6315			3585		

strates that the Quebec and the French-language effect were noticeably smaller in rural Canada.

DISCUSSION

The patterns of stature described by the estimations are for the most part anticipated. Earlier-born or lower parity children tended to be taller, consistent with previous evidence and with hypotheses about the biological status of the mother and intrafamily resource distribution.[26] Families with higher income, unsurprisingly, had taller sons. Men born in the closing years of the nineteenth century tended to be shorter, again consistent with previous evidence and with the widely entertained conjecture that growth in this period could be hazardous to health.[27] Farmers and white-collar workers were taller than labourers by as much as an inch – not surprising given previously documented patterns of inequality and differential access to resources favouring net nutrition.[28] Not all farmers were wealthy, but, generally, they experienced a lower relative price of food and greater isolation from endemic disease. Perhaps the biggest surprise is that the estimates are broadly robust to use of the soldier's occupation or his father's occupation in spite of intergenerational mobility.

The weak rural effect is unexpected. Coefficients were not significantly different than zero (albeit with a positive sign) and the constant terms in rural-only and urban-only estimations are very close (appendix: table 11.8). One explanation is that not every father born into rural Canada was a farmer; even among farmers many were relatively poor. A second line of explanation might be that the urban/rural health gap had already begun to close.[29] Pelletier et al. (1997) argue that urban/rural death rates began to converge after 1870; Harris and Mercier (2002) also suggest that suburban areas were nearly as unhealthy as the cities. Admittedly the precise definition of rural versus urban birth is unclear.

The regional effects conform to expectations. Those from Atlantic Canada were tall, in spite of lower incomes, because population density was low and reliance on fishing and animal husbandry gave easy access to dietary protein.[30] Those born in Western Canada were tallest, despite a higher cost of living, because wages were higher, population density was low, agricultural production was a regional specialty, and cities developed later.[31] Davies suggests that urbanization in British Columbia was informed by knowledge of sanitation unavailable at the time of building eastern cities.[32] The western height differential continued to exist well into the twentieth century.[33]

These results provide significant new detail about the patterns of Canadian stature and, by inference, childhood net nutrition. For example, the height advantage of the Atlantic region evident in other regressions disappears entirely if we restrict focus to the cities only. Those born in Atlantic Canadian cities were no taller than those born in Ontario cities. Our immediate interest, though, is to assess changes in the Quebec effect after introducing more powerful socioeconomic controls than were available previously. Inclusion of the language and urban/rural variables in table 11.3 reduces the Quebec height differential from 1.3 inches to 0.3 inches. It is clear that much of the variation otherwise attributed to province of birth is better ascribed to mother tongue. Those whose first language was French were 1.5 inches shorter than Anglophones, the largest of all influences investigated in our analysis. Separate regressions by province (not reported) imply a substantial Francophone height penalty everywhere in Canada. Separate rural and urban estimates also suggest that the effect was even larger in urban areas. The joint penalty for being born Francophone in a Quebec city was remarkably large.

It is not surprising that soldiers born in Quebec and, even more, Francophone soldiers were short. Food prices were higher in Quebec than Ontario.[34] Francophones in similar occupations had lower earnings.[35] Public health in Quebec City and Montreal was among the worst in North America.[36] Quebec industry employed large numbers of women and children at low wages.[37] Within Montreal, Francophones tended to live in less healthy conditions and had the highest infant mortality.[38] High infant mortality among Francophones is also reported for Ottawa.[39]

Nevertheless we are surprised that the broad range of demographic and socioeconomic controls does not reduce the combined effect of being Francophone and born in Quebec. We have introduced into the estimation various socioeconomic correlates of ethnic stratification: occupation, income, location, and family size. Undoubtedly we can improve further but remarkably the stature differential has increased rather than diminished as we controlled for more and more influences.

A measure of our ability to explain the stature differential with socioeconomic controls is available from a standard Oaxaca decomposition of stature differences by mother tongue that compares separate ethnicity-specific regressions.[40] The coefficients allow us to say how

Table 11.4
Oaxaca decomposition of mother tongue height differential

	Using French mother tongue coefficients		
	Estimate	*z*	*P>z*
Difference	1.638	21.81	0
Endowments/explained	0.397	2.28	0.023
Coefficients/unexplained	1.241	6.59	0
	Using English mother tongue coefficients		
	Estimate	*z*	*P>z*
Difference	1.638	21.81	0
Endowments/explained	0.177	1.77	0.077
Coefficients/unexplained	1.461	11.80	0

much of the average difference between language groups is explained by any tendency for Francophones to have been born disproportionately in less healthy areas (urban environment, Quebec) or to have had fathers with smaller incomes in lower socioeconomic status occupations or to have lived in larger families with more high parity children (i.e. birth order effects) or to have been born in a healthy decade (e.g., late 1890s). The calculations summarized in table 11.4 indicate that the "explained" share of mean stature difference is roughly 11 per cent or 24 per cent depending on whether we weight endowments by coefficients from the Anglophone or Francophone equation. The important conclusion, of course, is that even the most sensitive estimation that we can assemble explains only a small share of the Francophone stature difference. A disadvantaged socioeconomic status and other measurable characteristics contributed to the Francophone height penalty, but they explain at most a quarter of the differential. The remaining 75 per cent is still to be explained.

CONCLUDING COMMENTS: GENES, CLASS, AND CULTURE

We have argued that the prospect for an explanation of Canada's Quebec/French effect based in genetic differences is not promising. Socioeconomic or class-based determinants of net nutrition explain at most one-quarter of the gap. Might there be an explanation rooted in culture? Here, we use culture in the sense of systematic behavioural tendencies that are not the product of social, economic, demographic, or any of the other influences examined to date. A preference for smoking or living in large groups, or an aversion to healthy food consumption or sunlight, could be independent of socioeconomic circumstance and yet have a marked influence on net nutrition. This remains a somewhat speculative hypothesis. We know of no evidence supporting these or similar conjectures, with one important exception.

In 2001 two Quebec demographers, Sherry Olson and Patricia Thorton, reported birth-spacing evidence that breast-feeding in Montreal's Francophone population was more limited than in other cultural groups during the late nineteenth century.[41] They further argue that the difference in breast-feeding between Francophones and other groups (both Catholic and Protestant) can account for differences in infant mortality (which they also document). In this and other work, they emphasize the role of cultural distinctiveness independent of socio-economic differentiation.[42] We do not know if breast-feeding differed by cultural group outside Montreal but it seems possible, even if opportunities and constraints unique to the urban environment accentuated the contrast. An early withdrawal of breast-feeding, of course, may damage the growth potential of surviving children as well as causing elevated levels of infant mortality. Evidence is growing that scarring effects dominate selection effects in historical populations experiencing early life stress.[43] The coincidence of higher infant mortality and shorter adult stature among Francophones is consistent with this literature.

We are not in a position to test directly if cultural practices relating to breast-feeding may account for differential adult stature in Canada, but it seems possible. It also signals the possibility that a wide range of everyday cultural practice may have contributed to the Canadian Francophone stature puzzle. Further research would be useful in at least three directions: differences in breast-feeding and other cultural practices with implications for child health, improved socioeconomic controls in the multivariate analysis of adult stature, and genetic linkage studies of the Quebec population that will associate the genetic markers for height with observed phenotype variation. Ultimately, a multidimensional research strategy along these lines is needed to understand the single largest puzzle about the patterns of stature in nineteenth and twentieth-century Canada.

APPENDIX

Table 11.5
Estimated stature differentials, Quebec born and Quebec resident, various surveys, 1985–2005, by age and sex

		40–49 years		*30–39 years*		*20–29 years*	
Survey	*Characteristic*	*Coefficient*	*p-val*	*Coefficient*	*p-val*	*Coefficient*	*p-val*
MEN							
GSS 1985	Quebec born	-3.41	0.00	-1.14	0.05	-2.36	0.00
GSS 1985	Quebec residence	-3.64	0.00	-1.19	0.05	-2.40	0.00
GSS 1991	Quebec born	-2.90	0.00	-1.64	0.00	-2.01	0.00
GSS 1991	Quebec residence	-3.42	0.00	-1.94	0.00	-1.95	0.00
NPHS 1994	Quebec residence	-2.27	0.00	-1.96	0.00	-2.32	0.00
NPHS 1996	Quebec residence	-1.65	0.08	-1.21	0.17	-2.14	0.03
NPHS 1998	Quebec residence	-1.60	0.00	-2.06	0.00	-0.86	0.15
CCHS 2001	Quebec residence	-2.54	0.00	-2.19	0.00	-1.73	0.00
CCHS 2002	Quebec residence	-2.38	0.00	-1.65	0.00	-2.57	0.00
CCHS 2003	Quebec residence	-2.17	0.00	-1.88	0.00	-2.03	0.00
CCHS 2004	Quebec residence	-2.12	0.00	-1.72	0.02	-0.99	0.11
CCHS 2005	Quebec residence	-2.24	0.00	-1.90	0.00	-1.91	0.00
WOMEN							
GSS 1985	Quebec born	-2.41	0.00	-0.05	0.92	-1.94	0.00
GSS 1985	Quebec residence	-2.42	0.00	-0.02	0.97	-2.33	0.00
GSS 1991	Quebec born	-2.08	0.00	-1.61	0.00	-1.53	0.01
GSS 1991	Quebec residence	-1.76	0.00	-1.80	0.00	-1.76	0.00
NPHS 1994	Quebec residence	-1.72	0.00	-1.00	0.03	-1.83	0.00
NPHS 1996	Quebec residence	-1.58	0.09	-0.21	0.85	-0.77	0.49
NPHS 1998	Quebec residence	-2.43	0.00	-1.01	0.03	-1.02	0.06
CCHS 2001	Quebec residence	-1.64	0.00	-1.40	0.00	-1.38	0.00
CCHS 2002	Quebec residence	-1.67	0.00	-1.89	0.00	-1.11	0.00
CCHS 2003	Quebec residence	-1.70	0.00	-1.70	0.00	-1.04	0.00
CCHS 2004	Quebec residence	-0.64	0.22	-1.90	0.01	-0.60	0.26
CCHS 2005	Quebec residence	-1.37	0.00	-1.16	0.00	-1.22	0.00

Source: Statistics Canada, General Social Survey (GSS), National Population Health Survey (NPHS) and Canadian Community Health Survey (CCHS). The coefficients are estimated on records with more than $15,000 income and allowing for a distinctive effect of having an outdoor occupation.

Table 11.6
Estimated stature differentials, French origin and French language, various surveys, 1985–2005, by age and sex

Survey	Characteristic	*40–49 years*		*30–39 years*		*20–29 years*	
		coefficient	*p-val*	*coefficient*	*p-val*	*coefficient*	*p-val*
MEN							
GSS 1985	French origin	-3.08	0.00	-1.71	0.00	-1.46	0.00
GSS 1991	French origin	-2.76	0.00	-1.70	0.00	-1.88	0.01
GSS 1985	French language only	-3.70	0.00	-1.81	0.00	-2.78	0.00
GSS 1991	French language only	-3.39	0.00	-2.57	0.00	-2.27	0.00
NPHS 1994	French language only	-2.76	0.00	-3.38	0.00	-4.20	0.00
NPHS 1996	French language only	-1.64	0.24	-1.72	0.21	-3.57	0.01
CCHS 2001	French language only	-2.92	0.00	-2.85	0.00	-2.29	0.00
CCHS 2002	French language only	-2.60	0.00	-2.54	0.00	-3.33	0.00
CCHS 2003	French language only	-2.95	0.00	-2.84	0.00	-2.73	0.00
CCHS 2004	French language only	-3.62	0.00	-1.82	0.02	-2.11	0.00
CCHS 2005	French language only	-3.02	0.00	-2.72	0.00	-2.22	0.00
GSS 1991	French language plus	-3.24	0.00	-2.20	0.00	-2.11	0.00
NPHS 1994	French language plus	-2.19	0.00	-1.97	0.00	-1.78	0.00
NPHS 1996	French language plus	-1.56	0.00	-1.16	0.00	-0.78	0.02
CCHS 2001	French language plus	-2.22	0.00	-1.78	0.00	-1.11	0.00
CCHS 2002	French language plus	-1.96	0.00	-0.96	0.00	-1.10	0.00
CCHS 2003	French language plus	-1.72	0.00	-1.49	0.00	-1.23	0.00
CCHS 2004	French language plus	-1.53	0.01	-1.16	0.09	0.26	0.61
CCHS 2005	French language plus	-1.91	0.00	-1.26	0.00	-1.19	0.00
WOMEN							
GSS 1985	French origin	-1.84	0.01	-1.07	0.03	-2.13	0.00
GSS 1991	French origin	-2.06	0.00	-0.57	0.16	-1.56	0.01
GSS 1985	French language only	-2.05	0.01	-0.49	0.36	-2.47	0.00
GSS 1991	French language only	-2.17	0.00	-2.00	0.00	-1.76	0.00
NPHS 1994	French language only	-2.25	0.00	-1.85	0.00	-2.86	0.00
NPHS 1996	French language only	-1.48	0.25	0.53	0.71	0.17	0.93
CCHS 2001	French language only	-2.12	0.00	-1.59	0.00	-1.86	0.00
CCHS 2002	French language only	-2.18	0.00	-2.78	0.00	-2.00	0.00
CCHS 2003	French language only	-2.32	0.00	-2.05	0.00	-1.75	0.00
CCHS 2004	French language only	-0.66	0.27	-2.94	0.00	-1.47	0.02
CCHS 2005	French language only	-2.01	0.00	-1.81	0.00	-1.90	0.00
GSS 1991	French language plus	-2.11	0.00	-1.72	0.00	-1.65	0.00
NPHS 1994	French language plus	-1.57	0.00	-0.63	0.11	-1.17	0.01
NPHS 1996	French language plus	-1.19	0.00	-0.86	0.02	-0.10	0.80
CCHS 2001	French language plus	-1.39	0.00	-0.82	0.00	-0.66	0.00

Table 11.6 (*continued*)

Survey	Characteristic	40–49 years		30–39 years		20–29 years	
		coefficient	*p-val*	*coefficient*	*p-val*	*coefficient*	*p-val*
WOMEN (*continued*)							
CCHS 2002	French language plus	-0.98	0.00	-1.28	0.00	-0.14	0.63
CCHS 2003	French language plus	-1.42	0.00	-1.09	0.00	-0.35	0.03
CCHS 2004	French language plus	-0.57	0.23	-1.42	0.02	-0.26	0.54
CCHS 2005	French language plus	-1.36	0.00	-0.75	0.00	-0.93	0.00

Source: Statistics Canada, General Social Survey (GSS), National Population Health Survey (NPHS) and Canadian Community Health Survey (CCHS). The coefficients are estimated on records with more than $15,000 income and allowing for a distinctive effect of having an outdoor occupation. The GSS ethnic or cultural group variable is intended to identify the "roots" of the respondent; multiple responses are possible.

Table 11.7
Truncated regression results for linked soldiers with alternate sources for occupation

		Using soldier's occupation at enlistment			*Using father's occupation from 1901 census*		
		Coefficient	*z*	*P>z*	*Coefficient*	*z*	*P>z*
Cohort	Born pre-1880	Omitted			Omitted		
	Born 1880–85	-0.185	-0.678	0.498	-0.083	-0.26	0.795
	Born 1885–89	-0.371	-1.54	0.124	-0.335	-1.178	0.239
	Born 1890–95	-0.472	-2.026	0.043	-0.407	-1.473	0.141
	Born 1895+	-0.895	-3.748	0	-0.773	-2.772	0.006
Birthplace	Maritimes	0.315	3.563	0	0.243	2.636	0.008
	Quebec	-1.292	-13.685	0	-1.339	-13.478	0
	Ontario	Omitted			Omitted		
	West	0.693	5.756	0	0.614	4.864	0
Occupation	Farmer	Omitted			Omitted		
	White-collar	0.081	0.83	0.406	-0.07	-0.654	0.513
	Skilled	-0.537	-4.972	0	-0.53	-5.009	0
	Unskilled	-0.534	-4.991	0	-0.491	-4.524	0
	Labourer	-0.869	-5.981	0	-0.866	-6.724	0
	Other	0.316	1.914	0.056	-0.252	-1.053	0.292
Age	Under19	-0.208	-1.54	0.123	-0.15	-1.096	0.273
	Age 19	0.283	2.015	0.044	0.308	2.144	0.032
	Age 20	0.117	0.942	0.346	0.151	1.18	0.238
	21 and over	Omitted			Omitted		
	Constant	67.958	286.176	0	67.923	248.392	0
	Sigma	2.555	86.779	0	2.547	82.381	0
N		7387			6657		

Table 11.8
Truncated regression results with urban/rural split

		Rural only			*Urban only*		
		Coefficient	*z*	*P>z*	*Coefficient*	*z*	*P>z*
Cohort	Born pre-1880	Omitted			Omitted		
	Born 1880–85	0.204	0.498	0.618	-0.49	-0.913	0.361
	Born 1885–89	0.036	0.097	0.923	-0.746	-1.585	0.113
	Born 1890–95	-0.113	-0.315	0.752	-0.462	-1.009	0.313
	Born 1895+	-0.342	-0.951	0.341	-0.749	-1.57	0.116
Birthplace	Atlantic	0.482	4.38	0	0.086	0.449	0.653
	Quebec	-0.244	-1.499	0.134	-0.384	-1.74	0.082
	Ontario	Omitted			Omitted		
	West	0.627	3.863	0	0.553	2.711	0.007
Head's Occupation	Farmer	Omitted			Omitted		
	White-collar	-0.541	-3.028	0.002	0.482	1.451	0.147
	Skilled	-0.521	-3.257	0.001	-0.097	-0.295	0.768
	Unskilled	-0.5	-3.372	0.001	-0.097	-0.288	0.773
	Labourer	-0.772	-4.927	0	-0.526	-1.441	0.149
	Other	-0.341	-0.837	0.402	0.218	0.505	0.614
Mother Tongue	English	Omitted			Omitted		
	French	-1.502	-9.385	0	-1.856	-6.689	0
	Other	-0.045	-0.174	0.862	-1.169	-2.337	0.019
Age	Under 19	-0.399	-2.303	0.021	-0.378	-1.541	0.123
	Age 19	0.125	0.686	0.492	0.16	0.632	0.527
	Age 20	-0.053	-0.343	0.731	0.208	0.901	0.368
	21 and Over	Omitted			Omitted		
Earnings p.c.		1.436E-4	0.189	0.85	0.001	1.568	0.117
Birth order		-0.031	-0.941	0.346	-0.217	-3.942	0
	Constant	67.787	189.569	0	68.004	125.561	0
	Sigma	2.447	66.595	0	2.571	46.837	0
N		4,066			2,249		

12

Aboriginal and Mixed-Race Men in the Canadian Expeditionary Force, 1914–18[1]

ALLEGRA FRYXELL, KRIS INWOOD, AND AARON VAN TASSEL

INTRODUCTION

The uneasy relationship of First Nations communities with the British Empire did not stop them from contributing in important ways to the Canadian army in World War One (WWI). A considerable participation by Indians in the Canadian Expeditionary Force (CEF) was recognized at the time.[2] Some historians have argued that the government exaggerated Aboriginal participation by excluding communities with low attestation rates in order to demonstrate a positive response to the assimilationist policies of the Canadian government.[3] Other scholars note that Aboriginal attitudes to enlistment and the war effort differed greatly – even within communities.[4] Another complication is that the government appears to have reported on people for whom the Department of Indian Affairs (DIA) had administrative responsibility – Indians with "reserve status" under the provisions of the Indian Act – without considering First Nations outside the treaty system.

In this paper we provide a new portrait of Aboriginal participants in the CEF that differs from earlier work in two ways. First, we fashion a collective portrait that builds on the analysis of individual-level records. And, since we seek a broad view of Aboriginal experience, we do not limit our discussion to those who had taken treaty and thereby acquired "reserve status." Specifically, we examine soldiers who were identified as being Aboriginal in the enumeration records of the 1901 census.

The link between the census and military records allows us to identify differences in participation by tribal group, region, and mixed race versus pure blood. We see evidence of a considerable diversity of Aboriginal experience in the CEF, as historians have argued. The new evidence also suggests that Aboriginal contribution was even more extensive than originally claimed by the government because some mixed-race communities participated more actively than those with reserve status.

WHO IS ABORIGINAL?

The identification of an Aboriginal population in historical records is challenging. Canada's Indian Act defined who was and was not legally recognized for purposes of treaty payments and other entitlements and responsibilities. The legal definition changed over time and reflects the compromises of political and administrative process and bargaining between band leaders and the government.[5] Many researchers rely on this legal definition, understandably, because it identifies a population that is (i) politically significant and (ii) well-documented by the DIA. Nevertheless, policy-induced changes in criteria for "reserve status" complicate the use of this definition for some research purposes. Moreover, this definition excludes many people who had Aboriginal ancestry or lived within Aboriginal communities and yet more who self-identified as Aboriginal or behaved in a way that was identifiably Aboriginal according to cultural norms of the day. These exclusions reduce the overall size of the population identified as Aboriginal and may introduce biases inappropriate for some research purposes.

Fortunately, there are other ways to define indigeneity.[6] Government enumeration of ethnicity in many countries today relies on self-identification alongside a pragmatic recognition of political status for those whose standing is embedded in a treaty and/or legislation. Scholarly analysis of the causes and effects of particular socioeconomic characteristics may focus on those who grow up in Aboriginal communities and/or adopt culturally specific behaviour. Other kinds of research may require a family-based definition, for example if there is a genetic component for biomedical reasons or if ancestry and heritage figure in the analysis. Indeed, some research ideally might deploy a combination of the various definitions.

The definitions implicit in historical sources, of course, circumscribe what we can do. DIA sources do not provide individual-level detail on a systematic basis and in any case are limited to men with reserve status. Particularly worrisome is the exclusion of those whose childhood was Aboriginal even though as adults they might not have self-identified as Aboriginal. The census offers the potential for broader coverage. We are especially interested in the 1901 Canadian census because it records information when many of the WWI soldiers were still children. And, fortuitously, the 1901 census operated with a broader definition of Aboriginality than other pre-WWI censuses.

Hamilton demonstrates that enumeration of the First Nations was flawed in all years, although 1901 was less incomplete than earlier censuses.[7] The 1901 census instructions refer to "Treaty Indians" in a way that implies recognition of the presence of *non-Treaty* Indians.[8] Instructions for completion of the tribal origin and "colour" fields clearly invite the identification of Indians and mixed-race Aboriginals who would not have had treaty status. The post-WWI enumerations became *more* restrictive because the Census Bureau came to limit its enumeration of Indians to the reserve-based population, which was more easily identified. Nonreserve families of Aboriginal descent consequently faded into the general population without identification. The social deprecation of Aboriginal people undoubtedly encouraged some nonstatus people of Aboriginal descent to suppress evidence of their identity even in the 1901 census, but at least this enumeration made a comprehensive attempt to inventory the mixed-race community. Our strategy, therefore, is to begin with men and boys identified by 1901 census enumerators as Aboriginal or mixed race. We then ascertain which Aboriginal men enlisted in the CEF. Some of them were visibly Aboriginal in the context of the CEF, and others were not, but our identification of them as Aboriginal does not depend on any document generated during the war.

LINKING CENSUS TO CEF ATTESTATION PAPERS

We begin with 36,153 males under the age of thirty described as Aboriginal or partly so in the tribal origin field of the 1901 census. We have attempted to locate a CEF enlistment paper for all of them.[9] Individual attention to more than 36,000 records was complex and time consuming because of imprecision in both sources and particularly in the CEF reports of birth date and place. Young men are especially challenging because some lied about their age in order to enlist.

We look for soldiers with the same or similar names as in the census and then evaluate possible matches using information for next of kin, date of birth, and birthplace. After identifying soldiers with a consistent name and age, we discriminate among them and confirm matches using next of kin and, if that is not possible, place of birth.[10] By combining these indicators (age, name, date of birth, next of kin, and birthplace), we establish (i) if a CEF record can be found to match the individual extracted from the census and (ii) if the match can be made with "high," "medium," or "low" confidence.[11] We discard tenuous "medium" and "low" confidence links, triple check the remainder for transcription accuracy and linkage quality where this might make a difference, and in the end accept only those matched that are confirmed with "high" confidence.

We are confident in the matches made for 2,059 or 6 per cent of the individuals with which we began.[12] Undoubtedly we have failed to find many Aboriginal soldiers – because of name changes, errors or omissions in census-taking practice, and the enumerator's attempt to record Aboriginal names in English. Men whose names were not recorded clearly in one source or the other are harder to link. Someone who gave an Aboriginal name in 1901 and an Anglicized equivalent in the CEF is especially challenging. Men who married between 1901 and 1914 and thereby acquired a new next of kin are also more difficult to link. Because of these complications we express the enlistment data as an approximate rate of enlistment based on census-to-CEF linkage rather than as a comprehensive enlistment rate and use it mainly to gauge the relative enthusiasm for the war effort of different Aboriginal groups.

This process gives us a different set of soldiers than those identified by the DIA. The DIA records appear to record status Indians only, but they should be complete for that population.[13] We attempt to identify a broader Aboriginal population, but our records are incomplete insofar as they rely on the linkage between census and enlistment records. Two battalions with substantial Aboriginal participation illustrate the partial overlap between our men and soldiers known to Indian Affairs.[14] The 114th Canadian Infantry Battalion enlisted more than 200 Aboriginal men early in the war; many were from the 37th Haldimand Rifles militia unit based on the Six Nations reserve.[15] One hundred and twenty-six records in our database have regimental numbers associated with this battalion, implying that we have captured about two-thirds of the initial Aboriginal enlistment.[16] Only four soldiers in the 114th known from other sources to be Aboriginal are missing from our database. We identify fewer men from Winnipeg's 107th "Timber Wolf" Battalion, another largely Aboriginal unit,[17] perhaps in part because this unit relied more heavily on transfers from other units.[18]

ABORIGINAL PEOPLES AND THE CANADIAN EXPEDITIONARY FORCE

At the outbreak of war, Canada's professional army stood at only 3,000 soldiers. Few Aboriginal men were among the approximately 32,000 who answered the first call for volunteers.[19] Although no laws barred their enlistment, some Aboriginals were turned away because of social prejudice and their historical status as "wards" of the state.[20] Many believed that Aboriginal soldiers were not needed because the war would be over by Christmas and the first wave of enlistment was robust. The following year, however, as recruitment rates waned and casualties mounted, the CEF took more interest in the enlistment of Aboriginal men. The Canadian government ended uncertainty with an announcement 9 December that all Aboriginals were to be accepted as long as they met military regulations.[21] The decision in January 1916 to expand the CEF to 500,000 men further heightened interest in systematic recruitment from the First Nations.[22] Military and Indian Affairs officials were instructed to increase Aboriginal enlistment rates by recruiting on reserves.[23]

While some bands allowed eligible men to volunteer, others were hostile to the intrusion of recruitment officials into their communities.[24] They employed various tactics to counter the active recruitment campaigns. Talbot asserts that "attitudes against enlistment ... [had] hardened" by 1916 when only four of seventy Six Nations chiefs favoured enlistment and three even "publicly sympathized" with Germany.[25] The Manitoulin Island Aboriginal community circulated antienlistment pamphlets in an attempt to dissuade young men from enlisting – pamphlets were written in Ojibwa to avoid alerting Indian Affairs officials. At the Behawon Henvey Inlet Reserve eligible males hid in the forest while the chief argued that the communities' contributions to the Canadian Patriotic Fund should exempt his band from any compulsion to enlist.[26]

Resistance increased with the introduction of the Military Service Act. National debate over conscription ended in 29 August 1917 with the promulgation of the Military Service Act. The act did not mention the First Nations and was understood to apply to them. Unsurprising-

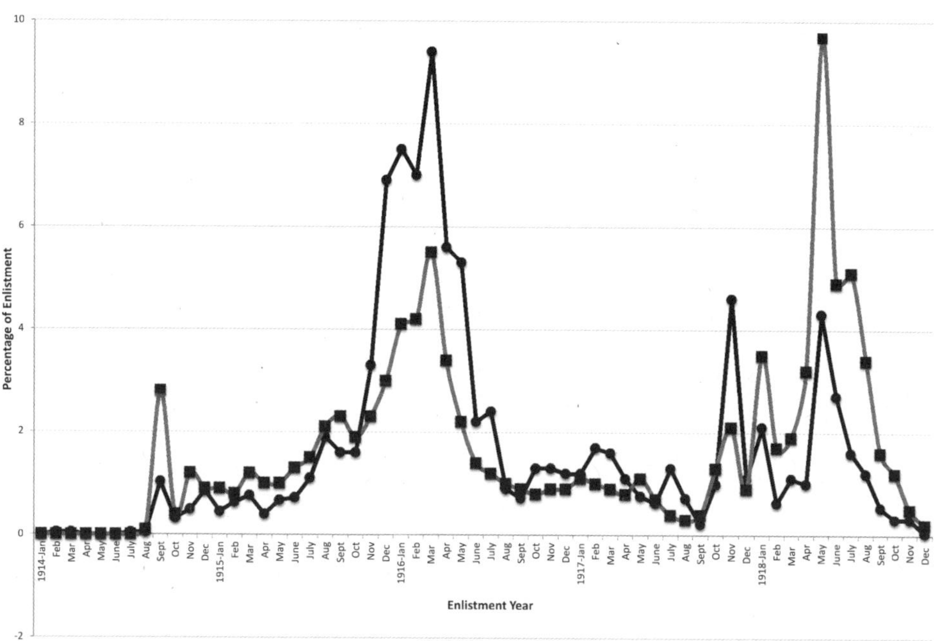

Figure 12.1 Rate of enlistment by attestation year

ly, this caused a strong reaction from many communities.[27] Aboriginals argued that they were not Canadian citizens but disenfranchised wards of the state who could not be forced to fight overseas for a government they did not elect.[28] Some communities were able to cite specific treaty rights; for example a passage in Treaty 3, signed in 1873, stipulated that they would not be forced to fight for Canada in the event of overseas warfare.[29] The Allied Indian Tribes of British Columbia wrote to the prime minister in the winter of 1917 explaining their resistance because of government unwillingness to resolve land claims, their status as "wards of the state," and the general inequality imposed on all Aboriginal peoples.[30] The petition also contained a threat of violence if the government attempted to implement conscription by force.[31]

After much deliberation, the Canadian government bowed to widespread pressure and by order-in-council on 17 January 1918 recognized an exemption of sorts for Aboriginal men. They could still be asked to fulfill noncombat duties in Canada, but they would not be sent overseas.[32]

Table 12.1
Distribution of ages at enlistment

Age (years)	*Aboriginals*	*All Canadian-born CEF*
10–19	20.9 %	18.0 %
20–29	57.3 %	64.2 %
30–39	16.2 %	13.7 %
40–49	3.6 %	4.0 %
50+	0.1 %	0.1 %

Table 12.2
Occupations of the heads of soldiers' households in 1901

	Aboriginals	*All Canadian-born CEF*
Agriculture and related	56 %	42 %
Unskilled labour	34 %	26 %
Professional, skilled, industrial and service	10 %	32 %

SIMILARITIES AND DIFFERENCES IN THE PATTERNS OF ABORIGINAL ENLISTMENT

The linked census-CEF data are largely consistent with this narrative. We chart in figure 12.1 the distribution of enlistment month by month for Aboriginal men and for all Canadian-born soldiers.[33] Both groups experienced an initial surge in the fall of 1914, fell back, and then began to increase again midway through 1915. The greater enthusiasm of Aboriginal response in 1915 can be understood as the response of a pent-up desire to serve following the shift to a policy of encouragement and then, on 9 December, recognition of the Aboriginal right to enlist freely. The highest rates of Aboriginal enlistment are visible during the winter and spring of 1916. Enlistment for both Aboriginal and others then dropped in 1917 until conscription came into effect on 29 August. At this point we see a second divergence: the rate of Canadian-born enlistment increases significantly while the Aboriginal upsurge was more subdued because of effective resistance by band leaders to the Military Service Act.

The same enlistment data allow us to report, in table 12.1, the personal and socioeconomic characteristics of Aboriginal soldiers. Most

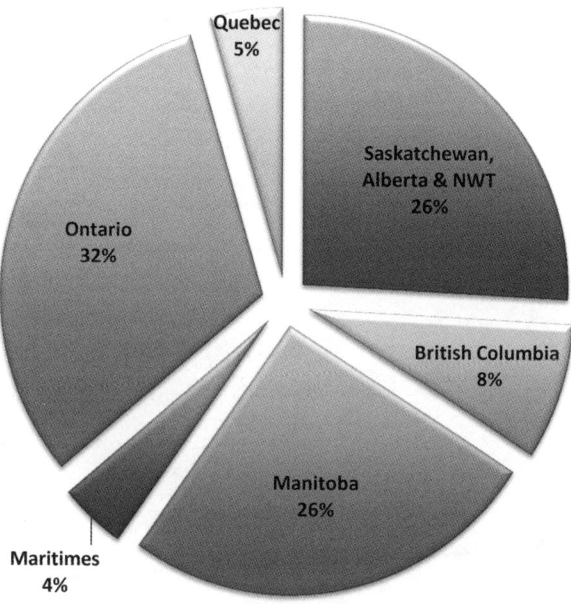

Figure 12.2 Province of birth for Aboriginal-born CEF

soldiers enlisted in their twenties; mean ages were 24.3 for Aboriginals and 24.5 for white Canadians. The patterns for marital status are also similar. For those reporting martial status, 76 per cent of the Aboriginals were single against 86 per cent for Canadian-born Caucasians.[34] Greater differences emerge in the comparison of socioeconomic background, as reflected in the occupations of heads of household in which soldiers were living in 1901. In table 12.2 we report these occupations in three broad groups: agriculture and related, unskilled labour, and higher-skilled roles in the professional, skilled labour, industrial and service sectors. Aboriginal soldiers came disproportionately from unskilled labouring families. Relatively few Aboriginal members of the CEF grew up in families whose head was active in professional, skilled trades, or the service sector. To a considerable extent this simply reflects the socioeconomic status of the First Nations in pre-WWI Canada.[35]

The birthplaces of Aboriginal soldiers also differed considerably from the pattern of birthplace for all Canadian-born (figures 12.2 and 12.3). Again, differences within the CEF mirror the patterns of Canadian society more broadly. The spatial distribution of origins for the soldiers roughly replicates their distributions in the Canadian population.

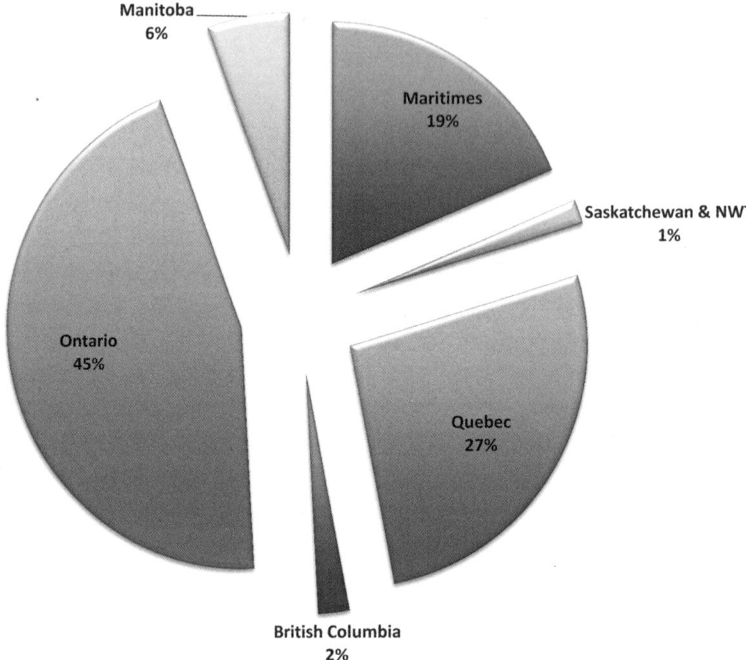

Figure 12.3 Province of birth for all Canadian-born CEF

Ontario contributed 32 per cent of Aboriginal soldiers, Manitoba 26 per cent, and Saskatchewan 18 per cent. Enlistment was less common among the more isolated Aboriginal populations on the West Coast and in the north.[36]

Table 12.3 reports the distribution of Aboriginal soldiers by reported tribe. Men of mixed Aboriginal-European ethnicity who identified a tribal group are reported with the relevant tribal group. This is important because 60 per cent of all census-linked Aboriginal soldiers described themselves as "mixed breeds" of Aboriginal and European descent, often simply recorded as "OB" for "Other Breed" under Tribal Origins. Most of the "half breeds" had one parent of French, English, or Scottish descent. A significant number of the mixed-race families gave a Caucasian surname in the census and in the CEF. Pure-blood Aboriginals, in contrast, were more likely to have an Aboriginal name in the 1901 census and a European name for military enlistment (especially if they wanted to enlist before December 1915). Thus, as a group, the mixed-race population was easier to link from the census to the

Table 12.3
Links and "Enlistment Rates" by Aboriginal Groups

Tribal Grouping	*1901 Eligible*	*Number*	*% Total Linked*	*"Enlistment Rate"*
Mi'kmaq, Malecite	1,076	101	4.5%	9.4%
Six Nations	4,384	247	11.1%	5.6%
Cree	7,789	480	21.5%	6.2%
Ojibwa, Chippewa, Saulteaux	3,694	231	10.4%	6.3%
Other Central Canada*	1,755	91	4.1	5.2%
Stoney, Sioux	1,294	22	0.99%	1.7%
Métis	920	126	5.7%	13.7%
BC Indian*	4,943	32	1.4%	0.7%
Slavey	350	1	0.45%	0.3%
Unspecified breed	7,155	746	33.5%	10.4%
Unspecified Aboriginal	2,792	143	6.4%	5.1%
Unclear / Not given	-	10		0.45%
Total	36,152	2,230		

*Other Central Canada includes Montagnais, Algonquin, Abenaki, Mississauga, Ottawa, Potawatomi, Huron, and respective "breeds."

attestation papers. This bias must be kept in mind when considering the pattern of tribal origins in table 12.3.

Thirty-three per cent of Aboriginal men linked from 1901 to CEF listed their tribal origins as some type of "breed" but did not give a specific tribal affiliation.[37] Cree Indians and Cree "breeds" comprise another 22 per cent of the sample, followed by Six Nations at 11 per cent, and Ojibwa/Chippewa/Saulteaux at 10 per cent. The broad category of "BC Indian" includes Salish, Kootenay, Shuswap, Kwaguilt, Carrier, Thompson, Yale, Nanaimo, and Cowichan natives as well as their respective "breeds," in addition to individuals simply listed as "BC Indian Breed." The low numbers of linked Stoney, Sioux, BC, and Slavey Indians may reflect lower quality enumeration (because of language barriers and the logistical challenge of enumerating remote communities) and of course the greater difficulty of linking them.

We express in table 12.3 and figure 12.4 the number of men identified in the CEF relative to the number from each tribal group returned in the 1901 census. For convenience we refer to this as an "approximate enlistment rate," but of course this is misleading to the extent that some men enumerated in 1901 did not remain in Canada and sur-

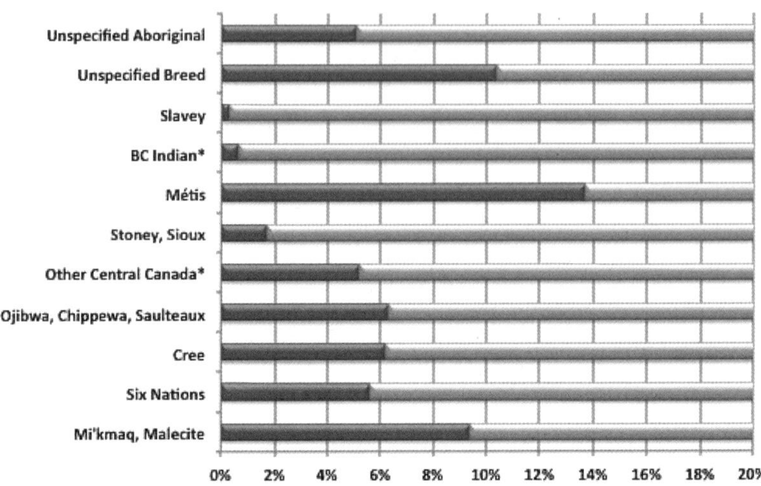

Figure 12.4 Aboriginal "enlistment rates"

vive until 1914, were not able-bodied in that year, or simply were not linked properly. The caveat is important because cross-border migration and mortality rates were high for Aboriginal men, and, as noted above, linking is a significant challenge. Accordingly some caution is needed to interpret these data. Our principal interest is the relative rates of apparent enlistment, i.e. comparing one Aboriginal group to others, rather than the absolute levels reported in table 12.2. Even this must be treated as an approximation because of intertribe differences in the ease of linking.[38]

The West Coast peoples appear to have had a very low enlistment rate – less than 1 per cent. While the difficulties of linking may have contributed to the low level, it resonates as well with other sources. Indian Agent Charles Cooke's anecdotes from his travels through the province include examples of hostility verging on violent threats to Indian Agents and military recruits, which historian R.J. Talbot attributes to "outstanding grievances against Canada and the Crown," as the encroachment of white settlers on native territory was particularly active in some parts of British Columbia during the early twentieth century.[39]

The Métis had the highest apparent enlistment rate, almost 14 per cent, in spite of the full-scale Riel Rebellion, which the parents of these soldiers lived through. Following the Métis were the unspecified "breeds" (10 per cent) and the Atlantic regional Mi'kmaq and Malecite (9 per cent) and then other central Canadian groups, which hovered between 4 and 6 per cent.[40]

Our enlistment rate for the Six Nations is lower than the 19 per cent speculated by the DIA in 1916.[41] We only record soldiers as Aboriginal if they can be securely linked to the census, while the DIA, on the other hand, may have been inclined exaggerate in order to demonstrate successful assimilation. It is less expected that the "approximate enlistment rate" of other groups is greater than that of the Six Nations. We believe the comparison to be roughly correct, in the absence of any reason to regard Six Nations men as more difficult to link than the Métis and other groups. Of course, much of the Six Nations leadership was hostile to enlistment and especially to conscription. Further, their location in southern Ontario and Quebec made it easy for Six Nations men to contribute in other ways, for example war-related work in agriculture and nearby factories.[42] It would be surprising if these factors did not have some impact. Among the Six Nations themselves, Mohawks comprised 43 per cent of positive links, followed by Delaware/Munsey (10 per cent), Cayuga (8 per cent) and the collective terms "Iroquois" (13 per cent) and "Six Nation" (13 per cent). Some have seen the Iroquois as the Queen's most ardent supporters, but these data do not suggest they were exceptional.[43]

Limited education made it unlikely that many Aboriginal men would become officers, and yet about 1 per cent of our census-linked soldiers entered the CEF as officers. George Black, of Chippewa heritage, had been an officer in the 13th Royal Regiment since 1902. He was living in Hamilton with his wife in January 1915 when he enlisted as a major. Another Aboriginal officer, Brantford native Lieutenant Oliver Milton Martin transferred from the 114th Battalion to the Royal Flying Corps in September 1917. After the war he remained in the militia and then in the Second World War rose to the rank of brigadier (the highest ranking Canadian Aboriginal in either war). Lieutenant Alexander Smith in the 20th Battalion received a Military Cross when his unit captured an enemy trench and took fifty prisoners during the Battle of the Somme. Smith survived the war despite being wounded three times and returned home to become a Six Nations chief.[44]

Other Aboriginal men distinguished themselves conspicuously. A member of the 1st Battalion, Francis Pegahmagabow received the Military Medal and two bars for his heroic efforts at Mount Sorrel, Passchendaele, and Amiens. After the war, Pegahmagabow returned to the Parry Island community to serve as a band councillor and chief.[45] Sev-

Table 12.4
Mother tongue and mixed race versus pure blood, by region and all Canada

	Number Observations	*% mixed*	*Mother tongue* *% Indian*	*% English*	*% French*
Southern Ontario & Eastern Canada					
Pure blood	568		89%	9%	2%
Mixed race	146	20%	34%	43%	23%
Northern Ontario and Manitoba					
Pure blood	98		82%	17%	1%
Mixed race	541	85%	20%	46%	34%
Western Canada					
Pure blood	78		86%	14%	0%
Mixed race	619	89%	45%	43%	13%
All regions					
Pure blood	744		88%	10%	2%
Mixed race	1,306	64%	33%	44%	23%

eral men of the 52nd or "Bull Moose" Battalion received decorations including the Distinguished Conduct Medal for Sergeant Leo Bouchard of the Nipigon First Nations and the Military Medal for Private Augustin Belanger.[46] The commanding officer of the 52nd described the Anishnawbe (Ojibwa) in his unit as among the "very best" of his soldiers.[47] This view was not uncommon; Winegard argues that race relations were generally good for Aboriginals in the CEF.[48]

Aboriginal soldiers shared with other members of the CEF a relatively high mortality rate. The Aboriginal death rate was 10 per cent – about the same as the loss in the B-surname sample of 9 per cent for a comparable length of service.[49] Admittedly, death may have arrived in different ways for Aboriginal soldiers.[50] Tuberculosis took a terrible toll in some prewar Aboriginal communities.[51] Not surprisingly, during the war the incidence of tuberculosis was higher for Aboriginal soldiers. The DIA Deputy Superintendent Scott observed, "The Indians are especially susceptible to tuberculosis, and many of their soldiers who escaped the shells and bullets of the enemy succumbed of this dreaded disease upon their return to Canada as a result of the hardships to which they were exposed at the front."[52]

THE DIVERSITY OF ABORIGINAL EXPERIENCE

The information presented above points to similarities and differences between Aboriginal and other soldiers and also to the considerable heterogeneity among Aboriginal troops themselves. Further diversity of region of birth, pure versus mixed blood, and language or mother tongue is reported in table 12.4.[53] We have constructed the regions to be of roughly equal size in order to retain sample sizes needed for statistically meaningful stratification and yet also capture some of the geographical and historical diversity.

One startling contrast is variation in the importance of mixed-race status. Nearly 90 per cent of Aboriginal soldiers born in northern Ontario and further west report some kind of mixed-race status, against only 20 per cent in southern Ontario, Quebec, and the Atlantic region. The information here does not allow us to say if the east-west difference simply mirrors the nature of regional Aboriginal communities or if it reflects some complex pattern of differences in the willingness to enlist. Another possibility is that mixed-race ethnicity may have a less socially acceptable response to 1901 enumerators in eastern Canada than in the West. Perhaps the long history of interaction between Aboriginals and relatively small numbers of Europeans in western Canada accommodated greater fluidity in both intermarriage and in the social acceptability of mixed-race identification.

The 1901 census also enquired about "mother tongue."[54] In all regions 90 per cent of those considered to be pure blood, defined here as tribal identification in 1901 with no indication of mixed race, reported one or another Indian language as their mother tongue. In contrast, among those described as mixed race, the proportion with an Aboriginal mother tongue varied from 20 per cent to 45 per cent and averaged one-third across Canada. The lowest proportion of Indian mother tongue among mixed race is seen in the large and long-standing mixed-race Aboriginal communities of northern Ontario and Manitoba. In this region, the historic heartland of the fur trade, there was a near equal balance of French and English mother tongue. Elsewhere, among mixed race who did not report an Aboriginal mother tongue, English was more widely used than French (as it was among pure bloods as well).

The evidence of mother tongue from the 1901 census suggests that the mixed-race soldiers were more closely integrated with immigrant

Table 12.5
Characteristics indicating the extent of social integration, by region

	Number Observations	*Previous military*	*Conscripted*	*Signed name*	*Christian church*
Southern Ontario & Eastern Canada					
Pure blood	568	25%	7%	86%	95%
Mixed race	146	23%	11%	96%	97%
Northern Ontario and Manitoba					
Pure blood	98	4%	10%	92%	93%
Mixed race	541	7%	30%	98%	99%
Western Canada					
Pure blood	78	6%	12%	99%	99%
Mixed race	619	11%	30%	88%	97%
All regions					
Pure blood	744	20%	8%	88%	95%
Mixed race	1,306	11%	28%	93%	98%

and settler-based Canadian society than pure-blooded Aboriginals. It seems likely that many men reporting mixed race did *not* have reserve status and, conversely, that most of the apparently pure-blooded soldiers did have treaty status. Unfortunately, there is no easy way to confirm this. Neither the census nor CEF attestation papers attempted to document status under the Indian Act. Some birthplaces were described as reserves, but the information is not systematically available, and in any case residence did not guarantee reserve status (just as reserve status did not guarantee residence).

Additional evidence of the extent of Aboriginal integration with immigrant and settler-based society is reported in table 12.5. About one-quarter of the soldiers from southern Ontario and eastern Canada had prior military and/or militia experience.[55] A cadet-training program introduced after the South African War of 1899–1902 may have contributed here since cadet training was widely adopted within the residential school system of most provinces.[56] By 1913, 4,655 Aboriginal students had received cadet training, and some of them undoubtedly enlisted in the CEF. Unexpectedly, there was no systematic difference in prior experience between mixed race and pure blood (except in the most westerly region where sample size undermines the significance of the contrast).

Almost all soldiers who enlisted in the CEF reported an attachment to one of the Christian churches. A small proportion indicated allegiance to an Indian faith or declined to answer the question (which would be consistent with rejection of the Christian churches). The non-Christian portion reached a maximum of 7 per cent among pure bloods in northern Ontario and Manitoba and 5 per cent in southern Ontario and eastern Canada. Literacy as defined by the ability to sign one's name is also available from the attestation documents. One in every ten soldiers made a mark rather than signed his name. Literacy, defined in this way, was lowest among pure bloods in the eastern and central regions and among the mixed race in the West.

About 10 per cent of pure bloods and 30 per cent of mixed race were conscripted, although the level was significantly lower in southern Ontario and eastern Canada. The lower incidence of conscription among pure bloods probably reflects an exemption to the Military Service Act available to many of them by virtue of having reserve status. A greater willingness to volunteer among Aboriginals in the eastern-most region is consistent with the suggestion that they were most closely integrated with immigrant and settler-based society.

CONCLUSIONS

We have examined participation in WWI through the characteristics and enlistment patterns of more than 2,000 Aboriginal members of the Canadian Expeditionary Force. Our survey employs a broader criterion for Aboriginal ethnicity than in most previous discussions. Nevertheless, pure-blooded Indians account for only one-third of our sample. Not surprisingly, given our broad definition of Aboriginality and our access to individual-level detail, we see considerable diversity among Aboriginal soldiers in the CEF.

Some of the patterns are unsurprising. The age profile for Aboriginal soldiers was broadly similar to that of other soldiers because war was predominantly an activity for young men (table 12.1). Other patterns reflect the distinct populations and communities from which the soldiers came. The spatial distribution of birthplace for Aboriginal soldiers differed from other soldiers in large part because in 1901 the Aboriginal population itself was located disproportionately in the Canadian west and north (figures 12.2 and 12.3). The occupations of the fathers of Aboriginal soldiers reflect the social and economic position of Aboriginal Canadians of that generation including, most obviously, a limited presence in white-collar, professional, and skilled labour (table 12.2).

Government policy also mattered. The ebb and flow of CEF recruiting influenced the timing of enlistment by Aboriginals as it did for other Canadians (figure 12.1). A policy aversion to Aboriginal enlistment held back attestations early in the war followed by a dramatic increase after the lifting of restrictions at the end of 1915. Intake resulting from the introduction of the Military Service Act was less dramatic in Aboriginal communities because of exemptions available to many treaty Indians and, perhaps more importantly, because conscription was introduced in a way that affronted Aboriginal sensibilities.

Our data confirm that Aboriginal communities under treaty with the Canadian government contributed large numbers of recruits to the CEF, as Scott argued in 1919. The military participation of the Six Nations in southern Ontario and western Quebec, for example, is widely recognized. We find that collectively the Six Nations accounted for 11 per cent of all Aboriginal soldiers (table 12.3). More surprising, though, may be the very large numbers of Aboriginal soldiers from other tribes. The mixed-race population, located largely in northern Ontario, Manitoba, and western Canada, had an especially high participation rate (figure 12.4). Taking account of Aboriginal groups outside of the DIA-administered reserve system reveals that Aboriginal participation in the war was considerably more extensive than has been recognized.

The data also reveal much about personal characteristics and socioeconomic circumstance. Large numbers of Aboriginal soldiers were born into families with an Aboriginal mother tongue. About a third of the mixed-race soldiers reported an Aboriginal mother tongue against nearly 90 per cent of apparently pure-blooded Indians (table 12.4). The relative importance of the mixed-race group was much greater in the West and in northern Ontario than in the east, although greater social acceptance of intermarriage and the emergence of the Métis as a recognized social group in the West may have exaggerated the contrast.

The language and enlistment patterns tend to suggest that mixed-race Aboriginal men were more closely integrated into the broader Canadian society than the pure blooded (most of whom probably had reserve status). Mixed-race Aboriginal soldiers were more likely to sign their name and to report affiliation with a Christian church (table 12.5). But the differences are not large, and the patterns varied regionally. A larger proportion in southern Ontario and eastern Canada had prior militia and/or military experience, but within each region there was little difference between pure bloods and the mixed race. The men described here learned thirty-one different native languages and five European languages as their first language.[57] This considerable heterogeneity is further complicated by sizeable differences across broadly defined regions of birth and between those reporting mixed race and those who apparently were pure bloods.

Our linked census-military data do not overturn or challenge current general understandings of Aboriginal participation in WWI. In fact, broadening the definition of Aboriginal from reserve status to include mixed-race communities reinforces evidence of the importance of Indians to the Canadian Expeditionary Force. Nevertheless, the patterns retrieved from individual-level data do add a new dimension. They document more extensively than before the complexity of Canada's First Nations communities and their varied contributions to the war. The variety of response to the war reminds us that the First Nations were remarkably diverse in terms of their history, location, and circumstances and that an uncritical use of the term "aboriginal participation" would be mistaken.

APPENDIX

Table 12.6
Appendix: quality codes for positive links from census to CEF

Match Quality	*Quantity*	*Qualitative Description*		
		Category	*Quantity*	*Description*
High	2,059	A01	255	Individuals who cannot be verified by NOK but who provide the exact, or close to exact, date of birth as that listed in the 1901 Census.
		A02	1318	Individuals whose next of kin can be confirmed in the 1901 census; most often, enlistees provided the names of their father, mother, brother, sister, or wife. The last is hardest to confirm because most soldiers married after 1901; in certain cases the wife's name can be confirmed by checking the 1911 census.
		A03	255	Individuals who cannot be verified by NOK but resided and/or were born in the same areas as listed in the 1901 census. Particular weight is given to individuals living on Aboriginal reserves or in towns/villages close to reserves.
		A04	231	Individuals whose DOB according to their CEF papers is within three years on either side of that provided in 1901 census (e.g. someone born in 1898 according to the census but anywhere between 1895 and 1901 in CEF), whose birthplace or current address is in the same region as their birthplace or current address in the 1901 census but cannot be verified by family members in 1901 and the NOK is a wife.
Med	58	Individuals whose CEF papers are incomplete, who cannot be linked by NOK, region or exact DOB, and often whose family members likewise enlisted and are considered "high" matches		
Low	102	Individuals whose CEF papers are not available online but whose names are unique within the region they gave as address/birthplace in the 1901 census. Further inquiry is required to verify these matches but, based on their uncommon first and surnames, the research team believes the majority of these will be "high" matches.		
Total	2,219			

Note: An additional 171 men known to be Aboriginal from other sources have been located in both the CEF and in the 1901 census. We expand our sample with these additional records.

Table 12.7
Average length of service for those who died

	N	*Average length of service to death*
Aboriginals	233	614 days
All CEF (linked B-surnames)	764	622 days

13

Tracing "The Trail of Infected Armies": Mobilizing for War, the Spread of the 1918 Influenza Pandemic, and the Case of the Polish Army Camp at Niagara-on-the-Lake, 1917–19

KANDACE BOGAERT, JANE VAN KOEVERDEN, AND D. ANN HERRING

The First World War was a time of unprecedented human mobility as millions of military personnel, along with the civilians who provided supplies and services to them, moved within and between continents and across oceans in support of the war effort. Between 1914 and 1919 in Canada alone, an army of 600,000 men was raised some 400,000 of whom were transported across the country and on to Europe.[1] Their story has become a defining element in the emergence of the modern Canadian state. Foreign troops also passed through Canada en route to the European theatre of war. Among them were more than 22,000 soldiers who volunteered to fight for the Polish Army in France, most of whom were recruited in the USA then sent to be trained by Canadian military officers at Camp Niagara at Niagara-on-the-Lake, Ontario.

In the fall of 1918 as Canada and the USA concentrated on sending replacement troops overseas as quickly as possible, the deadly second wave of the Spanish influenza spread around the globe. The spread of the epidemic was facilitated by the rapid movement of soldiers through crowded army camps and on packed troop trains and ships.[2] Influenza followed "the trail of infected armies": American soldiers from the Eastern Seaboard heading to Europe on Canadian transports, Canadian troops heading west to support the Siberian Expeditionary Force, and the Polish Army of America, training in southern Ontario, but destined for France.[3] The Polish Army Camp at Niagara-on-the-Lake was one of the first places in Canada to report an epidemic of influenza.[4] Military officials decided that stopping the movement of the Polish Army from the USA to Canada during the epidemic would be too heavy a blow to the Polish Army in France.[5] As a result of this decision, recruits continued to arrive in Canada from infected cities in the United States, and many soldiers were found to have influenza upon arrival at Niagara-on-the-Lake. This paper discusses how the Polish Army was mobilized in the USA, the routes by which the volunteers travelled to Niagara-on-the-Lake, and how the demand for fresh troops from North America to sustain World War I resulted in the transportation of sick soldiers across the Canadian border.

FROM POLAND TO NORTH AMERICA

Polish citizens began migrating to North America toward the end of the eighteenth century, in the wake of a series of civil uprisings in Eastern Europe. Many had moved to the United States and found work in northeastern or midwestern industrial cities such as New York, Pittsburgh, Cleveland, and Chicago. By 1914, some 2.2 million Poles had relocated to the United States.[6] In response to the influx of immigrants, Polish organizations formed to ease the difficult transition into the socially and environmentally harsh climate of North America.[7] The athletic society known as *The Sokóls* (The Falcons) emerged as one of the most influential organizations. The Falcons provided an environment that emphasized physical fitness, friendship based on Polish heritage, and loyalty to Poland.[8] The Falcons had begun mobilizing their membership in 1912 in anticipation of the potential need for soldiers in Poland and waited only for approval from the United States government to begin official recruitment.[9] The precedent of a Polish Army in America, however, had been set.

When the First World War began in 1914, loyalties were divided amongst Poles in America. Many longed for reunification of their homeland and saw supporting the Allied war effort as a means to achieve that end. Russia had been a longtime enemy, but, as liberal nationalists, American Poles held anti-German sentiments as well.[10] The French were drawn into the scheme because the staggering losses to its army created a shortage of soldiers as the war dragged on. In June of 1917, French President Raymond Poincaré announced his plans for the creation of a "Polish

Army in France,"[11] to be formed of volunteers from around the world, including the United States. The scheme would help replenish his forces while at the same time respond to French sympathies toward the cause of Polish independence.[12]

President Wilson had endorsed a free, united Poland in a speech to the American Senate in January 1917; in a speech on 2 April 1917, he argued that the United States must go to war against Germany. Building on the excitement of this declaration, on 3 April Ignacy Jan Paderewski, leader of American *Polonia*, spoke before a convention of the Polish Falcons in Pittsburgh, urging the Falcons to support the American military effort with the formation of *Kośiuszko's Army*, concluding with the rally cry, "Long live a free, independent and reconciled Poland!"[13] Paderewski lost no time in convincing Washington to support the army.[14]

RECRUITING A POLISH ARMY IN THE USA

To avoid inflaming public opinion and weakening its own armed forces, the United States War Department imposed a number of conditions on the recruiting efforts of the Polish Military Commission: no citizen of the United States of Polish Nationality eligible for the American Army draft could sign up; neither could someone whose family would be left without any means of support. To circumvent the problem of a foreign force training on American soil, the soldiers would be trained in Canada. Recruiting had to be conducted discreetly, using only small posters and signs (figure 13.1). The volunteer recruitment campaign began with great success on 9 October 1917; by the end of the day, 161 men from Chicago had volunteered, and the first sixty recruits had begun the journey to Niagara-on-the-Lake, the Canadian location where volunteers were trained.[15]

It was well understood that "recruiting [could] be successful only with the fullest cooperation of the local Polish clergy."[16] The Polish Roman Catholic Church was thus a key player in the success of the project, spearheading fundraising and recruiting. In the Pittsburgh Diocese, for instance, Reverend A. Pniak recruited twelve men for the army at a rally held at the Guardian Angels Roman Catholic Church.[17] Other effective strategies were used to spur young men to enlist. Advertisements and letters in local Polish language newspapers, such as one written by Jan Słociúski, presented appealing depictions of life at Niagara-on-the-Lake. According to Słociúski, "We only train six hours a day and we spend the rest of our time playing a variety of games so we're never

Figure 13.1 Recruiting poster, "Armia Polska we Francyi/Polish Army in France"

bored ... We have a theatre here thanks to the YMCA that shows concerts and moving pictures, which is completely free for us ... Many guests/friends come visit us from Buffalo since it's so close ... The town is small but has a lot of cheer."[18]

Polish artists supported the recruiting effort through music and film. In 1917, Ignacy Jan Paderewski composed the rousing battle hymn, *Leć, Orle Biały*, (*Soar, White Eagle*)[19] and a Polish Military Band was organized

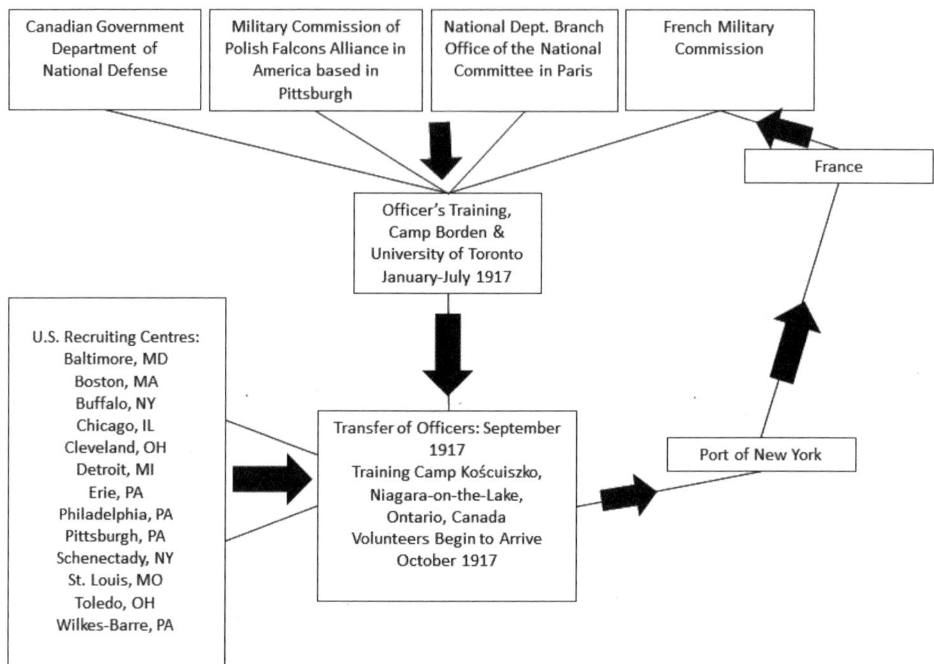

Figure 13.2 Emergence of the Polish Army in France, with information adapted from Valasek 2006, 408.

to bolster recruitment.[20] The Polish Military Commission's film, *Za Wolność i Ojczyznę (For Freedom and Fatherland)*, featured scenes from Niagara-on-the-Lake and the famous recruiter, Wacław Gasiorowski, speaking in front of a memorial to Kościuszko at Chicago's Humboldt Park.[21] When Polish volunteers were loaded onto trains headed for Niagara-on-the-Lake, care was taken to ensure that crowds of people cheered them off with patriotic sentiments, such as "Come back healthy and victorious!"[22]

Although the Polish Military Commission failed to muster the 100,000 men originally promised to President Wilson, its efforts were successful nonetheless. Recruiting centres in major US cities, such as Chicago, Detroit, New York, Philadelphia, and Boston and in smaller cities, such as Bridgeport, Connecticut, attracted 40,000 men for the Polish Army during the three years in which it operated (figure 13.2).[23] Only about 30,000 were accepted for training, and even fewer actually made it overseas.[24]

Recruits were required to undergo a medical examination to ensure that each man was fit to serve in the army.[25] Grounds for rejection included signs of tubercular disease and syphilis or evidence of corporal punishment or "defective intelligence."[26] A second medical examination was conducted by Canadian medical officials at Niagara-on-the-Lake.[27] At least one soldier who had tubercular disease managed to pass both medical tests, which calls into question the thoroughness with which the examinations were undertaken. He never reached Europe, perishing from tuberculosis at Niagara-on-the-Lake.[28] His body was sent home for burial to Greenwood, Pennsylvania.[29]

FROM THE USA TO NIAGARA-ON-THE-LAKE, CANADA

When sufficient numbers of men had signed up, the new recruits were sent by train to Camp Niagara where they received military training at Polish Camp (figure 13.3),[30] set up adjacent to the Canadian Army's Camp Niagara.[31] Niagara-on-the-Lake was chosen because of its history as a military centre and its proximity to Buffalo, NY, where recruits were mustered to be transported to Canada. The location was accessible from the USA via rail and from the Niagara River.[32] Polish American recruits began arriving at Niagara-on-the-Lake on 3 October 1917.[33]

The camp was headed by Lieutenant-Colonel Arthur D'Orr LePan, who served in the Canadian army from 1915 to 1919. He was appointed camp commandant when the Polish Army Camp at Niagara-on-the-Lake was formed and served in that capacity until 1919 with the dissolution of the camp.[34] Although a young officer, at the age of thirty-two Col. LePan was already distinguished as the superintendent of the University of Toronto prior to the war and as an instructor for the Canadian Officers Training Corps (COTC) since 1914.[35] LePan believed strongly in the Polish cause for independence and worked tirelessly on behalf of the volunteers in his camp, ceaselessly requesting extra blankets, jackets, and boots to outfit the Polish volunteers who often arrived poorly equipped to endure the cold climate.[36]

Recruits arrived after a long trip aboard crowded troop trains. Owing to the high cost of transportation, the Polish Military Commission aimed to send as many men as possible en masse to Niagara-on-the-Lake, since the price of train tickets was reduced with higher volume.[37] Sometimes as many as 350 volunteers were transhipped at a time.[38] When the US government took control of the railway system to facilitate troop movements on 28 December 1917, passenger trains operating on duplicate routes were eliminated. This reduced the number of

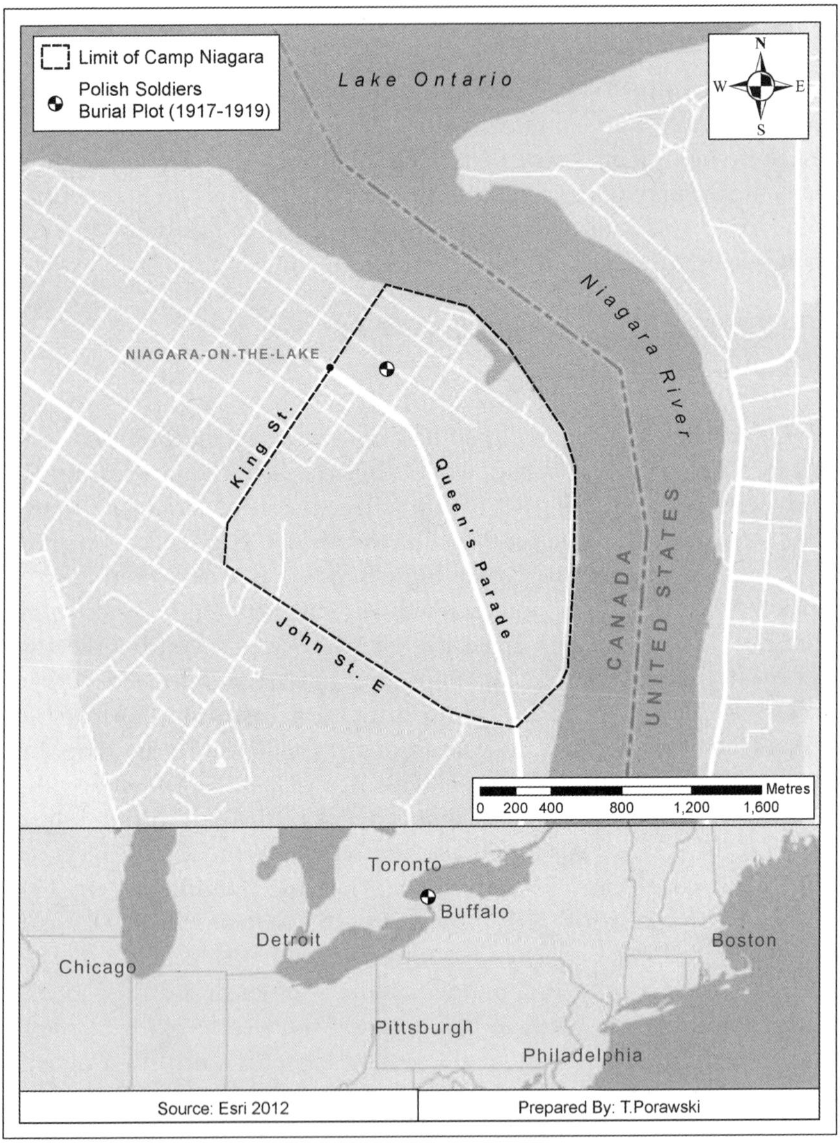

Figure 13.3 Niagara-on-the-Lake, Ontario, Camp Niagara and Polish soldiers cemetery

trains available for the Polish Military Commission. Sleeper car services had also been removed, worsening the crowding and making intolerable the jammed and stuffy conditions on trains.[39] With thousands of foreign soldiers crossing the US border into Canada, the Polish Military Commission was able to make arrangements with customs officers to expedite the process.[40]

Four wooden winter barracks had been constructed to house the recruits, however for most of the year they lived "under canvas," in tents.[41] Staff Captain of the 13th Division, Stanislaw Nastał, described his daily routine at the Polish Army Camp,[42] which included training in British drill, bayonet training (but without musketry or rifle drilling), mixed with calisthenics and sport.[43] New recruits were trained for three to four weeks then sent to Europe to enlist in the French army.[44]

The first few months did not proceed according to plan, however. The Allied forces had failed to make arrangements for the Polish soldiers to travel to Europe and were unable to spare any ships for that purpose. As a result, Polish recruits piled up at Niagara; with winter imminent, the camp faced a serious housing crisis.[45] To make matters worse, the winter of 1917 arrived unusually early and was exceptionally cold.[46] LePan's diary for November records chilly temperatures of 22 degrees Fahrenheit, the accumulation of "quite a lot of snow" by 23 November,[47] and his efforts to secure greatcoats and winter accommodation for the men. At this point, soldiers were living eight men to a tent, and by 1 December 1917 there were only sufficient barracks to house 1,200 of the 3,078 soldiers at the camp.[48] As more recruits continued to arrive, camp strength swelled to more than 4,000 men before the end of November.[49] As a stopgap measure to ease the unbearable over crowding, soldiers were shipped to military camps in St John, Quebec, and Fort Niagara in the USA.[50] Barracks were constructed by December, but they were not large enough to accommodate all of the volunteers. At this point, the citizens of Niagara-on-the-Lake agreed to billet the freezing soldiers.[51]

The residents of Niagara-on-the-Lake had initially dreaded the opening of a military camp for Polish soldiers. They were wary of a foreign army training in their midst,[52] even though the town was accustomed to the presence of large numbers of soldiers because of nearby Canadian Camp. Prejudice against eastern Europeans was long-standing in Canada[53] and only added to the anxiety and unease about the presence of the Polish Army so close to town. In a postwar speech, LePan mentions that an elderly lady captured the sentiments of community members during those early days: "Oh my God, those fellows will murder us in our beds."[54] This attitude changed, however, as the relationship between the soldiers and townspeople gradually warmed.

It is not clear when or how the Polish soldiers won over the residents of Niagara-on-the-Lake, but the soldiers became part of the daily life of the town. The Polish Army hosted dances and concerts that included the townsfolk and volunteered to assist the locals in a variety of ways, such as shovelling snow. When the owner of a local canning factory was short of men, Col. LePan offered to send Polish recruits to assist with the work.[55] By the winter of 1917, the townspeople had come around and many were prepared to help resolve the housing crisis at Polish Camp. Approximately 3,110 soldiers were billeted for free around the community; temporary residences included Western Home (a former courthouse), the town hall, a bathhouse, gymnasium, canning factory, steamboat shed, paint shop, and a few houses.[56]

Billeting was followed by community initiatives to enhance the Polish soldiers' stay in Canada. The Canadian YMCA organized sports tournaments and set up a canteen at Polish Camp, the profits of which were used to purchase goods for the soldiers.[57] The Polish Band was commissioned for performances in Toronto and New York and garnered high praise for its showmanship.[58] The positive attitude toward the Polish soldiers appears to have continued throughout the war. In a feature for the *Niagara Advantage*, one journalist writes nostalgically about the departure of the Polish soldiers and the disbanding of the camp on 11 March 1919,

> Our regret is that the Polish boys could not stay with us indefinitely. Both from a financial and social point of view, we have benefited greatly but it goes without saying that we regret the departure of our Polish friends, more because they were our friends than because their sojourn here was of financial benefit … our regret at parting is keen, not only because of our long and pleasant association with such a magnificent lot of men, but because they were, first, and always soldiers and above everything gentlemen.[59]

This sentiment is particularly poignant in light of the evidence that the 1918 influenza pandemic was unwittingly brought to the townspeople of Niagara-on-the-Lake by recruits for the Polish Army in France.

1918 INFLUENZA AND THE MOVEMENT OF SOLDIERS DURING WORLD WAR I

When the first cases of what scholars now believe to be influenza appeared among soldiers in Europe in the spring of 1918 (the first of three waves of the epidemic), there was considerable concern about what was causing the outbreak. The disease was first reported in early April among the American Expeditionary Forces at Brest and in a rest camp near Bordeaux;[60] it emerged subsequently amongst other armies in France. These two observations suggested to epidemiologists of the time that the disease had been brought by American soldiers to the European theatre of war.[61] Army and civilian records for the USA that spring show influenza moving with infected soldiers from army camp to army camp, then on to cities, such as New York.[62] From February to April 1918, regularly collected death certificates and statistics show that an early wave of influenza and/or pneumonia killed larger than expected numbers of New Yorkers.[63] New York was the port of disembarkation of the American Expeditionary Force to the western Front.

The aetiology of influenza, however, was poorly understood in 1918, even though the disease had been endemic in Europe and North America since the 1889 Russian pandemic.[64] When influenza surfaced in April among soldiers in the Second Army of the British Expeditionary Force in France, it was initially labelled as "PUO," pyrexia of unknown origin.[65] The Allies had been caught unprepared for chemical warfare in 1915, and when this seemingly new illness emerged in the spring of 1918 there were suspicions that it might have been caused by a biological or chemical weapon. The environment surrounding Étaples, France had already been contaminated with twenty-three gases including chlorine, phosgene, and mustard gas[66] and there were worries that enemy troops had aerosolized bubonic plague and dropped it on the Allied armies.[67] In 1918, viruses were neither filterable nor observable through microscopy, literally rendering them invisible.

By mid-May, however, "pyrexia of unknown origin" was recognized to be a mild form of influenza,[68] identified by the presence of a constellation of symptoms: high fever that lasted for several days, body aches, muscle and joint pain, headache, sore throat, sometimes leading to bleeding of the nasal membranes, and cough that sometimes produced a thin, brownish mucous. Thousands of soldiers fell ill with influenza that spring, but relatively few died.[69] Until the fall of 1918, for instance, influenza was but a minor illness among the Canadian Expeditionary Force in France, compared to the more serious problems of diarrhoea, dysentery, sexually transmitted diseases, trench foot, and war-related injuries.[70] Reports of influenza in army camps on both sides of the Atlantic received little public attention relative to the horrors of the trenches and growing opposition to a war of attrition that had dragged on far too long.[71]

Thus, when the recruits for the Polish Army in France were undergoing medical examinations in the USA, influenza was neither a major concern nor a reason to reject nor even detain volunteers from being transported on troop trains. Even after the spring and summer outbreaks of influenza, worrisome reports about epidemics in France, and recommendations by medical officers in the USA to reduce epidemics of respiratory diseases, influenza was not added to a list of possible threats issued in a 6 September 1918 memo from the medical department.[72] On the other side of the Canadian border, influenza was not a reportable disease under the 1912 Ontario Public Health Act.[73]

Influenza had been designated a reportable, quarantinable disease by federal maritime officials in July of 1918, but quarantine regulations only applied to ships arriving from overseas. Canadian quarantine policy at the time reflected concerns about defending the country from unwanted immigrants from Europe and the diseases they were believed to bring with them, such as had occurred in the mid-nineteenth century when cholera epidemics affected Montreal and other port cities. The border with the United States was viewed entirely differently and Americans, deemed to be so similar to Canadians, were not viewed as needing to be isolated and segregated in the same way as foreigners from abroad. Consequently, neither US coastal nor land borders were subject to federal quarantine regulations. At the time of the Spanish flu pandemic, therefore, Canadian-American land and sea borders were open, and wartime cooperation necessitated the transportation of American troops across those borders.[74] No one could have predicted that the second, more deadly, wave of influenza that erupted in the early fall of 1918 would threaten to overwhelm medical services at the Polish Army Camp at Niagara-on-the-Lake where thousands of Polish-American recruits had gathered for training.

SOLDIERS WITH INFLUENZA TRAVEL TO POLISH CAMP

The American Expeditionary Force under General John (Black Jack) Pershing had begun to increase troop movements to France in January of 1918; by May, some 200,000 men a month were being sent to France; by August Pershing's army had reached one million.[75] Although the Polish Army had been training in Canada and sending troops to France since October of 1917, camp strength in 1918 grew from some 1,200 men at the end of August to more than 2,500 by the week of 21 October (figure 13.4).

The need for replacement troops to maintain the war effort and support the largest campaign of the war, the Meuse-Argonne Offensive, meant that in the fall of 1918 Canada and the USA sent soldiers to Europe as quickly as possible, reducing training times, sending conscripted soldiers to the front, and filling spaces on Canadian troop ships departing from Montreal and Quebec City with American soldiers from the eastern seaboard.[76] The second wave of influenza emerged and spread in conjunction with these wartime conditions of rapid transportation, over-crowded training camps, troop trains and ships, and the wretched conditions of trench warfare on the Western front.[77] Boston has been consistently identified as the North American starting point for the second wave of influenza that erupted in the fall of 1918.[78]

The earliest well-documented evidence suggests the second wave of influenza arrived at Boston's Commonwealth Pier on 27 August 1918; by 8 September it had spread to the civilian population, as well as to the army's Camp Devens, located just outside the city. Within a fortnight, the base hospital and regimental infirmaries at Camp Devens were treating hundreds of sick trainees. The epidemic escalated such that on one day alone – Saturday, 14 September – more than 500 soldiers suffering from influenza were seen at the hospital.[79] The epidemic virtually exploded along the eastern seaboard, with several army camps (Devens, MA; Upton, NY; Lee, VA; Dix, NJ; Jackson, SC) reporting influenza during the first week of the fall wave.[80] By the week of 21 September, influenza was reported in civilian populations in Lowell, Massachusetts and in New York City.[81]

Boston was a primary recruiting centre for the Polish Army and was linked to Niagara-on-the-Lake by the New York Central Railway, which operated the Michigan Central Railway through southern Ontario.[82] This is likely the area from which the virus came to Niagara-on-the-Lake, brought inadvertently by Polish soldiers recruited by the Polish Military Commission from infected cities in the northeastern United States.[83]

There are some discrepancies in the reports about the first cases of influenza at Niagara-on-the-Lake. According to LePan,[84] the disease entered Polish Camp on 13 September 1918 along with American recruits. Dr J.L. Robinson, the camp's officer in charge of medical services, dates the entry of influenza to Polish Camp to 10 September 1918,[85] just two days after its identification at Camp Devens, Massachusetts. We are inclined to put more weight on Dr Robinson's opinion, given that he was in charge of medical services. Whichever date is correct, this is the earliest record of the second wave of the 1918 pandemic in Canada.[86] On 12 September, the battalions of the camp were assembled for panoramic photographs, bringing all of the men into close contact.[87] Given that influenza has on average a two-day incubation period, the infection could have spread easily from person-to-person during the gathering. On 17 September, the camp was put under quarantine; the first death from influenza occurred just one day later on 18 September.

It is unlikely that any single location can be identified as the origin of the pandemic in Canada. This highly contagious infectious disease could have easily percolated into southern Canada across the US border from many northeastern locations. After all, the disease emerged almost simultaneously in various locations around the world.[88] Around the time influenza appeared in Polish Camp, for instance, it was reported in a school in Victoriaville, Quebec, likely brought by visitors from the USA to a Eucharistic Congress.[89] On 20 September, soldiers at St Jean Barracks in Quebec fell ill with influenza; military officials linked the outbreak to the epidemic in Boston because the soldiers had been sent from there.[90] Another identified source of infection was Sydney, Nova Scotia, where an American Transport carrying soldiers to France arrived and docked with influenza in tow.[91] Within days, more than 660 soldiers had been removed from the ship into Sydney's small hospital, overwhelming the facility.

Once influenza had been introduced to Canada, however, the war effort influenced both the paths by which the disease spread and official responses to it.[92] Intensification of the war effort via the Siberian Expeditionary Force and the Meuse-Argonne Offensive trumped concerns about public health as sick soldiers were transported across the country and overseas.[93] Polish Camp had been put under quarantine on 17 September, a week after Dr Robinson marks the onset of the epidemic. Exemplifying how the military's priority to rush soldiers overseas outweighed public health concerns,[94] military officials decided that stopping the recruitment process would severely compromise the Polish Army in France. Recruits thus continued to arrive from infected cities in the United States, and many were found upon arrival to have influenza. On 1 October, for instance, Polish Camp received 180 soldiers; after an initial examination, sixty-two were sent to segregation and five to the hospital. By 19 October, all influenza admissions during the previous ten days were incoming recruits.[95] There are reports of troops travelling on "sealed" military trains to prevent the spread of influenza;[96] however, once sick recruits arrived at the camp they were sent to the camp hospital, continually reintroducing the virus to the camp. The health of recruits at the camp (and the surrounding civilian population) was deemed secondary to the push to get fresh troops overseas, and recruitment and transportation to Niagara-on-the-Lake continued unabated throughout the epidemic.

SICK AND DYING AT NIAGARA-ON-THE-LAKE

When influenza arrived at Polish Camp in the fall of 1918, soldiers were still being housed in a "city of tents."[97] During the height of World War I, more than 18,000 men in the Polish Camp and adjacent Canadian Camp were housed primarily in tents that slept eight or nine men, their heads facing in the same direction.[98] It is no wonder that influenza, an airborne infectious agent, rapidly overwhelmed the recruits and spread quickly from Polish Camp to Canadian Camp.[99]

During the period in which the camp was supposedly under quarantine, LePan's[100] diary mentions daily visits to inspect the crisis from majors, generals, and other military officials. This was clearly a very leaky quarantine. Major Morrison, who had advised LePan to quarantine the camp, visited on at least two occasions to assess the situation and to offer advice.[101] Medical officers from Fort Niagara, such as Major Fink and Major Hough, also came to observe the conditions.[102] To mitigate staff shortages in the hospital, two nurses arrived in the camp on 22 September.[103] Civilians also visited, often providing medical and other supplies requested by LePan.

Before quarantine was imposed, soldiers were permitted to obtain visitors passes to leave the camp, spend time in the town of Niagara-on-the-Lake, and circulate within the camp at recreation centres such as the YMCA tent. Clearly, there were plenty of opportunities for the epidemic to spread beyond the camp. The first civilian death from influenza in Lincoln County was recorded on 19 September, just one day after the first soldier death at Polish Camp.[104] By 30 September influenza was reported at the Armament School of the Royal Air Service in West Hamilton and soon spread to Hamilton's civilian population where the first influenza death occurred on 3 October 1918.[105]

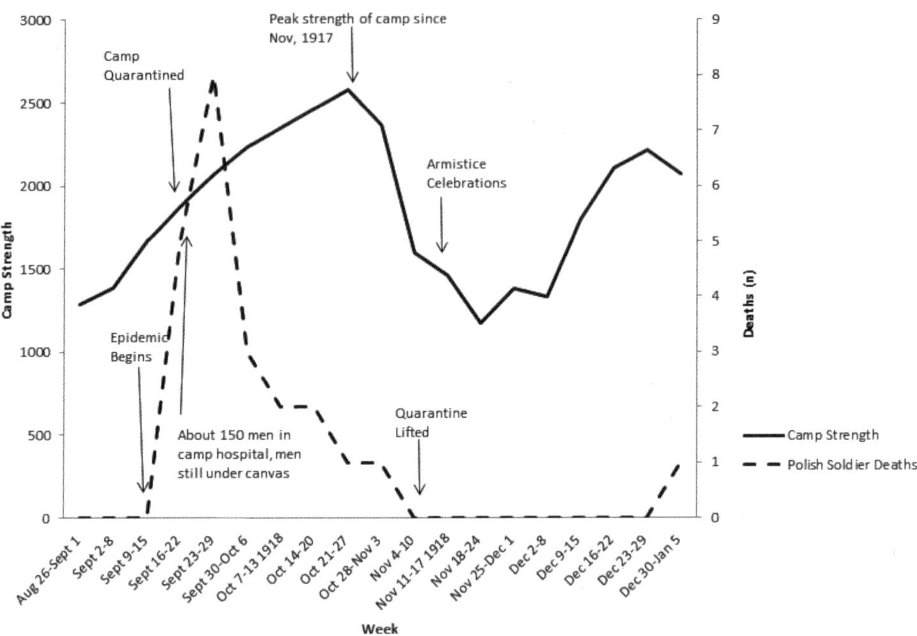

Figure 13.4 Polish soldier mortality and camp strength, from LePan's "War Diary," September to December, 1918

During the course of the fall wave of the epidemic, LePan maintained detailed death records of the names, officer numbers, place of burial, and date and cause of death for all fatalities that occurred at Polish Camp. His records match the soldier deaths listed for Polish Camp in the registered deaths for Ontario.[106] In all, twenty-five Polish soldiers died from influenza or influenza-related pneumonia during the fall wave of the epidemic, and in a subsequent recurrence during the third wave of the pandemic in January, six more perished. This represents about three-quarters of the forty-one deaths recorded from 1917 to 1918 among Polish recruits at Niagara-on-the-Lake.

Col. LePan's careful record of influenza deaths shows a rapid rise in mortality in September, peaking in the last week of September at nearly four deaths per 1,000, then a precipitous drop in November to only 0.42 deaths per 1,000, with none recorded for December. Morbidity was much higher, with 368 soldiers and eleven officers falling ill with influenza during the height of the epidemic between 10 September and 21 November.[107] Approximately 20 per cent of the Polish soldiers fell ill during the fall wave, and the virus was fatal for nearly 2.5 per

Figure 13.5 Polish soldiers memorial

cent of them.[108] As recruits died, they were buried together in a special plot set aside for the Polish army unless arrangements were made with the family to send their body home. LePan hand-drew a detailed plan of the cemetery indicating the location of each grave and where a larger cross of granite was placed with the inscription, "Died for Poland."[109]

INTERRUPTED JOURNEYS

The story of the Polish Army at Niagara-on-the-Lake is a little known piece of Canadian history. Our exploration of this relatively short, two-year period in which more than 22,000 Polish Americans moved to southern Ontario to train for military service was stimulated by Mark O. Humphries'[110] analysis of the role played by military priorities and decisions in the spread of the 1918 influenza in Canada and his contention that influenza came to Canada via American troop movements rather than from Canadian soldiers returning from Europe. Most research on the Polish Army in the United States has centered on the recruitment of soldiers and their subsequent military service in France; little has been written about their travel to Canada, their history within the Spanish Influenza pandemic, or how they touched the community in which they trained. The soldiers, however, have had a lasting and visible effect on Niagara-on-the-Lake. Most of the men from Polish Camp who died from influenza during the 1918 pandemic were buried at *Polski Cmentarz Hallerczyków* (Polish Soldiers Burial Plot), a small plot of graves in St Vincent de Paul cemetery dedicated to General Józef Haller's "Blue Army" (figure 13.5). Their story has become part of the local history of the town and their memorial an enduring symbol of their presence there.

One of the curiosities of the 1918 influenza pandemic lies in the paradox of a global toll of anywhere from fifty to one hundred million people[111] and the apparent forgetting of its occurrence over the subsequent decades.[112] Some authors have suggested the pandemic was omitted from official histories because it was overshadowed by the war[113] or because it was an affront to sensibilities about twentieth-century modernity and medicine[114] or because it was a relatively small blip against a larger backdrop of more persistent infectious diseases.[115]

The Polish Soldiers who perished from influenza at Niagara-on-the-Lake during the fall of 1918, however, have not been forgotten. Polish Americans and Canadians visit this site each year to remember the Polish Army that passed through this small town en route to the European theatre of war.[116] The soldiers whose lives ended at Niagara-on-the-Lake have come to represent the Polish odyssey to the Americas and the dream of an independent Poland;[117] the cemetery is now a site where Polish identity and nationalism are celebrated and performed. It is a singular site in Canada; to our knowledge it is the only special memorial for soldiers who died during the 1918 pandemic. Yet, the manner of their death means less than the cause for which they fought.

The graves of the Polish soldiers also draw attention to the priority placed by Canadian and American military officials on transporting sick soldiers across national borders despite the threat to public health posed by the deadly influenza pandemic. The effects of this decision were far-reaching. The impact of the Polish Army's fleeting migration to this small town was profound as Niagara-on-the-Lake became one of the first places in Canada to experience the 1918 pandemic, eventually losing seventeen of its residents during the fall outbreak.[118]

ACKNOWLEDGMENTS

We would first like to thank Dr Kris Inwood and Dr Peter Baskerville for including us in this project. Richard Kujawa, Małgorzata Kot, the helpful volunteers from the Polish Museum of America in Chicago,

Sara Maloney and staff at the Niagara Historical Society Museum generously gave their time and assistance during research visits to Chicago and Niagara-on-the-Lake. Tara Jenkins and Tom Porawski of Timmins Martelle Heritage Consultants Inc. produced the map. Paul Sulzycki and Lukas Magier provided assistance with Polish translations. David Earn provided the data files on influenza mortality in Lincoln County. Errors and omissions are entirely ours.

Notes

INTRODUCTION

1 The authors use the terms Indigenous, Aboriginal, Indian, and First Nation interchangeably.

CHAPTER TWO

1 This project was funded by the Australian Research Council. We thank the following researchers and volunteers for coding and tracing the ships: The Swing Rioters (Eliza II, Proteus, Lotus 1831): Jenny Elliston, Leanne Goss, David Noakes, Colin Tuckerman and Janet McCalman; Woodman 1826: Colin Tuckerman; Governor Ready 1827: Jenny Wells and Glad Wishart; Strathfieldsay 1831: Jenny Kisler; Atlas 1833: Colin Tuckerman; Enchantress 1833: Maureen Mann; Southworth 1834: Steve Rhodes; George III 1835, Bardaster 1836, The Royal Sovereign 1838: Geoff Brown. We also thank Claudine Chionh and Sandra Silcot for IT support.

2 Robson, *Convict Settlers*; Johnson and Nicholas, "Male and female living standards in England and Wales, 1812–1857"; Reid, *Gender, Crime and Empire*; Boyce, *Van Diemen's Land*; Maxwell-Stewart, *Closing Hell's Gates*; and Alexander, *Tasmania's Convicts.*

3 Alexander, *Tasmania's Convicts.*

4 Nicholas, ed., *Convict Workers*; and Oxley, *Convict Maids.*

5 Nicholas and Oxley, "The living standards of women during the industrial revolution, 1795–1820," 723; Johnson and Nicholas, "Male and female living standards in England and Wales."

6 Haines, "Skills, Origins and Literacy."

7 Founders & Survivors comprises two teams based at the universities of

Tasmania and Melbourne, as well as a number of collaborators in the United Kingdom and Canada. The Life Course project under discussion in this chapter has been funded by two grants from the Australian Research Council through the University of Melbourne and is building a population-level genealogical database of convicts and their descendants. For technical reasons this dataset is distinct from the male convict database that has been constructed by Hamish Maxwell-Stewart and funded through the University of Tasmania, and from the female convict database constructed by Trudy Cowley and the Female Convict History Centre. These three projects can share data and protocols, but the life course genealogical dataset requires customized software (Yggrasil) that manages relationships between convicts that can be disaggregated as families and aggregated as a population. It will eventually be archived by the Tasmanian Archives and Heritage Office and linked to their convict record index for public use.

8 Bradley, "The founders and survivors project."

9 The crowdsourcing was managed via a work platform using Google Docs. Volunteers were given a detailed instruction manual and entered coded data into Google Spreadsheets using fixed coding regimes. Workshops were held in Hobart and Melbourne where volunteers were trained in reading and interpreting the convict records, coding data, and filling out the spreadsheets. Telephone and email coaching supplemented the workshops. Volunteers were encouraged to work in teams and to communicate with each other. They also maintained their own chat room.

10 Haines, "Skills, Origins and Literacy."

11 Snell, *Annals of the Labouring Poor.*

12 Hobsbawm and Rude, *Captain Swing.*

13 Griffin, "The Violent Captain Swing?"

14 Meredith and Oxley, "Contracting Convicts."

15 Irish convicts were not transported in significant numbers until after 1840, when the first ship arrived direct from an Irish port. This paper focuses on comparing "like with like" during a prescribed chronological period, 1826–38 under the assignment system.

16 Boyce, *Van Diemen's Land.*

17 Preston and Haines, *Fatal Years.*

18 Founders & Survivors: Australian Life Courses in Historical Context 1803–1920, foundersandsurvivors.org/node/86912.

19 Mortlock, ed., *Experiences of a Convict.*

20 *The Cornwall Chronicle*, 10 January 1852, 19.

21 Karskens, "Death was in his Face."

CHAPTER THREE

1 Bullard, *Exile to Paradise*; and Doroshevich, *Russia's Penal Colony*.

2 Cobbett, *The Emigrant's Guide*, 40. For the dangers associated with migration to nineteenth-century New Zealand see Lenihan, "Wanderlust: The Multiple Migrations of New Zealand's Scots, 1840–1920" in this volume.

3 Christopher, "'The Slave Trade Is Merciful Compared to [This].'"

4 Haines and Shlomowitz, "Explaining the Mortality Decline," 273.

5 Bateson, *The Convict Ships*, 38–49.

6 McDonald and Shlomowitz, "Mortality on Convict Voyages," 291.

7 Cohen, "Determinants of Individual Immigrant Mortality," 378. Note that 94 per cent of male convicts landed in Australia were aged between fifteen and forty-four, Con 23/1 and 2, Tasmanian Archives and Heritage Office (henceforth TAHO).

8 Maxwell-Stewart, "Convict Transportation," 1,224; Ekirch, *Bound for America*, 23, 188; and Kelly, "Transportation from Ireland to North America."

9 Morgan, "The Convict Trade to Maryland," 213.

10 Eltis et al., *The Trans-Atlantic Slave Trade*; and Christopher, "'The Slave Trade is Merciful Compared to [This],'" 107–28.

11 Haines et al., "Mortality and Voyage Length," 507.

12 McKeown, *The Modern Rise of Population*; and McKeown, *The Role of Medicine*.

13 Haines and Shlomowitz, "Explaining the Mortality Decline."

14 Cohen, "Maritime Mortality"; Haines et al., "Maritime Mortality Revisited"; Haines and Shlomowitz, "Modern Mortality Decline"; Klein et al., "Transoceanic Mortality"; Steckel and Jensen, "New Evidence," 57; and Maxwell-Stewart and Shlomowitz, "Mortality and Migration."

15 Kippen and McCalman, "A Test of Character," in this volume.

16 Bateson, *The Convict Ships*, 338–96.

17 ADM 101 series, The National Archive, Great Britain (henceforth TNA).

18 ADM101/12/7, TNA; and ADM101/14/5, TNA.

19 Jackson, "Sickness and Health," 72, 76–7.

20 Haines and Shlomowitz, "Causes of Death."

21 Haines et al., "Mortality and Voyage Length."

22 Haines and Shlomowitz, "Causes of Death," 207.

23 Jackson, "Sickness and Health," 80; and Staniforth, "Diet, Disease and Death," 122.

24 The *East London* left Dublin for Van Diemen's Land in April 1844 with 133 female convicts and fifty of their children on board. Of these nineteen women and twelve children perished at sea. With the exception of

shipwrecks, this was by far the highest mortality rate encountered on any voyage to Van Diemen's Land. ADM 101/22/1, TNA.

25 ADM 101/32/9, TNA.

26 McIntyre, *Free Passage*; and Brand and Staniforth, "Care and Control," 34.

27 Rawley and Behrendt, *Transatlantic Slave Trade*, 258–9.

28 Haines and Shlomowitz, "Explaining the Mortality Decline," 259.

29 McDonald and Shlomowitz, "Mortality on Convict Voyages," 290.

30 Cohen, "Mortality on Immigrant Voyages."

31 Staniforth, "Diet, Disease and Death at Sea," 127.

32 Calculated using data from Con 31 series, TAHO and ADM 101 and HO 8 series, TNA.

33 ADM 101/25/2, TNA.

34 Carpenter, *The History of Scurvy and Vitamin C*, 99.

35 Inspectors of Prisons, Great Britain, *British Parliamentary Papers* (1837–38), vol. 31; Crawford, "The Irish Workhouse Diet"; and Carpenter, "Nutritional Studies in Victorian Prisons."

36 ADM 101/65/8, TNA; ADM 101/34/7, TNA; and ADM 101/25/2, TNA.

37 Horrell et al., "Measuring Misery."

38 Staniforth, "Diet, Disease and Death," 132.

39 ADM101/23/6, TNA. Fielding did not survive the voyage. She died twenty-one days after the ship had put to sea. Con 40/3, TAHO, 39.

40 ADM101/22/8, TNA.

41 ADM 101/74/06, TNA.

42 ADM 101/32/9, TNA.

43 Jackson, "Sickness and Health," 77.

44 Nicholas, "Unshackling the Past," 9.

45 Humphery, "A New Era of Existence"; and Foxhall, "From Convicts to Colonists."

46 Brand and Staniforth, "Care and Control," 24.

47 Jackson, "Sickness and Health," 84.

48 Johnson, *The Ghost Map*; and Curtin, *Death by Migration*, 50–6.

49 Bateson, *Convict Ships*, 68.

50 Brand and Staniforth, "Care and Control," 31; and Edward Caldwell, Surgeon R.N. to Sir William Burnett, Hobart Town, 1843, CSO 22/88/1859, TAHO.

51 Reid, "Setting Women to Work."

52 Frost, *Abandoned Women*, 46–65.

53 See Hinde, "Sex Differentials in Mortality," 22.

54 Reid, "Setting Women to Work," 9–11.

55 Frost, *Abandoned Women*, 80–97.

56 Con 41, TAHO, 1 in 25 systematic sample.
57 See for example McKeown, *The Modern Rise of Population*, 150.
58 Szreter, "Social Intervention," 32.
59 Colgrove, "The McKeown Thesis."
60 Szreter, "Social Intervention," 1–38.

CHAPTER FOUR

1 Belich, *Paradise Reforged*, 221.
2 See, for example, Prentis, *The Scots in Australia*; MacKenzie and Dalziel, *The Scots in South Africa*; Grosjean and Murdoch, *Scottish Communities Abroad*; Hunter, *A Dance Called America*; and Harper, *Adventurers and Exiles* among others.
3 These include Brooking and Coleman, *The Heather and the Fern*; Bueltmann, *Scottish Ethnicity*; and McCarthy, *Scottishness and Irishness*.
4 Of particular note regarding such methods is Baines, *Migration in a Mature Economy*.
5 The steady stream of migration research from Swedish scholars in the latter part of the twentieth century began with Thistlethwaite's 1960 contribution, but perhaps the most influential study came out of the "Sweden and America after 1860" project in 1976. Runblom and Norman, *From Sweden to America*.
6 See, for example: Foerster, *Italian Emigration*; Saloutos, *They Remember America*; and Cerase, "The Return to Italy.".
7 See, for example, Baines, *Migration in a Mature Economy*; and Harper, *Emigrant Homecomings*.
8 See Molloy, *Those Who Speak to the Heart*; and Robinson, *To the Ends of the Earth* among others.
9 Harper, *Adventurers and Exiles*; and Withers, *Urban Highlanders*, among others, provide good overviews of these flows.
10 The nature of the NZSG data is such that precise parish level information is not available for a significant number of the migrants, a level of precision that is necessary when defining "Highland" and "Lowland" based on cultural factors such as the *Gaidhealtachd*. It is simply not possible, utilising the NZSG data, to group the migrants as "Highlander" or "Lowlander" using such criteria. For more on the Highland/Lowland divide in cultural terms see Withers, *Urban Highlanders*, 16–19. The regions and counties of Scotland used here for analysis and discussion are based upon those used by Flinn, *Scottish Population History*, Map 2 (pxxiii) and discussion, 104–6.

11 Return Relating to the Population of Scotland at each Decennial Period, table II, 1881 Census of Scotland, 2–3.
12 The index of representation indicates figures for the whole period, 1840–1920, of 0.6, 0.5, 0.5, and 0.7 respectively for Ross and Cromarty, Angus, Aberdeen, and Lanarkshire and 3.3, 4.2, and 3.5 for Argyll, Nairn, and Moray.
13 Levitt and Smout, *The State of the Scottish Working-Class,* chapter 10, "Emigration."
14 Erickson, "Who Were the English and Scots Emigrants"; McClean, "Scottish Emigrants," 122.
15 A "relative" lack because the evidence of this even distribution does not mean that there is no evidence of any cluster or chain migration among Scots to New Zealand. A chain of migration from New Deer, Aberdeenshire has been found in Fordell, just south of Wanganui, for example, and migration from Shetland is a notable exception to this "even distribution" pattern. Lenihan, "From Alba to Aotearoa," 92, 186–94.
16 Withers, *Urban Highlanders,* 26; Campbell and Devine, "The Rural Experience," 46; Preliminary Report, table IV, 1871 Census of Scotland, 10–11.
17 Handley, *Scottish Farming,* 244, 258–61.
18 Devine, "Temporary Migration," 344.
19 Whittington et al., "Population from C.1600," 106; McClean notes the incidence of this in her thesis.
20 Richards, "Ironies of the Highland Exodus," 79. Between 1831 and 1841 Argyll's population decreased by 3.56 per cent, and between 1841 and 1851 the county lost a further 8.29 per cent of its population, a net population decrease of approximately 11,000 people over that decade alone. Withers, *Urban Highlanders,* table 2.1, 26; net population calculations based on Registrar General reports.
21 Calculations based on tables 4.1 and 4.2 in Withers, *Urban Highlanders,* 88, 92; Brock, *The Mobile Scot,* 100.
22 Personal communication with Linda Dunn, 21 October 2007; for more on the New Zealand Fencibles, see Alexander et al., *The Royal New Zealand Fencibles* – Donald's entry is on page 158.
23 Personal communication with Kae Lewis, 21 October 2007.
24 NZSG database, New Zealand Society of Genealogists, migrants 02047, 02048, 02049, 02050, 02051, 02052, 02053, 02055, 02056, 02057, and 02522.
25 Contributors were asked not to list more than three places of residence, but in this case the contributor filled the available space on the registra-

tion form instead. It is not impossible Harriet had more than these five places of residence in Scotland.

26 Moves within county of birth do not appear in the basic census enumeration tables of internal movement, at least at county level.

27 NZSG database, migrants 05437, 05538, 05544, 05553, 05558, and 05561.

28 NZSG database, migrant 01160.

29 NZSG database, migrant 01141.

30 Sinclair and Olssen, "Lands of Sheep and Gold," 34–51 provides a useful outline of the Australia-New Zealand relationship.

31 Mulligan, "Mary Edie's Biscuits," chapters 1 and 2.

32 Hearn, "Scots Miners," 74, 75, 77, 85.

33 NZSG database, migrant 01768.

34 Arnold, "Yeomen and Nomads"; and Arnold, "Trans-Tasman Migration" provide a useful introduction to this flow.

35 Regarding the destruction of the New Zealand census up to 1966 see, among others, Sinnott, "Census and Privacy in New Zealand"; and Olssen and Hickey, *Class and Occupation*, 29, 43.

36 Thwaites, "Berry, William – Biography."

37 "Mr William Berry," *The Cyclopedia of New Zealand* (Wellington, 1897, New Zealand ElectronicText Centre), accessed 13 August 2012, nzetc.victoria.ac.nz/tm/scholarly/tei-Cyc01Cycl-t1-body-d3-d13-d22.html,110; NZSG database, migrant 00482.

38 NZSG database, migrants 01848.

39 NZSG database, migrants 04946, 06648.

40 NZSG database, migrant 05916.

41 Tedebrand, "Remigration from America to Sweden," 201; Baines, *Migration in a Mature Economy*, 128–40; and Devine, *The Scottish Nation*, 475–6.

42 Richards, "Running Home," 83–4.

43 ibid., 79.

44 ibid.

45 ibid., 78.

46 As this sample is too small to draw upon conclusively, I have not directly compared the figures for Scots in New Zealand with figures related in studies of other migrant groups here. It is interesting to note, however, that these figures, as inconclusive as they are, nevertheless line up broadly with findings of a remigration study of Swedes in America where 75 per cent of remigrants were male, most of the migrants were between twenty and forty years of age, and around 30 per cent of men and 38 per

cent of women were married. Tedebrand, "Remigration from America to Sweden," 223–4.

47 Three have no age at arrival information.

48 NZSG database, migrant 03003.

49 William was still in New Zealand when his family moved to Domett when his youngest sibling was born in 1897, and he died in Glasgow in January 1901. NZSG database, migrant 02320.

50 NZSG database, migrants 03597, 04080.

51 NZSG database, migrant 00958.

52 Anderson, *Fasti Academiae*; Johnston, *Roll of the Graduates, 1860–1900*; Watt, *Roll of the Graduates, 1901–1925*; Mackintosh, *Roll of the Graduates, 1926–1955;* and Donald and MacDonald, *Roll of the Graduates 1956–1970.*

53 Watt, *Roll of the Graduates, 1901–1925,* 388; and *Aberdeen University Review* 20, no. 58 (November 1932).

54 *The Cyclopedia of New Zealand,* Wellington, 1897, New Zealand Electronic Text Centre 22 May 2009, 357–8; Johnston, *Roll of the Graduates, 1860–1900,* 228; and Watt, *Roll of the Graduates, 1901–1925,* 800.

55 Page, *Anatomy of a Medical School,* 20–1 and chapter 2; Buchan, *Capital of the Mind,* 273–4; and citing Dr William Buchan to Mr William Smellie, 20 August 1761, in Kerr, *Memoirs of the Life,* 238 (Ch. 1, n. 13).

56 Bueltmann's sample is based upon thirty-two travel accounts. Bueltmann, "'Brither Scots Shoulder Tae Shoulder,'" 203–17.

57 Richards, "Running Home," 97.

CHAPTER FIVE

1 A version of this paper was first presented at the Guelph University Conference, "Historical Inequality and Mobility: New Perspectives in the Digital Age," May 2012. I wish to very sincerely thank Kris Inwood and Peter Baskerville for organizing the conference and inviting the presentation. I thank Kris Inwood and an anonymous reviewer for thoughtful recommendations on the analysis.

2 Bogue, *From Prairie to Cornbelt,* 55–66; Winters, "Agricultural Tenancy."; and Atack, "The Agricultural Ladder Revisited." Also see Atack and Bateman, *To Their Own Soil,* chapter 7; Ferrie, "Up and Out or Down and Out?"; and Marr, "Distribution of Tenant Agriculture."

3 See Atack, "The Agricultural Ladder Revisited," 2–3. Lee Alston and Joseph Ferrie have suggested that tenancy might be better understood as

a stalled status for black Americans in the South in the early twentieth century; see, Alston and Ferrie, "Time on the Ladder."

4 See Winters, *Farmers without Farms*; Wilson, *A New Lease on Life*; and Wilson, *Tenants in Time.* Tenancy, Wilson shows, conferred some clear advantages: low entrance costs, long lease terms, affordable rates, protection in a culture of customary rights, and a role in family farm strategies. I think a largely unexamined advantage in areas with active land markets like Ontario was tenants' often strong negotiating position due to the relative ease of migration among farming communities.

5 The sample design and linkage procedures were developed with my colleague Michael Ornstein, whose expertise was critical to the work. For the most recent full account see Darroch, "Semi-Automated Record Linkage."

6 For example, the TRA samples in France or the Olson and Thornton samples of Montreal. See Dupâquier and Kessler, eds, *La société française au XIX siècle*; and Olson and Thornton, *Peopling the North American City.*

7 For examples of these estimates from linkage experiences, see Condron and Seaman, "Linkage"; Atack et al., "Matchmaker, matchmaker."

8 A version of the table appears in Darroch, "Semi-Automated Record Linkage."

9 For example, using life tables and age-specific population estimates from our samples gave a low estimate of overall decadal mortality of 11 per cent, while the lowest estimates of linkage failure due to enumeration problems and to problems of our procedures were each 10 per cent. See the details in Darroch, "Semi-Automated Record Linkage."

10 Darroch, "Semi-Automated Record Linkage."

11 The 1861 census explicitly instructed enumerators to record sons of farmers working on their father's farm as labourers, whereas the 1871 census instructions aimed to have them recorded as farmers. See the details of the reclassification in Darroch, "Class in nineteenth-century central Ontario," 57.

12 Baskerville and Sager, *Unwilling Idlers.* See chapter three where they show that toward the end of the nineteenth century the unemployed were recruited from many populations, but especially vulnerable were recent immigrants, older men, the illiterate, nonwhites, and those who had previously been general labourers.

13 Brookes, "'Doing the Best I Can'"; and Curtis, *The Politics of Population.*

14 See Gagan, *Hopeful Travellers*; and Bouchard, *Quelques Arpents.*

15 The farm entry pattern for this 1861 occupational category is based on

relatively small numbers, thirty-nine in total and just twelve representing those over age forty-nine. The pattern seems worth reporting.

16 The table includes farmers' sons, none of whom by definition were boarding or lodging in 1861. The 1 per cent reported in that year resulted from two farmer's sons misclassified as farm boarders. They are included in the table for completeness. The classifications were independently created.

17 Spillman, "The Agricultural Ladder," cited in Marr, "Distribution of Tenant Agriculture," 171.

18 The mean age of men who did not change labour force positions in the decade was thirty-eight years, of new farmers, twenty-nine and of new nonfarmers, thirty years. New farmers were, naturally enough, the most rural in their locations at the outset of the decade, with 93 per cent on the land in 1861, compared to 83 per cent of those remaining in their labour force locations. But only three-quarters of those entering or changing nonfarm occupations in 1871 were rural residents in 1861: urban life was beginning to be a launching pad for nonfarm occupational entry and tended to promote occupational change.

19 There were some interesting differences, however. A third of merchants, manufacturers, and professionals reported investments of $500 or more in 1861, followed by artisans and skilled workers with about half that number having what was significant investment capital in that year, compared to a low average of just 6 per cent of all men over age fifteen; those who did not change their labour force locations reported the largest holdings.

20 For example, as a direct consequence of age differences, larger numbers of both the younger streams of new farmers and nonfarmers than occupationally stable men had been in school in 1861 (10 and 12 per cent), although there were no detectable differences in reported literacy.

21 Four diverse references will serve here to illustrate the large literature on nineteenth-century migration: Norris, "Household and Transiency"; St.-Hilaire, *Peuplement et dynamique migratoire*; Hochstadt, *Mobility and Modernity*; and Hall and Ruggles, "'Restless in the Midst of their Prosperity.'"

22 Barman, *The West Beyond the West.*

23 Bouchard, *Quelques Arpents*; but also see, Widdis, *With Scarcely a Ripple.*

24 McInnis, "Marketable Surpluses"; Darroch, "Scanty Fortunes."

25 This differs very slightly from the proportions that I reported earlier, due to the differing populations under study. See Darroch, "Scanty Fortunes," table 3, where the comparable figure is 54.3.

26 See McCalla, *Planting the Province*, chapters 5 and 10; and Clarke, *Land, Power and Economics*, chapters 4 and 5.

27 The current analysis is insufficient to address the question of developing hierarchies of land ownership and of the associated advantages of "founding" families in some communities. This requires a more fine-grained geographic and social analysis, which I hope to undertake in continuing work. I note particularly that lands in the Mid-Northwest sub-region (figure 1), especially Huron and Bruce counties, were opened to farm settlement only in the 1850s and these properties were often of considerable size, if not greatly improved.

28 See Inwood and Reid, "Gender and Occupational Identity," where they report that most of those recorded as "industrial proprietors" in the schedules of the 1871 Ontario census lived in households engaging in agriculture as well as manufacturing. Nearly two-thirds owned a farm, and more than three-quarters reported some kind of agricultural production. Such pervasive occupational pluralism is also reported by Bouchard, *Quelques Arpents*, and by McCann, "Seasons of Labor." The last quotation is from Michael Katz's account of Wilson Benson's perambulations in social and geographic spaces in nineteenth-century Ontario; Katz, *The People of Hamilton*, 105. I thank two reviewers for reminding me about this very important issue.

29 Wilson, "Tenancy as Family Strategy"; and Wilson, *Tenants in Time.* Alternative estimates of tenure are conceivable employing a number of nominative sources that are available for some counties or townships, such as assessment rolls and abstract indexes to deeds, but given the size of the region under study, well beyond the scope of this inquiry. See Clarke's intricate estimates for Essex County in the southwest corner of the province (outside our study area): Clarke, *Land, Power and Economics*, 251–2. Nor can I duplicate an important US literature on land tenure, especially studies by Bogue, Winters, and Atack, that employed estimates of tenancy based on specific tabulations on the US population and real estate schedules: see Bogue, *From Prairie to Cornbelt;* Winters, *Farmers without Farms*; and Atack, "The Agricultural Ladder Revisited." See Peter Baskerville's more detailed, local account for Logan township, Ontario in this volume.

30 Among studies reporting age of farm entry, see Steckel, "The Age of Leaving Home"; Steckel, "Poverty and Prosperity"; Ferrie, "Up and Out or Down and Out"; Ferrie '*Yankees Now*'; and Darroch and Soltow, *Property and Inequality*, chapter 2. On age and tenancy in Ontario, see Marr, "Distribution of Tenant Agriculture"; and Wilson, *Tenants in Time.*

31 In a large literature, see Pooley and Whyte, eds. *Migrants, Emigrants and Immigrants*; Ferrie, "Up and Out or Down and Out?"; and Ferrie, *'Yankees Now,'* chapters 4 and 7.

32 The median ages in 1861 were: farmers, forty years; merchants, manufacturers, and other white-collar workers, thirty-six years; artisan and skilled workers, thirty-three years; labourers and semiskilled workers, twenty-nine years; and both farmers' sons and those not in the recorded labour force, twenty years.

33 The problem of multicollinearity is that two or more independent variables are so closely related that they are measuring the same phenomenon, so the statistical estimates of their effects are not well determined and the standard errors inflated. I examined the conventional diagnostics tests for collinearity in linear regression models employing the same variables as reported in table 7, which also inform a logistic regression. They give no evidence of collinearity.

34 For related interpretations, see Ferrie, "Up and Out or Down and Out?"; and Bonneuil and Rosntal, "Changing Social Mobility." Regarding movement from Ontario, see for example, Widdis, *With Scarcely A Ripple.*

35 See Marr, "Distribution of Tenant Agriculture." Also see Atack, "The Agricultural Ladder Revisited."

36 Wilson, *Tenants in Time*; Darroch and Soltow, *Property and Inequality*, chapter 2.

37 Marr "Distribution of Tenant Agriculture"; Marr, "Tenant vs. Owner Occupied"; and Atack, "The Agricultural Ladder Revisited." As Marr first reported for Ontario, I also find that those from England and Wales had a particular penchant for tenancy, suggesting a cultural and experiential preference. Exploring the data further sheds little additional light on this pattern. I do find evidence of sociocultural patterns beyond birthplace, for example, even among the Canadian-born farmers, those whose "origins" (traced through the male line in Ontario and only enumerated in 1871) were English more strongly tended to adopt tenant farming compared to men with any other origins. See Marr, "Tenant vs. Owner Occupied," 56.

38 Twice as many tenants as farm owners moved among regional towns or townships, 52 per cent versus 25 per cent.

39 Wilson, *Tenants in Time.*

40 Parkerson, *The Agricultural Transition.* He uses terms such as "countryside in motion" and "culture of mobility" (chapter 2).

41 Assumptions about some underlying hierarchy of status underlie almost every attempt at classifying historical occupations. For studies that explic-

itly consider their implications, see Bouchard, *Tous les métiers du monde*; and van Leeuwen, et al, *HISCO*.

42 For a detailed assessment of the sources of these differences, see Darroch, "Semi-automated record linkage."

CHAPTER SIX

1 Allen, *The British Industrial Revolution*.

2 Harley, "Ocean Freight Rates"; and Williamson, *Globalization and History*.

3 Inwood and Keay, "Trade Policy."

4 Darroch and Ornstein, "Ethnicity and Class"; Dillon, *The Shady Side of Fifty*; and Olson and Thornton, *Peopling the North American City: Montreal*.

5 Chambers, "Late Nineteenth Century Business Cycles"; and Forster, "The Coming of National Policy."

6 Harley, "Western Settlement"; and Marr, "The Wheat Economy in Reverse."

7 Forster and Inwood, "The Diversity of Industrial Experience"; Inwood and Keay, "Diverse paths"; and Inwood and Keay, "Trade Policy."

8 Green and Urquhart, "New Estimates of Output Growth"; and Urquhart, *Gross National Product*.

9 Gaffield, *Language, Schooling, and Cultural Conflict*; Gagan, *Hopeful Travellers*; and Widdis, "Tracing Eastern Ontarian Emigrants."

10 Drummond, *Progress Without Planning*, 29–30 and table 7.1.

11 Crowley, "Rural Labour," 44.

12 Prentice, *The School Promoters*, 95.

13 Urquhart, *Gross National Product*, table 1.1.

14 Emery et al., "Hecksher-Ohlin in Canada"; and McInnis, "The Population of Canada."

15 For example, see Inwood et al., "Labour Market Dynamics in Canada."

16 Darroch and Ornstein, "Ethnicity and Occupational Structure"; Steckel, "The Health and Mortality"; Ferrie, "A New Sample of Males"; Ruggles, "Linking Historical Censuses"; and Goeken et al., "New Methods."

17 Our approach has the added benefit of using real rather than with synthetic cohorts and is national in scope rather than regional.

18 Antonie et al., "Tracking People over Time."

19 The classification uses a "support vector machine" method; Richards demonstrates that this classification method produces the most correct links with the least errors on historical census data. Richards et al., "Applying Machine Learning."

20 Computing similarity between 3.5 million records (1871 census) and 4

million records (1881 census) on a single processor would give us a run-time estimate of close to 40 days: ((3.5M x 4M) record pairs x 2 attributes being compared) / (4M comparisons per second) / 60 (sec/min) / 60 (min/hour) / 24 (hours/day) = 40.5 days. See Antonie et al., "Tracking People over Time," for further detail.

21 Our use of manuscript occupational descriptions and aggregation to occupational groups and the three broad classes follows a well-defined set of rules within the framework of the NAPP-HISCO coding scheme (Roberts et al., "Occupational Classification"). Procedures used by the Census Bureau 140 years ago are not documented. Carter and Sutch document the "editing" of occupational returns by nineteenth century census staff: Carter and Sutch, "Fixing the Facts." We examine only those people who reported an occupation in both years, while the Census Bureau tallied occupations without regard for continuity.

22 Antonie et al., "Tracking People over Time."

23 The imprecision means that occasionally we will connect the wrong pair of records. A more damaging effect of imprecise or inconsistent reporting is to force us to broaden tolerance for declaring a match. For example, we must accept any 1881 age between twenty-eight and thirty-two for someone who reported twenty years in 1871, since someone is as likely to be one to two years off as to be exact in both years. Broadening tolerance, however, aggravates the problem of multiples links. Any classification system with census data must strike a balance between broadening tolerance to avoid mistakes arising from presuming more precision than is warranted and, on the other hand, diminishing unique links by expanding the pool of multiples.

24 The paper in this volume by Gordon Darroch provides a thorough and highly interesting analysis of the choice of young men to enter farming or not.

25 Census underreporting of occupations for women is documented by: Abel and Folbre, "A Methodology for Revising Estimates"; Inwood and Reid, "Gender and Occupational Identity"; and Carter and Sutch, "Fixing the Facts."

26 Roberts et al., "Occupational Classification," for the classification scheme.

27 Dunae finds that in some cases "dressmaker" was a coded way of identifying sex workers: Dunae, "Sex, Charades, and Census Records." Unfortunately, we cannot distinguish such cases. McDevitt, Irwin, and Inwood analyze gender differences in productivity and pay for clothing makers: McDevitt et al., J. Irwin, and K. Inwood, "Gender Pay Gap."

28 Among men aged fifteen to fifty-five, 87 per cent reported an occupation

in 1871 and 85 per cent in 1881. Enumerators had the option to record one or more occupations but rarely did so. We use the first-mentioned occupation. Canada, Department of Agriculture, *Manual Containing "The Census Act"… the First Census of Canada,* 23, and Canada, Department of Agriculture, *Manual Containing "The Census Act" … the Second Census of Canada,* 30.

29 Acheson, "The National Policy"; and Inwood and Stengos, "Discontinuities."

30 Drummond, *Progress Without Planning,* 30.

31 Charpentier et al., *Nouvelle histoire,* 240; and Heron, "Factory Workers," 511–16.

32 Darroch and Ornstein, "Ethnicity and Occupational Structure"; Darroch and Ornstein, "Ethnicity and Class"; and Akenson, *Small Differences,* 94–5.

33 Akenson notes that English immigrants had a similar experience comparable to Irish Roman Catholic immigrants: Akenson, *Small Differences.*

34 Darroch and Ornstein, "Ethnicity and Class"; and Darroch in this volume.

35 Admittedly, we examine the entire country while Darroch and Ornstein provide an in-depth analysis of the central regions of Ontario: see Darroch and Ornstein, "Ethnicity and Occupational Structure."

36 Marr, "The Wheat Economy in Reverse."

37 Future research will integrate these findings with the American experience, which is possible following the publication of newly available US census linkage.

CHAPTER SEVEN

1 Special thanks go to Sara Van Sligtenhorst and Jill Leslie for their diligent work linking "Loganites" across decades and countries. The People in Motion project is headed by Kris Inwood at Guelph University. I thank the Social Sciences and Humanities Research Council for financial support for the Perth Project.

2 Gagan, "Geographical and Social Mobility," 154; Houston and Smyth, "Geographical Transiency"; and Katz, *The People of Hamilton,* 94–111.

3 Parkerson, "How Mobile"; and Norris, "Migration, Pioneer Settlement, and the Life Course."

4 See Atack, "A Nineteenth Century Resource"; Parkerson, "How Mobile"; Darroch, this volume; and, from a slightly different perspective, Darroch, "Migrants in the Nineteenth Century" for surveys of this work. See also table 7.2 and its accompanying footnote.

5 Gordon Darroch led the way: see Darroch this volume; Ferrie, "The End of American Exceptionalism"; Steckel, "Household Migration"; Stewart, "Economic Opportunity or Hardship"; Ruggles, "Intergenerational Coresidence"; Goeken et al., "New Methods"; and Antonie et al., this volume.

6 Baskerville, "Chattel Mortgages"; and Johnston and Johnston, *History of Perth County*. Perth's population grew from 38,000 in 1861 to 46,553 in 1871 and to 53,700 in 1881. Acres occupied grew from 85.2 per cent in 1871 to 92.2 per cent in 1881.

7 For all of Ontario, see Wilson, *Tenants in Time*, 232. Logan figure is calculated from the 1871 census computerized file.

8 Karr, *The Canada Land Company*; Lee, *The Canada Company*; and Browde, "Settling the Canadian Colonies."

9 For the Canada Company's Annual Reports, see Reports of Court of Directors to the Proprietors, Box 3, Canada Company Papers, A–4–5, Ontario Archives. For Allan's report, see ibid., A–6–3, Commissioners to London Court, vol. 7, 30 August 1879; Stratford *Beacon*, 12 July 1878; and Listowel *Banner*, 29 November 1878.

10 Calculated from a complete computerized file of chattel mortgages for Perth County, 1871–1911.

11 Canada, House of Commons, *Debates*, C.F. Ferguson, 28 March 1890, 2662.

12 Correspondence with the Commissioners, vol. 8, 28 June 1877, Canada Company Papers, A–6–2, Ontario Archives; Commissioners to London Court, vol. 7, 18 January 1876, 9 June 1877 and 30 August 1879, Canada Company Papers, A–6–3, Ontario Archives.

13 For 1a and b in table 7.2, see Gagan, "Geographical and Social Mobility," 155; for 2a–4, see Galenson and Pope, "Economic and Geographic Mobility," 641; for 5–6c, see Stewart, "Economic Opportunity or Hardship," 240–1; for 7, see Parkerson, "How Mobile," 102. He includes several of the studies listed above.

14 Parkerson, "How Mobile," 99.

15 Linkage rules were as follows: name matches – where that was somewhat problematic the existence of relatives in both years would be checked, age matches within plus/minus three years, birthplace and sex matches. Two persons with similar identifiers were thrown out.

16 For reports of strikingly similar persistence rates, see Steckel, "Household Migration," 191; and Goeken et al., "New Estimates of Migration," 11.

17 Mortality rates do not affect our data since we only analyze *links* from one decade to the next and do not presume that missing links are movers. Nevertheless, we have also removed those we know died during the decade.

18 The LR was also run with birthplace only and there was no significant relationship.

19 Stewart, "Economic Opportunity or Hardship," 239.

20 This variable was constructed from the answers to two questions reported in Schedule Four of the 1871 census for Perth County: number of occupied acres and number of acres improved. Close to 95 per cent of Logan's farmers answered both questions.

21 The sig was .002 and .007 respectively. The regression was also run controlling for number of occupied acres (above and below fifty) and the findings remained as reported. A regression was run with just leaseholders and just owners, and the findings were similar in both cases. Finally, a regression was run with precedent years omitted in order to avoid any overlapping effect between time in Logan and per cent acres improved, and once again the finding that those with under 60 per cent improved acres were more likely to remain in Logan remained intact.

22 Hoffman and Richards, *Soil Survey of Perth County*. For an informed critique of applying twentieth-century soil appraisals to nineteenth-century agricultural practices, see Inwood and Irwin, "Land, Income and Regional Inequality," 166ff.

23 The variable ratio of dependents to earners was constructed in two ways. First, those without a stated occupation were deemed dependents. Secondly, those under the age of fifteen were deemed dependents. The second would catch those over fifteen who worked on farms but were not given an occupation. Neither construction yielded a significant result.

24 For a discussion of the merits of an agricultural ladder in Canadian agricultural historiography, see Darroch, this volume.

25 A logistic regression with move/stay as the dependent variable run with just tenants discarded age as insignificant.

26 For a summary of these findings, see Ferrie, "Up and Out or Down and Out," 39, fn 9.

27 Spennemann and Sutherland, "Late Nineteenth Century."

28 See "Historical Sketch of St Peter's Taken From the 125th Anniversary Directory, 1983," Pastor Arthur Horst and Mary Jane Schuessler, *St Peter's Lutheran Church in the Village of Brodhagen*, stpetershouse.ca/history_125booklet.html; and Carl R. Cronmiller, *A History of the Lutheran Church in Canada* (Toronto, 1961) 1:142–44.

29 Hoffman and Richards, *Soil Survey of Perth County*.

30 Brose, *German History*, 112–15.

31 For both tables, the data are for farms with owners for whom a link has been determined. German Lutheran farms number 126 and all other

farms number 287. The same contrasts are reflected if all farms are included, i.e., adding the farms for whom the owners could not be linked.

32 Jordan, *German Seed*, 35. See also Liebowitz, "The Persistence of Draft Oxen"; and Kauffman and Liebowitz, "Draft Animals."

33 *Listowel Banner*, 14 December 1877, 7.

34 See Spennemann and Sutherland, "Late Nineteenth Century"; Jordan, *German Seed*, 193; Conzen, "Peasant Pioneers," 284; and Atack, "Tenants and Yeomen," 26, 29.

35 Conzen, "Peasant Pioneers," used wills to help understand family strategies, but that research has yet to be undertaken in sufficient detail for this study. See also Salamon, *Prairie Patrimony*.

36 Karr, *The Canada Land Company*; Lee, *The Canada Company*; and Browde, "Settling the Canadian Colonies."

37 London Court to Commissioners 12 May, 4 and 29 December 1843; 15 April, 18 July, 8 Sept 1844; 4 January 1846, Correspondence with Commissioners, vol. 4, Canada Company Papers, A–6–2, vol. 4, Ontario Archives.

38 London Court to Commissioners, 4 December 1843, Correspondence with Commissioners, Canada Company Papers, A–6–2, vol. 4, Ontario Archives.

39 London Court to Commissioners, 17 November 1842, Canada Company Papers, A–6–2, vol. 4, Ontario Archives.

40 Friesen, "A German-Canadian Rarissimum"; Grenke, "German Land Settlement"; Lehmann, *The German Canadians*, 80–6; and Wagner, *A History of Migration*, 14–69.

41 For table 7.9 the selection is all household heads who leased in 1871. They have been linked by address coordinates and first and last name to the leasing data compiled from the Canada Company papers. Other Catholics are omitted.

42 Machan, ed., *Legacy of Logan*.

43 I was able to link 490 of the 555 heads, a linkage rate of 88 per cent.

44 See Darroch, this volume; Yoder, "Rethinking Midwestern"; and Wilson, *Tenants in Time*.

45 Letters to Court, Widder to Court, 12 October 1843, PAO, Canada Company Papers, A–6–3, Ontario Archives.

CHAPTER EIGHT

1 Humphrey, "Conflicting independence"; and Kulikoff, *From British*.

2 Danbom, *Born in the Country*; David B. Danbom, *The Resisted Revolution*; Gardner, *American Agriculture*; and Clarke, *Regulation And the Revolution*.

3 Engerman and Sokoloff suggest that the proportions of rural adult males owning land rose towards the end of the nineteenth century reaching an average of 75 per cent for the United States as a whole in 1900 and 83 per cent in the west compared to 72 per cent in the Midwest. In Canada, levels of ownership were even higher among adult males, reaching a national average of 87 per cent in 1901. See Engerman and Sokoloff, "Colonialism, Inequality," 21 and table 4; and Engermann and Sokoloff, "Debating the Role."

4 Gates, "The Homestead"; and Gates, *Frontier Landlords.*

5 Atack, "The Agricultural Ladder Revisited."

6 LeDuc, "The Disposal"; Curti, *The Making*; Bogue, *Patterns from the Sod*; Saloutos, "Land policy"; Bogue, *From Prairie to Corn Belt*; and Winters, "Tenancy as an Economic Institution."

7 Atack, "The Agricultural Ladder Revisited," 2.

8 For a discussion of the literature, and a life cycle analysis of the data used in this chapter, see Leonard et al., "Household and Farm."

9 The details of the disposal in the late 1960s and early 1970s are cited in Atack "A Nineteenth Century Resource."

10 See for instance, Hargis, "Name Games"; and Sylvester, *The Limits of Rural Capitalism.*

11 Kansas State Board of Agriculture. *Biennial Report* (Topeka, 1873–1976).

12 Sylvester et al., "Demography and Environment."

13 Rabe-Hesketh and Skrondal, *Multilevel*; and Snijders and Boskers, *Multilevel Analysis.*

14 Jordan, *North American.*

15 Malin, *Winter.*

16 Buchanan et al., *Roadside Kansas.*

17 Knights, "Potholes"; Adams and Kasakoff, "Estimates"; Reid, "The 1870 United States Census"; and Anderson and Fienberg, *Who Counts.*

18 Agricultural Statistics Rolls, 1865–1940, Kansas State Historical Society.

19 Some idea of the pace of western settlement can be seen in tables previously published (reporting on the number of farms and total acres in farms) in Leonard et al., "Drought," table 2; and in Sylvester, "Ecological Frontiers," appendix table 2 (reporting on the number of households in each township by census year).

20 Atack notes the ambiguity of the "farmers without farms" category in the work of Bogue, *From Prairie to Corn Belt*, and Curti, *The Making*. See Atack, "The Agricultural Ladder Revisited," 7–8. In Canada, McInnis notes the inconsistency of the occupational categories assigned to the landless rural population between federal censuses, arguing that the differences were not representative of economic trends. See McInnis, "The Changing Structure."

21 Atack, "The Agricultural Ladder Revisited," 3–5.

22 Gray, "Farm Ownership."

23 Leonard et al., "Household and Farm," 287–317.

24 Black and Allen, "The Growth of Farm Tenancy."

25 Atack, "The Agricultural Ladder Revisited," 19; for the original description of the Bateman Foust sample, see Bateman and Foust, "A Sample of Rural Households."

26 For discussions of tenancy and cotton cultivation see Daniel, *Breaking the Land*; Aiken, *The Cotton Plantation*; and Giesen, *Boll Weevil Blues*. Various USDA maps from the early twentieth century detail the spatial extent of the cotton belt, noting the northernmost range extending to the southeastern border of Kansas but no further. See for example figure 2 in Giesen, *Boll Weevil Blues*, page ix, which reproduces a graphic from the *New York Times* in 1910.

27 Atack, "The Agricultural Ladder Revisited," table 3, 19.

28 Worster, *Dust Bowl*; Miner, *Harvesting the High Plains*; Fitzgerald, *Every Farm a Factory*; and Sherow, *The Grasslands*.

29 The patterns of family proprietorship and mixed farming have been described in greater detail in other publications that use these data. See Sylvester and Cunfer, "An Unremembered Diversity"; and Sylvester, "Ecological Frontiers."

30 Sylvester et al., "Demography and Environment," 31–60.

31 Miner, *Harvesting the High Plains*, 286.

32 The US Census Bureau reported the highest ever Gini coefficient for income in 2006 of 0.47, a substantial increase from the coefficient in 1967 of .397, when it was first reported. Gini indices tend to be lower in Europe and Canada, generally ranging between .26 and .33. See Amiel and Cowell, *Thinking About Inequality*; and *World Development Indicators*.

33 The distributions are presented using farm-size categories in an appendix for readers who prefer to examine the data in more detail.

34 Singer and Willett, *Applied Longitudinal Data*; and Snijders and Boskers, *Multilevel Analysis*, 2012.

CHAPTER NINE

1 See the remarkable suite of intercensal links for Quebec City compiled by St-Hilaire and Marcoux, at www.phsvq.cieq.ulaval.ca/.

2 Of all marriages 1881–1901, about 5 per cent crossed the linguistic divide, 2.5 per cent the religious divide. See also Gauvreau et al., "Le jumelage."

3 Data in both the census of 1881 and the index to the census of 1901 are well controlled with respect to order and geographic location. For the 1881 data, see www.genealogie.umontreal.ca. The 1901 index is accessible at automatedgenealogy.com/ and reliably linked to digital images of both the population schedule and the property schedule at www.collectionscanada.gc.ca/ archivianet/.

4 Use of the computer is akin to that described by Darroch in chapter five, this volume, and in greater detail in Darroch, "Semi-Automated Record Linkage."

5 Vital events 1840–1920 were grounded in matches to censuses, tax rolls, and city directories. For details of the surname sample, and for matching procedures in three birth cohorts (1859, 1879, and 1899) and a death cohort (1881), see Olson and Thornton, *Peopling the North American City*, chapter two and appendix B. On household contours, sometimes ambiguous in the duplex and triplex habitat of Montreal, and practices of 1871 and 1881 census takers, see Lauzon, "Cohabitation et déménagements"; on surname sampling strategies, see Bardet, *Rouen aux XVIIe et XVIIIe siècles*; Perrenoud, *La population de Genève*; Oris et al., "Les solitudes urbaines"; and Darroch, "Domestic Revolution."

6 An address is reported for 92 per cent of households; for the remainder, usually a second family living in the same house, the street segment can be interpolated. For a fruitful use of the house or property in compilation of diverse sources, see Johansen, "Urban Social and Demographic Reconstitution."

7 By situating resident owners, I recreated the undocumented boundaries of the sixty-seven census divisions. Confining the search for tenant families to a particular division reduces the number of homonyms. Since most annual leases began and moves occurred 1 May, *Lovell's Montreal Directory of 1880–81* and the municipal tax roll of occupants (both compiled in June 1880) correspond best to the census of April 1881.

8 Although the tax roll of a given year shows some units as vacant or not yet canvassed (8 percent in 1880), it has consistently proved a less biased source than census or directory with respect to low-rent households.

9 See Hanna and Olson, "Social landscape." The segments are similar to twin block faces, 442 in 1881 and 772 in 1901. The neighbourhood rent median is more comprehensive than assignment of status by occupation, since it can be applied to households headed by women or the retired.

10 Gilliland and Olson, "Residential Segregation"; and Gilliland et al., "Did Segregation Increase." The published census data refer to "divisions," which were ephemeral subdivisions of the administrative wards of the

city; they are hereafter referred to by the more familiar term "census tracts." Maps in colour can be accessed at www.mun.ca/mapm/.

11 In a "simple" household, the 1901 rubric "relation to head" clarifies relationships among all the members. For 1881, Gauvreau created variables "household type" and "individual situation" by an algorithm based on age, sex, marital status, order of appearance, and shared surname, as employed in the Canadian Families Project.

12 For review of that literature see Hall and Ruggles, "'Restless in the Midst of their Prosperity.'" Among the first to point out the magnitude of the mortality effect on the estimates of mobility was Parkerson, "How Mobile."

13 Thornton and Olson, "Mortality." The life table is based on a cohort of 7,000 deaths at ages over twelve months, in the year 1881, and 3,400 infant deaths in the cohort born April 1879 to April 1880.

14 Projet Balsac supplied Catholic marriages for the Island of Montreal (www.uqac.ca/balsac/). These records proved as valuable for men as for women because of the potential for distinguishing among homonyms, detecting the remarried (more frequent among men), and confirming the identities of stepchildren. The Quebec Family History Society provided a compilation of Protestant marriages (www.qfhs.ca/), as well as a carefully verified digital version of the register from Christ Church, the Anglican cathedral. Because local Protestant registers rarely report the full names of parents, they leave many ambiguities, but a compensating effect, buttressing recovery of Protestants, is their greater variety of surnames.

15 The estimate for 1861 is derived from a search for families of infants born in 1859; improvement is apparent from improved matches for households enrolled to pay the municipal "water tax" and is consistent with census-taking efforts after Confederation, as discussed by Curtis, *The Politics of Population.*

16 City dwellers have been considered harder to match. To penetrate the massive literature of record matching, see Darroch, "Semi-Automated Record Linkage"; and Dillon, *The Shady Side of Fifty.* Darroch discusses the limitations of Soundex, and Dillon, "Challenges and Opportunities," provides extensive discussion of French and English name stocks in Quebec and overstatement of ages of the elderly.

17 On standardization of street names, common first names, French Canadian surnames, double names, and occupation titles, see Olson and Thornton, *Peopling the North American City*, 367–71.

18 Transcriptions for 1881 were a pioneering venture carried out by a cross-

country mobilization of volunteers, remarkably successful but still scarred by limitations of language skills and keyboard options for French accents. The more recent 1901 index was compiled also by volunteers but with interactive checks.

19 Dillon, "Challenges and Opportunities"; Darroch, "Semi-Automated Record Linkage"; and Guest, "Notes from the National Panel Study."

20 Dillon, "Challenges and Opportunities."

21 Especially useful here is the work of Darroch on "pockets" of surnames ("Semi-Automated Record Linkage") and relation to head of household ("Constructing Census Families"). See also Darroch, "Domestic Revolution" and "Home and Away."

22 Olson and Thornton, *Peopling the North American City*, 153–6.

23 Gilliland, "Modeling Residential Mobility in Montreal."

24 Gilliland and Olson, "Residential Segregation"; and Gilliland et al., "Did Segregation Increase."

25 Gauvreau et al., "Mobilité sociale." The sample of occupations demonstrated the substitutability of occupation data from either marriage register or census. See also Long and Ferrie, "The Path to Convergence."

26 Thernstrom, *The Other Bostonians.*

27 Kok and Mandemakers, "A Life-Course Approach"; Ruggles, "Confessions of a Microsimulator"; and Ruggles, "Multigenerational Families."

28 On the coresident nuclear family in both rural and urban habitats of North America, see Darroch, "Domestic revolution"; Darroch and Ornstein, "Family Coresidence"; and Ruggles, "The Decline."

29 Ingenious strategies are emerging for samples that will enhance recovery and minimize bias; see Ruggles, "Linking Historical Censuses"; Ferrie, "A New Sample of Males"; Long, "Rural-Urban Migration"; Long and Ferrie, "The Path to Convergence"; Reid et al., "Nineteenth-Century Scottish Demography"; Rosental, *Les Sentiers Invisibles.*

30 Darroch, "Home and Away."

31 Ruggles, "Demography of the Unrelated." Not all were truly unrelated; apparent in 1901 are numerous "in-laws" reported as lodgers, detectable once we have recovered wives' maiden names from marriage records.

32 Contributions to these areas of research locally are Baskerville, "Familiar Strangers"; Bradbury, *Wife to Widow*; Dillon, *The Shady Side of Fifty*; Harris, "The End Justified"; Harvey, "'Dealing'"; and Laflamme, *Vivre en Ville.*

33 Retrieval of nuns and novices, for example, can be enhanced by revisiting directories of religious communities. A database of female vocations shows that a very high proportion of those in Montreal communities were of rural origins; they entered novitiates in Montreal at about age

eighteen; a large share left after a stay of a month or a year, and those who stayed were likely to survive (relative to other women of the same age) and to move among institutions. Rousseau and Remiggi, eds., *Atlas historique*; Danylewicz, *Taking the Veil*; Payette, "Les vocations féminines"; and MacDonald, "Who Counts."

34 See Baskerville and Sager, *Unwilling Idlers;* and Olson and Thornton, *Peopling The North American City*, 190–8. Immigrants were, of course, shock absorbers as well and added to the competition for entry-level jobs.

35 Maternal mortality averaged about 1 per cent of births, higher at a first birth and among mothers under twenty. Childhood rickets contributed to risk of a woman's death at a first birth.

36 See van Poppel et al., "The Effects."

37 Thornton and Olson, "Mortality," 169–70; and Myers and Elman, "Morbidity."

38 See Shackle, *Decision*; and Beck, *Risk Society*.

39 Gilliland, "Modeling Residential Mobility"; and Gilliland and Olson, "Claims."

40 Lewis, *Manufacturing Montreal*. The central role of kinship in one of the country's largest corporations is apparent in Austin, "Life Cycles"; and Sennett, *Families Against the City*. See also Granovetter, "The Strength," and subsequent debates on social networks.

41 Historical demographers have always been attentive to kinship among villagers, urban élites, and individuals on the move. Since the 1970s, studies of factory towns have provided insights into the way kin relations penetrated workplaces (Hareven, *Family Time*) and served families even at long distance (Bras, "Maids to the City"). On endogamy and inheritance among "non-coresident families," see White and Jorion, "Representing"; Brudner and White, "Class"; and on relational networks as a "non-material legacy," see Levi, *Inheriting Power*.

42 Dufaux and Olson, "Reconstruire." On advance of real estate values, see Linteau, *Maisonneuve*; on risk-avoidance strategies of property owners, see Rodger, *The Transformation*; Sweeny, "Spatial"; on oversight of minors, see Nootens, "'What a Misfortune,'" pointing to narrative sources in court records and notarial repertories.

43 Notable are Lenihan's sources for chapter 4, and the Founders and Survivors project referred to in chapter 2, this volume.

CHAPTER TEN

1 Acknowledgments: I thank the University Research Fund at Victoria University of Wellington for funding the data collection for this paper, and

the Special Collections Research Center at the Regenstein Library, University of Chicago for permission to make digital photographs of the data. Charlie Russell, Sarah Bryant, Megan Zacher, and Anthony Gerbi provided exemplary research assistance. I have used the Houghteling survey manuscripts with students in HIST234 (Introduction to Social History) at Victoria University of Wellington in 2008 and 2009 and HIST3869 (Urban American History, 2010) and HIST1907W (Living, working, and dying in Chicago, 2011) at the University of Minnesota. Their impressions and comments about the families have been very informative for this research. I acknowledge further support from the Minnesota Population Center (5R24HD041023), funded through grants from the Eunice Kennedy Shriver National Institute for Child Health and Human Development (NICHD).

2 Roberts, "The Entry into Employment."

3 Slichter, *The Turnover.*

4 Goldin and Katz, *The Race*; and Sundstrom, "Internal."

5 Long and Ferrie, "Intergenerational."

6 Lee and Solon, "Trends."

7 Grawe, "Intergenerational Mobility'; and Beller and Hout, "Intergenerational Social Mobility."

8 Converse, *Survey Research*; and Ward, *Poverty.*

9 Booth, *Life and Labour*; Du Bois, *The Philadelphia Negro*; and Kellogg, *Wage-Earning Pittsburgh.*

10 Aronovici, *The Social Survey*; and Eaton and Harrison, *A Bibliography.*

11 Gazeley and Newell, "The End of Destitution"; and Williams and Zimmerman, *Studies of Family.*

12 Bulmer, *The Chicago School*; Park et al., *The City*; and Sampson, *Great American City*, 34–5.

13 Hunter, *Symbolic Communities*; Smith and White, *Chicago*; and Venkatesh, "Chicago's Pragmatic Planners."

14 Zorbaugh, *The Gold Coast*; O'Connor, 81–3; and Shaw and McKay, *Juvenile Delinquency.*

15 Sibley, "Invisible Women."

16 See for example, Abbott, *Women in Industry*; Abbott, *The Tenements*; and Breckinridge, *New Homes for Old*, among others.

17 Burgess and Cottrell, *Predicting*; and Burgess, "Factors."

18 "Chicago Heiress, 'Friend of the Friendless,' Dies," *Chicago Tribune*, 3 January 1927, 3.

19 Houghteling, *The Income*, 20–2.

20 Bureau of Labor Statistics, *The Cost of Living in the United States*, Bls Bulletin. Vol. 357 (Washington, DC: GPO, 1924).

21 Houghteling, *The Income and Standards.*
22 Survey of Income and Cost of Living of Study, 1924–25, MS–1011, Special Collections Research Center, University of Chicago Library.
23 Martha May, "The "Good Managers": Married Working Class Women and Family Budget Studies, 1895–1915," *Labor History* 25, no. 3 (1984): 351–72.
24 Houghteling, "Study," 165.
25 I am indebted to my students in HIST234, HIST3869, and HIST1907W for these observations and summarizing the notes on the Houghteling surveys.
26 Mokyr, "Why More Work for Mother."
27 Schedule A2, Survey of Income and Cost of Living of Study, 1924–25, MS–1011, Special Collections Research Center, University of Chicago Library.
28 Schedule M20, Survey of Income and Cost of Living of Study, 1924–25, MS–1011, Special Collections Research Center, University of Chicago Library.
29 Schedules A13 and J81, Survey of Income and Cost of Living of Study, 1924–25, MS–1011, Special Collections Research Center, University of Chicago Library.
30 Neckerman, "Divided Households."
31 Grossman, *Land of Hope.*
32 Coale and Rives, "A Statistical Reconstruction," 21.
33 King and Magnuson, "Perspectives," 458; and Hacker, "New Estimates," 88.
34 I have also saved images of the 1880, 1900, and 1910 censuses and World War I and World War II enlistment files for husbands. Going back before 1920, I "lose" many more European migrants to Europe, and many of the men are not yet married to their spouse.
35 Douglas, *Real Wages*; Carter et al., *Historical Statistics*, table Ba4323.
36 Ihrke and Faber, *Geographical Mobility.*
37 Claude S. Fischer, "Ever-More," 188.
38 Simmons, "Changing Residence."
39 Bigott, *From Cottage to Bungalow.*
40 Houghteling, *The Income*, 110–13.
41 Craig, *Fireside Politics*, 13; and Bowden and Offer, "Household Appliances."
42 Chad Ronnander, "The Classification of Work."
43 Benson, *Household Accounts.*
44 Jacoby and Sharma, "Employment Duration."

CHAPTER ELEVEN

1 Ginsburg et al., "Major Gene Control"; Luo et al., *Pediatric Research*; Silventoinen,"Determinants"; Visscher et al., "Heritability"; and Morris et al., "Familial Concordance."

2 Floud, "Secular Changes"; Haines, "Growing Incomes"; Komlos, "Anomalies"; Steckel and Haurin, "Health and Nutrition"; and Tanner, *A History*.

3 Cranfield and Inwood, "A Tale of Two Armies"; and Inwood et al., "Physical Stature."

4 Haines et al., "The Short and the Dead."

5 Cranfield and Inwood, "The Great Transformation."

6 Davenport and Love, *The Medical Department*, 108, 1130.

7 Cranfield and Inwood, "The Great Transformation."

8 Mielke et al., *Human Biological Variation*, 239ff; Habicht et al., "Height and weight"; and Hermannusen et al., "Micro and Macro."

9 Bielicki, "Physical Growth"; Fogel, "Physical Growth as a Measure"; Komlos, "Anomalies"; Komlos, "Shrinking"; Steckel, "Stature; " Steckel, "Biological Measures"; Steckel, "Heights"; Tanner, *Foetus in Man*; and Tanner, *A History*.

10 Hatton and Bray, "Long Run Trends."

11 Komlos, "An anthropometric history."

12 Floud et al., *The Changing Body*, 69, 226.

13 Thornton and Olson, "A Deadly Discrimination."

14 Kirk-Elleker, "A Measure of Well-Being."

15 Morton, *When Your Number's Up*.

16 Fogel, "Physical Growth as a Measure"; Lamm, "British Soldiers."

17 Guest, "Notes"; and Emery and McQuillan, "A Case Study Approach."

18 Dillon, "Challenges and Opportunities."

19 Clarke, "Unwanted Warriors"; and Clarke, "'You Will Not.'"

20 Morton, *When Your Number's Up*, 60.

21 Even soft or "fuzzy" truncation requires a maximum likelihood truncated regression technique that ignores all observations with height less than the truncation point. In this case OLS and truncated regressions produce very similar coefficients; we report the latter because it is in principle preferable; see Fogel et al., "Exploring"; Fogel, "Physical Growth as a Measure"; Komlos and Kim, "Estimating Trends"; and Komlos, "How to."

22 Green et al., "Conspicuous"; and Inwood et al., "Labour Market Dynamics in Canada."

23 Ghosh and Bandyopadhyay, "Income"; Hatton and Martin, "The Effects"; Horton, "Birth Order"; and Li and Power, "Influences."

24 Uncertainty arises with families who reported no income at all. Undoubtedly some were drawing down savings in the absence of income during the current year. Nevertheless, some own-account workers and farmers may not have reported income consistently despite the best efforts of census staff (Minns and Risov, "The Spirit of Capitalism"). Census instructions were clear, but 1901 was the first Canadian enumeration of income. In recognition of possible inconsistencies, we reestimate on only those who reported positive income. We lose valuable information about many low-resource families, but this model is useful as a robustness check. While sample size is smaller, the estimated coefficients for the French and Quebec effects are qualitatively identical (see the right hand column in table 8).
25 Canadian Families Project, 23.
26 Horton, "Birth Order"; and Hatton and Martin, "The Effects."
27 Steckel, "Stature"; and Haines, "Growing Incomes."
28 Darroch, "Occupational Structure"; Darroch and Ornstein, "Ethnicity and Occupational Structure"; Darroch and Soltow, *Property and Inequality*; and Emery and Levitt, "Cost of Living."
29 Bielicki, "Physical Growth"; and Thibault et al., 1985, 113.
30 Norrie et al., *A History*, 229.
31 Emery and Levitt, "Cost of Living"; and Minns and MacKinnon, "The Costs."
32 Davies, "Night Soil."
33 Jette, "A Regional Analysis."
34 Yool, "An Anthropometric Study."
35 Green et al., "Conspicuous"; and Inwood et al., "Labour Market Dynamics in Canada."
36 Copp, *The Anatomy of Poverty*; and McInnis, "The Population of Canada."
37 Brown and Cook, *Canada 1896–1921*, 128.
38 Gilliland et al., "Did Segregation Increase"; Olson and Thornton, *Peopling the North American City*; Thornton and Olson, "A Deadly Discrimination"; and Ward and Ward, "Infant Birth Weight."
39 Mercier and Boone, "Infant Mortality."
40 Here we estimate with ordinary least squares rather than truncated regression to simplify the decomposition (OLS and maximum likelihood truncation models produce near-identical coefficients).
41 Thornton and Olson, "A Deadly Discrimination."
42 Olson and Thornton, *Peopling the North American City*, 89–129.
43 Bozzoli et al., "Adult Health"; Hatton, "Infant mortality"; and Klemp and Weisdorf, "The Lasting Damage."

CHAPTER TWELVE

1 In this paper we use the terms Aboriginal, Indigenous, Indian, and First Nations interchangeably, although we employ Aboriginal with more frequency as, according to Section 35 of the Constitution Act, 1982, its definition includes the Indian, Inuit, and Métis peoples of Canada. We are grateful for financial support from the Social Sciences and Humanities Research Council of Canada and comments from Kandace Bogaert, Michelle Hamilton, Richard Holt, and participants at the 2012 Record Linkage Workshop at the University of Guelph.

2 Scott, "The Indians," 73–88.

3 Talbot, "'It Would Be Best,'" 110–11.

4 Lackenbauer and McGowan, "Competing Loyalties."

5 Miller, *Lethal Legacy*, 1–49; and Hamilton, "'Anyone Not.'"

6 Axelsson and Sköld, *Indigenous Peoples.*

7 Hamilton, "'Anyone Not.'" See also Hamilton and Inwood, "The Aboriginal Population"; and Gaffield, "Language."

8 Canada, Census 1901, *Instructions to Enumerators*, articles 9, 47, and 53.

9 Soldiers of the First World War, Canadian Expeditionary Force, Library and Archives Canada, www.collectionscanada.gc.ca/databases/cef/index-e.html; and The Canadian Great War Project, www.canadiangreatwarproject.com/.

10 We consider all soldiers with a consistent name and a date of birth range plus or minus three years from the census birth date (and plus or minus five years for the youngest children in 1901). Connecting next of kin listed at attestation to family members in the 1901 census is an imperfect process because titles and initials obscure some first names, and marriage and remarriage changed surname for many women. If next of kin in the attestation paper was a friend or distant relative, the 1901 census search could be time consuming. For some men, identification in the 1911 census was a helpful intermediate step. Many enumerators record birthplace province or territory in contrast to individual communities identified during attestation. As a supplement to birthplace, therefore, when no other basis for confirmation is available, we also consider location in 1901. Additional military information describing complexion, medical, or occupation notes was occasionally useful (e.g. descriptors such as "copper skin" or "Mighty Hunter").

11 We match census and attestation records with three levels of confidence using criteria reported in appendix: table 12.6. Our process gives more weight to potential matches with uncommon names than to otherwise

comparable matches with common names. Many medium-confidence matches reflect the complication of multiple possible links for a common name. Some matches cannot be confirmed (i.e. remain low confidence) because documents are missing from the library and archives web-based collection.

12 We add records for 171 men identified as Aboriginal in some other source and then located in both the census and attestation records.

13 Some lists of soldiers survive in the DIA records, but there does not appear to be a comprehensive inventory; see Winegard, *For King and Kanata,* 76, 91, 137. For this reason it is impossible to assess any of the DIA-derived estimates of participation. Equally, there is no reason to doubt the contemporary tally of 3,500 Indian soldiers (Scott, "The Canadian Indians").

14 Proposals to create segregated Aboriginal units were by and large resisted in Canada, as in the United States. See Gaffen, *Forgotten Soldiers,* 11; Winegard, *For King and Kanata,* 51ff; and Walker, "Race and Recruitment," 7. On the US see Holm, "Fighting," 71; Holm, "Strong Hearts," 138–9; and Tate, "From Scout to Doughboy," 424–6.

15 Sheffield, "Indifference," 62–3; Lackenbauer et al., *A Commemorative History,* 123; and Summerby, *Native Soldiers,* 7.

16 We compare regimental numbers of our census-linked soldiers with the numbers apparently assigned to the 114th ("Regimental Number List," Library and Archives Canada, 32, www.collectionscanada.gc.ca/archivianet/02015203_e.html, accessed Sept. 2011; and "Utilities," Canadian Great War Project, www.canadiangreatwarproject.com, accessed 17 Sept. 2011). The regimental numbering is not well understood. Comparison is further imprecise because some soldiers may not have been enumerated in 1901 or did not declare Aboriginal ethnicity or could not be linked securely. Winegard reports that by the end of the war 287 men from the Six Nations alone had joined this unit: see Winegard, *For King and Kanata,* 67.

17 Although not an exclusively Aboriginal unit, the 107th Battalion had more than 500 Aboriginal soldiers when it was sent to England prior to 1917: see Lackenbauer, *A Commemorative History,* 124.

18 Our method finds only sixty-five members among the first enlistment into the 107th. About 500 Aboriginals joined this unit but many later in the war. See Annual Report 1919, Department of Indian Affairs (Ottawa: 1920), 26; Gaffen, *Forgotten Soldiers* 10; Talbot, "It Would Be Best," 100; Summerby, *Native Soldiers,* 7; Lackenbauer, *A Commemorative History,* 124; and Winegard, *For King and Kanata,* 68ff. A Saskatchewan Cree in the

107th, Private Andrew W. Anderson received the Military Medal for his courage in laying communication lines under heavy shell fire.

19 Morton and Hitsman, *Broken Promises*, 23; and Rutherdale, *Hometown Horizons*, 46.

20 Talbot, "It Would Be Best," 99–100; Walker, "Race and Recruitment"; Winegard, *For King and Kanata*; and Hapbkirk, "Militarism," 76–92. Talbot quotes a letter by the Tsimshian of BC sent to the Prime Minister objecting to the Militia Act "on the grounds that at no time have our Indians had any say in the making of the laws of Canada. We have always been treated by the Government as minors and wards of the Government, and we contend that under these circumstances we should not be subject to conscription ... until we receive just treatment at the hands of the Canadian government and are recognized as citizens and given a say in the making of the laws of Canada we consider that we should not be subject to conscription." From the Fort Simpson Band Council of 1917, cited in Talbot, "It Would Be Best," 107.

21 Dempsey, *Warriors of the King*, 22; and Winegard, *For King and Kanata*, 43ff. Of course, since 1914 the First Nations had been donating to the Canadian Patriotic Fund, and they expanded agricultural production. See Gaffen, *Forgotten Soldiers*, 24; and Titley, *A Narrow Vision*, 39.

22 Dempsey, *Warriors of the King*, 22–3; and Winegard, *For King and Kanata*, 77.

23 Encouragement also came from private citizens such as the anonymous individual who offered to fund an entire Six Nations regiment; see Lackenbauer, *A Commemorative History*, 122.

24 Talbot, "It Would Be Best"; and Dempsey, *Warriors of the King*, 31–2.

25 Talbot, "It Would Be Best," 101.

26 ibid., 104.

27 Gaffen, *Forgotten Soldiers*, 20; and Dempsey, *Warriors of the King*, 41.

28 Dempsey, *Warriors of the King*, 38–9.

29 ibid.

30 McGowan, "'Until We Receive Just Treatment,'" 62–4; and Titley, "Duncan Campbell Scott," 56. The Allied Indian Tribes of British Columbia frequently petitioned the government for resolution on outstanding native land claims, to the annoyance of Scott and the DIA.

31 McGowan, "'Until We Receive Just Treatment,'" 58, 62–4.

32 Lackenbauer, *A Commemorative History*, 128. This exemption allowed Aboriginals to contribute through agricultural or industrial work, though some Status Indians served overseas as volunteers.

33 Detail for all Canadian-born is taken from a database of 8,900 soldiers

whose surname began with the letter B and who have been linked from CEF to the 1901 census; see Cranfield and Inwood, "The Great Transformation"; and Kirk-Elleker, "A Measure of Well-being."

34 These data may understate the married share of Aboriginal solders because ethnicity is known only through linking to the census, which as noted in the text is more difficult for married men.

35 The proportion of Aboriginal soldiers from families with agricultural and related experience is lower than expected. Either our preconceptions about Aboriginal families (as defined in this paper) are mistaken or men with nonagricultural backgrounds were more likely to enlist or both.

36 Both Summerby and Scott emphasize the "serious difficulties of a high obstructive nature" in recruiting among Indians who resided in "remote and inaccessible localities," often unfamiliar with the English language: see Summerby, *Native Soldiers,* 7; and Scott, "The Canadian Indians," 289.

37 Someone who was reported as a "Cree Breed," for example, is assigned to the "Cree," not "breed," category.

38 Fortunately, the factors making linkage more difficult (language differences, limited contact with white Canadians) probably also inhibited enlistment, implying that our data may exaggerate differences but not change the ordering across tribal groups.

39 Talbot, "It Would Be Best," 105, 112.

40 The group "Other Central Canada" comprises individuals who recorded Mississauga, Montagnais, Algonquin, Abenaki, Ottawa, Potawatomi, Huron or Wyandot ethnicity.

41 Talbot, "It Would Be Best," 102.

42 Lackenbauer, *A Commemorative History,* 94 and 102; and Hapbkirk, *Militarism,* 80–1.

43 Talbot, "It Would Be Best," 101–2.

44 Gaffen, "Forgotten Soldiers," 13.

45 Scott, "The Canadian Indians," 76; and Gaffen, *Forgotten Soldiers,* 16–17.

46 Bouchard was recommended for honour seven times. Belanger was killed in action. See Scott, "The Canadian Indians," 293.

47 Gaffen, *Forgotten Soldiers,* 31; and Lackenbauer, *A Commemorative History,* 123. All First Nations men in Hay's unit died in the battle for Hill 70 north of Lens, France in 1917.

48 Winegard, *For King and Kanata,* 134–5. While some mixed-race men would have blended into these units, most full-blooded Aboriginals would have been easily identifiable.

49 We link the Commonwealth War Grave Commission record (Debt of Honour Register, 1914–20, www.cwgc.org) to Aboriginal and B-surname

soldiers. The linking relies on name and regimental number and the dates for enlistment and death: see Truta, "Linking Casualties"; and Van Tassel, "Death Rates." Length of service is reported in appendix: table 12.7. The overall CEF death rate reported by Vance is similar: Vance, *Death So Noble*, 11.

50 Walker ("Race and Recruitment," 26) suggests that there was some tendency to place Aboriginals in noncombatant roles. In order to assess the overall importance of this tendency, we classify the military units of casualties as combat or noncombat in their primary function. Admittedly, the distinction between combat and noncombat units is difficult and we do not know roles *within* units. We see no evidence of a significant difference. 95 per cent of the identifiably Aboriginal casualties served in regular combat units (e.g. "1st Canadian Mounted Rifles" or "Princess Patricia's Canadian Light Infantry") and 5 per cent served in noncombatant or support units (e.g. "Canadian Forestry Corps" or "Canadian Railway Troops"). The proportions for B-surname casualties were comparable: 96 per cent and 4 per cent.

51 One DIA medical superintendent noted of the Norway House Reserve, "Disease here means one malady, and one only, for practical purposes. That is tuberculosis. Practically nobody dies of anything else." See Waldram et al., *Aboriginal Health*, 30–2, 191.

52 Scott, "The Canadian Indians," 74. See also Shewell, *Enough to Keep Them Alive*, 108–11; and Lackenbauer, *A Commemorative History*, 126–7. Apart from exposure to contagious disease and injury in combat, the soldiers may have been reasonably healthy. CEF soldiers were sufficiently well fed that on average they gained weight during the war: see Clarke et al., "Fighting Fit?"

53 Western Canada is Saskatchewan and more westerly locations, Eastern Canada is Quebec and the Atlantic region, and Lake Nipissing divides northern from southern Ontario. Birthplace is taken from the census (unless attestation paper disagrees, and the sibling birth pattern indicates family relocation shortly after birth, in which case we use location on the attestation paper). Each person is assumed to be pure blood unless the report of tribal origin indicates mixed race (following appendix 12.6). Mother tongue or first language is that reported in the 1901 Census.

54 Gaffield, "Language."

55 Reserve status soldiers had a higher proportion; see Winegard, *For King and Kanata*, 67.

56 Winegard, *For King and Kanata*.

57 This is an underestimate because we cannot count entries that simply

specified Indian, reported no language, or were unrecognizable. The following are reported – Abenaquis, Algonquin, Assinaboine, Carrier, Cayuga, Chippewa, Cowichan, Cree, Delaware, English, French, Gaelic, German, Iroquois, Kootenay, Kwaquist, Micmac, Millicete, Mississagua, Mohawk, Montagnais, Munsee, Ojibeway, Onandaga, Oneida, Otchipwe, Potich, Pottawamis, Saulteaux, Scotch, Slave, Slave, Squamish, Stoney, Tuscarora, Watian.

CHAPTER THIRTEEN

1 Busch, *Canada and the Great War,* xii.
2 Oxford et al., "World War I."
3 Humphries, *The Last Plague,* 130–48.
4 Humphries, "The Horror at Home," 249–50.
5 LePan, "War Diary," 1:54; and LePan, Letter from LePan to the Chief of General Staff, 8, "War Diary," 2.
6 Ruskoski, "The Polish Army," 12.
7 Brannigan and Lin, "'Where east meets west.'"
8 Ruskowski, "The Polish Army," 15.
9 Hapak, "The Polish Military," 28.
10 Ibid., 29.
11 Ruskoski, "The Polish Army," 23.
12 Rzepniewski, *The General,* 2.
13 Hapak, "Recruiting," 46.
14 Biskupski, "Paderewski," 39. At the helm of the Polish National Department during the Great War, Ignacy Jan Paderewski was instrumental in forming the Polish Army in France: "I collected a considerable sum of money for the relief of the hungry, I reconciled and united the huge Polish immigration of four million, I gained for Poland the ardent help of the United States, [and] I created the Polish Army in France from Polish volunteers."
15 Hapak, "Recruiting," 97–8.
16 Borkowski, "City of Pittsburgh's," 41.
17 Ibid., 40–1.
18 Jan Słociúski, "Z Obozu Kosciuszki."
19 Hapak, "Recruiting," 143.
20 Ibid., 143–5.
21 Ruskoski, "The Polish Army," 43; and Hapak, "Film," 27. The film told the story of a young Polish man who was reluctant to volunteer for the Polish Army in France. Labeled a coward by his friends, family, and

fiancée (who broke off their engagement), he was reconciled with them after he joined up. In another patriotic storyline, a young man secretly joined the army with the help of his sister, a decision accepted with resignation by his widowed mother.

22 Skarzyński, "The Polish Army," 116; and Nastał, "The Blue Division," 263.
23 Pliska, "The 'Polish American Army,'" 56.
24 Ibid., 56.
25 Valasek, "Medical Examination."
26 Ibid., 73–9.
27 LePan, "War Diary," 2:7.
28 LePan, List of Deaths at Polish Army Camp, "War Diary," 2.
29 Ibid.
30 Jerzy et al., *Czyn*, 219.
31 Merritt, *On Common Ground*, 134.
32 Hapak, "Recruiting," 103; and LePan, "War Diary," 1. LePan's War Diary contains many references to organizing transportation via train. Often these remarks express frustration at having no warning of a troop train's arrival, or having had prior warning, no train arrived.
33 LePan, Polish Army Camp Strength, "War Diary," 2:1.
34 LePan, Remarks of Col. LePan at Banquet at Closing of Camp, "War Diary," 2.
35 Carnochan,"The Polish Army," 8.
36 LePan, "War Diary," 1. LePan's Diary is full of instances where he requested supplies for the Polish soldiers (ranging from boots, blankets and jackets, to underwear), usually by telephone.
37 Jerzy et al., *Czyn*, 219.
38 LePan, "War Diary," 1:11.
39 Stover, *The Routledge Historical Atlas*, 54–5; LePan "War Diary," 1:31. One Canadian officer discovered this problem the hard way when he refused to get back on a crowded troop train after a stop at Niagara Falls and realized there was no sleeper car. After a firm telephone call from Col. LePan, the officer was quickly back on the packed train.
40 LePan, "War Diary," 2:10; and Jerzy et al., *Czyn*, 165. Arrangements were made with the superintendent of immigration, W. Scott, to allow bearers of a card or document signed by recruiting authorities in the United States to be shown every consideration and allowed into Canada at the border.
41 Hawkings et al., *Toward a History*, 6–12; LePan, "War Diary," 1:64; and Nastał, "The Blue Division," 263.
42 Nastał, "The Blue Division," 263.

43 Ibid., 264; and LePan, "War Diary," 2:4.
44 Hawkings et al., *Toward a History,* 6–12.
45 Hapak, "The Polish Military," 29.
46 Merritt, *On Common Ground,* 136.
47 LePan, "War Diary," 1:7.
48 Ibid., 2:1.
49 LePan, Daily Strength, "War Diary," 2:2.
50 LePan, LePan's letter to the Chief of General Staff, Militia & Defense, "War Diary," 2:5.
51 LePan, "War Diary," 1:9.
52 Carnochan, "The Polish Army," 9.
53 Brannigan and Lin, "'Where East Meets West,'" 87–108.
54 LePan, Remarks of Lt-Col. LePan at Banquet at Closing of Camp, "War Diary," 2:2.
55 LePan, "War Diary," 1:50.
56 Ibid., 1:9.
57 LePan, LePan's letter to the Chief of General Staff, Militia & Defense, "War Diary," 2:10; and LePan, Remarks of Lt-Col. LePan at Banquet at Closing of Camp, "War Diary," 2:6; and Ascher, "Polish Relief," 25. The American Red Cross provided care kits for soldiers who were being sent overseas and set up facilities that enabled them to communicate with relatives in enemy countries. LePan also commends the American Red Cross and the YMCA for providing aid during the influenza outbreak of 1918, which included the provision of medical supplies, visiting the hospital to cheer the inmates, and writing letters home for them.
58 LePan, "War Diary," 1:48, 49.
59 LePan, LePan's letter to the Chief of General Staff, Militia & Defense, "War Diary," 2:9.
60 Burnett and Clark, *Influenza,* 70–1.
61 Patterson and Pyle, "The geography," 8.
62 Crosby, *America's Forgotten Pandemic,* 62; and Barry, *The Great Influenza,* chapter 14, 1.
63 Olson et al., "Epidemiological."
64 Bristow, *American Pandemic,* 36; Patterson and Pyle, "The geography," 8.
65 Herring and Padiak, "The geographical epicentre."
66 Oxford et al., "World War I."
67 Crosby, *America's Forgotten Pandemic,* 9.
68 Soltau, Note on mild Pyrexial Epidemic, Resembling Influenza, May 12, 1918, WO 95 47, National Archives of the United Kingdom.

69 Byerly, *Fever of War*, 6.
70 Herring and Padiak, "The geographical epicentre," 1–8.
71 Byerly, *Fever of War*, 69–74.
72 Ibid., 73.
73 MacDougall, "Toronto's Health Department," 229.
74 Humphries, *The Last Plague*, 91–108.
75 Byerly, *Fever of War*, 70.
76 Humphries, "The Limits of Necessity," 22–6.
77 Oxford et al., "World War I," 111–14; and Ewald, "Transmission modes."
78 Byerly, "The U.S. Military."
79 Byerly, *Fever of War*, 74.
80 Smallman-Raynor and Cliff, *War Epidemics*, fig. 7.19.
81 Ibid., 406, fig. 7.12.
82 Hapak, "Recruiting," 148; and Solomon and Schafer, *The New York Central Railway*, 14.
83 LePan, Letter to the Chief of General Staff, Militia & Defense, "War Diary," 2:8.
84 Ibid., 2:7.
85 Robinson, Polish Camp Hospital, vol. 2, File 15-2-73.
86 Humphries, "The Horror at Home," 250.
87 LePan, "War Diary," 1:50.
88 Patterson and Pyle, "The Geography," 4–21.
89 Humphries, "The Horror at Home," 250.
90 Ibid., 252.
91 Ibid., 252.
92 Ibid., 235–60; and Humphries, "The Limits of Necessity," 21–47.
93 Humphries, "The Horror at Home," 252; and Humphries, "The Limits of Necessity," 21–47.
94 Humphries, "The Limits of Necessity," 22; and Humphries, "The Horror at Home," 253.
95 LePan, "War Diary," 1:50; and Byerly, *Fever of War*, 75.
96 Humphries, "The Limits of Necessity," 27.
97 Hawkings et al., *Toward a History*, 22.
98 Ibid., 22; Nastał, "The Blue Division," 264; and Byerly, *Fever of War*, 83. In the United States, however, medical officers made the men alternate head and feet direction in order to prevent contagion.
99 LePan, "War Diary," 1:50–64; and Humphries, "The Limits of Necessity," 38. LePan was frustrated when quarantine was put into effect because the assistant director of medical services (ADMS), Major Morrison, would not

allow Polish soldiers living without heat and under canvas to be billeted in the town. Throughout the epidemic, LePan describes the weather as very cold with frequent heavy rains. It must have been a miserable time to be under canvas. Aware of the influenza outbreak at Camp Niagara and Polish Camp, the mayor of Toronto, Thomas Church, protested that despite the wet autumn weather, soldiers were still being housed in tents and requested they be provided with warmer, more sanitary conditions in Toronto. On 20 September, LePan made arrangements to house incoming recruits at the O'Neill Canning Factory. Sick recruits were taken to the camp hospital.

100 LePan, "War Diary," 1: 51–64.

101 Ibid., 1:51–2.

102 Ibid., 1:52–53, 81–2. The ever pressing need for more resources became more urgent during the epidemic. LePan authorized any expenditure that would bring succor for the Polish soldiers, including the purchase of extra milk and other food for the sick. Some men received as many as six to eight eggs per day and up to six pints of milk. A court of inquiry was called after the epidemic to investigate these extra expenses, but LePan was resolute. The lack of supplies frustrated LePan to the point he would "accept assistance from God, man or the devil" in dealing with the epidemic.

103 LePan, "War Diary," 1:53.

104 "Lincoln County Registration of Deaths," MS 935, Reels 244-245, Archives of Ontario (AO).

105 Shen, "Origins and spread."

106 Based on a comparison of "Lincoln County Registration of Deaths," MS 935, Reels 244–45, Archives of Ontario and LePan, List of Deaths at Polish Army Camp for deaths occurring between September-December 1918, "War Diary," 2.

107 Robinson, Polish Camp Hospital, n.p.

108 This estimate of the influenza attack rate is based on the average strength of the camp September to November, 1918, which was 1,879 men. Smallman-Raynor and Cliff, *War Epidemics*: 405, table 7.11, provide estimates of attack rates for a sample of US Army Camps. On average, the estimated influenza attack rate for the sample was 21.6 per cent, very close to the estimated attack rate for Polish Camp, though rates at US camps were as low as 0.8 (Wheeler, GA) and as high as 49.8 per cent (Cody, NM).

109 LePan, Plan of Grave Plot of Polish Army, "War Diary"; and Ascher, "Polish Relief," 23.

110 Humphries, "The Horror at Home," 235–60; Humphries, "The Duty of the Nation," 172–274; and Humphries, "The Limits of Necessity," 21–47.

111 Johnson and Mueller, "Updating the Accounts."

112 Fahrni and Jones, "Introduction," 8: note, however, that scholarship on the pandemic has "exploded" since the 1990s.

113 Crosby, *America's Forgotten Pandemic*, 295.

114 Byerly, *Fever of War*, 21–3; Bristow, *American Pandemic*, 8; and Kelm, "Flu Stories."

115 Swedlund, "Everyday mortality."

116 Ascher, "Polish Relief," 23.

117 Craggs, "Remembering"; and Mosse, *Fallen Soldiers*, 70–106.

118 "Lincoln County Registration of Deaths," MS 935, Reels 244–5, Archives of Ontario (AO).

Bibliography

ARCHIVAL SOURCES

ADM 101 series. The National Archive of the United Kingdom.

Agricultural Statistics Rolls, 1865–1940. Kansas State Historical Society.

Canada Company Papers. Archives of Ontario, Canada.

Con 23 and 31 series. Tasmanian Archives and Heritage Office.

HO 8 series. The National Archive of the United Kingdom.

Lincoln County Registration of Deaths (1918). Vol. 23, MS 935, Reels 244–45. Archives of Ontario (AO).

LePan, Aurther D'Orr. "War Diary." Vols. 1–2, 1917–19. Library and Archives Canada.

Military Personnel Records WWI (Canadian Expeditionary Force) and WWII (Killed In Action only for WWII). Library and Archives Canada.

Robinson, J.L. Polish Camp Hospital (21 November 1918). Outbreak of Spanish Influenza, vol. 2. Department of National Defense, Military District 2. Library and Archives Canada.

Soltau, B. Note on a mild Pyrexial Epidemic, Resembling Influenza, May 12, 1918. National Archives of the United Kingdom.

Survey of Income and Cost of Living of Study, 1924–25. MS–1011. Special Collections Research Center. University of Chicago Library.

DATABASES

1871 Canadian Census (5 per cent sample). University of Guelph, 2005.

1881 Canadian Census (100 per cent sample). University of Ottawa and PRDH.

BALSAC Population Database. www.uqac.ca/balsac.

Canada, Census 1901. Individual manuscripts accessed through www.ancestry.ca and *Automated Genealogy*. Accessed August 2012. www.automatedgenealogy.com/census/.
Canadian Families Project, Eric W. Sager, director. *The National Sample of the 1901 Census of Canada User's Guide*. University of Victoria, 2002.
The Canadian Great War Project. www.canadiangreatwarproject.com/.
Commonwealth War Graves Commission. www.cwgc.org.
Eltis, David, Stephen D. Behrendt, David Richardson and Herbert S. Klein. *The Trans-Atlantic Slave Trade: A Database on CD-ROM*. Cambridge: Cambridge University Press, 1999.
Founders & Survivors: Australian Life Courses in Historical Context, 1803–1920. www.foundersandsurvivors.org/node/86912.
NZSG Database. New Zealand Society of Genealogists.
"Regimental Number List of the Canadian Expeditionary Force." Library and Archives Canada. Accessed September 2011. www.collectionscanada.gc.ca/archivianet/02015203_e.html.
"Soldiers of the First World War – CEF Search." Library and Archives Canada. Accessed December 2006. www.collectionscanada.gc.ca/databases/cef/001042-100.01-e.php.
The Quebec Family History Society. www.qfhs.ca/.
Table 075–0010 (Historical statistics, urban and rural population, every 10 years (persons)), CANSIM, Statistics Canada (2012).

GOVERNMENT PUBLICATIONS

Bureau of Labor Statistics. *The Cost of Living in the United States*. Bls Bulletin. Vol. 357. Washington: Government Printing Office, 1924.
Canada, Census 1901, *Instructions to Enumerators*.
Canada, Department of Indian Affairs. *Annual Report,* various years.
Canada, Department of National Health and Welfare. *The Report on Canadian Average Weights, Heights and Skinfolds,* Canadian Bulletin on Nutrition 5:1, 1957.
Canadian Community Health Survey (2001–5). Statistics Canada, Canada.
Census of Canada, 1870–1 (1873) Ottawa: I.B. Taylor.
Davenport, C. and A.G. Love. *The Medical Department of the U.S. Army in the World War. Vol. 15, Statistics, Part One, Army Anthropology*. Washington: Government Printing Office, 1921.
Department of Agriculture, Census Branch. *Manual Containing "The Census Act" And The Instructions To Officers Employed In The Taking Of The First Census Of Canada*. Ottawa: Brown Chamberlin, 1871.

Department of Agriculture, Census Branch. *Manual Containing "The Census Act" And The Instructions To Officers Employed In The Taking Of The Second Census Of Canada.* Ottawa: Brown Chamberlin, 1881.

General Report of the Census of Canada, 1880–81. Ottawa: MacLean, Roger, 1885.

Inspectors of Prisons, Great Britain. *British Parliamentary Papers* (1837–8). Vol. 31.

Kansas State Board of Agriculture. *Biennial Report.* Topeka, 1873–1976.

National Population Health Survey (1994, 1996, 1998). Statistics Canada, Canada.

Social Survey, Health Module (1985,1991). Statistics Canada, Canada.

SECONDARY SOURCES

Aberdeen University Review 20, no. 58 (November 1932).

Abbott, Edith. *The Tenements of Chicago, 1908–1935.* Chicago: University of Chicago Press, 1936.

– *Women in Industry, a Study in American Economic History.* New York: D. Appleton, 1910.

Abel, Marjorie, and Nancy Folbre. "A Methodology for Revising Estimates: Female Market Participation in the U.S. Before 1940." *Historical Methods* 23, no. 4 (Fall, 1990): 167–76.

Acheson, T.W. "The National Policy and the Industrialization of the Maritimes, 1880–1910." *Acadiensis* 1, no. 2 (1972): 3–28.

Adams, John W. and Alice Bee Kasakoff. "Estimates of Census Underenumeration Based on Genealogies." *Social Science History* 15, no. 4 (1991): 527–43.

Adams, John W., Alice Bee Kasakoff, and Jan Kok. "Migration Over the Life Course in XIXth Century Netherlands and the American North: A Comparative Analysis Based on Genealogies and Population Registers." *Annales de Démographie Historique* 2, no. 104 (2002): 5–27.

Aiken, Charles S. *The Cotton Plantation South Since the Civil War.* Baltimore: Johns Hopkins University Press, 1998.

Akenson, Donald H. *The Irish in Ontario: A Study in Rural History.* 2nd ed. Montreal & Kingston: McGill-Queen's University Press, 1999.

– *Small Differences: Irish Catholics and Irish Protestants, 1815–1922: An International Perspective.* Montreal & Kingston: McGill-Queen's University Press, 1988.

Alexander, A. *Tasmania's Convicts: How Felons Built a New Society.* Crows Nest, NSW: Allen & Unwin, 2010.

Alexander, Ruth, Gail Gibson, and Alan J. La Roche. *The Royal New Zealand Fencibles, 1847–1852*. Auckland: New Zealand Fencible Society, 1997.

Allen, Robert C. *The British Industrial Revolution in Global Perspective.* Cambridge: Cambridge University Press, 2009.

Alston, Lee and Joseph Ferrie. "Time on the Ladder: Career Mobility in Agriculture, 1890–1938." *Journal of Economic History* 65, no. 4 (2005): 1058–81. www.nber.org/papers/w11231.

Amiel, Yoram and Frank A. Cowell. *Thinking About Inequality: Personal Judgment And Income Distributions.* Cambridge: Cambridge University Press, 1999.

Anderson, Margo J. and Stephen E. Fienberg. *Who Counts?: The Politics of Census-taking in Contemporary America.* New York: Russell Sage Foundation, 1999.

Anderson, P.J., ed. *Fasti Academiae Mariscallanae Aberdonensis. Selections from the Records of the Marischal College and University MCXCII–MDCCCLX.* Aberdeen: Printed for the New Spalding club, 1889.

Antonie, L., P. Baskerville, K. Inwood, J.A. Ross. "An Automated Record Linkage System – Linking 1871 Canadian Census to 1881 Canadian Census." Unpublished manuscript, 2010.

Antonie, L., K. Inwood, D. Lizotte, and J.A. Ross. "Tracking People over Time in 19th Century Canada." *Machine Learning,* 95, no. 1 (2014): 129–46.

Arnold, Rollo. "The Dynamics and Quality of Trans-Tasman Migration, 1885–1910." *Australian Economic History Review* 26, no. 1 (1986): 70–8.

Aronovici, Carol. *The Social Survey.* Philadelphia: Harper Press for Seybert Institution Bureau for Social Research, 1916.

– "Yeomen and Nomads: New Zealand and the Australasian Shearing Scene, 1886–1896." *New Zealand Journal of History* 18, no. 2 (1984): 117–42.

Ascher, Elizabeth "Polish Relief Work in Niagara." *Niagara Historical Society,* no. 35 (1923): 14–25.

Atack, Jeremy. "The Agricultural Ladder Revisited: A New Look at an Old Question with Some Data for 1860." *Agricultural History* 63, no. 1 (1989): 1–25.

– "A Nineteenth Century Resource for Agricultural History Research in the Twenty-first Century." *Agricultural History* 78 (2004): 389–412.

– "Tenants and Yeomen in the Nineteenth Century." *Agricultural History* 62 (1988): 6–32.

Atack, Jeremy and Fred Bateman. *To Their Own Soil: Agriculture in the Antebellum North.* Ames: Iowa State University Press, 1987.

Atack, Jeremy, Fred Bateman, and M. Eschelbach Gregson. "Matchmaker, matchmaker, make me a match: a general personal computer-based matching program for historical research." *Historical Methods* 25 (1992): 53–65.

Austin, Barbara J. "Life Cycles and Strategy of a Canadian Company: Dominion Textile, 1873–1983." PhD thesis, Concordia University, 1985.

Axelsson, Per and Peter Sköld, eds. *Indigenous Peoples and Demography: The Complex Relation Between Identity and Statistics.* New York: Berghahn, 2011.

Baines, Dudley. *Migration in a Mature Economy: Emigration and Internal Migration in England and Wales 1861–1900.* Cambridge: Cambridge University Press, 1985.

Bardet, Jean-Pierre. *Rouen aux XVIIe et XVIIIe siècles: Les mutations d'un espace social.* Paris: SEDES, 1983.

Barman, Jean. *The West Beyond the West: A History of British Columbia.* Toronto: University of Toronto Press, 1996.

Barry, John. *The Great Influenza: The Epic Story of the Deadliest Plague in History.* New York: Penguin, 2004.

Baskerville, Peter. "Chattel Mortgages and Community in Perth County Ontario." *Canadian Historical Review* 87 (2006): 583–619.

– "Familiar Strangers: Urban Families with Boarders in Canada, 1901." *Social Science History* 25, no. 3 (2001): 32–46.

– *A Silent Revolution? Gender and Wealth in English Canada, 1860–1930.* Montreal & Kingston: McGill-Queen's University Press, 2008.

Baskerville, Peter and Eric Sager. *Unwilling Idlers: The Urban Unemployed and Their Families in Late Victorian Canada.* Toronto: University of Toronto Press, 1998.

Bateman, Fred and James D. Foust. "A Sample of Rural Households Selected from the 1860 Manuscript Censuses." *Agricultural History* 48, no. 1 (1974): 75–93.

Bateson, Charles. *The Convict Ships.* Sydney: Library of Australian History, 2004.

Beck, Ulrich. *Risk Society: Towards a New Modernity.* London: Sage, 1992.

Belich, James. *Paradise Reforged: A History of the New Zealanders, from the 1880s to the Year 2000.* Auckland: Allen Lane, 2001.

Beller, Emily and Michael Hout. "Intergenerational Social Mobility: The United States in Comparative Perspective." *The Future of Children* 16, no. 2 (2006): 19–36.

Benson, Susan Porter. *Household Accounts: Working-Class Family Economies in the Interwar United States.* Ithaca: Cornell University Press, 2007.

Bielicki, T. "Physical Growth as a Measure of the Economic Well-Being of Populations: The Twentieth Century." In *Human Growth, vol. III,* 2nd edition, edited by F. Falkner and J.M. Tanner, 283–306. New York: Plenum Press, 1986.

Bigott, Joseph C. *From Cottage to Bungalow: Houses and the Working Class in Metropolitan Chicago, 1869–1929.* Chicago: University of Chicago Press, 2001.

Biskupski, M.B. "Paderewski as Leader of American Polonia, 1914–1918." *Polish American Studies* 43, no.1 (1986): 37–56.

Black, John D. and R.H. Allen. "The Growth of Farm Tenancy in the United States." *Quarterly Journal of Economics* 51 (1937): 393–425.

Bogue, Allan G. *From Prairie to Corn Belt: Farming on the Illinois and Iowa Prairies in the Nineteenth Century.* Chicago: University of Chicago Press, 1963.

Bogue, Margaret Beattie. *Patterns from the Sod: Land Use and Tenure in the Grand Prairie, 1850–1900.* Springfield: Illinois State Historical Library, 1959.

Bonneuil, Noël and Paul-André Rosental. "Changing Social Mobility in Nineteenth-Century France." *Historical Methods* 32, no. 2 (1999): 53–73.

Booth, Charles. *Life and Labour of the People in London.* New York: Macmillan, 1903.

Borkowski, Edward. "City of Pittsburgh's Part in Formation of Polish Army World War I 1917–1920." In *Haller's Polish Army in France,* translated and edited by Paul Valasek, 21–70. United States of America: Whitehall Printing, 2006. Originally published in Edward Borokowski, *City of Pittsburgh's Part in Formation of Polish Army World War I, 1917–1920.* Pittsburgh: Central Council of Polish Organizations of Pittsburgh, PA, 1956.

Bouchard, Gérard. *Quelques arpents d'Amérique : Population, économie, famille au Saguenay, 1838–1971.* Montréal: Boréal, 1996.

– *Tous les métiers du monde : Le traitment des données professionnelles en histoire sociale.* Québec: Les Presses de l'Université Laval, 1996.

Bowden, Sue and Avner Offer. "Household Appliances and the Use of Time: The United States and Britain since the 1920s." *Economic History Review* 47, no. 4 (1994): 725–48.

Boyce, J. *Van Diemen's Land.* Melbourne: Black Inc, 2008.

Bozzoli, C., A. Deaton, and C. Quintana-Domeque, "Adult Health and Childhood Disease." *Demography* 46 (2009): 647–69.

Bradbury, Bettina. *Wife to Widow: Lives, Laws, and Politics in Nineteenth-Century Montreal.* Vancouver: UBC Press, 2011.

Bradley, J., Rebecca Kippen, Hamish Maxwell-Stewart, Janet McCalman, and Sandra Silcot. "Research note: The founders and survivors project." *History of the Family* 15, no. 4 (2010): 467–77.

Brand, Ian and Mark Staniforth. "Care and Control: Female Convict Transportation Voyages to Van Diemen's Land." *Great Circle* 16, no. 1 (1994): 23–42.

Brannigan, A. and Lin, A. "'Where east meets west': Police, immigration, and public order in the settlement of Canada from 1896 to 1940." *The Canadian Journal of Sociology* 4, no.1 (1999): 87–108.

Bras, Hilde. "Maids to the City: Migration Patterns of Female Domestic Servants from the Province of Zeeland, the Netherlands (1850–1950)." *The History of the Family* 8 (2003): 217–46.

Breckinridge, Sophonisba Preston. *New Homes for Old.* New York and London: Harper & Brothers, 1921.

Bristow, Nancy. *American Pandemic: The Lost Worlds of the 1918 Influenza Pandemic.* Oxford and New York: Oxford University Press, 2012.

Brock, Jeanette M. *The Mobile Scot: A Study of Emigration and Migration, 1861–1911.* Edinburgh: J. Donald Publishers, 1999.

Brookes, A. "'Doing the Best I Can': The Taking of the 1861 New Brunswick Census." *Histoire sociale/Social History* IX, no.1 (1976): 70–91.

Brooking, Tom and Jennie Coleman. *The Heather and the Fern: Scottish Migration & New Zealand Settlement.* Dunedin: University of Otago Press, 2003.

Brose, Eric. *German History, 1789–1871: From the Holy Roman Empire to the Bismarckian Reich.* Oxford: Berghahn Books, 1997.

Browde, Anatole. "Settling the Canadian Colonies: A Comparison of Two Nineteenth-Century Land Companies." *Business History Review* 76 (2002): 299–335.

Brown R. and Cook, R. *Canada 1896–1921: A Nation Transformed.* Toronto: McClelland & Stewart Limited, 1974.

Brudner, Lilyan A. and Douglas R. White. "Class, Property, and Structural Endogamy: Visualizing Networked Histories." *Theory and Society* 26, no. 2/3 (1997): 161–208.

Buchan, James. *Capital of the Mind: How Edinburgh Changed the World.* London: John Murray, 2003.

Buchanan, Rex, J.R. McCauley, and Kansas Geological Survey. *Roadside Kansas: a Traveler's Guide to its Geology and Landmarks.* Lawrence: University Press of Kansas for the Kansas Geological Survey, 1987.

Bueltmann, Tanja. "'Brither Scots Shoulder Tae Shoulder': Ethnic Identity, Culture and Associationism Among the Scots in New Zealand to 1930." PhD thesis, Victoria University of Wellington, 2008.

– *Scottish Ethnicity and the Making of New Zealand Society, 1850–1930.* Edinburgh: Edinburgh University Press, 2011.

Bullard, Alice. *Exile to Paradise: Savagery and Civilization in Paris and the South Pacific.* Stanford: Stanford University Press, 2000.

Bulmer, Martin. *The Chicago School of Sociology: Institutionalization, Diversity, and the Rise of Sociological Research.* Chicago: University of Chicago Press, 1984.

Bulmer, Martin, Kevin Bales, and Kathryn Kish Sklar. *The Social Survey in Historical Perspective, 1880–1940.* Cambridge and New York: Cambridge University Press, 1991.

Burgess, Ernest W. "Factors Determining Success or Failure on Parole." In *The Workings of the Indeterminate Sentence Law and the Parole System in Illinois,* edited by A.A. Bruce, 221–34. Springfield: Illinois State Board of Parole, 1928.

Burgess, Ernest W. and L.S. Cottrell. *Predicting Success or Failure in Marriage.* New York: Prentice Hall, 1939.

Burnet, F.M. and E. Clark. *Influenza.* London: Macmillan, 1942.

Busch, Briton C., ed. *Canada and the Great War: Western Front Association Papers.* Montreal & Kingston: McGill-Queen's University Press, 2003.

Byerly, Carol. *Fever of War.* New York: New York University Press, 2005.

Byerly, Carol. "The U.S. Military and the Influenza Pandemic of 1918–1919." *Public Health Reports* 125, S3 (2010): 82–91.

Campbell, R.H. and T.M. Devine. "The Rural Experience." In *People and Society in Scotland, 1830–1914,* edited by William Hamish Fraser and R.J. Morris, 46–72. Edinburgh: J. Donald, 1990.

Carnochan, Janet. "The Polish Army in Niagara." *Niagara Historical Society,* no. 35 (1923): 7–12.

Carpenter, Kenneth J. *The History of Scurvy and Vitamin C.* Cambridge: Cambridge University Press, 1986.

– "Nutritional Studies in Victorian Prisons." *Journal of Nutrition* 136, no. 1 (2006): 1–8.

Carter, Susan B. and Richard Sutch. "Fixing the Facts: Editing of the 1880 U.S. Census of Occupations with Implications for Long-Term Labor Force Trends and the Sociology of Official Statistics." NBER Historical Paper 74, (October, 1995).

Carter, Susan B., Scott Sigmund Gartner, Michael R. Haines, Alan L. Olmstead, Richard Sutch, and Gavin Wright, eds. *Historical Statistics of the United States.* New York: Cambridge University Press, 2006.

Cerase, F.P. "Nostalgia or Disenchantment: Considerations on Return Migration." In *The Italian Experience in the United States,* edited by Silvano M. Tomasi and Madeline H. Engel, 217–39. New York: Center for Migration Studies, 1970.

Chambers, Edward J. "Late Nineteenth Century Business Cycles in Canada." *Canadian Journal of Economics and Political Science* 30, no. 3 (August, 1964): 391–412.

Charpentier, Louise, René Durocher, Christian Laville, and Paul-André Linteau. *Nouvelle histoire du Québec et du Canada.* Anjou: Centre éducatif et Culturel, 1990.

Christopher, Emma. "'The Slave Trade is Merciful Compared to [This]': Slave Traders, Convict Transportation and the Abolitionists." In *Many Middle Passages: Forced Migration and the Making of the Modern World,* edited by

Emma Christopher and Marcus Rediker, 107–28. Berkeley: University of California Press, 2007.

Clarke, John. *Land, Power and Economics on the Frontier of Upper Canada.* Montreal & Kingston: McGill-Queen's University Press, 2001.

Clarke, Nic. "'You Will Not Be Going to This War': The Rejected Volunteers of the First Contingent of the Canadian Expeditionary Force." *First World War Studies* 1 (2010): 161–83.

– *Unwanted Warriors: The Rejected Volunteers of the Canadian Expeditionary Force.* PhD thesis, University of Ottawa, 2009.

Clarke, Nic, John Cranfield, and Kris Inwood. "Fighting Fit? Diet, Disease and Disability amongst Canadian Expeditionary Force Recruits, 1914–1918." *War and Society* 33, no. 2 (2014): 79–96

Clarke, Sally H. *Regulation And the Revolution In United States Farm Productivity.* Cambridge: Cambridge University Press, 1994.

Coale, Ansley J. and Norfleet W. Rives. "A Statistical Reconstruction of the Black Population of the United States 1880–1970: Estimates of True Numbers by Age and Sex, Birth Rates, and Total Fertility." *Population Index* 39, no. 1 (1973): 3–36.

Cobbett, William. *The Emigrant's Guide; in Ten Letters Addressed to the Tax-payers of England.* London: Knight and Lacy, 1826.

Cohen, Raymond L. "The Determinants of Individual Immigrant Mortality on Sailing Ships, 1836–1853." *Explorations in Economic History* 24 (1987): 371–91.

– "Maritime Mortality in the Eighteenth and Nineteenth Centuries: A Survey." *International Journal of Maritime History* 1, no. 1 (1989): 159–91.

– "Mortality on Immigrant Voyages to New York, 1836–1853." *Journal of Economic History* 44, no. 2 (1984): 289–300.

Colgrove, James. "The McKeown Thesis: A Historical Controversy and Its Enduring Influence." *American Journal of Public Health* 95, no. 5 (2002): 725–29.

Condron, G.A. and J. Seaman. "Linkage in the 1880–81 Philadelphia Death Register to the 1880 Manuscript Census: a Comparison of Hand- and Machine-Record Linkage Techniques." *Historical Methods* 14 (1981): 73–84.

Converse, Jean M. *Survey Research in the United States: Roots and Emergence 1890–1960.* Berkeley: University of California Press, 1987.

Conzen, Kathleen Neils. "Peasant Pioneers: Generational Succession among German Farmers in Frontier Minnesota." In *Countryside in the Age of Capitalist Transformation,* edited by Steven Hahn and Jonathon Prude, 259–92. Chapel Hill: University of North Carolina Press, 1985.

Copp, T. *The Anatomy of Poverty*. Toronto: McClelland & Stewart Limited, 1974.

Craig, Douglas B. *Fireside Politics: Radio and Political Culture in the United States, 1920–1940*. Baltimore: Johns Hopkins University Press, 2003.

Craggs, S. "Remembering Polish soldiers who trained in Niagara-on-the-Lake 90 years ago." *St Catharines Standard*, 3 June 2008. www.stcatharinesstandard.ca/2008/06/03/remembering-polish-soldiers-who-trained-in-niagara-on-the-lake-90-years-ago

Cranfield, John and Kris Inwood. "The Great Transformation: A Long-Run Perspective on Physical Well-Being in Canada." *Economics and Human Biology* 5, no. 2 (2007): 204–28.

– "A Tale of Two Armies: The Stature of Australian and Canadian Soldiers in World War One." *Australian Economic History Review* 55, no. 2 (July, 2015).

Crawford, E. Margaret. "The Irish Workhouse Diet, 1840–90." In *Food, Diet and Economic Change Past and Present*, edited by C. Geissler and D.J. Oddy, 83–100. Leicester: Leicester University Press, 1993.

Cronmiller, Carl R. *A History of the Lutheran Church in Canada*. Toronto, 1961.

Crosby, Alfred. *America's Forgotten Pandemic*. Cambridge: Cambridge University Press, 2003.

Crowley, Terry. "Rural Labour." In *Labouring Lives: Work and Workers in Nineteenth-century Ontario*, edited by Paul Craven, 13–102. Toronto: University of Toronto Press, 1995.

Curti, Merle. *The Making of an American Community: a Case Study of Democracy in a Frontier County*. Stanford: Stanford University Press, 1959.

Curtin, P.D. *Death by Migration: Europe's Encounter with the Tropical World in the Nineteenth Century*. Cambridge: Cambridge University Press, 1989.

Curtis, Bruce. *The Politics of Population: State Formation, Statistics, and the Census of Canada, 1840–1975*. Toronto: University of Toronto Press, 2001.

The Cyclopedia of New Zealand. Wellington, 1897. New Zealand ElectronicText Centre. Accessed 13 August 2012. nzetc.victoria.ac.nz/tm/scholarly/tei-Cyco1Cycl-t1-body-d3-d13-d22.html.

Danbom, David B. *Born in the Country: A History of Rural America*. Baltimore: Johns Hopkins University Press, 2006.

– *The Resisted Revolution: Urban America and the Industrialization of Agriculture, 1900–1930*. Ames: Iowa State University Press, 1979.

Daniel, Pete. *Breaking the Land: the Transformation of Cotton, Tobacco, and Rice Cultures Since 1880*. Urbana: University of Illinois Press, 1985.

Danylewycz, Marta. *Taking the Veil: An Alternative to Marriage, Motherhood and Spinsterhood in Quebec, 1840–1920*. Toronto: McClelland & Stewart Limited, 1988.

Darroch, Gordon. "Class in Nineteenth-Century Central Ontario: A Reassessment of the Crisis and Demise of Small Producers During Early Industrialization, 1861–1871." *Canadian Journal of Sociology* 13, nos. 1 and 2 (1988): 49–71.

– "Constructing Census Families and Classifying Households: 'Relationship to Head of Family or Household' in the 1901 Census of Canada." *Historical Methods* 33, no. 4 (2000): 10–26.

– "Domestic Revolution and Cultural Formation in Nineteenth-Century Ontario, Canada," *The History of the Family* 4, no. 4 (1999): 427–45.

– "Home and Away: Patterns of Residence, Schooling, and Work Among Children and Never Married Young Adults, Canada, 1871 and 1901." *Journal of Family History* 26, no. 2 (2001): 22–50.

– "Migrants in the Nineteenth Century: Fugitives or Families in Motion?" *Journal of Family History* 6 (1981): 257–77.

– "Occupational Structure, Assessed Wealth and Homeowning during Toronto's Early Industrialization, 1861–1899." *Histoire Sociale* 16 (1983): 381–410.

– "Scanty Fortunes and Rural Middle-class Formation in Nineteenth-century Rural Ontario." *Canadian Historical Review* 79, no. 4 (1998): 621–59.

– "Semi-Automated Record Linkage with Surname Samples: A Regional Study of "Case Law" Linkage, Ontario, 1861–1871." *History and Computing* 14, nos. 1 and 2 (2006): 153–83.

Darroch, Gordon and Michael Ornstein. "Ethnicity and Class, Transitions over a Decade: Ontario, 1861–1871." *Canadian Historical Association, Historical Papers* (1984): 111–37.

– "Ethnicity and Occupational Structure in Canada in 1871: The Vertical Mosaic in Historical Perspective." *Canadian Historical Review* 61, no. 3 (1980): 305–33.

– "Family Coresidence in Canada in 1871: Family Life-Cycles, Occupations, and Networks of Mutual Aid, Canadian Historical Association." *Historical Papers* (1983): 30–55.

Darroch, Gordon and Lee Soltow. *Property and Inequality in Victorian Ontario: Structural Patterns and Cultural Communities in the 1871 Census.* Toronto: University of Toronto Press, 1994.

Davies, M. "Night Soil, Cesspools, and Smelly Hogs on the Streets: Sanitation, Race, and Governance in Early British Columbia." *Histoire Sociale* 38 (2005): 1–35.

Deaton, A. "Height, Health and Development." *Proceedings of the National Academy of Sciences* 104, no. 33 (2007): 13,232–37.

Dempsey, L. James. *Warriors of the King: Prarie Indians in World War I.* Regina: Canadian Plains Research Center, 1999.

Devine, T.M. *The Scottish Nation 1700–2000.* London: Penguin, 1999.

– "Temporary Migration and the Scottish Highlands in the Nineteenth Century." *The Economic History Review* 32, no. 3 (1979): 344–59.

Dickin-McGinnis, Janice. "The Impact of Epidemic Influenza: Canada, 1918–1919." *Historical Papers* 12, no. 1 (1977): 120–40.

Dillon, Lisa. "Challenges and Opportunities for Census Record Linkage in the French and English Canadian Context." *History and Computing* 14, no. 12 (2002): 185–212.

Dillon, Lisa. *The Shady Side of Fifty: Age and Old Age in Late Victorian Canada and the United States.* Montreal & Kingston: McGill-Queen's University Press, 2008.

Donald, Louise and W.S. MacDonald, eds. *Roll of the Graduates of the University of Aberdeen 1956–1970: With Supplement 1860–1955.* Aberdeen: Aberdeen University Press, 1982.

Doroshevich, Vlas. *Russia's Penal Colony in the Far East.* London: Anthem Press, 2011.

Douglas, Paul H. *Real Wages in the United States, 1890–1926.* Boston: Houghton Mifflin, 1930.

Drummond, Ian. *Progress Without Planning: The Economic History of Ontario from Confederation to the Second World War.* Toronto: University of Toronto Press, 1987.

Du Bois, W.E.B. *The Philadelphia Negro: A Social Study.* New York: Schocken Books, 1899.

Dufaux, François and Sherry Olson. "Reconstruire Montréal, rebâtir sa fortune." *Revue de Bibliothèque et Archives Nationales du Québec* 1 (2009): 44–57.

Dunae, Patrick A. "Sex, Charades, and Census Records: Locating Female Sex Trade Workers in a Victorian City." *Histoire Sociale/Social History* 42, no. 84 (2009): 267–97.

Dupâquier, Jacques and Denis Kessler, eds. *La société française au XIXe siècle.* Paris: Fayard, 1992.

Eaton, Allen H. and Shelby M. Harrison. *A Bibliography of Social Surveys: Reports of Fact-Finding Studies Made as a Basis for Social Action, Arranged by Subjects and Localities: Reports to January 1, 1928.* New York: Russell Sage Foundation, 1930.

Ekirch, A.R. *Bound for America: The Transportation of British Convicts to the Colonies, 1718–75.* Oxford: Clarendon, 1990.

Emery, G. and K. McQuillan. "A Case Study Approach to Ontario Mortality

History: the Example of Ingersoll, 1881–1972." *Canadian Studies in Population* 15 (1986): 135–58.

Emery, Herb, K. Inwood and H. Thille. "Hecksher-Ohlin in Canada: New Estimates of Regional Wages and Land Prices." *Australian Economic History Review* 47, no. 1 (2007): 22–48.

Emery, J. and C. Levitt. "Cost of Living, Real Wages and Real Incomes in Thirteen Canadian Cities, 1900–1950." *Canadian Journal of Economics* 35 (2002): 115–37.

Engerman, Stanley and Kenneth Sokoloff. "Colonialism, Inequality, and Long-Run Paths of Development." NBER Working Paper 11507, January 2005.

– "Debating the Role of Institutions in Political and Economic Development: Theory, History and Findings." *Annual Review of Political Science* 11 (2008): 119–35.

Erickson, C.J. "Who Were the English and Scots Emigrants to the United States in the Late Nineteenth Century?" In *Population and Social Change*, edited by D.V. Glass and Roger Revelle, 347–81. London: E. Arnold and New York: Crane, Russak, 1972.

Ewald, P.W. "Transmission modes and the evolution of virulence." *Human Nature* 2, no.1 (2005): 1–30.

Fahrni, M. and E.W. Jones, eds. *Epidemic Encounters: Influenza, Society, and Culture in Canada, 1918–20*. Vancouver and Toronto: University of British Columbia Press, 2012.

Ferrie, Joseph. "The End of American Exceptionalism?: Mobility in the United States since 1850." *Journal of Economic Perspectives* 19 (2005): 199–215.

– "A New Sample of Males Linked from the Public-Use-Microdata-Sample of the 1850 US Federal Census of Population to the 1860 US Federal Census Manuscript Schedules." *Historical Methods* 29 (1996): 141–56.

– "Up and Out or Down and Out? Immigrant Mobility in the Antebellum United States." *Journal of Interdisciplinary History* 26, no. 1 (1995): 33–55.

– *Yankees Now: European Immigrants in the Antebellum U.S., 1840–1860*. New York: Oxford University Press, 1999.

Fischer, Claude S. "Ever-More Rooted Americans." *City & Community* 1, no. 2 (2002): 177–98.

Fitzgerald, Deborah Kay. *Every Farm a Factory: The Industrial Ideal in American Agriculture*. New Haven: Yale University Press, 2003.

Flinn, Michael W., ed. *Scottish Population History: From the 17th Century to the 1930s*. Cambridge: Cambridge University Press, 1976.

Floud, R.W. "Secular Changes in American and British Stature and Nutrition." *Journal of Interdisciplinary History* 14 (1983): 445–81.

Floud, R.W., R.W. Fogel, B. Harris, and S.K. Hong. *The Changing Body: Health, Nutrition, and Human Development in the Western World since 1700*. Cambridge: Cambridge University Press, 2011.

Fogel, R.W. "Physical Growth as a Measure of the Economic Well-Being of Populations." In *Human Growth, vol. III*, edited by F. Falkner and J.M. Tanner, 263–81. New York: Plenum Press, 1986.

Fogel, R.W., S. Engerman, and T. Trussell. "Exploring the Uses of Data on Height." *Social Science History* 6 (1982): 401–21.

Fogel, R.W., S. Engerman, R. Floud, G. Friedman, R. Margo, K. Sokoloff, R. Steckel, T. Trussell, G. Villaflor, and K. Wachter. "Secular Changes in American and British Stature and Nutrition." *Journal of Interdisciplinary History* 14 (1983): 445–81.

Foerster, Robert F. *The Italian Emigration of Our Times*. Cambridge: Harvard University Press, 1919.

Forster, Ben. "The Coming of National Policy: Business, Government and the Tariffs, 1876–1879." *Journal of Canadian Studies* 3, no. 3 (1979): 39–49.

– *A Conjunction of Interests: Business, Politics, and Tariffs, 1825–1879*. Toronto: University of Toronto Press, 1986.

Forster, Ben and Kris Inwood "The Diversity of Industrial Experience: Cabinet and Furniture Manufacture in Late Nineteenth-Century Ontario." *Enterprise and Society* 4, no. 2 (2003): 326–71.

Foxhall, Katherine. "From Convicts to Colonists: The Health of Prisoners and the Voyage to Australia, 1823–53." *The Journal of Imperial and Commonwealth History* 39, no. 1 (2011): 1–19.

Friesen, Gerhard. "A German-Canadian Rarissimum: Briefe von Ansiedlern in Huron Trackt, Canada." *German-Canadian Yearbook* 10 (Toronto, 1988): 11–31.

Frost, Lucy. *Abandoned Women: Scottish Convicts Exiled Beyond the Seas*. Sydney: Allen and Unwin, 2012.

Gaffen, Fred. *Forgotten Soldiers*. Penticton: Theytus Books, 1985.

Gaffield, Chad. "Language, Ancestry, and the Competing Constructions of Identity in Turn-of-the-century Canada." In *Household Counts: Canadian Households and Families in 1901*, edited by Eric W. Sager and Peter Baskerville, 420–33. Toronto: University of Toronto Press, 2007.

– *Language, Schooling, and Cultural Conflict: The Origins of the French-Language Controversy in Ontario*. Montreal & Kingston: McGill-Queen's University Press, 1987.

Gagan, David. "Geographical and Social Mobility in Nineteenth-Century Ontario: A Microstudy." *Canadian Review of Sociology and Anthropology* 13, no. 2 (1976): 152–64.

– *Hopeful Travellers: Families, Land, and Social Change in Mid-Victorian Peel County, Canada West.* Toronto: University of Toronto Press, 1981.

Galenson, David W. and Clayne Pope. "Economic and Geographic Mobility on the Farming Frontier: Evidence from Appanoose Country, Iowa, 1850–1870." *The Journal of Economic History*, 49, no. 3 (1989): 635–55.

Gardner, Bruce L. *American Agriculture in the Twentieth Century: How it Flourished And What it Cost.* Cambridge: Harvard University Press, 2002.

Gates, Paul W. *Frontier Landlords and Pioneer Tenants.* Ithaca: Cornell University Press, 1945.

– "The Homestead Law in an Incongruous Land System." *American Historical Review* 41 (1936): 652–81.

Gauvreau, Danielle, Patricia Thornton, and Sherry Olson. "Mobilité sociale dans une ville industrielle nord-américaine, Montréal 1881 à 1901." *Annales de Démographie Historique*, 2008 no. 1: 89–114.

Gauvreau, Danielle, Patricia Thornton, and Hélène Vézina. "Le jumelage des recensements aux mariages du fichier BALSAC, présentation de l'approche et étude exploratoire des enfants de couples mixtes à la fin du XIXe siècle." *Cahiers québécois de démographie* 39 (2010): 357–81.

Gazeley, Ian and Andrew Newell. "The End of Destitution: Evidence from Urban British Working Households 1904–37." *Oxford Economic Papers* 64, no. 1 (2012): 80-102.

Ghosh, J.R. and A.R. Bandyopadhyay. "Income, Birth Order, Siblings, and Anthropometry." *Human Biology* 78 (2006): 733–41.

Giesen, James C. *Boll Weevil Blues: Cotton, Myth, And Power In the American South.* Chicago: The University of Chicago Press, 2011.

Gilliland, Jason. "Modeling Residential Mobility in Montreal, 1860–1900." *Historical Methods* 31, no. 1 (1998): 27–42.

Gilliland, Jason and Sherry Olson. "Claims on Housing Space in Nineteenth-Century Montreal." *Urban History Review* 26, no. 2 (1998): 3–16.

– "Residential Segregation in the Industrializing City: A Closer Look." *Urban Geography* 31, no. 1 (2010): 29–58.

Gilliland, Jason A., Sherry H. Olson, and Danielle Gauvreau. "Did Segregation Increase as the City Expanded? The Case of Montreal, 1881–1901." *Social Science History* 35, no. 4 (2011): 465–503.

Ginsburg, E., G. Livshits, K. Yakovenko, and E. Kobyliansky. "Major Gene Control of Human Body Height, Weight and BMI in Five Ethnically Different Populations." *Annals of Human Genetics* 62 (1998): 307–22.

Goeken, Ron, Lap Huynh, Tom Lenius, and Rebecca Vick. "New Estimates of Migration for the United States, 1850–1900." Unpublished paper, Recordlink Conference, Guelph, Ontario, 2010.

Goeken, Ron, Lap Huynh, T.A. Lynch, and Rebecca Vick. "New Methods of Census Record Linking." *Historical Methods* 44, no. 1 (2011): 7–14.

Goldin, Claudia and Lawrence Katz. *The Race between Education and Technology.* Cambridge: Harvard University Press, 2008.

Granovetter, Mark S. "The Strength of Weak Ties." *American Journal of Sociology* 78, no. 6 (1973): 1,360–80.

Grawe, Nathan D. "Intergenerational Mobility for Whom? The Experience of High- and Low- Earning Sons in International Perspective." In *Generational Income Moblity in North America and Europe,* edited by Miles Corak, 813–27. Cambridge: Cambridge University Press, 2004.

Gray, Louis C. "Farm Ownership and Tenancy." In *Agricultural Yearbook, 1923,* United States Department of Agriculture, 507–600. Washington, DC: Government Printer, 1924.

Green, A.G. and M.C. Urquhart. "New Estimates of Output Growth in Canada: Measurement and Interpretation." In *Perspectives on Canadian Economic History,* edited by D. McCalla, 182–99. Toronto: Copp Clark Pitman, 1987.

Green, A.G., M. MacKinnon, and C. Minns. "Conspicuous by their Absence: French Canadians and the Settlement of the Canadian West." *Journal of Economic History* 65 (2005): 822–49.

Grenke, Arthur. "German Land Settlement in Eastern Canada and its Influence on Community Development and Assimilation." *German-Canadian Yearbook* 14 (Toronto, 1998): 31–56.

Grosjean, Alexia and Steve Murdoch, eds. *Scottish Communities Abroad in the Early Modern Period.* Leiden and Boston: Brill, 2005.

Grossman, James R. *Land of Hope: Chicago, Black Southerners, and the Great Migration.* Chicago: University of Chicago Press, 1989.

Griffin, C.J. "The Violent Captain Swing?" *Past and Present* 209 (2010): 149–80.

Guest, Avery. "Notes from the National Panel Study: Linkage and Migration in the Late Nineteenth Century." *Historical Methods* 20, no. 2 (1987): 63–77.

Habicht, J.P., C. Yarbrough, R. Martorell, R.M. Malina, and R.E. Klein. "Height and weight standards for preschool children. How relevant are ethnic differences in growth potential?" *Lancet* (April 6, 1974): 611–14.

Hacker, J. David. "New Estimates of Census Coverage in the United States, 1850–1930." *Social Science History* 37, no. 1 (2013): 71–101.

Haines, Michael R. "Growing Incomes, Shrinking People – Can Economic Development Be Hazardous to Your Health? Historical Evidence for the United States, England, and the Netherlands in the Nineteenth Century." *Social Science History* 28 (2004): 249–70.

Haines, Michael R., Lee A. Craig, and Thomas Weiss. "The Short and the Dead: Nutrition, Mortality, and the "Antebellum Puzzle" in the United States." *Journal of Economic History* 63 (2003): 382–413.

Haines, Robin and John McDonald. "Skills, Origins and Literacy: A comparison of the Bounty Immigrants Into New South Wales in 1841, With the Convicts Resident in the Colony." *Australian Economic History Review* 42, no. 2 (2002): 132–59.

Haines, Robin, John McDonald, and Ralph Shlomowitz. "Mortality and Voyage Length in the Middle Passage Revisited." *Explorations in Economic History* 38 (2001): 503–33.

Haines, Robin and Ralph Shlomowitz. "Causes of Death of British Emigrants on Voyages to South Australia, 1848–1885." *Social History of* Medicine 16, no. 2 (2003): 201–07.

– "Explaining the Modern Mortality Decline: What Can We Learn from Sea Voyages?" *Social History of Medicine* 11, no. 1 (1998): 15–48.

– "Explaining the Mortality Decline in the Eighteenth-Century British Slave Trade." *Economic History* Review 53, no. 2 (2000): 262–83.

Haines, Robin, Ralph Shlomowitz, and Lance Brennan. "Maritime Mortality Revisited." *International Journal of Maritime History* 8, no. 1 (1996): 133–72.

Hall, Patricia Kelly and Steven Ruggles. "'Restless in the Midst of their Prosperity:' New Evidence on the Internal Migration of Americans, 1850–2000." *Journal of American History* 91, no. 3 (2004): 829–46.

Hamilton, Michelle A. "'Anyone Not on the List Might As Well Be Dead': Aboriginal Peoples and the Censuses of Canada, 1851–1916." *Journal of the Canadian Historical Association* 18 (2007): 57–79.

Hamilton, Michelle A. and Kris Inwood. "The Aboriginal Population and the 1891 Census of Canada." In *Indigenous Peoples and Demography: The Complex Relation Between Identity and Statistics,* edited by Per Axelsson and Peter Sköld. 95–116. New York: Bergahn, 2011.

Handley, James E. *Scottish Farming in the 18th Century.* London: Faber and Faber Ltd., 1953.

Hanna, David and Sherry Olson. "Social Landscape of Montreal 1901." In *Historical Atlas of Canada.* Plate 30 and Plate 49, Vols II and III. Toronto: University of Toronto Press, 1990 and 1993.

Hapak, Joseph. "Film in the Service of Polish Independence." *Polish American Studies* 44, no. 1 (1987): 25–37.

– "The Polish Military Commission, 1917–1919." *Polish American Studies* 38, no. 2 (1981): 26–38.

– "Recruiting a Polish Army in the United States, 1917–1918." PhD thesis, University of Kansas, 1985.

Hapbkirk, J. Evan. "Militarism, Sovereignty, and Nationalism: Six Nations and the First World War." MA thesis, Trent University, 2010.

Hareven, Tamara K. *Family Time and Industrial Time.* New York: Cambridge University Press, 1982.

Hargis, Peggy G. "Name Games: Deeds, Mortgages, and the Conventions of Race." *Historical Methods* 35, no. 2 (2002): 53–61.

Harley, C. Knick. "Ocean Freight Rates and Productivity, 1740–1913: The Primacy of Mechanical Invention Reaffirmed." *The Journal of Economic History* 48, no. 4 (December, 1988): 851–76.

– "Western Settlement and the Price of Wheat, 1872–1913." *The Journal of Economic History* 38, no. 4 (December, 1978): 865–78.

Harper, Marjory. *Adventurers and Exiles: The Great Scottish Exodus.* London: Profile, 2003.

– *Emigrant Homecomings: The Return Movements of Emigrants, 1600–2000.* Manchester: Manchester University Press, 2006.

Harris, Richard. "The End Justified the Means: Boarding and Rooming in a City of Homes, 1890–1951." *Journal of Social History* 26, no. 2 (1992): 331–58.

Harris, Richard and Michael Mercier. "How Healthy Were the Suburbs?" *Urban History Review* 31 (2005): 767–98.

Harvey, Janice. "'Dealing with the Destitute and the Wretched': The Protestant House of Industry and Refuge in Nineteenth-Century Montreal." *Journal of the Canadian Historical Association* 12 (2001): 73–94.

Hatton, T.J. "Infant mortality and the health of survivors: Britain, 1910–50." *Economic History Review* 64 (2011): 951–72.

Hatton, T.J. and B. Bray. "Long Run Trends in the Heights of European Men, 19th–20th Centuries." *Economics and Human Biology* 8 (2010): 405–13.

Hatton, T.J. and R.M. Martin. "The Effects on Stature of Poverty, Family Size and Birth Order: British Children in the 1930s." *Oxford Economic Papers* 62 (2010): 157–84.

Hatton, T.J. and Jeffrey G. Williamson. *Migration and the international labor market, 1850–1939.* London: Routledge, 1994.

Hawkings, Trevor, Robert Mayer, and Lynne Richard-Onn. *Toward a History of Camp Niagara.* Niagara-on-the-Lake, Ontario, Canada: Parks Canada, 1990.

Hearn, Terry. "Scots Miners in the Goldfields, 1861–1870." In *The Heather and the Fern: Scottish Migration & New Zealand Settlement,* edited by Tom Brooking and Jennie Coleman, 67–86. Dunedin: University of Otago Press, 2003.

Hermannusen, M., C. Thiel, E. von Büren, M.A. Rol de Lama, A. Pérez Romero, C. Ariznaverreta Ruiz, J. Burmeister, and J.A. Tresquerres. "Micro and Macro Perspective in Auxology: Findings and Considerations upon the Variability of Short Term and Individual Growth and the Stability of Population Derived Parameters." *Annals of Human Biology* 25 (1998): 359–85.

Heron, Craig. "Factory Workers." In *Labouring Lives: Work and Workers in Nineteenth-century Ontario*, edited by Paul Craven, 479–590. Toronto: University of Toronto Press, 1995.

Herring, D.A and Padiak, J. "The geographical epicentre of the 1918 influenza pandemic." In *Written in Bone*, edited by M. Smith and M. Brickley, 1–18. British Archaeological Report International Series 1743. London: Archaeopress, 2008.

Hinde, Andrew. "Sex Differentials in Mortality in Nineteenth-Century England and Wales." Paper presented to the Economic History Society Conference, Cambridge, 1–3 April 2011. www.ehs.org.uk/ehs/conference2011/Assets/HindeFullPaper.pdf.

Hitsman, J.M. and J.L. Granatstein. *Broken Promises: A History of Conscription in Canada*. Toronto: Oxford University Press, 1977.

Hobsbawm, E.J. and George Rude. *Captain Swing*. London: Lawrence and Wishart, 1969.

Hochstadt, Steve. *Mobility and Modernity: Migration in Germany, 1820–1889*. Ann Arbor: University of Michigan Press, 1999.

Hoffman, D.W. and N.R. Richards. *Soil Survey of Perth County*. Guelph: Report Number 15 of the Ontario Soil Survey, 1952.

Holm, Tom. "Fighting a White Man's War: the Extent and Legacy of American Indian Participation in World War II." *The Journal of Ethnic Studies* (Summer, 1981): 69–81.

Holm, Tom. "Strong Hearts: Native Service in the U.S. Armed Forces." In *Aboriginal Peoples and Military Participation: Canadian and International Perspectives*, edited by P. Whitney Lackenbauer, R. Scott Sheffield and Craig Leslie Mantle, 127–51. Kingston: Canadian Defence Academy Press, 2007.

Horrell, Sara, David Meredith, and Deborah Oxley. "Measuring Misery: Body Mass, Ageing and Gender Equality in Victorian London." *Explorations in Economic History* 46 (2009): 93–119.

Horton, S. "Birth Order and Child Nutritional Status: Evidence from the Philippines." *Economic Development and Cultural Change* 36 (1988): 341–54.

Houghteling, Leila. *The Income and Standards of Living of Unskilled Laborers in Chicago*. Chicago: University of Chicago Press, 1927.

– "Study of the income and standard of living of unskilled laborers in Chicago." PhD thesis, University of Chicago, School of Social Service Administration, 1926.

Houston, C.J. and W.J. Smyth. "Geographical Transiency and Social Mobility: The Illustrative Odyssey of Irish Immigrant William Benson, a Well Known Canadian Unknown." *British Journal of Canadian Studies* 7, (1992): 345–55.

Humphery, Kim. "A New Era of Existence: Convict Transportation and the Authority of the Surgeon in Colonial Australia." *Labour History* 59 (1990): 59–72.

Humphries, M.O. "The Duty of the Nation: Public Health and the Spanish Influenza in Canada, 1918–19." PhD thesis, University of Western Ontario, 2008.

– "The Horror at Home: The Canadian Military and the "Great" Influenza Pandemic of 1918." *Journal of the Canadian Historical Association* 16, no. 1 (2005): 235–60.

– *The Last Plague: Spanish Influenza and the Politics of Health and War.* Toronto: University of Toronto Press, 2013.

– "The Limits of Necessity: Public Health, Dissent, and the War Effort During the 1918 Influenza Pandemic." In *Epidemic Encounters: Influenza, Society, and Culture in Canada, 1918–20*, edited by M. Fahrni and E.W. Jones, 21–47. Vancouver and Toronto: University of British Columbia Press, 2012.

Humphrey, Thomas J. "Conflicting independence: land tenancy and the American Revolution." *Journal of the Early Republic* 28, 2 (2008): 159–82.

Hunter, Albert. *Symbolic Communities: The Persistence and Change of Chicago's Local Communities.* Chicago: University of Chicago Press, 1974.

Hunter, James. *A Dance Called America: The Scottish Highlands, the United States and Canada.* Edinburgh: Mainstream Publishing, 1994.

Ihrke, David K. and Carol S. Faber. *Geographical Mobility: 2005 to 2010.* Washington: US Census Bureau, 2012.

Inwood, Kris and Jim Irwin. "Land, Income and Regional Inequality: New Estimates of Regional Incomes and Growth in Canada, 1871–1891." *Acadiensis* 31, no. 2 (2002): 157–84.

Inwood, Kris and Ian Keay. "Diverse paths to industrial development: Evidence from late nineteenth century Canada." *European Review of Economic History* 16, no. 3 (2012): 311–33.

– "Trade Policy and Industrial Development: Iron and Steel in a Small Open Economy, 1870–1913." *Canadian Journal of Economics,* 46, no. 4 (2014): 1,264–94

Inwood, Kris, Mary MacKinnon, and Chris Minns. "Labour Market Dynamics in Canada, 1891–1911: A First Look from New Census Samples." in *The Dawn of "Canada's Century": Hidden Histories,* edited by G. Darroch, 361–96. Montreal & Kingston: McGill-Queen's University Press, 2013.

Inwood, Kris, L. Oxley, and E. Roberts. "Physical Stature in Nineteenth Century New Zealand – a Preliminary Interpretation." *Australian Economic History Review* 50 (2010): 282–83.

Inwood, Kris and Richard Reid. "Gender and Occupational Identity in a Canadian Census." *Historical Methods* 34, no. 2 (2001): 57–70.

Inwood, Kris and Thanasis Stengos. "Discontinuities in Canadian economic growth, 1870–1985." *Explorations in Economic History* 28, no. 3 (1991): 274–86.

Jackson, R.V. "Sickness and Health on Australia's Female Convict Ships, 1821–1840." *International Journal of Maritime History* 18, no. 2 (2006): 65–84.

Jacoby, Sanford M. and Sunil Sharma. "Employment Duration and Industrial Labor Mobility in the United States 1880–1980." *Journal of Economic History* 52, no. 1 (1992): 161–79.

Jerzy, W., J. Praga, and Z. Kumoz. *Czyn Zbrojny Wychodzstwa polskiego w Ameryce: zbior dokmentow I materialow historycznych.* Warsaw: Wydawnictwo Conandor, 2001.

Jette, M. "A Regional Analysis of Anthropometric Measurements in a Canadian Employee Population Study." *Canadian Journal of Public Health* 71 (1980): 32–36.

Johansen, Hans Christian. "Urban Social and Demographic Reconstitution. The Case of Eighteenth Century Odense." *History and Computing* 11, nos. 1 and 2 (1999): 115–28.

Johnson, N.P. and J. Mueller. "Updating the Accounts: Global Mortality of the 1918–1920 "Spanish" influenza pandemic." *Bulletin of the History of Medicine* 76, 1 (2002): 105–15.

Johnson, Paul and Stephen Nicholas. "Male and female living standards in England and Wales, 1812–1857." *The Economic History Review* 48, no. 3 (1995): 1–13.

Johnson, Steven. *The Ghost Map.* London: Penguin, 2006.

Johnston, William, ed. *Roll of the Graduates of the University of Aberdeen, 1860–1900.* Aberdeen, 1906.

Johnston, W.S. and Hugh J.M. Johnston. *History of Perth County to 1967.* County of Perth, Stratford, Ontario, 1967.

Jones, H. "Population Patterns and Processes From c.1600." In *An Historical Geography of Scotland,* edited by G. Whittington and I.D. Whyte, 93–118. London and New York: Academic Press, 1983.

Jordan, Terry. *German Seed in Texas Soil: Immigrant Farmers in Nineteenth Century Texas.* Austin: University of Texas Press, 1966.

Jordan, Terry. *North American Cattle-Ranching Frontiers: Origins, Diffusion, and Differentiation.* Albuquerque: University of New Mexico Press, 1993.

Karr, Clarence. *The Canada Land Company: The Early Years, An Experiment in*

Colonization. Ottawa: Ontario Historical Society, Research Publication, No. 3, 1974.

Karskens, G. "Death was in his Face: Dying, Burial and Remembrance in Early Sydney." *Labour History* 74 (1998): 21–39.

Katz, Michael. *The People of Hamilton, Canada West.* Cambridge Mass: Harvard University Press, 1975.

Kauffman, Kyle D. and Jonathon J. Liebowitz. "Draft Animals on the United States Frontier." *Overland Journal* 15, no. 2 (1997): 13–26.

Kellogg, Paul Underwood. *Wage-Earning Pittsburgh.* New York: Survey Associates, 1914.

Kelly, James. "Transportation from Ireland to North America, 1703–1789." In *Refiguring Ireland,* edited by David Dickson and Cormac Ó Gráda, 112–35. Dublin: Lilliput Press, 2003.

Kelm, Mary Ellen. "Flu Stories: Engaging with Disease, Death, and Modernity in British Columbia, 1918–1919." In *Epidemic Encounters: Influenza, Society and Culture in Canada, 1918–1920,* edited by M. Fahrnia and E.W. Jones, 167–92. Vancouver and Toronto: University of British Columbia Press, 2012.

Kerr, Robert, ed. *Memoirs of the Life, Writings, and Correspondence of William Smellie.* Bristol: Thoemmes Press, 1996.

King, Miriam L. and Diana L. Magnuson. "Perspectives on Historical U.S. Census Undercounts." *Social Science History* 19, no. 4 (1995): 455–66.

Kirk-Elleker, Asher. "A Measure of Well-being: An Anthropometric Study of Living Conditions in Canada at the Turn of the Twentieth Century" MA thesis, University of Guelph, 2008.

Klein, H.S., *The Middle Passage: Comparative Studies in the Atlantic Slave Trade.* Princeton: Princeton University Press, 1978.

Klein, H.S., S.L. Engerman, R. Haines, and R. Shlomowitz. "Transoceanic Mortality: The Slave Trade in Comparative Perspective." *William and Mary Quarterly* 58, no. 1 (2001): 93–117.

Klemp, M. and J. Weisdorf. "The Lasting Damage to Mortality of Early-Life Adversity." *European Review of Economic History* 16 (2012): 233–46.

Knights, Peter R. "Potholes in the Road of Improvement? Estimating Census Underenumeration by Longitudinal Tracing: US censuses, 1850–1880." *Social Science History* 15, 4 (1991): 517–26.

Kok, Jan and Kees Mandemakers. "A Life-Course Approach to Co-residence in the Netherlands, 1850–1940." *Continuity and Change* 25, no. 2 (2010): 285–312.

Komlos, J. "Anomalies in Economic History: Toward a Resolution of the" Antebellum Puzzle." *Journal of Economic History* 56 (1996): 202–14.

– "Shrinking in a Growing Economy? The Mystery of Physical Stature during the Industrial Revolution." *Journal of Economic History* 58 (1998): 779–802.

– "An anthropometric History of Early-Modern France." *European Review of Economic History* 7 (2003): 159–89.

– "How to (and How Not to) Analyze Deficient Height Samples." *Historical Methods* 37 (2004): 160–73.

Komlos, J. and J. Kim. "Estimating Trends in Historical Heights." *Historical Methods* 23 (1990): 116–20.

Kulikoff, Allan. *From British Peasants to Colonial American Farmers.* Chapel Hill: University of North Carolina Press, 2000.

Lackenbauer, P. Whitney and Craig Leslie Mantle, eds. *Aboriginal Peoples and the Canadian Military: Historical Perspectives.* Kingston: Canadian Defence Academy Press, 2007.

Lackenbauer, P. Whitney and Katharine McGowan. "Competing Loyalties in a Complex Community: Enlisting the Six Nations in the Canadian Expeditionary Force, 1914–1917." In *Aboriginal Peoples and the Canadian Military: Historical Perspectives*, edited by P. Whitney Lackenbauer and Craig Leslie Mantle, 89–115. Kingston: Canadian Defence Academy Press, 2007.

Lackenbauer, P. Whitney with John Moses, Scott Sheffield, and Maxime Gohier. *A Commemorative History of Aboriginal People in the Canadian Military.* Ottawa: Department of National Defense, 2010.

Laflamme, Valérie. *Vivre en ville et prendre pension à Québec aux XIXe et XXe siècles.* Paris: L'Harmattan, 2007.

Lamm, D. "British Soldiers of the First World War: Creation of a Representative Sample." *Historical Social Research* 13 (1988): 55–98.

Laslett, Peter and Richard Wall, eds. *Household and Family in Past Time: Comparative Studies in the Size and Structure of the Domestic Group over the Last Three Centuries.* Cambridge: Cambridge University Press, 1972.

Lauzon, Gilles. "Cohabitation et déménagements en milieu ouvrier montréalais: Essai de réinterprétation à partir du cas du village Saint-Augustin (1871–1881)." *Revue d'histoire de l'Amérique française* 46, no.1 (1992): 115–42.

LeDuc, Thomas. "The Disposal of the Public Domain on the Trans-Mississippi Plains: Some Opportunities for Investigation." *Agricultural History* 24 (1950): 199–204.

Lee, Chul-In and Gary Solon. "Trends in Intergenerational Income Mobility." NBEW Working Paper No. 12007, February 2006.

Lee, Robert C. *The Canada Company and the Huron Tract, 1826–1853: Personalities, Profits and Politics.* Toronto, Ontario: Natural Heritage, 2004.

Lenihan, Rebecca A. "From Alba to Aotearoa: Profiling New Zealand's Scots Migrants, 1840–1920." PhD thesis, Victoria University of Wellington, 2010.

Lehmann, Heinz. *The German Canadians, 1750–1937: Immigration, Settlement and Culture.* St John's, Newfoundland: Jesperson Press, 1986.

Leonard, Susan Hautaniemi, Myron P. Gutmann, and Glenn D. Deane. "Household and Farm Transitions in Environmental Context." *Population and Environment* 32, 4 (2011): 287–317.

Leonard, Susan Hautaniemi, Myron P. Gutmann, Glenn Deane, and Kenneth M. Sylvester, "Drought and the lifecycle/landuse trajectory in agricultural households," in Satomi Kurosu, Tommy Bengtsson, Cameron Campbell, eds., *Demographic Responses to Economic and Environmental Crises* (Kashiwa, Japan, Proceedings of IUSSP Seminar at Reitaku University 2010),

Levi, Giovanni. *Inheriting Power: the Story of an Exorcist.* Chicago: University of Chicago Press, 1988.

Levitt, Ian and T.C. Smout. *The State of the Scottish Working-Class in 1843: A Statistical and Spatial Enquiry Based on the Data from the Poor Law Commission Report of 1844*. Edinburgh: Scottish Academic Press, 1979.

Lewis, Robert D. *Manufacturing Montreal: The Making of an Industrial Land scape, 1850 to 1930.* Baltimore: Johns Hopkins University Press, 2000.

Li, L. and C. Power. "Influences on Childhood Height: Comparing Two Generations in the 1958 British Birth Cohort." *International Journal of Epidemiology* 33 (2004): 1,320–28.

Liu, Y.Z., P. Xiao, Y.F. Guo, D.H. Xiong, L.J. Zhao, H. Shen, Y.J. Liu, V. Dvornyk, J.R. Long, H.Y. Deng, J.L. Li, R.R. Recker, and H.W. Deng. "Genetic Linkage of Human Height is Confirmed to 9q22 and Xq24." *Human Genetics* 119 (2006): 295–304.

Liebowitz, Jonathan J. "The Persistence of Draft Oxen in Western Agriculture." *Material History Review* 36 (1992): 29–37.

Linteau, Paul-André. *Maisonneuve ou Comment des promoteurs fabriquent une ville, 1883–1918.* Montreal: Boréal Express, 1981.

Long, Jason. "Rural-Urban Migration and Socioeconomic Mobility in Victorian Britain." *Journal of Economic History* 65, no. 1 (2005): 1–35.

Long, Jason, and Joseph Ferrie. "British, American, and British-American Social Mobility: Intergenerational Occupational Change Among Migrants and Non-Migrants in the Late 19th Century." Workshop paper, University of Guelph, 17 May 2012.

– "Intergenerational Occupational Mobility in Britain and the U.S. Since 1850." *American Economic Review*, 104, no. 4 (2013): 1,109–37.

– "The Path to Convergence: Intergenerational Occupational Mobility in

Britain and the US in Three Eras." *The Economic Journal* 117 (March 2007): C61–C71.

– "Grandfathers Matter(ed): Occupational Mobility Across Three Generations in the U.S. and Britain, 1850–1910." Working paper, 2012.

Lovell, J. *Lovell's Montreal Directory of 1880–81: Containing an alphabetical directory of the citizens, a street directory, an advertisers classified business directory and a miscellaneous directory ... corrected to June 11th 1880.* Montreal: J. Lovell, 1880.

Luo, Z.C., K. Albertsson-Wikland, and J. Karlberg. *Pediatric Research* 44 (1998): 563–71.

MacDonald, Heidi. "Who Counts? Nuns, Work and the Census of Canada." *Histoire Sociale/ Social History* 43, no. 86 (2010): 369–91.

MacDougall, Heather. "Toronto's Health Department in Action: Influenza in 1918 and SARS in 2003." In *Epidemic Encounters: Influenza, Society, and Culture in Canada, 1918–20,* edited by M. Fahrni and E.W. Jones, 225–65. Vancouver and Toronto: University of British Columbia Press, 2005.

Machan, Hilary, ed. *Legacy of Logan: Logan Township, 1850–2000.* Logan: Logan Township History Book Committee, 2000.

MacKenzie, John M. and Nigel Dalziel. *The Scots in South Africa: Ethnicity, Identity, Gender and Race, 1772–1914.* Manchester: Manchester University Press, 2007.

MacKinnon, Mary. "Unilingues ou bilingues? Les Montréalais sur le marché du travail en 1901." *L'Actualité économique* 76, no. 1 (2000): 137–58.

Mackintosh, John, ed. *Roll of the Graduates of the University of Aberdeen, 1926–1955; with Supplement 1860–1925.* Aberdeen: Aberdeen University Press, 1960.

Malin, James Claude. *Winter Wheat in the Golden Belt of Kansa: A Study in Adaption to Subhumid Geographical Environment.* Lawrence: University of Kansas Press, 1944.

Marr, William. "The Distribution of Tenant Agriculture, Ontario, Canada, 1871." *Social Science History* 11, no.2 (1987): 169–86.

– "Tenant vs. Owner Occupied Farms in York County, Ontario, 1871." In *Canada Papers in Rural History, vol. 4,* edited by Donald Akenson, 50–7. Gananoque, Ontario: Langdale Press, 1984.

– "The Wheat Economy in Reverse: Ontario Wheat Production 1887–1917." *Canadian Journal of Economics* 14 (1981): 136–45.

Maxwell-Stewart, Hamish. *Closing Hell's Gates: the Death of a Convict Station.* Crows Nest, NSW: Allen & Unwin, 2008.

– "Convict Transportation from Britain and Ireland, 1615–1870." *History Compass* 8, no. 11 (2010): 1221–42.

Maxwell-Stewart, Hamish and R. Shlomowitz. "Mortality and Migration: A Survey." In *Health and Medicine at Sea, 1700–1900*, edited by D. Haycock and S. Archer, 128–42. London: Boydell and Brewer, 2009.

May, Martha. "The 'Good Managers': Married Working Class Women and Family Budget Studies, 1895–1915." *Labor History* 25, no. 3 (1984): 351–72.

McCalla, Doug. *Planting the Province: The Economic History of Upper Canada, 1784–1870*. Toronto: University of Toronto, 1993.

McCann, Larry. "Seasons of Labor: Family, Work, and Land in a Nineteenth-century Nova Scotia Shipbuilding Community." *The History of the Family: An International Quarterly* 4, no. 4 (1999): 485–527.

McCarthy, Angela. *Scottishness and Irishness in New Zealand Since 1840*. Manchester: Manchester University Press, 2011.

McDevitt, C., J. Irwin, and K. Inwood. "Gender Pay Gap, Productivity Gap and Discrimination in Canadian Clothing Manufacturing in 1870." *Eastern Economic Journal* 35 (2009): 24–36.

McDonald, John and Ralph Shlomowitz. "Mortality on Convict Voyages to Australia, 1788–1868." *Social Science History* 13, no. 3 (1989): 285–313.

McGowan, Katharine. "'In the Interests of the Indians'. The Department of Indian Affairs, Charles Cooke and the Recruitment of Native Men in Southern Ontario for the Canadian Expeditionary Force, 1916." *Ontario History* 52, no. 1 (2010): 109–24.

– "'Until We Receive Just Treatment': The Fight Against Conscription in the Naas Agency, British Columbia." *BC Studies* 167 (2010): 47–70.

McInnis, Marvin. "The Changing Structure of Canadian Agriculture, 1867–1897." *Journal of Economic History* 4, 1 (1982): 191–8.

– "Marketable Surpluses in Ontario Farming, 1860." *Social Science History* 8, no. 4 (1984): 395–424.

– "The Population of Canada in the Nineteenth Century." In *A Population History of North America*, edited by Michael Haines and Richard Steckel, 371–432. New York: Cambridge University Press, 2000.

McIntyre, Perry. *Free Passage: The Reunion of Irish Convicts and their Families in Australia 1788–1852*. Dublin: Irish Academic Press, 2011.

McKeown, Thomas. *The Modern Rise of Population*. New York: New York Academic Press, 1976.

– *The Role of Medicine: Dream, Mirage, or Nemesis?* London: Nuffield Provincial Hospitals Trust, 1976.

McClean, R.R. "Scottish Emigrants to New Zealand, 1840–1880: Motives, Means and Background." PhD thesis, Edinburgh University, 1990.

Mercier, M. and C. Boone. "Infant Mortality in Ottawa, Canada, 1901: Assessing Cultural, Economic and Environmental Factors." *Journal of Historical Geography* 28 (2002): 486–507.

Meredith, D. and D. Oxley. "Contracting Convicts: The Convict Labour Market in Van Diemen's Land 1840–1857." *Australian Economic History Review* 45, no. 1 (2005): 45–72.

Merritt, Richard. *On Common Ground: The Ongoing Story of the Commons in Niagara-on-the-Lake.* Toronto: Dundurn, 2012.

Mielke, J., L.W. Konigsberg, J.H. Relethford. *Human Biological Variation*, 2nd ed. Oxford: Oxford University Press, 2011.

Miller, Jim R. *Lethal Legacy: Current Native Controversies in Canada.* Toronto: McClelland & Stewart Limited, 2004.

Miner, H. Craig. *Harvesting the High Plains: John Kriss And the Business of Wheat Farming, 1920–1950.* Lawrence: University Press of Kansas, 1998.

Minns, C. and M. MacKinnon. "The Costs of Doing Hard Time: A Penitentiary-based Regional Price Index for Canada, 1883–1923." *Canadian Journal of Economics* 40 (2007): 528–60.

Minns, C. and M. Risov. "The Spirit of Capitalism? Ethnicity, Religion, and Self-employment in Early 20th Century Canada." *Explorations in Economic History* 42 (2005): 259–81.

Mokyr, Joel. "Why More Work for Mother? Knowledge and Household Behavior, 1870–1945." *Journal of Economic History* 60, no. 1 (2000): 1–41.

Molloy, Maureen. *Those Who Speak to the Heart: The Nova Scotian Scots at Waipu, 1854–1920.* Palmerston North: Dunmore Press, 1991.

Morgan, Kenneth. "The Organization of the Convict Trade to Maryland: Stevenson, Randolph and Cheston, 1768–1775." *The William and Mary Quarterly*, 3rd Series, 24, no. 2 (1985): 201–27.

Morris, D.H., M.E. Jones, M.J. Schoemaker, A. Ashworth, and A.J. Swerdlow. "Familial Concordance for Height and its Components: Analyses From the Breakthrough Generations Study." *American Journal Of Human Biology* 24 (2012): 22–7.

Mortlock, J., ed. *Experiences of a Convict, Transported for Twenty-One Years.* Sydney: Sydney University Press, 1864 and 1965.

Morton, Desmond. *When Your Number's Up: the Canadian Soldier in the First World War.* Toronto: Vintage Canada, 1994.

Morton, Desmond and J.L. Granatstein. *Marching to Armageddon: Canadians and the Great War, 1914–1919.* Toronto: Lester & Orpen Dennys, 1989.

Morton, Desmond and J.M. Hitsman. *Broken Promises: A History of Conscription in Canada.* Toronto: Oxford University Press, 1977.

Mosse, George L. *Fallen Soldiers: Reshaping the Memories of the World Wars.* Oxford: Oxford University Press, 1990.

Mulligan, Desiree. "Mary Edie's Biscuits and Other Interesting Information About the Edie Family of Edievale." Unpublished family history, Wellington, NZ, 1996.

Murphy, M. "Where have all the children gone? Women's reports of more childlessness at older ages than when they were younger in a large-scale continuous household survey in Britain." *Population Studies* 63 (2009): 115–33.

Myers, George C. and Cheryl Elman. "Morbidity, Disability and Mortality in the United States in the Late Nineteenth Century: Differentials and Social Implications." *Cahiers de la Société de Démographie Historique* 2 (2000): 93–109.

Nastał, Stanisław. "The Blue Division." In *Haller's Polish Army in France*, translated and edited by Paul Valasek, 80-149, United States of America: Whitehall Printing, 2006. Originally published in Stanislaw Nastal, *The Blue Division.* Cleveland: Polish Army Veterans' Association in America, 1922.

Neckerman, Kathryn M. "Divided Households: Extended Kin in Working-Class Chicago, 1924." *Social Science History* 19, no. 3 (1995): 371–98.

Nicholas, Stephen, ed. *Convict Workers: Reinterpreting Australia's Past.* Oakleigh, Australia: Cambridge University Press, 1988.

– "Unshackling the Past." In *Convict Workers: Reinterpreting Australia's Past*, edited by S. Nicholas, 3–13. Cambridge: Cambridge University Press, 1988.

Nicholas, Stephen and Deborah Oxley. "The Living Standards of Women During the Industrial Revolution, 1795–1820." *Economic History Review* 46, no 4. (1993): 723–49.

Nootens, Thierry. "'What a Misfortune that Poor Child Should Have Married Such a Being as Joe': Les fils prodigues de la bourgeoisie montréalaise, 1850–1900." *Canadian Historical Review* 86, no. 2 (2005): 225–56.

Norrie, K., D. Owram, and J. Emery. *A History of the Canadian Economy.* Scarborough: Thomson/Nelson, 2002.

Norris, Darrell A. "Household and Transiency in a Loyalist Township: The People of Adolphustown, 1784–1822." *Histoire Sociale/Social History* 8, no. 26 (1980): 399–415.

– "Migration, Pioneer Settlement, and the Life Course: The First Families of an Ontario Township." *Canadian Papers in Rural History* 4 (1982): 130–52.

O'Connor, Alice. *Poverty Knowledge: Social Science, Social Policy, and the Poor in Twentieth-Century U.S. History.* Princeton: Princeton University Press, 2001.

Olson, D.R, L. Simonsen, P.J. Edelson, and S.S. Morse. "Epidemiological Evidence of an Early Wave of the 1918 Influenza Pandemic in New York City." *Proceedings of the National Academy of Science usa* 102, no. 31 (2005): 11,059–63.

Olson, Sherry and Patricia Thornton. *Peopling the North American City: Montreal 1840–1900*. Kingston & Montreal: McGill-Queen's University Press, 2011.

Olssen, Erik and Maureen Hickey. *Class and Occupation: The New Zealand Reality*. Dunedin, NZ: Otago University Press, 2005.

Oris, Michel, Gilbert Ritschard, and Grazyna Ryczkowska. "Les solitudes urbaines, structures et parcours dans la Genève des années 1816–1843." *Annales de Démographie Historique*, 2006, no. 1: 59–87.

Oxford, J.S., A. Sefton, R. Jackson, W. Innes, R.S. Daniels, and N.P. Johnson. "World War I May Have Allowed the Emergence of "Spanish" Influenza." *Lancet Infectious Disease* 2, no. 2 (2002): 111–14.

Oxley, D. *Convict Maids: The Forced Migration of Women to Australia*. Melbourne: Cambridge University Press, 1996.

Page, Dorothy. *Anatomy of a Medical School: A History of Medicine at the University of Otago, 1875–2000*. Dunedin: Otago University Press, 2008.

Park, Robert Ezra, Ernest W. Burgess, Roderick Duncan McKenzie, and Louis Wirth. *The City*. Chicago: University of Chicago Press, 1925.

Parkerson, Donald H. *The Agricultural Transition in New York State: Markets and Migration in Mid-Nineteenth-Century America*. Ames: Iowa State University Press, 1995.

– "How Mobile were Nineteenth Century Americans?" *Historical Methods* 15 (1982): 99–110.

Patterson, K.D, and G.F. Pyle. "The Geography and Mortality of the 1918 Influenza Pandemic." *Bulletin of the History of Medicine* 65, no. 1 (1991): 4–21.

Payette, Céline. "Les vocations féminines de la région montréalaise au XXe siècle." MA thesis, Université du Québec à Montréal, 1991.

Pelletier, F., J. Légaré, and R. Bourbeau. "Mortality in Quebec During the Nineteenth Century: From the State to the Cities." *Population Studies* 51 (1997): 93–103.

Perrenoud, Alfred. *La population de Genève du seizième au début du dix-neuvième siècle: Étude démographique*. Genève: Jullien, 1979.

Pliska, Stanley. "The "Polish-American Army" 1917–1921." *The Polish Review* 10, no. 3 (1965): 46–59.

Prentice, Alison. *The School Promoters: Education and Social Class in Mid-Nineteenth Century Upper Canada*. Toronto: McClelland & Stewart Limited, 1977.

Prentis, Malcolm D. *The Scots in Australia: A Study of New South Wales, Victoria and Queensland, 1788–1900*. Sydney: Sydney University Press, 1983.

Preston, Samuel H. and Michael Haines. *Fatal Years: Child Mortality in Late Nineteen-Century America*. Princeton, New Jersey: Princeton University Press, 1991.

Pooley, Colin G. and Ian D. Whyte, eds. *Migrants, Emigrants and Immigrants: A Social History of Migration.* London and New York: Routledge, 1991.

Rabe-Hesketh, Sophia and Anders Skrondal. *Multilevel and Longitudinal Modeling Using Stata.* College Station, Texas: Stata Press, 2005.

Rawley, James and Stephen D. Behrendt. *The Transatlantic Slave Trade: A History.* Lincoln: University of Nebraska Press, 2005.

Reid, Alice, Ros Davies, and Eilidh Garrett. "Nineteenth-Century Scottish Demography from Linked Censuses and Civil Registers: a 'Sets of Related Individuals' Approach." *History and Computing* 14, nos 1–2 (2002): 61–86.

Reid, Kirsty. *Gender, Crime and Empire: Convicts, Settlers and the State in Early Colonial Australia.* Manchester: Manchester University Press, 2007.

– "Setting Women to Work: The Assignment System and Female Convict Labour in Van Diemen's Land, 1820–1839." *Australian Historical Studies* 34, no. 121 (2003): 1–25.

Reid, Richard. "The 1870 United States Census and Black Underenumeration: A Test Case from North Carolina." *Social History / Histoire Sociale* 28, 56 (1995): 487–99.

Richards, Eric. "Ironies of the Highland Exodus, 1740–1900." *The Journal of Australian Studies* no. 68 (2001): 74–86.

– "Running Home from Australia: Intercontinental Mobility and Migrant Expectations in the Nineteenth Century." In *Emigrant Homecomings: The Return Movement of Emigrants, 1600–2000*, edited by Marjory Harper, 77–104. Manchester: Manchester University Press, 2005.

Richards, L., L. Antonie, S. Areibi, and G. Grewal. "Applying Machine Learning Techniques to a Record Linkage Problem." Poster presented at Women in Machine Learning Workshop, Lake Tahoe, Nevada, December 2012.

Roberts, Evan, Matthew Woollard, Chad Ronnander, Lisa Dillon, and Gunnar Thorvaldsen. "Occupational Classification in the North Atlantic Population Project." *Historical Methods* 36, no. 2, Part 2 (2003): 89–96.

Roberts, Kenneth. "The Entry into Employment: An Approach Towards a General Theory." *Sociological Review* 16 (1968): 168–84.

Robinson, Neil. *To the Ends of the Earth: Norman Mcleod and the Highlanders Migration to Nova Scotia and New Zealand.* Auckland: HarperCollins, 1997.

Robson, L.L. *The Convict Settlers of Australia.* Melbourne, Melbourne University Press, 1994.

Rodger, Richard. *The Transformation of Edinburgh, Land, Property and Trust in the Nineteenth Century.* Cambridge: Cambridge University Press, 2001.

Ronnander, Chad. "The Classification of Work: Applying 1950 Census Occupation and Industry Codes to 1920 Responses." *Historical Methods* 32, no. 3 (1999): 151–55.

Rosental, Paul-André. *Les sentiers invisibles, espace, familles et migrations dans la France du 19e siècle.* Paris: EHESS, 1999.

Rousseau, Louis and Frank Remiggi, eds. *Atlas historique des pratiques religieuses: le Sud-Ouest du Québec au XIXe siècle.* Ottawa: Presses de l'University d'Ottawa, 1998.

Ruggles, Steven. "Confessions of a Microsimulator: Problems in Modeling the Demography of Kinship." *Historical Methods* 26, no. 4 (1993): 161–69.

– "The Decline of Intergenerational Coresidence in the United States, 1850–2000." *American Sociological Review* 72 (2007): 962–89.

– "The Demography of the Unrelated Individual 1900–1950." *Demography* 25, no. 4 (November 1988): 521–36.

– "Intergenerational Coresidence and Family Transitions in the United States, 1850–1880." *Journal of Marriage and the Family* 73, no. 1 (2011): 138–48.

– "Linking Historical Censuses: a New Approach." *History and Computing* 14, no. 12 (2002): 213–24.

– "Multigenerational Families in Nineteenth-Century America," *Continuity and Change* 17, no. 1 (2003): 139–65.

Ruggles, Steven and Susan Brower. "Measurement of Household and Family Composition in the United States, 1880–2000." *Population and Development Review* 29, no. 1 (2003): 73–101.

Runblom, Harald and Hans Norman. *From Sweden to America: A History of the Migration.* Minneapolis: University of Minnesota Press, 1976.

Ruskoski, David Thomas. "The Polish Army in France: Immigrants in America, World War I Volunteers in France, Defenders of the Recreated State in Poland." PhD thesis, Georgia State University, 2006.

Rutherdale, Robert. *Hometown Horizons: Local Responses to Canada's Great War.* Vancouver: UBC Press, 2004.

Rzepniewski, Andrzej. *The General Haller's Polish Army in France, 1917–1919.* Warsaw: US Army Military History Institute, 1995.

Sager, Eric W. and P. Baskerville, eds. *Household Counts: Canadian Households and Families in 1901.* Toronto: University of Toronto Press, 2007.

Salamon, Sonya. *Prairie Patrimony: Family, Farming and Community in the Midwest.* Chapel Hill: University of North Carolina Press, 1992.

Saloutos, Theodore. "Land policy and its Relation to Agricultural Production and Distribution, 1862 to 1933." *Journal of Economic History* 22 (1962): 445–60.

– *They Remember America; the Story of the Repatriated Greek-Americans.* Berkeley: University of California Press, 1956.

Sampson, Robert J. *Great American City: Chicago and the Enduring Neighborhood Effect.* Chicago: University of Chicago Press, 2012.

Scott, Duncan Campbell. "The Canadian Indians and the Great World War." Reprinted in *Aboriginal Peoples and the Canadian Military: Historical Perspectives,* edited by P. Whitney Lackenbauer and Craig Leslie Mantle. 73–88. Kingston: Canadian Defence Academy Press, 2007.

Sennett, Richard. *Families Against the City, Middle Class Homes of Industrial Chicago, 1872–1890.* Cambridge: Harvard University Press, 1970.

Shackle, G.L.S. *Decision, Order, and Time in Human Affairs.* Cambridge: Cambridge University Press, 1969.

Shaw, Clifford R. and Henry D. McKay. *Juvenile Delinquency and Urban Areas: a Study of Rates of Delinquency in Relation to Differential Characteristics of Local Communities in American Cities.* Rev. ed. Chicago: University of Chicago Press, 1969.

Sheffield, Scott R. "Indifference, Difference and Assimilation: Aboriginal People in the Canadian Military Practice, 1900–1945." In *Aboriginal Peoples and the Canadian Military: Historical Perspectives,* edited by P. Whitney Lackenbauer and Craig Leslie Mantle, 57–71. Kingston: Canadian Defence Academy Press, 2007.

Shen, L.W. "Origins and Spread of the 1918 Influenza Pandemic." In *Anatomy of a Pandemic: The 1918 Influenza in Hamilton,* edited by D. Ann Herring, 5–15. Hamilton: Allegra Press, 2005.

Sherow, James Earl. *The Grasslands of the United States: an Environmental History.* Santa Barbara: ABC-CLIO, 2007.

Shewell, Hugh. *Enough to Keep Them Alive: Indian Welfare in Canada 1873–1965.* Toronto: University of Toronto Press, 2004.

Sibley, D. "Invisible Women? The Contribution of the Chicago School of Social Service Administration to Urban Analysis." *Environment and Planning A* 22 (1990): 733–45.

Silventoinen, M. "Determinants of Variation in Adult Body Height." *Journal of Biosocial Science* 35 (2003): 263–85.

Simmons, James W. "Changing Residence in the City: A Review of Intraurban Mobility." *Geographical Review* (1968): 622–51.

Sinclair, Keith and Erik Olssen. "Lands of Sheep and Gold: The Australian Dimension to the New Zealand Past, 1840–1900." In *Tasman Relations: New Zealand and Australia, 1788–1988,* edited by. Keith Sinclair, 34–51. Auckland: Auckland University Press, 1987.

Singer, Judith D. and John B. Willett. *Applied Longitudinal Data Analysis: Modeling Change and Event Occurrence.* Oxford: Oxford University Press, 2003.

Sinnott, Rex. "The Census and Privacy in New Zealand: Do Privacy Concerns Justify Destruction of Name-Identified Census Forms?" *Archifacts* (April 2000): 25–50.

Skarzyński, Wincenty. "The Polish Army in Light of the Facts." In *Haller's Polish Army in France*, translated and edited by Paul Valasek, 80–149. United States of America: Whitehall Printing, 2006. Originally published in *Armja Polska We Francji we Swietle Faktow*. Warszawa: Tłoczono w Zakładach graficznych Straszewiczów, 1929.

Slichter, Sumner H. *The Turnover of Factory Labor*. New York: D. Appleton and Company, 1919.

Słociúski, Jan. "Z Obozu Kosciuszki." *Dziennik Zwiazkowy – Zgoda Poniedzialek* (26 November, 1917): 5.

Smallman-Raynor, M.R and A.D. Cliff. *War Epidemics: An Historical Geography of Infectious Diseases in Military Conflict and Civil Strife, 1850–2000*. Oxford: Oxford, 2004.

Smith, Andrew. *British Businessmen and Canadian Confederation: Constitution Making in an Era of Anglo-Globalization*. Montreal & Kingston: McGill-Queen's University Press, 2008.

Smith, Thomas Vernor and Leonard Dupee White. *Chicago, an Experiment in Social Science Research*. Chicago: University of Chicago Press, 1929.

Snell, K.D.M. *Annals of the Labouring Poor: Social Change and Agrarian England, 1660–1900*. Cambridge: Cambridge University Press.

Snijders, Tom and Roel J. Boskers. *Multilevel Analysis: An Introduction to Basic and Advanced Multilevel Modeling*. Thousand Oaks, California: Sage, 2012.

Solomon, Brian and Mike Schafer. *The New York Central Railroad*. St Paul: MBI Publishing, 2007.

Spennemann, Dirk H.R. and Gaye Sutherland. "Late Nineteenth Century German Immigrant Land and Stock Holdings in the Southern Riverina: An Exploration of Large Scale Spatial Patterns." *Journal of the Royal Australian Historical Society* 94 (2008): 74–90.

Spillman, W.J. "The Agricultural Ladder." *American Economic Review Proceedings* 9, no.1 (1919): 170–9.

St Peter's Lutheran Church in the Village of Brodhagen. "Historical Sketch of St Peter's Taken From the 125th Anniversary Directory, 1983." Researched and written by Pastor Arthur Horst and Mary Jane Schuessler. stpetershouse.ca/history_125booklet.html

St-Hilaire, Marc. *Peuplement et dynamique migratoire au Saguenay, 1840–1960*. Sainte-Foy: Les Presses de l'Université Laval, 1996.

Staniforth, Mark. "Diet, Disease and Death at Sea on the Voyage to Australia, 1837–1839." *International Journal of Maritime History* 8, no. 2 (1996): 119–56.

Steckel, Richard H. "The Age of Leaving Home in the United States, 1850–1860." *Social Science History* 20, no. 4 (1996): 507–31.

– "Biological Measures of the Standard of Living." *Journal of Economic Perspectives* 22 no. 1 (2008): 129–52.

– "The Health and Mortality of Women and Children, 1850–1860." *The Journal of Economic History* 48 no. 2 (1998): 333–45.

– "Heights and Human Welfare: Recent Developments and New Directions." *Explorations in Economic History* 46 (2009): 1–23.

– "Household Migration and Rural Settlement in the United States, 1850–1860." *Explorations in Economic History* 26 (1989): 190–218.

– "Poverty and Prosperity: A Longitudinal Study of Wealth Accumulation, 1850–60." *Review of Economics and Statistics* 72, no. 2 (1990): 275–85.

– "Stature and the Standard of Living." *Journal of Economic Literature* 33 (1995): 1,903–40.

Steckel, Richard H. and Roderick Floud, eds. *Health and Welfare During Industrialization.* Chicago: University of Chicago Press, 1997.

Steckel, Richard H. and R.A. Jensen. "New Evidence on the Causes of Slave and Crew Mortality in the Atlantic Slave Trade." *Journal of Economic History* 46 (1986): 57–77.

Steckel, Richard H. and D.R. Haurin. "Health and Nutrition in the American Midwest: Evidence from the Height of Ohio National Guardsmen, 1850–1910." In *Stature, Living Standards, and Economic Development,* edited by J. Komlos, 117–28. Chicago: University of Chicago Press, 1995

Stewart, James I. "Economic Opportunity or Hardship?: The Causes of Geographic Mobility on the Agricultural Frontier, 1860–1880." *The Journal of Economic History* 69, no. 1 (2009): 238–68.

Stover, John. *The Routledge Historical Atlas of the American Railroads.* New York: Routledge, 1999.

Summerby, Janice. *Native Soldiers, Foreign Battlefields.* Ottawa: Veterans Affairs, 2005.

Sundstrom, William A. "Internal Labor Markets before World War I: On-the-Job Training and Employee Promotion." *Explorations in Economic History* 25, no. 4 (1988): 424–45.

Swedlund, A. "Everyday Mortality in the Time of Plague: Ordinary People Under Extraordinary Circumstances in Massachusetts Before and During the 1918 Flu Epidemic." In *Plagues and Epidemics: Infected Spaces Past and Present,* edited by D.A. Herring and A.C. Swedlund, 153–78. New York: Berg, 2010.

Sweeny, Robert C.H. "Spatial and Social Dynamics of Rentier Capital in an Industrializing Town: The Case of 19th Century Montreal." Paper presented at Economic History Association, Austin, 6 September 2007. Accessed 4 December 12. www.eh.net/eha/system/files/eha-meeting-2007/pdf/robert-c-h-sweeny-paper.pdf.

Sylvester, Kenneth M. "Ecological Frontiers on the Grasslands of Kansas: Changes in Farm Scale and Crop Diversity." *Journal of Economic History* 69, 4 (2009): 1,040–61.

– *The Limits of Rural Capitalism: Family, Culture, and Markets in Montcalm, Manitoba, 1870–1940*. Toronto: University of Toronto Press, 2001.

Sylvester, Kenneth M. and Geoff Cunfer. "An Unremembered Diversity: Mixed Husbandry and the American Grasslands." *Agricultural History* 83, 3 (2009): 352–83.

Sylvester, Kenneth M., Susan Hautaniemi Leonard, Myron P. Gutmann, and Geoff Cunfer. "Demography and Environment in Grassland Settlement: Using Linked Longitudinal and Cross-Sectional Data to Explore Household and Agricultural Systems." *History and Computing* 14, 1 (2006): 31–60.

Szreter, Simon. "The Importance of Social Intervention in Britain's Mortality Decline c. 1850–1914: A Reinterpretation of the Role of Public Health." *Social History of Medicine*, no. 1 (1988): 1–38.

Tanner, J.M. *Foetus in Man: Physical Growth from Conception to Maturity*. Cambridge: Harvard University Press, 1978.

– *A History of the Study of Human Growth*. Cambridge: Cambridge University Press, 1981.

Talbot, Robert J. "'It Would Be Best to Leave Us Alone': First Nation Responses to the Canadian War Effort, 1914–1918." *Journal of Canadian Studies* 45, no. 1 (2011): 91–120.

Tate, Michael L. "From Scout to Doughboy: The National Debate over Integrating American Indians into the Military, 1891–1918." *The Western Historical Quarterly* 17, no. 4 (1986): 417–37.

Tedebrand, Lars-Goran. "Remigration from America to Sweden." In *From Sweden to America: A History of the Migration*, edited by Harald Runblom and Hans Norman, 201–27. Minneapolis: University of Minnesota Press, 1976.

Thernstrom, Stephan. *The Other Bostonians: Poverty and Progress in the American Metropolis, 1880–1970*. Cambridge: Harvard University Press, 1973.

Thibault, Harold W., Lise LaPalme, Richard Tanguay, and Arto Demirjian. "Anthropometric Differences Between Rural and Urban French-Canadian Schoolchildren." *Human Biology* 57, no. 1 (1985): 113–29.

Thornton, Patricia and Sherry Olson. "A Deadly Discrimination Among Montreal Infants, 1860–1900." *Continuity and Change* 18 (2001): 95–135.

– "Mortality in Late Nineteenth-Century Montreal: Geographic Pathways of Contagion." *Population Studies* (2011): 1–25.

Thwaites, Ian. "Berry, William – Biography." From the *Dictionary of New Zealand Biography. Te Ara: The Encyclopedia of New Zealand.* Accessed 1 September 2010. www.TeAra.govt.nz/en/biographies/2b19/1.

Titley, E. Brian. "Duncan Campbell Scott and the Administration of Indian Affairs." *Canadian Story and History, 1885–1985: Papers Presented at the Tenth Annual Conference of the British Association for Canadian Studies.* Edited by Colin Nicholson and Peter Easingwood. 47–69. Edinburgh: University of Edinburgh Press, 1985.

– *A Narrow Vision: Duncan Campbell Scott and the Administration of Indian Affairs in Canada.* Vancouver: University of British Columbia Press, 1986.

Truta, Ramona C. "Linking Casualties to Soldiers." Working Paper, University of Guelph, Historical Data Research Unit, 7 November 2011.

Urquhart, M.C. *Gross National Product, Canada, 1870–1926: The Derivation of the Estimates.* Montreal & Kingston: McGill-Queen's University Press, 1993.

Urquhart, Malcolm C. "New Estimates of Gross National Product Canada, 1870–1926: Some Implications for Canadian Development." In *Long Term Factors in American Economic Growth,* edited by Stanley L. Engerman and Robert E. Gallman, 9–94. Chicago: University of Chicago Press, 1986.

van Leeuwen, Marco H.D., Ineke Maas, and Andrew Miles. *HISCO: Historical International Standard Classification of Occupations.* Leuven: Leuven University Press, 2002.

van Poppel, Frans, Jurjen de Jong, and Aart C. Liefbroer. "The Effects of Paternal Mortality on Sons' Social Mobility." *Historical Methods* 31, no. 3 (1998): 101–13.

van Tassel, Aaron. *Death Rates Among Aboriginal Soldiers in the Canadian Expeditionary Force.* Course Paper, University of Guelph, December 2011.

Valasek, Paul, trans. and ed. *Haller's Polish Army in France.* United States of America: Whitehall Printing, 2006.

– ed. "Medical Examination of Recruits," in *Haller's Polish Army in France,* translated and edited by Paul Valasek. United States of America: Whitehall Printing, 2006: 73–79.

Vance, Jonathan. *Death So Noble: Memory, Meaning, and the First World War.* Vancouver: UBC Press, 1997.

Vapnik, Vladimir N. *The Nature of Statistical Learning Theory.* Springer Verlag: Heidelberg, 1995.

Venkatesh, Sudhir. "Chicago's Pragmatic Planners: American Sociology and the Myth of Community." *Social Science History* 25, no. 2 (2001): 275–317.

Visscher, P.M., W.G. Hill, N.R. Wray. "Heritability in the Genomics Era – Concepts and Misconceptions." *Nature Reviews: Genetics* 9 (2008): 255–66.

Wagner, Jonathan. *A History of Migration from Germany to Canada, 1850–1939.* Vancouver: UBC Press, 2006.

Waldram, James, D. Ann Herring, and T. Kue Young. *Aboriginal Health in*

Canada: Historical, Cultural, and Epidemiological Perspectives, 2nd edition. Toronto: University of Toronto Press, 2006.

Walker, James, "Race and Recruitment in World War I: Enlistment of Visible Minorities in the Canadian Expeditionary Force," *Canadian Historical Review* 70, no. 1 (1989): 1–26.

Ward, David. *Poverty, Ethnicity, and the American City, 1840–1925: Changing Conceptions of the Slum and the Ghetto.* Cambridge: Cambridge University Press, 1989.

Ward, W. and P. Ward. "Infant Birth Weight and Nutrition in Industrializing Montreal." *American Historical Review* 89 (1984): 324–45.

Watt, Theodore, ed., *Roll of the Graduates of the University of Aberdeen, 1901–1925, with Supplement, 1860–1900.* Aberdeen: Aberdeen University Press, 1935.

White, Douglas R. and Paul Jorion. "Representing and Computing Kinship: a New Approach." *Current Anthropology* 33, no. 4 (1992): 454–63.

Widdis, Randy W. "Tracing Eastern Ontarian Emigrants to New York State, 1880–1910." *Ontario History* 81, no. 3 (1989): 201–23.

– *With Scarcely A Ripple: Anglo-Canadian Migration into the United States and Western Canada, 1880–1920.* Montreal & Kingston: McGill-Queen's University Press, 1998.

Williams, Faith M. and Carle C. Zimmerman. *Studies of Family Living in the United States and Other Countries.* Washington: United States Department of Agriculture Miscellaneous Publication No. 223, 1935.

Williamson, Jeffrey. *Globalization and History: The Evolution of a Nineteen-Century Atlantic Economy.* Cambridge: MIT Press, 1999.

Wilson, Catherine Anne. *A New Lease on Life: Landlords, Tenants and Immigrants in Ireland and Canada.* Montreal & Kingston: McGill-Queen's University Press, 1994.

– "Tenancy as Family Strategy in Mid-Nineteenth Century Ontario." *Journal of Social History* 31 no. 4 (1998): 875–96.

– *Tenants in Time: Family Strategies, Land and Liberalism in Upper Canada, 1799–1871.* Montreal & Kingston: McGill-Queen's University Press, 2009.

Winegard, Timothy C. *For King and Kanata: Canadian Indians and the First World War.* Winnipeg: University of Manitoba Press, 2012.

Winters, Donald L. "Agricultural Tenancy in the Nineteenth-Century Middle West: The Historiographic Debate." *Indiana Magazine of History* 78, no. 2 (1982): 128–53.

– *Farmers without Farms: Agricultural Tenancy in Nineteenth-century Iowa.* Westport, Conn: Greenwood Press, 1978.

– "Tenancy as an Economic Institution: The Growth and Distribution of

Agricultural Tenancy in Iowa, 1850–1900." *Journal of Economic History* 37, 2 (1977): 382–409.

Withers, Charles W.J. *Urban Highlanders: Highland-Lowland Migration and Urban Gaelic Culture, 1700–1900*. East Linton, East Lothian, Scotland: Tuckwell Press, 1998.

World Development Indicators. Washington: World Bank Publications, 2007.

Worster, Donald. *Dust Bowl: The Southern Plains in the 1930s*. New York: Oxford University Press, 1979.

Yoder, Frank. "Rethinking Midwestern Farm Tenure: A Cultural Perspective." *Agricultural History* 71 (1997): 457–78.

Yool, J. "An Anthropometric Study of the Standard of Living and Degree of Marginality in Ontario and Quebec, 1870–1900." Unpublished MA Paper, University of Guelph, Department of Economics, 2006.

Zorbaugh, Harvey Warren. *The Gold Coast and the Slum: A Sociological Study of Chicago's near North Side*. Chicago: University of Chicago Press, 1929.

Contributors

LUIZA ANTONIE is a postdoctoral fellow at University of Guelph. She is the lead computer scientist for the People in Motion project, which links people across historical Canadian censuses. She received her PhD in computing science from the University of Alberta with specialization in data mining. Her research interests include associative classifiers, health informatics, and record linkage. She has published several articles on these topics.

PETER BASKERVILLE holds a research chair in modern Western Canadian history at the University of Alberta and is professor emeritus at the University of Victoria. He has written on nineteenth and twentieth-century Canadian gender, business, labour, and social history. He published *A Silent Revolution?: Gender and Wealth in English Canada, 1860–1930*, McGill-Queen's University Press, in 2008. He is currently writing on social relations in nineteenth and twentieth-century Perth County, Ontario and on the homesteading process in Alberta.

KANDACE BOGAERT is a PhD candidate in the Department of Anthropology at McMaster University. Her dissertation research focuses on the impact and spread of the 1918 influenza pandemic among soldiers training in Ontario and on troopships in Canadian harbours. She is currently a research assistant for an interdisciplinary project investigating the links between the 1890 Russian influenza pandemic and the 1918 influenza pandemic in Canada.

JOHN CRANFIELD is a professor in the Department of Food, Agricultural, and Resource Economics at the University of Guelph. His research focuses on the economics of food demand, innovation in the agri-food and biotechnology sectors, and anthropometric history. John has published in outlets such as the *Journal of Development Economics, Economics and Human Biology*, and the *World Bank Economic Review.*

GORDON DARROCH is professor of sociology, emeritus, York University. He has been involved in the development and dissemination of a variety of national historical databases and has published historical studies of ethnicity, social mobility, inequalities, and of families and households. A recent contribution appeared in *Popolazione e Storia* (Italian Society of Historical Demography, 2010). He is the editor of and a contributor to *The Dawn of Canada's Century: Hidden Histories*, McGill-Queen's University Press, 2014. Currently he is examining migration and mobility in nineteenth-century Ontario.

ALLEGRA FRYXELL is currently completing her PhD in modern European history at Gonville & Caius College, University of Cambridge, supervised by Peter Mandler and Christopher Clark. Her MPhil (Cambridge) explored Egyptomania in interwar Britain, and in addition to her interest in twentieth-century Canadian history, she has written on the archaeology of smell in the experience of pilgrimage in medieval Europe. Her thesis research explores ideas of nonlinear temporalities in Western Europe and North America in the affective sciences and arts, circa 1880–1930.

ANN HERRING is professor of anthropology at McMaster University. She has written on the anthropology of infectious disease, syndemics, the 1918 influenza pandemic, and historic epidemics among Aboriginal people in Canada. She coedited *Plagues and Epidemics: Infected Spaces Past and Present* (with A.C. Swedlund), Berg Press, in 2010. She is currently collaborating on a transdisciplinary project investigating the relationship between the Russian influenza pandemic (1889–90) and the 1918 influenza pandemic in Canada.

KRIS INWOOD is a professor of economics and of history at the University of Guelph. He has published widely on industrialization, the standard of living, and labour mobility in the *Journal of Economic History, Machine Learning, Economics and Human Biology*, and other journals. He directs the Historical Data Research Unit and the People in Motion project at the University of Guelph.

REBECCA KIPPEN is a senior research fellow and Australian Research Council Future fellow in the Melbourne School of Population and Global Health at the University of Melbourne. Her research interests include historical demography and population futures for Australia. She is currently researching the life courses and demography of nineteenth-century Tasmanians.

REBECCA LENIHAN is an historian of nineteenth and early twentieth-century New Zealand and Scotland with a particular interest in migration and settlement. She has written several articles about the New Zealand Scots, is a coauthor of *Unpacking the Kists*, McGill-Queen's University Press, 2013, and author of *From Alba to Aotearoa* (working title), under contract with Otago University Press for 2014 publication.

SUSAN HAUTANIEMI LEONARD is associate research scientist in the Institute for Social Research, University of Michigan, research affiliate at the Population Studies Center, and coeditor of *Continuity and Change*. Her work is centered on the relationship between human populations and their environments. Recent publications in *Population and Environment*, *Women and Health*, and *Continuity and Change* speak to her interests in household dynamics and farming practices in grasslands environments, female reproductive senescence, and historical epidemiology and mortality. She is currently working on connecting household-level processes to farm sustainability.

HAMISH MAXWELL-STEWART is an associate professor in the School of Humanities, University of Tasmania. He has authored or coauthored a number of books on convict transportation to the Australian colonies including *Chain Letters: Narrating Convict Lives*, Melbourne University Press, 2001; *American Citizens, British Slaves: Yankee Political Prisoners in an Australian Penal Colony*, Melbourne University Press, 2002; and *Closing Hell's Gates: The Death of a Convict Station*, Allen and Unwin, 2008. He is currently working on the long-run impacts of forced migration on the health and social mobility of convicts and their descendants.

JANET MCCALMAN is a professor in the Centre for Health & Society in the Melbourne School of Population and Global Health, University of Melbourne. She is the author of three award-winning social histories of private life and health in Australia: *Struggletown* (1984), *Journeyings* (1993), and *Sex and Suffering* (1998). She has pioneered demographic prosopography for the building of cradle-to-grave studies and has published on women's health, colonial and indigenous health transitions. She is a founder of Founders & Survivors: Australian life courses in historical context 1803–1920.

SHERRY OLSON is professor of geography at McGill University and a member of the Centre interuniversitaire d'Études québécoises (CIÉQ). Her papers address questions in historical demography and ethnicity. She authored an environmental history of Baltimore and coauthored with Patricia Thornton a social history titled *Peopling the North American City, Montreal 1840–1900*, McGill-Queen's University Press, 2011. She is now absorbed in the challenges of building geobases for the historical analysis of urban environments.

EVAN ROBERTS is an assistant professor of history at the University of Minnesota and previously taught at Victoria University of Wellington. He has written on women's work in the United States, stature, and well-being in New Zealand, and methodological issues in constructing historical datasets. He is currently writing a book about married women's work in the United States between the Civil War and World War II, research for which contributed to his chapter in this volume.

J. ANDREW ROSS is a postdoctoral fellow in the departments of history and economics at the University of Guelph. His book, *Joining the Clubs: The Business of the National Hockey League to 1945*, is forthcoming from Syracuse University Press.

KEN SYLVESTER is research associate professor, Institute for Social Research, University of Michigan, and coeditor of *Historical Methods*. He has written on social, agricultural, and environmental history in the North American Great Plains. Recent publications in *Agricultural History*, *Journal of Economic History*, *Environmental History*, and *Agriculture, Ecosystems and Environment* focus on household-level social and land-use behaviour. He is currently writing on the transformation of the plains agriculture and society in the green revolution era.

JANE VAN KOEVERDEN holds a master of arts in journalism from Western University, as well as a bachelor of arts & science from McMaster University. She is currently involved in research on experiential education at the University of Waterloo and works casually as an associate producer and online reporter for CBC radio.

AARON VAN TASSEL holds a BA from the University of Guelph and an MA from the University of Western Ontario. His research focuses on Canadian cultural and business history in the late nineteenth and early twentieth centuries. His major research paper, "'An Unique Institution of Extraordinary Magnitude': Eaton's and the Construction of a Modern Department Store, 1920–1940," examines the Eaton Company's rapid national expansion and the formation of its new corporate identity during the 1920s and '30s.

Index

Aboriginal. *See* ethnicity
African Americans. *See* ethnicity
age structure, 53–4
agricultural, 10, 77, 87, 261; crisis, 121–2, 138; ladder, 9, 93–4, 104, 109–12, 114–15, 117–18, 152,166, 171, 173
antibiotics, 45
anticontagionists, 63
antiscorbutics, 45, 55
artisans, 94, 99, 102, 108, 117

bankruptcies, 144
boarders and lodgers, 104, 191, 195, 206–8, 215, 219, 229
boarding/lodging, 12–13, 281–82
breast-feeding, 249
Burgess, Ernest, 214

calorific value, 55–6
Canada Company, 145–5, 157–61, 163–4
census, 4, 6, 9–14, 34, 72, 75, 84, 89, 93–4, 96–9, 102, 106, 111, 118, 121–5, 126–9, 141–2, 145, 148, 157, 162, 166–71, 173–7, 181, 184–5, 189–97, 202, 209–10, 213, 215, 238–42; families, neighbouring and kinship, 204–5; enumeration and administration, 125, 127, 129, 166–9, 256; evaluations of, 170–4, 256; intercensal linkages, 191
Chicago, 11–12, 201, 208–9, 211–30, 241, 244–5, 275–6, 278, 290–1
child birth, 52, 54, 56, 59, 62–3, 65
children, 8, 12, 21, 31, 33–5, 41, 48, 52, 59, 61, 65, 69, 70, 74, 78, 79, 86, 87, 103–4, 108, 114, 128, 171, 195, 218–20, 229, 243, 246–9, 256–7
cohorts, 5–6, 246
convicts, 19–41; discipline of, 21–4, 29–33; transportation of, 19–29
cost and standard of living, 243–4, 248
crowding, 44–7, 49, 51–3, 58, 64
cultural communities. *See* ethnicity

data mining, 123
disease/illness: accidents, 56, 59–60, 62, 65; catarrhs, 57; constipation, 59; diarrhoea, 51, 56–7, 59, 65;

dysentery, 56–7, 59; influenza, 14, 282–90; pandemic, 282–4, 286, 288–90; pyrexia, 283; scurvy, 48, 54–6, 59, 64; smallpox, 45; syphilis, 279; tuberculosis, 56, 208, 266, 279; typhus, 57
Dolben Act, 45
domestic service, 61

ethnicity, 133–5, 247, 249; Aboriginal, 13–14, 254–73; African Americans, 245, 247; British, 45; English and Welsh, 19–42, 128, 129, 136, 139, 153–64, 237, 240, 247, 249; French, 12, 13, 128, 129, 134–5, 136, 233–53, 262, 267; German, 128, 134, 138, 153–64; Indian, 14, 254, 256, 257, 263, 266–7, 269, 270–1; Irish, 12, 45, 57, 128, 134–5, 136, 137, 138, 153–64, 262; Métis, mixed race, 13–14, 256–71; of Montreal, 183–205; Origin (census category), 129; Polish, 13–15, 274–91; Scottish, 10, 71–90, 128, 134, 136, 138, 153–64
execution, 62

families, 94, 106, 108–9, 111, 238–49; composition, 5, 71, 128 (*see also* household); family reconstitution, 33–8; formation, 33–8; strategies, 77, 89, 102, 120, 169, 184, 205
famine, 57, 72, 74
farm, 97, 98 103, 120, 121, 130–9, 241, 246; acquisition, 103, 112, 115, 117–18, 179–80; labourers, 23–9, 61; occupiers, 108–9, 111, 115–16, 166–7; owners, 104, 109, 111–12, 117, 151–2, 175–6. *See also* farmer and farming
farmer(s), 97, 98 103, 120, 121, 130–9, 241, 246; sons of, 98–9, 101–2, 103, 107, 109, 112, 113–14, 116–18, 121, 171, 241; immigrant, 102, 133, 135; middling, 109; new, 101–2, 104–5, 106, 111, 116–17, 121, 131, 132, 133, 138; religion of, 135; yeoman, 166. *See also* farm and farming
farming, 97, 98 103, 120, 121, 130–9, 246; households, 108, 114, 117, 171, 173–4, 176–7, 184; Improve (acreage), 109, 110–11, 112, 117. *See also* farm and farmer
food. *See* nutrition

genealogical/genealogist, 7–8, 73, 79, 86, 126
genetic, 13, 233, 236–37, 249, 255
Gini coefficient, 177, 179
gold rush, 28, 81

height, 13, 19, 25–6, 40, 47, 233–53
home ownership, 12, 105, 209, 250–1
hospitals, 48–9, 54, 58, 63. *See also* sickbay
Houghteling, Leila, 242–4
household, 94, 105–6, 108, 114, 117, 238–49; composition, 195–6, 261; of unrelated persons, 205–7
hulks, 54–5, 65
human capital, 40
hygiene, 46, 59, 65

illiteracy. *See* literacy
immigration and emigration, 123;

American-Canadian and Canadian-American, 44, 47, 53–4, 57; Australian, 51, 57; English, 44; Irish, 47, 57, 135; Polish, 275–90; Scottish, 8, 71–90
income, 120, 243, 246; indicators, 193.
Indian. *See* ethnicity
industry/industrial, second revolution, 120
inequality, 10–11, 183–5, 238–49
insult accumulation, 20–1, 29–33, 38–41
insurance rating, 48–9, 53
intergenerational, 88, 166, 237–41, 261; mobility, 203

journey to work, 204, 250

labourers/labouring, 94, 97–9, 100–1, 105, 106, 108, 110, 112, 113, 115, 116–17, 118–19, 132, 241, 246, 261
labour force, 9–10, 28–9, 97–9, 101, 103, 105, 107, 113–15, 116–19, 121, 131–7
labour markets, 106, 121, 125, 130
landed tenancy, 10, 94, 111–12, 116–17, 117, 173–4
land markets, 103, 105, 109, 114, 117, 118
land ownership, 11, 94, 113, 116, 166–7, 173–6
language, 240–8, 267–8, 271
lease holders, 102, 112, 116, 156–64
life cycle/life course, 3–8, 13, 21, 33, 103, 105, 111, 112, 117, 118, 166, 173, 175, 181, 184; transitions, 3, 33–8, 196–7, 201–2, 206
linkage, methods, 3–6, 8–9, 34, 73, 89, 90, 94–7, 118, 124–9, 141–2, 146–51, 163, 178, 243, 256–8; obstacles, 191–3, 196–9; retrieval rates, 191–3, 200
literacy, 240, 269
living standard, 12, 13, 236, 238–49; rents as indicator, 193–5

McKeown theory, 45, 63
methodology: ANOVA, 69–70; coding, 29–33; linear regression, 69–70; logistic regression, 113, 148–9; longitudinal analysis, 47, 64; multilevel estimation, 166, 169, 182–3
Métis. *See* ethnicity
miasmas, 63–4
microdata, 95, 111, 123, 125, 126, 140
migration, 93, 96, 106–8, 111, 113, 114, 117, 120, 123, 135, 264; chain, 76, 79; government assisted, 20; interregional, 72, 73, 74, 76–9, 83–4, 89, 90; intraurban, 11, 190, 201–3, 249, 256; local, 72, 73, 74, 76–9, 83–4, 89, 90; outmigration, 71–6, 80–3, 85–90, 96–7, 109, 119, 129, 196; return, 72, 73, 74, 82; step, 8, 72, 73, 79, 80–3, 84, 85–9; urban (migrants), 240, 249. *See also* mobility
military, 13, 238, 240, 254–73, 274–81, 285–91
mobility, 93–4; age selection, 190; career, 9–10, 11–12; culture of, 9, 71, 72, 116; geographic, 9, 12, 71–90, 106, 107–8, 112, 115, 196; historiography of, 9–10, 11, 142–3, 146–51, 196, 208; land owners, 166–7, 173–6; occupa-

tional, 9–10, 12, 94, 97, 99, 100, 105, 107–8, 112, 114, 115, 121, 139, 193–5, 240–2, 253–5; tenants, 10, 152–3, 173–4. *See also* migration
Montreal, 11, 12, 125, 139, 189–210, 247, 249, 284, 285
morbidity, famine related, 65; female, 51, 56, 58; male, 51, 56; on convict vessels, 48–50, 54, 56–8, 60, 65; postvoyage, 46, 50, 51, 60, 61; prevoyage, 57–8
mortality, Aboriginal, 264, 266; famine related, 57, 65; female, 49–51, 54, 56, 58–9, 61, 65, 67–8; infant, 247, 249; male, 50–1, 56, 61, 67–8; on convict vessels, 43–4, 51–4, 56, 63–4, 67–8; on immigrant vessels, 51, 53–4, 57; postvoyage, 50, 61, 65; slave trade, 45–6, 53, 63; survival, 37–8
mortgage, 145

New Deal, 173
Nightingale reforms, 63
nurseries, 63
nutrition, 54–7, 65, 236–47

occupation(al), 98, 100, 102, 108, 109, 122, 126, 239–46; change, 71, 87, 88, 121–4, 125, 126–40; pluralism, 303n28; reporting, 125, 129–31; status, 12, 99, 102, 111, 193–5, 203, 261
orphan schools, 63
owners, 209. *See also* farm, owners

People in Motion project, 141, 371, 372
political protest, 23
potatoes, 55
pregnancy, 56, 60, 63
prevoyage screening, 46, 59, 65
prison, 7, 47, 54–7
property, 109. *See also* farm; farmer; and farming

radio, 252
regional differences, 75, 76, 78, 83, 131, 233, 239, 242–6, 262–8
religion and church, 131, 239, 242–6, 269–70; Anglican, 153–64; as cultural identifier, 190, 195, 198, 202, 204; Lutheran, 153–64; Presbyterian, 153–64; Protestant, 135; recording standards, 199; Roman Catholics, 12, 135, 137, 138, 153–64, 276
road gangs, 61

sampling, 73, 123, 125, 170, 190, 209
scattergrams, 180–1
sickbay, 51, 61, 66–70. *See also* hospitals
social persistence, 176, 178, 181–3, 241; of coresidence, 203; of segregation, 203
stress, 20–1, 38–41
succession, 167
sulphonamides, 45
surgeon-superintendent system, 44
surname samples, 95, 196, 238, 266
surveys, social, 124, 234–5, 238, 240, 243–4

tenancy/tenants, 10, 94, 109–13, 115–17; rates, 142, 173–4. *See also* mobility
tonnage, 49, 52

University of Chicago: Sociology Department, 241; School of Social Service Administration, 242; Press, 243

Van Diemen's Land Company, 28
ventilation, 44
vitamin C, 47, 55
voyage length, 50–1, 53–4

wage, 246. *See also* income
weight, 56–7
women, 117; employment, 61, 97, 111, 255; married, 62–3, 97, 255